Early Childhood Education
Building a Philosophy for Teaching

C. Stephen White
George Mason University

Mick Coleman
The University of Georgia

Merrill
an imprint of Prentice Hall
Upper Saddle River, New Jersey   *Columbus, Ohio*

Library of Congress Cataloging-in-Publication Data

White, C. Stephen.
  Early childhood education: building a philosophy for teaching /
C. Stephen White, Mick Coleman.
      p.   cm.
  Includes bibliographical references and index.
  ISBN 0–02–427222–1
  1. Early childhood education.   2. Child development.   I. Coleman,
Mick.   II. Title.
LB1139.23.W55   2000   99–11342
372.21--DC21   CIP

Cover photo: FPG.
Editor: Ann Castel Davis
Developmental Editor: Hope Madden
Production Editor: Sheryl Glicker Langner
Production Management: Kate Scheinman, Carlisle Communications
Design Coordinator: Diane C. Lorenzo
Cover Designer: Curt Besser
Production Manager: Laura Messerly
Editorial Assistant: Pat Grogg
Photo Coordinator: Sandy Lenahan
Electronic Text Management: Karen L. Bretz
Director of Marketing: Kevin Flanagan
Marketing Manager: Meghan McCauley
Marketing Coordinator: Krista Groshong

This book was set in Palatino by Carlisle Communications, Ltd. and was printed and bound by R. R. Donnelley & Sons Company. The cover was printed by Phoenix Color Corp.

©2000 by Prentice-Hall, Inc.
Pearson Education
Upper Saddle River, New Jersey 07458

Photo Credits: pp. 2, 140, 160, 191, 358, and 364 by Scott Cunningham/Merrill; pp. 8, 102, 146, 226, 241, and 289 by Barbara Schwartz/Merrill; pp. 11, 18, 62, 66, 108, 133, 183, 206, 210, 264, 272, 286, 305, 315, 347, 352, and 372 by Anthony Magnacca/Merrill; pp. 22 and 43 by Library of Congress; p. 50 by PhotoDisc; pp. 59 and 89 by Simon & Schuster/PH College; p. 70 by Todd Yarrington/Merrill; p. 79 by National Education Association; pp. 86, 114, 123, 151, 165, 230, 234, 249, 256, 278, 296, 330, and 340 by Anne Vega/Merrill; p. 178 by Corbis/Bettmann-UPI; p. 187 by Pennsylvania Dutch Visitors Bureau; p. 198 by Silver Burdett Gin; and p. 382 by Dallas Police Department.

Printed in the United States of America

10 9 8 7 6 5 4 3 2 1

ISBN: 0-02-427222-1

Prentice-Hall International (UK) Limited, *London*
Prentice-Hall of Australia Pty. Limited, *Sydney*
Prentice-Hall of Canada, Inc., *Toronto*
Prentice-Hall Hispanoamericana, S. A., *Mexico*
Prentice-Hall of India Private Limited, *New Delhi*
Prentice-Hall of Japan, Inc., *Tokyo*
Prentice-Hall (Singapore) Pte. Ltd., *Singapore*
Editora Prentice-Hall do Brasil, Ltda., *Rio de Janeiro*

Preface

Early childhood teachers in the 21st century face unique educational, family, and societal challenges. Changes in educational policies and practices are leading to new ideas about how to organize and deliver educational programs. We think it is important to help student teachers develop a sense of professional identity and confidence in their ability to respond to the educational needs of young children in contemporary society. It is equally important that teachers recognize the diversity of childhood life experiences represented within their classrooms. It is for these reasons that we take an ecological perspective in this textbook to address the different contexts that influence the care and education of children from birth through age 8:

- **Childhood development.** We examine the physical, cognitive, language, and social-emotional development of children from birth to age 8 in relationship to both theory and research. Likewise, the implications of developmental trends are addressed in regard to family influences and educational practices.
- **Historical precedents.** It is important that students develop a sense of professional continuity with past, current, and emerging educational practices. Subsequently, we review the historical precedents of early childhood education to place current educational issues within a historical perspective.
- **Classroom organization.** We address the design elements associated with organizing child-centered learning centers for both classroom and playground settings. Again, readers are guided through activities in which they apply organizational principles presented in the textbook.
- **Curriculum integration.** Finally, we emphasize how an early childhood curriculum can be integrated across subject-matter content and incorporate families, developmental theories, and issues of diversity. We thus consider the chapter on curriculum integration as a capstone to current trends that challenge teachers to integrate information from various contexts in their planning and facilitation of early childhood educational practices.

TEXTBOOK FEATURES

The features of this textbook are designed to assist readers in achieving these goals:

- In each chapter, students are asked to reflect upon key ideas as a means of developing one theme associated with their philosophy of teaching. Students are asked to save their philosophy of teaching. Students are also asked to save their reflective exercises. These are discussed as a whole in the final chapter when students finalize and defend their personal philosophy of teaching.
- Issues of diversity are integrated into discussions of history, childhood development, assessment, classroom organization, behavior management, and curriculum models. The integration of diversity across chapters allows students to better understand and appreciate the diverse abilities and life experiences of young children.
- **Educational policies.** We discuss a range of educational policies and their influence on educational practices. Students are encouraged to consider how these emerging policies might impact their professional lives.
- **Family-school relations.** Chapters on family development and family-school relations provide students with theoretical guides for understanding family lives, communicating with families, and involving families in planning and implementing early childhood educational practices.
- **Assessment.** Readers are encouraged to consider multiple assessment approaches when assessing children's development and educational gains. Subsequently, various assessment strategies are summarized.
- **Behavior management.** The guidance of children's behavior in group settings can be controversial. We therefore examine multiple perspectives of behavior management to provide readers with insight into the various views held on this topic by professionals and families.
- **Curriculum models.** We also review multiple early childhood curriculum models and their relevance to addressing families and issues of diversity. Readers are encouraged to consider how various curriculum models relate to their own philosophy of early childhood education.

Pedagogical Elements

- Chapter-opening questions help students define essential developmental and educational concepts.
- Case studies allow students to see the personal side of children's family and school lives. The case studies also encourage students to examine their personal reactions to complex situations.

- "Checklists" and "Tips for Teachers" provide quick summaries of factors to consider when assessing or implementing educational practices.
- Figures and tables clarify and extend the key ideas presented in the textbook.
- Boxes provide further examples of how research and theory influence teaching practices in early childhood classrooms.
- End-of-chapter activities encourage students to apply, investigate, or discuss contemporary educational issues.

ACKNOWLEDGMENTS

There are numerous people who have assisted us in the completion of this textbook. We thank the many teachers, teacher assistants, family-school coordinators, and administrators in Georgia and Virginia who offered ideas and opportunities for us to be in a variety of child-care, preschool, kindergarten, and primary-grade settings. We are also indebted to our faculty colleagues and support staff at The University of Georgia and George Mason University. We appreciate the specific contributions of Barbara Benson, Marilyn Rahilly, and Carlos Toledo for their assistance in conducting research, developing ideas for case studies, and securing permissions. We especially recognize Ruth Steinbrenner for her contributions to the cognitive development, assessment, and classroom organization chapters; Rachel Sweeney for allowing us to use many of her integrated lesson and unit plans; and Becky Olson for her advice on inclusion within different early childhood settings.

We thank the following reviewers for their helpful comments: Georgianna Cornelius, *New Mexico State University*; Sandra B. Decosta, *Indiana State University*; Natalie L. Delcamp, *Rollins College (FL)*; Barbara N. Duffield, University of Toledo; Esther H. Egley, *Mississippi State University*; Ione M. Garcia, *Illinois State University*; Barbara G. Graham, *Norfolk State University*; Joan E. Herwig, *Iowa State University*; Joan M. Hildebrand, *Towson State University*; Florence Leonard, *Towson State University (Retired)*; Elaine S. Lyons, *Luzerne County Community College (PA)*; and Colleen K. Randel, *The University of Texas at Tyler*.

We thank Ann C. Davis, Senior Editor, for her assistance, vision, and knowledge while developing, refining, and revising this textbook. We especially appreciate the extensive efforts of Hope Madden, Developmental Editor, and Kate Scheinman, Editorial Director at Carlisle Publishers Services, in assisting us in the book's completion and publication. The support provided by our department heads and deans was central in allowing us to focus on text development. We are therefore appreciative of the support and guidance provided by Drs. Denise Glynn, Sharon Price, Patsy Skeen, and George Stanic at the University of Georgia and Associate Dean Martin Ford, Dean Gary Galluzzo, and Dean Gustavo Mellander at George Mason University.

Discover Companion Websites
A Virtual Learning Environment

Technology is a constantly growing and changing aspect of our field that is creating a need for content and resources. To address this emerging need, we have developed an online learning environment for students and professors alike–Companion Websites–to support our textbooks.

In creating a Companion Website, our goal is to build on and enhance what the textbook already offers. For this reason, the content for each user-friendly website is organized by chapter and provides the professor and student with a variety of meaningful resources. Common features of a Companion Website include:

For the Professor

Every Companion Website integrates **Syllabus Manager™**, an online syllabus creation and management utility.

◆ **Syllabus Manager™** provides you, the instructor, with an easy, step-by-step process to create and revise syllabi, with direct links into Companion Website and other online content without having to learn HTML.

◆ Students may logon to your syllabus during any study session. All they need to know is the web address for the Companion Website and the password you've assigned to your syllabus.

◆ After you have created a syllabus using **Syllabus Manager™**, students may enter the syllabus for their course section from any point in the Companion Website.

◆ Class dates are highlighted in white and assignment due dates appear in blue. Clicking on a date, the student is shown the list of activities for the assignment. The activities for each assignment are linked directly to actual content, saving time for students.

- ♦ Adding assignments consists of clicking on the desired due date, then filling in the details of the assignment—name of the assignment, instructions, and whether or not it is a one-time or repeating assignment.

- ♦ In addition, links to other activities can be created easily. If the activity is online, a URL can be entered in the space provided, and it will be linked automatically in the final syllabus.

- ♦ Your completed syllabus is hosted on our servers, allowing convenient updates from any computer on the Internet. Changes you make to your syllabus are immediately available to your students at their next login.

For the Student

- ♦ **Chapter Objectives**—outline key concepts from the text

- ♦ **Interactive self-quizzes**—complete with hints and automatic grading that provide immediate feedback for students

  After students submit their answers for the interactive self-quizzes, the Companion Website **Results Reporter** computes a percentage grade, provides a graphic representation of how many questions were answered correctly and incorrectly, and gives a question by question analysis of the quiz. Students are given the option to send their quiz to up to four email addresses (professor, teaching assistant, study partner, etc.).

- ♦ **Message Board**—serves as a virtual bulletin board to post–or respond to–questions or comments to/from a national audience

- ♦ **Net Searches**—offer links by key terms from each chapter to related Internet content

- ♦ **Web Destinations**—links to www sites that relate to chapter content

To take advantage of these resources, please visit the *Early Childhood Education: Building a Philosophy for Teaching* Companion Website at www.prenhall.com/white

Contents in Brief

Contents

chapter 5 *Cognitive and Language Development*   **114**

----

chapter **11** *Organizing Classroom and Outdoor Learning Environments*   **286**

chapter 1

Building a Personal Philosophy of Teaching:
Concepts of Development and Education

After reading this chapter you should be able to discuss the following questions:

❖ In what ways are developmental concepts, principles, and perspectives reflected in early childhood classrooms?
❖ What is education?
❖ Why are educational philosophies important?
❖ Why are family-school-community partnerships important?

CHAPTER OVERVIEW

A primary goal of this textbook is to help you develop your own philosophy of early childhood education. This is not an easy task. As you will see, teachers must consider a range of issues when planning for the education of young children. In the chapters that follow, we provide you with guidance in developing a professional philosophy that will allow you to:

- Understand, and explain to others, how children develop;
- Place contemporary educational objectives within historical perspective;
- Adjust to new trends and practices occurring in the field of education;
- Relate effectively to the families of young children;
- Assess children's educational progress;
- Justify your choice of an early childhood educational curriculum;
- Organize a developmentally appropriate learning environment;
- Plan and facilitate children's learning experiences; and
- Guide children's behavior in a professional manner.

In this chapter, we respond to a series of reflective questions that will allow you to begin developing your personal teaching philosophy as it relates to early childhood education. We conclude by providing examples of teaching philosophies for you to consider and perhaps discuss with your peers.

UNDERSTANDING THE LINKS BETWEEN DEVELOPMENT AND EDUCATION

Translating and making sense of the enormous amount of information about children that is available today can be overwhelming. Two factors contribute to this situation. First, as noted in Table 1.1, a number of professionals from different fields contribute to our understanding of how children develop and learn. Second, researchers are constantly asking new questions and providing us with additional information about children's development and education.

TABLE 1.1	Professions Contributing to Early Childhood Education	
Education	**Human Services**	**Health**
Teachers	Social workers	Nurses
Parent educators	School and community mental health counselors	Physicians
Family life educators	Psychologists	Nutritionists
Youth ministers	Psychometrists	Child life specialists
Youth specialists (youth organizations, children's museums)	Marriage and family therapists	Physical therapists
Researchers	Recreation specialists	Youth coaches

 A personal philosophy of early childhood education can help you to place new information about children's development and education within an applied perspective. Our experiences in the early childhood field, both as teachers and as consultants to schools, have led us to identify five reflective questions for developing a philosophy of early childhood education:

- How do children develop?
- What is education?
- What is the relationship between children's development and education?
- How do children learn?
- Who has responsibility for educating young children?

How Do Children Develop?

Student teachers sometimes ask us, "Why is it important to study child development in order to teach?" The answer is simple. Only by understanding children's development can teachers meet the educational needs of young children. Without such an understanding, teachers run the risk of constructing a learning environment that at best meets the needs of only some children, and at worst is harmful to all children. Relating children's development to educational practices begins with an understanding of basic developmental concepts.

Development.   This concept refers to the orderly, sequential and increasingly more complex levels of functioning that children display as they advance in age (Holt, 1991; Vaughan & Litt, 1990). As noted in Figure 1.1, children's development takes place across three major *domains* or areas of development. The *physical domain* reflects children's physical growth, perceptual skills, and motor skills.

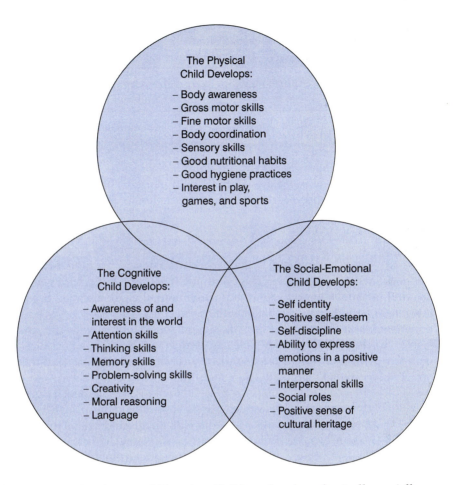

The Physical
Child Develops:

– Body awareness
– Gross motor skills
– Fine motor skills
– Body coordination
– Sensory skills
– Good nutritional habits
– Good hygiene practices
– Interest in play,
  games, and sports

The Cognitive
Child Develops:

– Awareness of and
  interest in the world
– Attention skills
– Thinking skills
– Memory skills
– Problem-solving skills
– Creativity
– Moral reasoning
– Language

The Social-Emotional
Child Develops:

– Self identity
– Positive self-esteem
– Self-discipline
– Ability to express
  emotions in a positive
  manner
– Interpersonal skills
– Social roles
– Positive sense of
  cultural heritage

FIGURE 1.1   *Developmental Domains.* Children develop physically, socially-emotionally, and cognitively

Adapted from "Ages and Stages," *Serving child care needs: Developmental and curriculum issues,* by Coleman, M. (1988). University of Georgia Cooperative Service, Athens, GA.

The *cognitive domain* reflects children's language development and thinking and problem-solving skills. The *social-emotional domain* reflects children's self-identity, interpersonal skills, and their expression of feelings.

Ages and stages of development.   In order to make sense of the continuous process of development, most teachers and other child professionals categorize children's development into distinct stages. It is important to note that the categories are arbitrary, and can therefore be misleading when viewed as fixed and

TABLE 1.2   Ages and Stages of Early Childhood Development and Education

Stage	Approximate Age	Developmental Challenge	Educational Challenge
Infancy	Birth to age 1	Self-regulation	Trust and support
Toddlerhood	Age 1 to age 3	Social adjustment	Social limits
Preschool	Age 3 to age 5	Exploration	Guided learning
Primary grades	Age 5 to age 8	Inquiry	Structured learning

universal. For example, in upcoming chapters you will find that theorists categorize the ages and stages of children's development in different ways. Likewise, we use the age categories presented in Table 1.2 only as a general indicator of the relationship between the developmental challenges faced by children and the resulting educational challenges faced by teachers.

Infants have the task of regulating a number of bodily and social functions during their first year of life (e.g., refinement of reflexes, communicating, sleeping, feeding), as well as making discoveries about themselves and others. Yet, they are also heavily dependent upon others for their care. As you will see in Chapter 6, the manner in which adult caregivers respond to these developmental challenges can influence infants' trust in others. Such trust is important in the formation of positive interpersonal relationships. Adults who work with infants understand this developmental challenge and respond to infants' need for guidance and assistance with patience and support.

An important developmental task for toddlers is to adjust their behavior to conform to social expectations. Teachers assist toddlers in achieving this task by respecting, but placing age-appropriate limits on, their need to explore their world. For example, limits on such behaviors as hitting, running, biting, and pushing protect the well-being of others, as well as help toddlers learn to exercise self-control.

The world of preschoolers gradually expands as they more actively explore their surroundings, ask questions, and attempt to understand how things work. Children are most successful in these endeavors when teachers guide learning activities by asking questions, providing labels for objects, introducing new materials for exploration, and presenting new learning experiences.

Primary-age children begin to make more formal inquiries about their world. Their activities involve more cooperation, they take place for longer periods of time, and they challenge children to use more sophisticated problem-solving and communication skills. Teachers now begin providing more structure in facilitating children's learning activities by providing a wider range of more sophisticated materials and activities, arranging short- and long-term group projects, and encouraging children to cooperate in solving problems.

Growth. "Growth" refers to the increase in children's physical size (e.g., length and weight) (Holt, 1991; Vaughan & Litt, 1990). Pediatricians, nutritionists, and other health specialists are most often concerned with this aspect of children's development. For example, school nurses rely upon growth charts to assess children's height and weight. Nutritionists ensure that school menus reflect the dietary needs of young children.

Maturation. "Maturation" refers to the biological processes that underlie and influence children's growth and development (Holt, 1991). Although unobservable, these biological processes support the observable motor skills that children display. Muscles and nerves do not just grow in size, they also become better organized and more efficient. This maturational process in turn results in more complex skills like running faster, jumping higher, and throwing more efficiently.

Normal. "Normal" refers to typical patterns of growth and development (Allen & Marotz, 1994; Holt, 1991). Normal is a relative term. We refer to children as displaying normal patterns of growth and development when their behaviors and skills are characteristic of most children their age.

Average. "Average" is a statistical term that indicates the specific standing of a particular child within a distinct group. For example, the score that results from a math test can be classified as average, below average, or above average, depending upon where the score falls within a distribution of scores.

Atypical. "Atypical" refers to growth and development patterns that fall above or below the norm. Atypical patterns of development are not necessarily detrimental to children's adjustment. For example, children with atypically low cognitive skills may compensate by spending more time on tasks or may use their atypically high social skills to get the extra help they need to complete tasks.

At-risk. "At-risk" refers to growth and development patterns that place children's life adjustment in jeopardy. At-risk is also a relative concept, since children's living circumstances can influence the degree to which a particular behavior or physical condition may jeopardize their development. For example, two children with the same emotional problem may not be at the same level of risk, depending upon their families' willingness and ability to seek out community help to address their child's emotional needs.

On the other hand, certain developmental conditions are routinely used by child professionals as potential at-risk indicators. Low birth weight is often used as one criterion for identifying young children who may need early intervention services in order to keep their development within a normal range. Schools and human service agencies may use a combination of childhood indicators (e.g., low birth weight, early patterns of growth and development) and family indicators (e.g., teenage parent, low socioeconomic standing) as criteria for identifying children who are at-risk.

Teachers plan learning environments that reflect the diversity of children's lives.

Diversity.   "Diversity" is not often mentioned as a developmental term. Nevertheless, we include it in our list to reflect the fact that children develop in different environments. Children come from different ethnic and racial backgrounds. They are of different genders. They live in families with different structures, incomes, and lifestyles. They come from different geographic areas and cultural backgrounds. These are issues that we will repeatedly return to throughout this textbook, highlighting the important responsibility that teachers have for planning learning environments that reflect the diversity of children's life experiences.

As you may already have guessed, these developmental concepts do not stand alone. Rather, they are used by child professionals from different fields to communicate with one another and to plan their own work with young children. Education is one such field that makes active use of these developmental concepts.

What Is Education?

Education, like development, has many dimensions. In the most general sense, the education of young children is reflected in teachers' interpretation and application of the developmental concepts previously discussed. We thus define *education* as an endeavor in which developmentally appropriate learning objectives are defined and pursued for individual children and groups of children.

In a more applied sense, education can refer to any number of administrative units (e.g., child care, nursery school, prekindergarten, kindergarten, primary grades), sponsors (e.g., public and private schools), and programs (e.g., teacher-centered approach involving formal instruction, child-centered approach involving children's self-selection of activities) that seek to support and advance children's development (Seefeldt & Barbour, 1990). The choice of an early childhood educational curriculum is one key to linking children's development to educational practices.

Curriculum.   As you will discover in Chapter 10, there are different types of curricula for guiding children's early education. As reflected in our definition of education, all educational curricula deal with the complex process of identifying, planning, facilitating, and assessing educational goals. Some teachers follow a curriculum that is provided by their school, while others develop their own curriculum. In any case, it is important that you understand the connection between the particular curriculum that you use and the developmental principles upon which it is based.

What Is the Relationship Between Children's Development and Education?

The following principles are especially useful for appreciating the link between child development and early childhood educational curricula. We therefore have included an example of an educational issue for each of the following developmental principles.

Development is holistic.   You will note that in Figure 1.1 the three developmental domains overlap. This overlap reflects the principle that, rather than developing in isolation, all three domains are integrated. That is, children develop as a whole with each domain influencing all other domains. For example, children who are physically small for their age may not be able to participate in games at the same level as their larger peers (physical domain). As a result, some of these children may develop a sense of inadequacy that negatively impacts their relationship with others (social-emotional domain). These children may subsequently develop a poor self-esteem that also negatively impacts their social skills outside of school and their academic performance within the classroom (social-emotional and cognitive domains).

An educational application of this principle is that teachers must plan for the education of the whole child. This principle is reflected in the concept of the "integrated curriculum," in which reading, writing, music, science, and other subject-matter areas are integrated into all activities throughout the day rather than being divided into different time slots. We discuss strategies for developing an integrated curriculum in Chapter 13.

Development is orderly and sequential.

Children usually follow a similar pattern of growth and development. For example, most children sit before they stand, stand before they walk, and walk before they run.

An educational application of this principle is that decisions about children's growth and development should be made using developmentally appropriate assessments. Different assessment strategies are often needed for different developmental domains and even for different types of behaviors within developmental domains. For example, assessing children's height and weight (physical domain) through the use of standardized growth charts is appropriate, since the charts reflect observable characteristics of young children. In contrast, assessing young children's intelligence (cognitive domain) and interpersonal skills (social-emotional domain) only through the use of tests and scales is inappropriate. Cognitive and social-emotional development can take many different forms and can be measured in many different ways. Also, it has long been established that the use of standardized tests is less reliable when used with small children (Shepard & Smith, 1986). Early childhood teachers therefore rely more heavily upon informal observations of children's classroom behavior and work to assess their development and educational progress. We provide guides for making such observations throughout this book, and give special attention to assessment issues in Chapter 9.

Children develop at their own pace.

Although children's development and education are orderly and sequential, we also expect variations to occur in individual children. Physical, family, school, and community factors can influence children's development and their educational progress. In what ways might the following factors potentially influence the pace at which children develop and learn?

- **Physical.** Nutrition, disease, pollution, and access to health services;
- **Family.** Family structure, family interactions, and family economics;
- **School.** Early intervention programs, teacher qualifications, choice of curriculum, class size, and classroom organization; and
- **Community.** Size of community, support of schools, crime statistics, and quality of social services.

An educational application of this principle is that educational settings for young children should reflect both group and individual interests and skill levels. Certainly, a toddler room should look different from a kindergarten classroom, which should in turn look different from a third-grade classroom. Classroom organization must also take into account the interests and needs of individual children. We discuss organizational strategies for balancing the interests and needs of groups and individual children in Chapter 11.

Children develop best in a supportive environment.   Children's self-esteem and sense of confidence are reinforced by supportive parents and teachers. Children who receive emotional support feel safe, and feeling safe has many educational benefits. It gives children the courage to seek out and adapt to new learning situations. It reinforces children's right to assert their feelings. It also encourages children to work cooperatively with peers and adults.

An educational application of this principle is that effective teachers are willing and able to work with families to construct mutually supportive home-school learning environments in which children feel safe to ask questions and explore their world. We review strategies for achieving supportive home-school learning environments in Chapters 7 and 8.

Children develop within an ecological context.   Children do not develop in a vacuum; instead they develop in a world that is in constant flux. Children are influenced directly or indirectly by environmental, social, business, religious, and legislative events.

An educational application of this principle is that teachers have a professional responsibility to help shape the world in which young children develop. They also have a professional responsibility to empower parents to become advocates for their children. This idea is relatively new in early childhood education,

Children develop in a world that is in constant flux.

but it is one that has become increasingly important during the past two decades. We examine the relationships among social policy, advocacy, and early childhood education in Chapter 3.

Just as ideas about education are linked to children's development, so too are ideas about how children learn. In the following section we examine three developmental perspectives that guide teachers' views of childhood learning.

How Do Children Learn?

The following perspectives have different implications for how children develop, and, therefore, the role of teachers in structuring children's learning experiences. As you will see, each perspective has both advantages and disadvantages.

Nature perspective. The nature perspective emphasizes the genetic makeup of children as the major contributor to their growth and development. Both are viewed as innately driven processes that unfold naturally (see Figure 1.2a). *Canalization*, a term originally developed by Waddington (1957), is sometimes used to describe the strength of genetic factors in directing children's growth and development. Simply put, the more canalized a behavior, the more it unfolds naturally due to maturational forces. For example, sitting, standing, and walking unfold naturally in an orderly and sequential manner, indicating that they are easily learned and thus are more highly canalized (Zigler & Stevenson, 1993). Printing and writing are less canalized in that they do not occur naturally but instead require instruction and practice.

Teachers who adopt a strong nature perspective of development tend to assume a passive approach toward early childhood education. Children's development is seen as biologically predetermined; therefore the teacher's role is to support children's "natural" learning skills.

There are positive and negative aspects associated with this educational approach. On the positive side, teachers respect and are eager to support children's natural abilities, including their ability to demonstrate "natural" learning skills in different subject areas. On the negative side, teachers may make decisions about children's learning abilities based solely upon their classroom behaviors or the statistical averages that result from standardized tests. Teachers may fail to take into account the individual variations that occur in young children's growth and development, children's behavior outside the classroom, or the influence of children's living environments.

Nurture perspective. The nurture perspective is the opposite of the nature perspective, emphasizing the power of the environment in shaping children's development (see Figure 1.2b). For example, a behavior that is considered normal in one family (e.g., a child who shows an early interest in the arts) may be viewed as atypical in another family. Teachers who follow a nurture perspective of child

FIGURE 1.2   Nature, Nurture, and Interactionist Perspectives

a. **Nature Perspective.** The child's genetic makeup drives the child's development.

Child's genetic makeup

↓

Child's development

b. **Nurture Perspective.** The child's environment drives the child's development.

Child's environment

↓

Child's development

c. **Simple Interaction.** The child's genetic makeup and environment interact to influence the child's development.

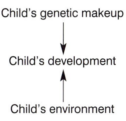

Child's genetic makeup

↓

Child's development

↑

Child's environment

d. **Reciprocal Interaction.** The child and the environment influence each other.

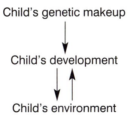

Child's genetic makeup

↓

Child's development

↓↑

Child's environment

e. **Regulatory Interaction.** Social institutions like family and school regulate the child's reciprocal interactions.

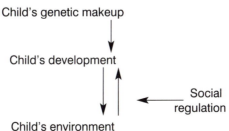

Child's genetic makeup

↓

Child's development

↓↑

Child's environment

Social regulation ⟶

development and education strive to understand the norms and expectations associated with different families, communities, and cultures.

The nurture perspective, like the nature perspective, has both positive and negative aspects. On the positive side, this perspective is empowering in that teachers take a proactive stance in shaping children's learning environments. On the negative side, it is difficult to design a classroom environment that meets the needs of every child. It also is difficult to construct a classroom environment that is equally supportive of every child's home environment. These challenges can become frustrating for beginning teachers as they learn to develop realistic expectations of the limits to shaping children's learning environments.

Interactionist perspective.

The interactionist perspective is based on the assumption that nature and nurture interact to influence children's development (see Figure 1.2c). Development is viewed as a holistic process involving the integration of all developmental domains. Within each domain there is a *reaction range*, or developmental potential. A particular child's adjustment within his or her reaction range is set by the interacting forces of biology and environment. That is, children's genetic makeup defines the lower and upper limits of their developmental potential (i.e., reaction range), with their environment influencing the level at which they make a final adjustment.

For example, two children born with the same physical disability may make different developmental and educational adjustments depending upon the environments in which they live. While the upper and lower limits of adjustment are similar for both children, the child who receives more positive support and encouragement from parents and teachers can be expected to make a better adjustment than the child who receives less support and encouragement. One case study of interaction between genetic and environmental forces is presented in Box 1.1.

The interactionist perspective has evolved over the past few decades. As noted in Figure 1.2c, the initial interactionist model simply noted that children's biological makeup and environment interacted across time to shape their development. During the 1960s and 1970s, researchers extended the model to reflect the reciprocal interaction between children and their environments (Bell, 1968, 1971; Thomas & Chess, 1977) (see Figure 1.2d). Rather than being passive respondents to the environment, children were viewed as active players in helping to shape their environments (Scarr & McCartney, 1983). For example, a child's gender, temperament, or physical appearance may lead parents and teachers to hold certain expectations about that child's interests and learning abilities.

The most recent modification of the interactionist perspective involves social regulatory institutions (family, education, religion, government) that structure the reciprocal relationship between children and their environment (Sameroff, 1987) (see Figure 1.2e). For example, the regulatory functions of home and school may be similar or different, depending in part upon the level of communication and coop-

BOX 1.1   *Biology and Environment: The Case of Juan and Mary Beth*

As you read about Juan and Mary Beth, think about how biology and environment have interacted to influence their lives. As a teacher, how might you respond to questions regarding the inclusion of children like Juan and Mary Beth in school, home, and community life?

Juan

Juan's disability was obvious from birth. Because Juan was diagnosed with cerebral palsy, his father, Juan Sr., left full-time employment to care for his son, picking up part-time work as finances necessitated. To accommodate Juan as he grew, Juan Sr. built ramps into his house and remodeled its interior, including the bathrooms, to create the most accessible environment possible for his son. Although Juan is confined to a wheelchair, he fishes regularly with his father, and the two excitedly follow NASCAR racing, attending races several times a year. Juan now attends public high school, where he receives high marks in science, history, and math; in his spare time he manages the school's basketball team.

Mary Beth

Mary Beth was also diagnosed with cerebral palsy as a young child. She is the fourth of seven children living in a roomy two-story farmhouse. Mary Beth's condition was also clear at a very early age, and she has subsequently been confined to a wheelchair for most of her life. As a young child, her father carried her up the steps to her room. Eventually he partitioned off an area of the family room for her bedroom so she could remain on the ground floor. Mary Beth attended a government-funded school for children with special needs until she was 16. Now 28, she spends the day on the farm with her retired parents. Mary Beth does not help with the chores; it's difficult to traverse the often muddy acreage in her wheelchair. She helps her parents plan meals, enjoys visits from her brothers and sisters and their children, and has collected more than 400 videotapes of her favorite cartoons and movies.

eration that exists between parents and teachers. A child who is able to adjust to the regulatory functions of multiple settings like family, school, and peer group can be expected to make a better developmental and educational adjustment than a similar child who is able to successfully adapt to only one setting.

Teachers who adopt the interactionist perspective have a flexible and reflective approach toward education and early childhood learning. Rather than holding all children accountable to one standard, teachers take into account the social context of children's lives and its possible influence on their development and classroom performance. For example, teachers who adopt this perspective are more likely to use norms, not averages, in assessing children's development and learning skills. Norms provide more flexibility in presenting children's skills in the best possible light. An "at-risk" child who performs in the lower end of what is considered normal may have accomplished as much or perhaps even more than a child with a similar performance who is not judged to be "at-risk."

The interactionist perspective can also be frustrating for teachers. Perhaps the most obvious frustration is that it is impossible to precisely identify the relative importance of all genetic factors and environmental events that influence children's development and education. Learning is a complex endeavor that does not easily lend itself to a detailed interactionist analysis. Nevertheless, it is important to keep in mind the potential influences of biology and environment in any learning environment.

Combining perspectives.   In reality, few teachers identify strongly with only one of the perspectives. Most teachers combine elements of all three to develop their ideas about early childhood development and education. This is a practical approach, since adhering to only one perspective would result in a much narrower approach to arranging learning environments and facilitating children's learning experiences. It is for this reason that a combination of developmental perspectives is often reflected in teachers' educational philosophies.

A final question remains before we ask you to make your first attempt at writing your own philosophy of early childhood education. We now turn to the issue of responsibility for children's education.

Who Has Responsibility for Educating Young Children?

The answer to this question is rather simple. Early childhood education today is widely viewed as a responsibility of schools, families, and the community at large. As you will see in the following chapters, schools are forming partnerships with both community agencies (see Chapter 3) and families (see Chapter 8). The idea of family-school-community "partnerships" is a valid one, having a connection to the past (see Chapter 2), and reflecting current concerns regarding the education of young children.

Two factors in particular underlie the need for family-school-community partnerships. First, as American society becomes more diverse, greater input is needed from families and communities in creating learning environments that are responsive to the educational needs of all children. As we have already noted, classrooms today include children who represent different cultures, religions, and family lifestyles (Coleman & Churchill, 1997). Furthermore, only during the past two decades have we really begun to address the meaning and impact of such factors upon educational environments (Harry, 1992; Ogbu, 1992; Patterson, 1992; Procidano & Fisher, 1992; Slonim, 1991). This makes it necessary to call upon families and communities to inform teachers and school administrators about the aspirations they hold for children and their expectations of early childhood education in helping to fulfill those aspirations (Coleman & Wallinga, 1998).

Second, family-school-community partnerships have the potential to do more than support the education of young children. They can also benefit families, schools, and communities themselves (Sanders & Epstein, 1998). A few of the benefits associated with family-school-community partnerships include the following (Kelley-Laine, 1998):

- **Democracy.**   Some countries (e.g., France, Germany) view family involvement as a legal right. In this country, families and community groups are being recruited to assist in making educational policies that will prepare children for adult life in a democratic society.
- **Accountability.**   Both families and communities are increasingly holding schools accountable for student achievement at all educational levels. Such accountability is seen as vital to ensuring a socially responsible and economically productive society.
- **Social problems.**   Families and communities view schools as part of the solution to correcting social problems like violence, teenage pregnancy, and substance abuse.
- **Resources.**   Education is becoming more expensive. Schools are looking to families and communities to assist in raising school funds, purchasing computers and other expensive equipment, and providing staffing support.

We have addressed all of the questions presented at the beginning of this chapter. You are now ready to take a practice turn at writing your own philosophy of early childhood education.

DEVELOPING A TEACHING PHILOSOPHY

As a teacher, you will be asked by parents and school administrators to explain your classroom practices. It is difficult to respond to such requests without a philosophy of early childhood education that reflects the developmental and educational concepts, principles, and perspectives reviewed in this chapter. Your philosophy of education will not only guide your interactions with children, it will also help you to better understand and justify the differences between your teaching practices and those of other teachers.

We recognize that you may not feel ready to write your personal teaching philosophy. We also recognize that the philosophy you write today will change as you learn more about early childhood theories, acquire factual knowledge about children's development and teaching practices, and gain practical experience in the classroom. Nevertheless, the information that you have read so far gives you a good beginning point from which to construct a working draft of your philosophy.

A personal philosophy of education guides teachers' professional practices and interactions.

Take a moment to consider the following reflective questions, then read our examples of philosophies of teaching.

- How do children develop?
- What is education?
- What is the relationship between development and education?
- How do children learn?
- Who is responsible for educating young children?

Developmental Philosophy

The following philosophy is based upon a developmental perspective that we outlined in this chapter along with a document entitled "Developmentally Appropriate Practices" (DAP)(Bredekemp & Copple, 1997). We refer to the DAP document throughout this textbook, and give particular attention to it in Chapters 3 and 10.

I believe that children develop in an orderly fashion with each child accomplishing developmental tasks at his or her own pace. The goal of education is to support and advance children's development by following developmentally appropriate practices that are supportive of children's physical, cognitive, and social-emotional needs.

Instructional Philosophy

The following teaching philosophy is pragmatic, emphasizing the organizational and instructional components of early childhood education. We address instructional aspects of teaching throughout the following chapters. Special attention is given to curriculum models in Chapter 10. The organizational components of teaching are discussed in Chapter 11; the concept of an "integrated classroom" is discussed in Chapter 13.

> I believe that education is a life-long pursuit that begins during the early years. Setting the stage for early interest in learning is best achieved by organizing a classroom that is stimulating and developmentally appropriate. Special attention should be given to integrating children's learning experiences so that subject matter concepts like reading and math are embedded in all activities throughout the day.

Ecological Philosophy

The following philosophy is based upon the idea that children have a human "ecology" that is made up of their home, school, and community lives. Teachers who follow an ecological philosophy of teaching are most interested in making sure that the separate lives of children are interconnected and harmonious. We first address the implications of family-school-community connections in Chapter 3. We specifically address the ecological model in Chapter 8.

> I believe that early childhood education is the responsibility of schools, families, and communities. Families are responsible for encouraging children to adopt a positive attitude toward learning. It is therefore important that they take an active role in their children's school activities. Teachers are responsible for planning educational objectives to facilitate children's learning. To do this effectively, they must ensure that the classroom learning environment is supportive of children's home learning environments. Social service professionals are responsible for coordinating their services with families and schools so that developmental and educational problems can be identified and addressed.

Humanistic Philosophy

Finally, the following philosophy reflects a teaching approach in which teachers are totally accepting of children. They also strongly believe that the school day should reflect an atmosphere in which teachers follow—rather than lead—children through learning activities. We compare this "humanistic" approach to other teaching and behavior management approaches in Chapter 12.

> I believe that effective teaching is tailored to the needs of each child. Understanding and accepting the individual worth of each child is crucial to facilitating that child's particular learning interests. Teachers thus serve as educational guides, taking the lead of children to organize the classroom, develop educational objectives, and facilitate learning activities that have personal meaning and value to the children involved.

Now consider a final series of questions as you reflect back on these examples. Make notes as you think about the questions. Use your notes to write your own teaching philosophy.

- Can you identify which reflective questions asked at the beginning of this section are reflected in the examples?
- With which example do you most agree? Why?
- What modifications would you make in the examples to make them more personally appealing?

Save the first draft of your teaching philosophy, as you will return to it as you read the following chapters. Students often find that the philosophies they first write serve as useful reference points for tracking their professional development as a teacher.

CHAPTER SUMMARY

Teachers who understand early childhood development are better able to construct effective learning environments and communicate with child professionals from different fields. Developing a personal philosophy of early childhood education that links children's development to educational practices is especially important in applying new information about childhood learning and development, explaining the importance of children's behaviors to others, and justifying personal teaching practices.

ACTIVITIES

1. Compare your teaching philosophy with those of your classmates. In what ways are your philosophies alike, and in what ways do they differ? In small groups, discuss the different educational implications of your philosophies. Will some philosophies be easier to implement than others?

2. Using Figure 1.1, describe your physical, social-emotional, and cognitive development as a young child. You may want to ask your parents, teachers, grandparents, or other significant adults to help you with this task. Did you develop "evenly" across all three developmental

domains, or were you more advanced in one area? In small groups, compare your developmental profile with the profiles of others in your classroom. Describe some of the challenges for a teacher faced with the developmental profiles represented in your group.

3. One of the most important developmental principles of early childhood education is that "development is holistic." Reflect upon your own early education. How was this principle implemented by your teachers? In small groups, discuss your responses to this question.

4. Ask three or more early childhood professionals from different fields to define the terms "development" and "education." Identify the ways in which their definitions are alike and different. Which definitions do you like best? Compare the definitions that resulted from your interviews with those of your classmates.

chapter 2

Historical Perspectives on Early Childhood Education

After reading this chapter you should be able to discuss the following questions:

❖ Who are the people who have influenced current practices and beliefs in early childhood education?

❖ How have historical events such as the Industrial Revolution, the Great Depression, and the Civil Rights Movement influenced early childhood education?

❖ Why have federal policies and practices been important in the evolution of early childhood education?

❖ How have attitudes and beliefs about children changed over time?

CHAPTER OVERVIEW

In this chapter we examine a number of different influences on current theory, research, and practice in early childhood education. These influences include significant people, events, and contextual factors such as political events and demographic and sociological trends. We also consider how issues related to diversity, educators' beliefs about children and child nature, and society's beliefs about the capabilities and needs of children have evolved and expanded over time. This chapter is organized by time periods beginning with the 15th century. In each time period, we focus on the events, people, and issues that we feel have had a major influence on current early childhood beliefs and practices. Since there are many other events, people, issues, and questions that could be considered, we have carefully selected historical information that best fits the scope and purpose of this text.

In Activity 1 at the end of this chapter, you can discuss how one of the instrumental early childhood educators profiled in this chapter fits with the philosophy of education you developed in Chapter 1.

1400–1600:
BEGINNINGS OF EARLY CHILDHOOD EDUCATION

Time line

1423 The printing press was invented. Prior to this event, all books in Western Europe were reproduced by hand.

1439 Movable type was invented. The emergence of printing allowed books to spread across Europe and provided more people access to books.

1440   The Hornbook, a small book for children that usually contained the alphabet, vowels and consonants, and biblical verse, was created.

1444   The first public library was established in Italy.

1505–1560   Martin Luther led the Reformation.

During the 15th century, the Medieval period was drawing to a close and the Renaissance was beginning to spread across Europe. During Medieval times, the Christian church dominated all aspects of life, including schools and systems for educating children (Bowen, 1981). Childhood was not recognized as a unique period of life until the end of the 15th century (Trawick-Smith, 1997). In fact, once children developed past infancy they were considered to be miniature adults (Osborn, 1991; Trawick-Smith, 1997). In the society of the 15th century, there was a clearly defined class system in which the privileged classes maintained power and control over commoners or peasants (Zaller, 1984). Children of the upper classes were often provided with educational opportunities through study with a tutor or in schools in the homes of prominent families. Middle-class children left home for vocational apprenticeship, and poorer children often had to go to the streets to work (Wilds & Lottich, 1961).

The Renaissance during the 15th and 16th centuries was important to education because of achievements in the arts and literature and scientific advances that eventually influenced how children were educated (Palmer & Colton, 1992). For example, the introduction of the symbol of zero, the current symbols used in algebra, and the publication of the heliocentric theory by Copernicus all contributed to the expansion of education in Europe (Eby, 1952). During this time period, there was little, if any, attention paid to the education of young children. Those children who did receive an education were from the more privileged economic class. Younger children were considered expendable because of high rates of infant and child mortality (Wilds & Lottich, 1961; Wortham, 1992). Girls were rarely provided with the same opportunities and experiences that were available to boys (Eby, 1952; Butts, 1973).

The Reformation

The major historical event of the 16th century that influenced early childhood education was the Reformation. In 1517, Martin Luther protested practices of the Catholic Church that he believed to be greedy and corrupt. His challenge led to a protest that changed the social and educational structures across Europe and eventually influenced educational practices in the United States (Eby, 1952; Wilds & Lottich, 1961). Luther's call for reform led to the establishment of Protestantism, which gained the support of lower economic classes. As the control of schools in Germany passed from the church to lay people, schools became accessible to all economic classes (Hewes, 1995). The establishment of state-supported schools available to all people eventually spread throughout Europe. During the 16th century, schools became organized in patterns more similar to the ways schools are organized today

(Wilds & Lottich, 1961). For example, in Holland, religious groups began to conduct classes with 1 teacher for a group of 10 students (Boyd, 1965).

Martin Luther (1483–1546).   Luther is commonly referred to as the "Father of the Reformation" and is credited with a number of educational reforms. Luther opposed the power and authority of the Catholic Church by advocating that the state should control both the church and the schools. The central purpose of schooling for Luther was to learn about religion through study of the scriptures (Osborn, 1991). Many of Luther's beliefs about education reflected his strong religious convictions. For example, he considered the commandment "Honor thy Father and Mother" as the foundation of society (Eby, 1952) and believed that home training and obedience were central to all social order. Additional beliefs credited to Luther that continue to influence early childhood education include: 1) the importance of the home and family as being essential to good government and social order; 2) compulsory school attendance; 3) the importance of music in education, and 4) equal rights for all citizens (Eby, 1952; Osborn 1991; Wilds & Lottich, 1961).

Although few European Americans had settled in what was to become the United States at this time, Native Americans were living in various parts of the country. Box 2.1 briefly describes Native American family life during this time period and the ways that Native Americans instructed their children in tribal customs and practices.

1600–1800:
EMERGING AWARENESS OF THE IMPORTANCE
OF EARLY CHILDHOOD EDUCATION

Time line

1628   John Comenius wrote *The School of Infancy.*

1660   Mashpee reservation in Massachusetts became one of the first reservations set up for Native Americans.

1690   *The New England Primer,* which concentrated on Christian doctrine and was presented in rhyme, was written by Benjamin Harris. This primer was used as a textbook for young children.

1697   The famous collection of stories, *Mother Goose Tales,* appeared in France. The collection of stories included "Little Red Riding Hood," "Sleeping Beauty," "Cinderella," and "Puss in Boots."

1700   Relying on Native American labor, Spanish priests established missions from the Atlantic to the Pacific. The Native American population declined by as much as 45% during Spanish occupation in California, mostly as a result of sickness.

1744   John Newberry, the first English publisher of children's books, published the children's book *Pocketbook.*

BOX 2.1   *Native Americans in Early America*

Although Europeans regarded all Native Americans as a single group, it is estimated that no less than 240 distinct Native American groups existed during the 17th century (Mintz & Kellogg, 1988). These groups, later called "nations" by treaty writers, often consisted of a number of distinct villages or tribes that were comprised of large, extended kin networks (Coontz, 1988).

One of the most impressive values held by Native Americans was a belief in sharing and reciprocity (Coontz, 1988; Trawick-Smith, 1997). Private ownership of land or property did not exist. Instead, individual merit was tied to one's generosity with others. This view of life resulted in a flexible society in which family and community functions were interconnected, but without the presence of social institutions like the police or hospitals.

Within the family system, most marriages were monogamous. Marriage was based on individual choice, and divorce was possible. Gender roles were differentiated but flexible (Coontz, 1988). Women sometimes accompanied their husbands on hunting expeditions

and men often cared for children and assisted their wives while in camp. Children were considered to be a significant part of the natural order and, consequently, were highly cherished and valued (Trawick-Smith, 1997).

Parent-child relations among Native Americans were significantly different from those of colonial American families. Unlike the strict, repressive environment of colonial life, Native Americans adopted a more permissive style of parenting (Coontz, 1988; Mintz & Kellogg, 1988). Children were taught independence and self-discipline primarily through praise and public reward for achievement. Spanking was rarely used as a discipline technique, since it was believed that physical punishment made children timid.

Among some tribes, mothers and grandmothers were responsible for child rearing, while among other tribes, fathers and other males assumed this role. Children were active participants in family life, beginning work at an early age. Gender roles and life skills were gradually learned through modeling, stories, ceremonies, and rituals.

1769 Rev. Eleazer Wheelock opened Dartmouth College as a school for Native American youth; the Spanish established the California mission system.

1770s Thomas Jefferson influenced the development of public education in the United States by advocating local control of lower schools, rather than domination by a central government, and the separation of church and state.

1777 Vermont became the first state to abolish slavery.

During the 17th and 18th centuries, the education of children under 6 years of age was not thought of as distinctly different from that of older children (Trawick-Smith, 1997; Weber, 1984). However, the basis of many of the ideas, practices, and theories that continue to influence early childhood education were established as a developing awareness of the importance of the early years in education evolved. In Europe, educational opportunities continued to be influenced by social class during the 17th century (Wilds & Lottich, 1961). For example, upper-class children pursued a cultural education while lower-class children were engaged in religious education and apprenticeship training (Bowen, 1981; Eby, 1952).

During this time, educational opportunities became available to more people. An increased interest in educating all people, including lower economic groups, was a consequence of the growth of Protestantism (Butts, 1973). An awareness of the unique nature of childhood also emerged as writers of the period described children as fragile creations of God who needed to be safeguarded and reformed (Cleverly & Phillips, 1986, p. 7). As children began to be perceived as being different from adults, games and clothes were designed for children, and institutions designed for children's education emerged (Cleverly & Phillips, 1986; Trawick-Smith, 1997).

In the United States, the early European colonists of the 1600s valued the labor of children and believed that it kept them from growing up in idleness (Elkind, 1987; Osborn, 1991). Some children were sent to the American colonies in bondage as servants or apprentices to relieve European societies from supporting them if they were orphaned or illegitimate (Wortham, 1992). Children could also be sold or taken from families and placed as servants or apprentices in a home to learn a craft or trade. Different religious groups such as the Lutherans, the Society of Friends, The Dutch Reformed Church, and the Roman Catholics established and supported their own schools (Bowen, 1981). These schools maintained a strong focus on religion and emphasized basic skills such as reading and writing. In the Southern Colonies, European American plantation owners and aristocrats used private schools or hired tutors (Osborn, 1991). The belief that children could be used as economic tools continued to exist throughout this time period. Many children did not attend school since there was no established school system available to all (Bowen, 1981; Eby, 1952; Elkind, 1987). The early European colonists' need for laborers is also linked to the arrival of African American immigrants to the United States in the 1600s.

The first African Americans settled in the Virginia colony in 1619 and arrived in America as indentured servants (Osborn, 1991). As indentured servants, African Americans were freed after serving their term (Coontz, 1988; Mintz & Kellogg, 1988). Free African Americans could hold property, bear arms, travel freely, and even purchase slaves and white indentured servants (Coontz, 1988). However, as the need for labor expanded, it was not long before African Americans were brought to the colonies as slaves. Education was available for some African Americans in New England and there were a few schools in the South for African American children prior to the Revolutionary War (Grotberg, 1976). For example, the Virginia Colony established a public school for "Negroes and Indians" in 1620, but by 1640 the importation of slaves had become commonplace and no further provision was made for their education on any systematic basis (Osborn, 1991). By the end of the 1700s, most African American children were enslaved with little or

BOX 2.2 — *African Americans in Colonial America*

Many of the white people in these provinces take little or no care of Negro marriages; and when Negroes marry after their own way, some make so little account of these marriages that with views of outward interest they often part men from their wives by selling them far asunder, which is common when estates are sold by executors. . . . (Calhoun, 1945, p. 237).

This observation by a 1757 traveler after a trip through Maryland and Virginia reflects three challenges that confronted children in African American families (Coontz, 1988; Dill, 1988; Gutman, 1976, 1983; Mintz & Kellogg, 1988). Children lost ties to their kin and community when they were forcibly removed from their native homelands. Families were disrupted by the death and sale of family members. Male slaves lacked family and paternal authority due to their social status.

Even though these challenges were real, it is a mistake to view slave families as passive in their response to slavery. In fact, slave families took proactive steps to maintain their cultural and family lives (Trawick-Smith, 1997). For example, although it is true that slave marriages could be easily disrupted, most slaves living on larger plantations lived in two-parent households. Although male slaves lacked authority, they often attempted to prevent the sexual exploitation of their daughters, wives, and mothers (Staples, 1981). Fathers also overcame challenges to their authority by serving as role models by teaching their sons crafts, fishing, hunting, and farming skills (Genovese, 1981).

Perhaps one of the most important ways in which parents attempted to instill in their children a sense of family and community was through *fictive kin* networks. These networks granted family status to unrelated slaves, allowing children to receive support from adoptive parents or godparents. Fictive kin thus served as one strategy by which African American families maintained a sense of family unity. Fictive kin also demonstrates that few other immigrants to the colonies experienced the unique, life-threatening challenges faced by African American families.

no opportunity for formal school experiences. After the Revolutionary War, the teaching of African Americans was forbidden by law, and schools disbanded (Grotberg, 1976). Box 2.2 provides a brief description of African American family life in colonial America.

One of the most significant events during the 17th and 18th centuries was the Industrial Revolution. The Industrial Revolution began in England in the early 1700s and led to a dramatic change in the economic life of people in England, Western Europe, and the United States (Palmer & Colton, 1992). Simple, hand-operated tools were replaced by machines, and goods were no longer made at home by individual workers. People gradually moved from rural areas to cities where factories were being built and jobs were offered (Crabtree, Nash, Gagnon, & Waugh, 1992). The emergence of the factories produced harsh living and working conditions for many workers. Laborers, including children as young as 10 years of age, often spent 12 to 13 hours a day, 6 days a week, performing monotonous tasks

(Wortham, 1992). Although these inventions saved both time and money, they also indirectly created problems. For example, the invention of the cotton gin created a situation in which cotton could be cleaned and made ready for factory use faster, but more slaves were needed to pick the cotton, which increased the demand for slaves (Palmer & Colton, 1992; Wortham, 1992).

Influential People

During the 16th and 17th centuries, four men were responsible for the gradual emergence of the recognition of the early years as a distinctive area of education. Comenius, Pestalozzi, Locke, and Rousseau wrote books on education and included specific reference to the education of the young child. The works of these four men helped establish early childhood education and formed the foundation for many of our current theories and practices in early childhood education (Hewes, 1995; Weber, 1984).

Comenius (1592–1670). Comenius's beliefs about education focused on nature and the natural tendencies and experiences of childhood. That is, he contended that the natural growth of the child must be the basis for education and schooling. Many educators believe that his ideas on education have had a profound impact on general educational practices as well as on specific practices related to early childhood education. For example, Comenius asserted that there should be educational opportunities for all people. According to Comenius, schools were the best agencies for educating society and the individual. He also believed that carefully planned experiences were needed to unfold innate ideas, and that children learn through action on objects (Hewes, 1995; Weber, 1984).

A number of Comenius's beliefs continue to influence early childhood practice and theory today:

- The recognition of the concept of individual differences and delineation of stages of development (Comenius, 1956; Wilds & Lottich, 1961).
- The ideas presented in the book *School of Mother's Knee* on the significance of children's interests (Hewes, 1995). According to Comenius, the content of teaching should be drawn from children's interest in things, language, manipulation, and people.
- The belief that young children should be engaged in different types of activities consisting of the very things children love to do, such as run, jump, pour out water, lift things up, and carry things from place to place (Wilds & Lottich, 1961).
- A detailed program for young children consisting of play, games, rhymes, tales, music, and manual activity (Comenius, 1956).

John Locke (1632–1704). In the late 17th century, John Locke formulated and elaborated a theory of education that continues to influence early childhood education (Weber, 1984). The focus of Locke's ideas is on character building and the development of the moral, physical, and mental aspects of people (Osborn, 1991). Locke applied a scientific approach to human nature with an emphasis on the influence of the environment upon learning. Locke emphasized that the ultimate goal of education should be on the process of learning rather than on the products of learning (Locke, 1964).

According to Locke, human nature is not pre-formed at birth, but rather is a result of the impact of the environment upon the unformed and pliable raw material of the human organism (Locke, 1964). The idea that individuals acquire knowledge and concepts as the result of their experience is associated with the term *tabula rosa,* or blank slate (Osborn, 1991). Locke asserted that children should be considered blank slates on which learning can be influenced by experience. He was one of the first to point out that there could be no true education that did not take the nature of the individual learner into consideration (Locke, 1964; Osborn, 1991). Attention to the development of the total child through the senses of sight, taste, smell, and hearing expanded the education methods commonly used at this time (Weber, 1984). Locke also recognized the advantages of play. He felt that play was a method of learning and that children would learn much quicker when doing something they enjoyed (Locke, 1964).

Locke believed that the intellectual powers of memorizing and reasoning are developed through the study of the right kind of subject matter, such as classical languages and mathematics. This application of a discipline-based philosophy eventually led to a severe authoritarian methodology. This methodology was supported by the belief that physical and mental powers could come about only as a result of rigorous exercises of body, mind, and conduct (Locke, 1964). This authoritarian methodology developed despite Locke's opposition to severity and his original contention that the educational process should be made as pleasant as possible for the child (Weber, 1969).

Jean Jacques Rousseau (1712–1778).

Rousseau was a French philosopher who wrote a number of works that continue to influence how we view young children and their education. As with Luther and Locke, Rousseau's ideas were unique and quite provocative for the period of time in which he lived. Rousseau's writings were reactions against the absolutist monarchy, closed economic systems, religious authoritarianism, and rigid social stratification of his day (Weber, 1984). Rousseau believed that feeling was more important than reason and spontaneity and that self-indulgence and impulsive behavior were more important than reason (Boyd, 1914).

A central belief of Rousseau's philosophy was that human nature is essentially good and education must allow that goodness to unfold. According to Rousseau, people should live in a natural state without the corrupting influences or evils of society. In terms of early education, Rousseau believed that children are essentially good at birth and they should be allowed to freely express their instincts and feelings (Boyd, 1914). That is, a child should be free from all unnatural restraints of objects such as clothing and should not be controlled through punishment. It was important to Rousseau that each individual fully develop his or her own unique potential.

Rousseau believed that social and emotional adjustment were more important than the accumulation of information or skills. He contended that inner development and self-direction were key elements of education and that a central objective of education is preparation for successful human relationships. Several of the key ideas of Rousseau's philosophy were *freedom, growth, interest,* and *activity.* According to Rousseau, since the child is the center of the educational process, his or her needs and spontaneous growth processes are a starting point for learning educational concepts.

A major contribution by Rousseau was his description of the natural characteristics of children at different age levels. These stages of development were clearly delineated by special characteristics or functions (Eby, 1952; Wortham, 1992). Consequently, Rousseau's type of education was made up of a curriculum that was ordered by different age levels and was based on the interests and activities of children (Hewes, 1995). Since education should provide a firm base of experience with objects coming before symbols, textbooks had no place in education until the age of 12. According to Rousseau, the role of the teacher should be that of a guide who allows children to discover knowledge on their own rather than one who relies on teaching from textbooks. He also advocated a general education in which learning occurred through direct observation of concrete objects (Boyd, 1914).

Since Rousseau was concerned with the natural development of children, his curriculum contained activities that were based on natural experiences that relied on the senses. For example, arithmetic and geometry were not taught as formal studies but as experiential activities. Rousseau believed that children should work with a variety of objects that would become useful in counting, measuring, weighing, or comparing. By allowing children to use their natural impulses when handling and exploring objects, they would begin to perceive physical properties such as heat, hardness, size, and shape. Rousseau is also noted for his belief that a child's education should begin at birth.

Rousseau's philosophy and writing had a major impact on early childhood education. As you will see, his ideas about organizing what one teaches are based on levels of development, allowing children to explore objects before reading textbooks, and on building instruction on activities that involved the manipulation of objects. Rousseau's philosophy also influenced Pestalozzi, Froebel, Dewey, and Piaget, as well as other theorists who have contributed to present early childhood theories and practices.

Johann Pestalozzi (1746–1827).

Pestalozzi was a Swiss educator who developed theories that have influenced many current educational practices in Europe and the United States. Like Rousseau, he believed that education should be based on natural development and that every person, regardless of economic status, had the right to an education. Pestalozzi opened a school in 1774 for poor children in which he incorporated Rousseau's beliefs that children's natural instincts should be the basis for teaching. He also believed that teaching techniques such as memorization and rote learning were ineffective. He urged the use of natural objects and self-discovery to teach children through object lessons (Hewes, 1995; Weber, 1984).

One of Pestalozzi's notable contributions was his development of teaching methods that allowed him to adapt instruction to fit individual needs. He believed that children should be involved in activities that were meaningful to them, based on their own interests and experiences (Gutek, 1968). Pestalozzi adapted several of Rousseau's original ideas because he felt that Rousseau's methods were too informal. He thought that teachers should plan activities and students should be grouped with children of different ages so that the older children could help the younger ones (Gutek, 1968). He also wrote two books, *Leonard and Gertrude,* in 1885, and *How Gertrude Teaches Her Children,* in 1894, which explained his beliefs and theories.

Comenius, Rousseau, and Pestalozzi were pioneers in early childhood education because they focused on the study of children, the nature of children, and on how children learn (Hewes, 1995; Weber, 1984; Wortham, 1992). These theorists influenced efforts to improve conditions for children in Europe and early childhood education in America (Wortham, 1992). Their ideas and theories on recognizing stages of development, teaching individuals instead of groups, and using objects to teach concepts and ideas before introducing symbols and print influenced beliefs about the nature of young children and provided effective ways to teach them throughout the 18th and 19th centuries.

1800–1900:
EXPANSION AND CHANGE IN EARLY CHILDHOOD EDUCATION

Time line

1801 Johann Pestalozzi wrote *How Gertrude Teaches Her Children,* emphasizing home education and learning by discovery.

1803 The Louisiana Purchase. The United States bought territories west of the Mississippi River from France and President Jefferson proposed that many of the Indian nations living east of the Mississippi River be moved west.

1812 Public schools were established in New York state.

1816 Robert Owen set up a nursery school in Great Britain at the New Lanark Cotton Mills, believing that early education could counteract bad influences at home.

1817 Thomas Galludet founded the first residential school for the deaf in Hartford, Connecticut.

1827 Schools were made entirely free for all children in Massachusetts as support of schools by taxation was established and school attendance was made compulsory.

1830   Congress approved the Indian Removal Act, permitting the U. S. Army to force thousands of Native Americans to lands west of the Mississippi River.

1836   William McGuffey began publishing the *Eclectic Reader* for elementary school children; his writing had a strong impact on moral and literary attitudes in the 19th century.

1837   Friedreich Froebel established the first kindergarten in Blandenburgh, Germany.

1837   Horace Mann began his job as secretary of the Massachusetts State Board of Education. He believed that the growth of the common school lay in its power to prevent children from becoming criminals, which was better than trying to reform them after they had fallen.

1850   There were approximately 80,000 European Americans, 8,000 Mexicans, and 5,000 South Americans in California.

1851   The Chinese population in California grew from 4,000 to 25,000 within 1 year.

1853-1856   More than 52 treaties were made with Native American tribes and the United States gained 174 million acres of Native American lands.

1856   Mrs. Carl Shurz established the first kindergarten in the United States in Watertown, Wisconsin; the school was founded for children of German immigrants who spoke German.

1860   Elizabeth Peabody opened a private kindergarten in Boston, Massachusetts for English-speaking children.

1863   President Lincoln signed the Emancipation Proclamation.

1863   The U. S. Office of Education was established by Congress.

1864   Chinese people were recruited to work on the transcontinental railroad. At the peak of its construction, more than 10,000 Chinese workers were hired; by 1869 the railroad was completed and nearly 15,000 Chinese workers were no longer wanted in the West.

1867   Howard, Morehouse, and Talladega colleges were founded.

1869   The first special education class for the deaf was conducted in Boston.

1873   Susan Blow opened the first public school kindergarten in the United States in St. Louis, Missouri as a cooperative effort with William Harris, Superintendent of Schools.

1879   The Carlisle Indian School opened in Pennsylvania. Similar schools were founded in other states in an effort to educate Native Americans in American culture.

1880   The first teacher-training program for teachers of kindergarten, the Oshkosh Normal School, was established in Philadelphia.

1882   The first federal exclusion law aimed at a specific nationality, the Chinese Exclusion Act of 1882, was passed by Congress and signed into law by President Arthur; the law suspended Chinese immigration for the next 10 years.

1884 The American Association of Elementary, Kindergarten, and Nursery School Educators was founded to serve in a consulting capacity for other educators.

1884–1885 The National Education Association made a general recommendation that kindergartens become a part of all public schools.

1893 The San Francisco Board of Education decided to send all Japanese children to a segregated Chinese school.

1896 The U.S. Supreme Court upheld "separate but equal" doctrine in *Plessy v. Ferguson.*

1896 John Dewey started the Laboratory School at the University of Chicago, basing his program on child-centered learning with an emphasis on life experiences.

At the beginning of the 19th century, social conditions continued to change dramatically as the United States continued to move from a primarily agricultural society to an industrial society (Crabtree et al., 1992). The changing social conditions were influenced by a population that grew continuously and changed because of the geographical expansion of the country and an increase of immigrants. A growing number of Americans no longer believed the European educational system to be the best system for a democracy (Wilds & Lottich, 1961). Rather, Americans began to see the European system as one that perpetuated class distinctions rather than one that would provide educational opportunities for all people (Wortham, 1992). Educational expectations were also changing to incorporate the belief that there should be general development of all capacities for everyone rather than only trade or vocational training for some (Eby, 1952). As the industrial civilization and culture took industry out of the home and transferred it to specialized shops, the population shifted from open, country villages and small towns to cities (Crabtree et al., 1992). As described in Box 2.3, all of the members of working-class immigrant families provided needed labor for the expanding industrial economy.

In the early 1800s, children continued to be viewed as an economic asset; as a result, not all children attended schools. However, as an industrial culture developed, the changing social structure influenced how young children lived (Wilds & Lottich, 1961). In the urban areas of the East, there were different social and economic classes that included wealthy merchant families, middle-income artisans practicing trades, and lower-income apprentices and laborers. Children of the wealthy and tradesman classes were provided with access to school while the children of the labor class often had to work.

Conditions began to change during the second half of the 19th century, and children were no longer considered to be a feasible economic asset. As immigration continued to bring more people to America, adults began competing with children for jobs. Toward the end of the 19th century, the child development movement was established, which triggered a change in how children were perceived and treated (Cremin, 1988). However, after the Civil War, children continued to be needed to work in places such as mines and textile mills (Osborn, 1991).

BOX 2.3 — *European American Immigrants in Industrial America*

Working-class immigrants provided much of the skilled and unskilled labor needed to support the industrialization of America. Women and children joined men in working outside the home, often in poverty conditions. Kin and nonkin networks provided assistance in overcoming language barriers, inadequate income, substandard housing, and the sense of losing the customs and values of one's native country (Mintz & Kellogg, 1988). For example, extended kin provided support by helping relatives find employment and helping them adjust to the work environment of industrial America (Hareven, 1984). Nonkin support came from neighbors who provided job information and protected neighborhood children (Coontz, 1992).

Husband and wife relations were less differentiated than those in middle- and upper-income families. Husbands often assumed household responsibilities while their wives were away at work. Nevertheless, the value attached to the labor force employment of men and women was different. Like women today, those who worked outside the home commiserated about the lower wages attached to their work.

Parent-child relations among working-class families were less child-centered than those of higher income families, in part because of the importance of child labor to family income. Parents sometimes even worked alongside their children and supervised their work (Mintz & Kellogg, 1988). The overriding importance of work to the family lives of working-class children and adults in industrial America is reflected in an 1834 advertisement placed by a textile company in Milledgeville, Georgia:

> To hire twenty to thirty suitable laborers to work in the factory. White women, girls and boys are such as will be wanted, aged ten years and upwards. Entire families may find it to their interest to engage in our service. A good house of entertainment will be kept near the factory (Calhoun, 1945, p. 177).

The dependent period of adolescence within working-class families extended well beyond the teenage years. Adult children sometimes deferred marriage, remained at home, and continued their contribution to the family's income. Young men and women often were unable to establish households of their own until their early thirties (Mintz & Kellogg, 1988).

African Americans under slavery had no rights, and few, if any, educational opportunities; they could be separated from family members. After slaves were freed, conditions improved only slightly for African American children since their parents often worked as sharecroppers or tenant farmers for very low wages (Wortham, 1992). African American children were commonly used for child labor in the South, and not until the 20th century were educational opportunities provided to most African American children and their families. During the early 1800s, most educational opportunities for slaves were available through African American churches and philanthropic groups. Church Sunday schools provided training in literacy skills through Bible reading and memorization of biblical verses (Grotberg, 1976).

Attempts were made to establish schools for African Americans after the Civil War, which enabled some of them to pursue an education. However, they were forced to form schools without the resources available to European Americans. Several African American colleges and universities were founded between 1861 and 1890 and schools for younger children became more commonplace (Anderson, 1988; Grotberg, 1976). As the early childhood education movement began to grow and expand in the years following the Civil War, it grew along separate color lines with African Americans being excluded from the schools available to European Americans.

For Native American children, daily life was difficult as the settlement of the East Coast caused them to move west of the Mississippi River. Treaties made with Native Americans were frequently broken, their rights commonly ignored, and there was a high death rate due to susceptibility to European diseases (Grotberg, 1976). Relocation of tribes was frequent, and toward the end of the 19th century, Native Americans were moved to reservations where they were governed and controlled by the U.S. government. Education for Native American children continued to take place in the context of their tribe during westward expansion. Schools were eventually established on reservations and nearby communities. For the most part, these schools were segregated and of lower quality when compared to European American schools. A system of boarding schools was established by the end of the 19th century to educate students away from their Native American culture, values, and customs (Wortham, 1992).

The abolition of slavery, which created a new demand for inexpensive labor, led to an increase in immigration that included Asians and Southern Europeans. Chinese and Japanese immigrants settled in the western United States, while European immigrants tended to move to the eastern and midwestern sections of the country (Wortham, 1992). During the latter part of the 19th century, all ethnic groups were confronted with constant change as the country continued to change from a rural agrarian society to an urban, industrialized society (Grotberg, 1976). Not all ethnic and cultural groups were treated equally, nor did they have access to equal educational opportunities.

The Child Study Movement

After 1860, there was a dramatic rise in the child population, and as more children were visible, their needs drew more attention. The child study, or child development, movement was established as the biological sciences laid the foundation for a new psychology that approached growth and development through a series of several well-marked stages (Osborn, 1991). G. Stanley Hall, who is considered the "Father of child psychology and child development," associated child study experiments to the actual teaching of young children (Trawick-Smith, 1997). The child study movement was a natural outgrowth of the new psychology. Educators began to believe that in order for education to be valid, it should be aligned to the different stages of growth (Wortham, 1992).

Before Hall's studies, there had been little systematic investigation of child nature. As the child study movement spread into schools and throughout society, attitudes about the effects of stress on children, such as working under poor conditions, changed (Wortham, 1992). These pressures were believed to impede growth, to affect children during important stages of development, and ultimately to influence their adult lives. The need for early school experiences became apparent as the child study movement spread and people acknowledged the existence of developmental stages. Even though the practice of child labor began to decline at the end of the 19th century, there continued to be situations in which children worked in potentially damaging conditions with no opportunity for early school experiences (Cremin, 1988).

Froebel and the Growth of Kindergarten

One of the most important developments in early childhood education was the conceptualization and establishment of the kindergarten. Until the 19th century, early childhood education was not recognized as separate from education in elementary and secondary schools. Comenius, Rousseau, and Pestalozzi were pioneers in the study of children, their nature, and how they learn. Friedreich Froebel, a German, was influenced by the writings of these three men and expanded their theories as he established himself as the "Father of kindergarten" (Hewes, 1995).

Friedreich Froebel (1782–1852).

In his book *Education of Man*, Froebel described a system of kindergarten education that provided a specific direction for early childhood education. Froebel is considered to be the "great organizer of the ideas and much of the practice relating to early childhood education" (Weber, 1984, p. 33). His comprehensive work regarded education as a process and established the importance of early education in the development of personality (Eby, 1952). The need for social education that engaged children in group activities was also described. Froebel studied with Pestalozzi and incorporated many of Pestalozzi's ideas into his philosophy of education. Specifically, he believed that human growth takes place in stages, that education should focus on the child's interests and activities, and that young children should be allowed to manipulate real objects that are useful (Hewes, 1995; Weber, 1969, 1984). Froebel began the first kindergarten in 1837 in Germany.

In the kindergarten, or "child's garden," he stressed the belief that children should be allowed to choose activities of interest to them. He developed a variety of curriculum materials that he called "gifts and occupations" (Osborn, 1991; Spodek, 1991). The gifts were materials that represented symbolic ideas in a concrete form (Weber, 1969, 1984). These materials were designed with a definite sequence and clear direction for their use. Occupations were sequences of activities designed for developing different skills such as sewing, cutting, bead stringing, weaving, drawing, and pasting (Osborn, 1991; Weber, 1969).

The following ideas, originally formulated by Froebel, have influenced our beliefs about how young children develop and learn:

- Specific stages of growth occur in the following sequence: infancy, childhood, "boyhood," youth, and maturity (Froebel, 1887).
- Children's growth and learning begin in the family setting and extend in an orderly manner into school life (Eby, 1952; Elkind, 1987).
- Observation of children's behavior provides opportunities to examine the spontaneity of their actions and products (Eby, 1952; Froebel, 1887).
- Children learn by doing through activities that focus on the idea of unfolding (Hewes, 1995; Weber, 1969, 1984).
- The purpose of instruction is to provide activities in which children build habits, skill, power of will, and character rather than acquire knowledge (Weber, 1984).
- The child's inner world will be awakened through the manipulation of objects (Froebel, 1887). By manipulating objects through play, children will have opportunities for self-expression.
- Play is an important function in the development and education of young children. Play materials and objects facilitate the unfolding of the child's consciousness (Weber, 1969, 1984). According to Froebel, play was "the perfect medium for self-activity for the release of the child's inner powers" (Weber, 1984, p. 37).

By designing materials with a definite sequence and by supplying explicit directions for their use, Froebel provided an educational system with clear directions for the teacher. Froebel was an associate of Comenius, Locke, and Pestalozzi in marking the beginning of the development of education methodology appropriate for training teachers (Eby, 1952; Hewes, 1995). Since Froebel believed that training depended upon carefully elaborated and communicable methods, his kindergarten procedures were presented in complete detail (Weber, 1969). Froebel's educational ideas spread quickly throughout Europe and into the United States. A number of influential educational leaders who were interested in kindergarten, such as William T. Harris, Susan Blow, Henry Barnard, and Elizabeth Peabody, studied and applied Froebelian philosophy to the rapidly growing American kindergarten movement.

Growth of the Kindergarten in the United States

Henry Barnard, who is commonly referred to as the "Father of the American kindergarten," published the first article on kindergarten in the United States (Osborn, 1991). Barnard, who was influenced by Rousseau, believed that all citizens had a right to an education and viewed schools as agencies of social change

(Weber, 1969). The kindergarten movement in the United States was heavily influenced by Froebel, with the first kindergartens reflecting his philosophy and practices. After the first German kindergarten was established in Wisconsin in 1856, the movement began to spread to other parts of the country (Hewes, 1995; Weber, 1969). Elizabeth Palmer Peabody established an English-speaking kindergarten in 1860 and published the first text on kindergarten, which she wrote with Mary Mann (Hewes, 1995; Osborn, 1991; Weber, 1969).

Following the Civil War, the kindergarten movement grew and developed, with the majority of growth taking place in large cities (Wortham, 1992). The first public school kindergarten was established in St. Louis, Missouri under the direction of Susan Blow, who worked with the Superintendent of the St. Louis schools, William T. Harris (Eby, 1952; O'Connor, 1995; Osborn, 1991). In 1870 there were only 11 kindergartens; by 1900 there were over 5,000 kindergartens throughout the country (Wortham, 1992). The curriculum of the early kindergartens included exercises, field trips, nature study, and the use of different materials (O'Connor, 1995; Weber, 1969). Toward the end of the 19th century, conflicts related to the nature and organization of the kindergarten experience emerged (Hewes, 1995). Patty Smith Hill was one of the pioneers in the kindergarten and nursery school movement in the late 1800s and early 1900s (O'Connor, 1995; Osborn, 1991; Weber, 1969). Hill moved away from the Froebelian philosophy and was influenced by G. Stanley Hall and the child study movement (Hewes, 1995; Osborn, 1991).

In the late 1800s and early 1900s a major influence on early childhood education, the progressive movement, emerged. A central belief of this movement was that traditional schools were not keeping pace with the rapid changes of life in the United States. Advocates of progressive education believed that classrooms should be child-centered and organized around the interests of children. This belief was in opposition to the prevailing classroom practices in which the teacher was the sole authority while children sat quietly except during the recitation period.

1900–1950:
ESTABLISHMENT OF EARLY CHILDHOOD EDUCATION

Time line

1900 After 1900, Mexican and Mexican American labor made up a majority of workers on 18 western railroads and constituted 60% of the labor in southwestern mines.

1904 Asian Indians began to relocate to the United States; by 1923 there were approximately 7,000 Asian Indians living primarily on the West Coast.

1906 The San Francisco School Board ordered children of Japanese and Korean residents to attend the segregated Oriental Public School.

1907 Maria Montessori started her first preschool in Rome, Italy.

1909 The first White House Conference on Children was convened by Theodore Roosevelt.

1911 Margaret and Rachel McMillan founded an open-air nursery school in Great Britain, where the class met outdoors and there was an emphasis on healthy living.

1912 Arnold and Beatrice Gesell wrote *The Normal Child and Primary Education*.

1917 The Immigration Act of 1917 included a head tax; however, it was waived for Mexican Americans during World War I.

1918 The first public nursery schools were started in Great Britain.

1919 Harriet Johnson started the Nursery School of the Bureau of Educational Experiments, later called the Bank Street College of Education.

1923 Congress granted all Native Americans the rights of U.S. citizenship.

1924 *Childhood Education*, the first professional journal in early childhood education, was published by the International Kindergarten Union (IKU).

1924 The Immigration Act of 1924, which excluded the immigration of all Asian laborers, was signed into law.

1926 The National Committee on Nursery Schools (now called the National Association for the Education of Young Children) was initiated by Patty Smith Hill at Columbia Teachers College.

1933 The Works Projects Administration (WPA) provided money to start nursery schools so that unemployed teachers would have jobs.

1935 The National Council of Negro Women was founded.

1940 The Lanham Act provided funds for child care during World War II, mainly for day-care centers for children whose mothers worked in the war effort.

1940–1946 Demands for foreign labor increased because World War II drew domestic farm workers into industry and military service.

1942 President Roosevelt signed an Executive Order that was responsible for removing and relocating more than 110,000 persons of Japanese ancestry from the West Coast.

1943 Kaiser Child Care Centers opened in Portland, Oregon to provide 24-hour care for children.

1944 Tribal leaders met in Denver to form the National Congress of American Indians, which was dedicated to guarding Native American rights and preserving their culture, reservations, and lands.

1946 Dr. Benjamin Spock wrote the *Common Sense Book of Babies*.

At the beginning of the 20th century, American society continued to evolve as changes caused by urbanization and industrialization influenced daily life. There was an increase in the standard of living for some Americans as mechanization and agricultural and industrial development continued to create a demand for labor (Crabtree et al., 1992). As the number of immigrants increased, the rapid expansion of cities helped to create a society divided by economic class. Poor laborers were concentrated in the factory districts, the rising middle class in the suburbs, and the wealthy on country estates or in exclusive urban neighborhoods (Wortham, 1992). Americans continued to move to towns and cities as more and more job opportunities became available in larger businesses and factories (Crabtree et al., 1992). After World War I, there was a period of economic expansion and prosperity in the 1920s. However, economic conditions changed drastically as a result of the Great Depression beginning in 1929 and continuing until World War II.

The federal government's role in the provision of social and economic benefits changed dramatically in the 1930s. A precedent was set during the Depression for providing assistance to different groups of people such as farmers, the poor, the elderly, and children (Crabtree et al., 1992). The Social Security Act of 1935 resulted in the provision of services such as protection and care of the homeless, old-age pensions, and unemployment insurance. Since the beginning of the 20th century, a concern for the health, welfare, and education of children influenced federal and state policies and laws (Datta, 1976). For example, the use of children as laborers and the conditions children worked under had been a social issue among organized labor and child development advocates since the late 1800s (Osborn, 1991; Wortham, 1992). Federal laws that established minimum standards for child labor and methods for enforcement were finally enacted in 1938 (Osborn, 1991). As the number of children living in poverty increased dramatically during the Depression, agencies outside the family became more involved in establishing and implementing policies designed to improve the health and overall welfare of children.

For ethnic minorities such as African Americans, Asian Americans, Hispanics, and Native Americans, the practice of separate but unequal schools continued until the 1950s. We describe common experiences of Asian Americans during the first half of the 20th century in Box 2.4. During the early part of the 20th century, schools were not always available to African Americans. However, during the 1920s and 1930s, more schools were established in the rural South. By 1935, enough elementary schools had been built to enroll the majority of African American children (Anderson, 1988). For many African American children, separate schools meant schools that were funded at a lower level than schools for European American children. This practice was especially prevalent in the South, where services available to European American children, such as transportation, had to be provided by the parents and teachers of African American children (Wortham, 1992).

Native American children continued to attend the reservation schools that were established around the turn of the century for their first years of schooling (Wortham, 1992). After the first years of schooling, they attended boarding schools located off of the reservation for the remainder of their elementary and secondary education. Many students had difficulty adjusting to life in a different culture away from their family and native practices. Educational policies of segregation by race and the placement of disabled children in separate facilities continued to exist throughout the country during the first half of the 20th century (Wortham, 1992).

BOX 2.4 Asian Americans in Early 20th-Century America

During the latter part of the 19th century and early part of the 20th century, the Chinese and Japanese dominated Asian immigration to the United States. The first Chinese immigrants came to America to build the transcontinental railroad in the West, and later were largely employed in small businesses and service industries, such as restaurants and laundries, which did not compete with European American enterprises. The early Japanese immigrants were heavily involved in agriculture and food processing industries, especially in California (Kitano & Daniels, 1988).

The Chinese had immigrated in large numbers before the Japanese. Both the Chinese and Japanese immigrations were characterized by an initial wave of young men. Their families, left behind in China and Japan, expected to join them in America after they had established a financial foothold. However, this did not always occur. The Chinese Exclusion Act of 1882 prohibited the entry of any new Chinese workers into the United States, but more importantly, also prohibited the entry of family members of Chinese Americans already in the country. This resulted in a Chinese American community that was largely characterized by an aging, male-dominated population (Kitano & Daniels, 1988).

Japanese American immigrants were somewhat more fortunate as they were shielded from the most flagrant discriminatory practices through the support of the Japanese government (Kitano & Daniels, 1988). Japan's emerging status as a world power gave them political influence within the United States that the weak Chinese government was un-able to provide Chinese immigrants. For this reason, there were no formal limitations placed on Japanese immigration. This allowed for the entry of wives and children into the United States, which led to the Japanese community being populated by predominately intact family units. Their ability to establish families in the United States gave them stronger social and economic networks (Hing, 1993).

The isolationist period that the United States entered following World War I started a reversal of fortunes for both groups. In 1924 the Japanese were formally given the same immigration treatment the Chinese had faced since 1882—no entry (Hing, 1993). The attack on Pearl Harbor in 1941 completed this reversal of policy. As a result, the Chinese were elevated to the status of valiant allies while the Japanese were viewed as the embodiment of evil. In 1943 Congress passed the Chinese Repealer Act, which repealed the discriminatory immigration policies established in 1882. At the same time, over 120,000 Japanese Americans living on the West Coast of the United States were interned in POW camps throughout the country (Hing, 1993).

The family lives of Japanese and Chinese Americans share many characteristics. The traditional parenting style is authoritarian and patriarchal (Schwartz & Scott, 1994). The father is considered the authority figure and maintains a certain emotional distance from the children (Devore & Schlesinger, 1991; Kitano & Daniels, 1988). The mother assumes a more submissive and nurturing role, especially when the children are very young (Hing, 1993). Harsh discipline of young children is generally not practiced, but children

BOX 2.4

Asian Americans in Early 20th-Century America continued

are expected to obey and conform to family rules. However, after the child reaches school age, the schools play a greater role in shaping the expectations and behavior of children. In addition, Asian mothers are responsible for seeing that their children receive a good education. Male children are generally more valued by Asian families than girls, especially among the Chinese. As a result of children's socialization into the American cultural mainstream, second and third generation Asian children often experience conflicts with their family's traditional cultural beliefs.

Native American children often attended reservation schools in the early to mid-20th century.

Beliefs About Young Children

During the first half of the 20th century, different beliefs and perspectives about how young children learn and should be educated continued to be formulated and discussed. The child study movement begun by Hall in the late 1800s gained momentum. Individuals such as Thorndike (1910) and Gesell (1924) provided new knowledge on the measurement of intelligence, stages of growth and development, and the role of genetics in growth and development (Trawick-Smith, 1997; Weber, 1984). There was also a growing concern and sensitivity to the needs of disabled and minority children.

The progressive movement that influenced the kindergarten movement at the end of the 19th century was led by John Dewey. Dewey believed that kindergarten should move away from the religious philosophy of Froebel to a more scientific and pragmatic approach (Osborn, 1991). Dewey and other educators who were identified with the progressive movement, such as Alice Temple, had a major impact on early childhood education during the 1920s, 1930s, and 1940s (Weber, 1969, 1984). Although the progressive methods of project activities, field trips, and group work were accepted as viable teaching practices, a number of educators began to question the progressive movement. The use of standardized test results as a basis for deciding what should be taught and how instruction should be organized became a viable practice during this time period. The move away from child-centered education to practices influenced by standardized tests and predetermined curriculum was in conflict with Dewey's progressive ideas and continues to influence educational practices today.

John Dewey (1859–1952).

John Dewey was one of the first Americans whose theories had a major impact on American education. The term "child-centered curriculum" is associated with the progressive movement, which was led by Dewey while he was at the University of Chicago in the late 1890s and early 1900s (Weber, 1984). Dewey's ideas and beliefs about kindergarten challenged the Froebelian philosophy, which continued to influence many kindergarten practices at the end of the 19th century. Dewey believed that the Froebelian philosophy was too rigid, too outdated, and that the teacher dominated and initiated too many of the activities (Wortham, 1992).

A number of ideas that emerged from Dewey's reinterpretation of Froebel's activities have had a lasting impact on early childhood education. The following beliefs about the role of early childhood teachers and how young children learn continue to influence educational practice:

- The realities of everyday life should be the basis for all classroom activities in which children participate (Weber, 1984). According to Dewey, all activity should start with the child and not by the child's imitation of teacher-initiated activities (Cremin, 1964; Cuffaro, 1995; Weber, 1984).
- Children's interests should be tapped by providing opportunities to engage in daily living activities or occupations such as cooking and carpentry (Dewey, 1938).
- Children's social interests and interactions with others should also be incorporated into daily classroom life. Dewey believed that children learn about society by participating in a democratically run classroom that starts with the already familiar experiences of the home and school (Cuffaro, 1995; Weber, 1984). Children should then be introduced gradually to the community

and larger social world through outdoor games, nature study, and walks in the community (Cremin, 1964).

- Participation in play activity contributes to children's intellectual and social development. Play that relates to daily experiences and elicits problem solving on the part of the child is highly valued (Dewey, 1938). Play situations in which the child is free to choose how to play with blocks or how to use an object such as a broom are ways to enhance children's development.
- The teacher's role is that of a facilitator who encourages social skills by providing opportunities to practice them (Cuffaro, 1995). As a facilitator, the teacher includes children in planning, organizing, and evaluating their own experiences as a way to create a democracy in the classroom (Dewey, 1938).
- Social development can be encouraged in classrooms that contained children of mixed ages. Dewey believed that the divisions between grades are artificial, unnecessary, and work against social growth and development (Cremin, 1964).

Dewey's philosophy continues to influence early childhood practice, however, his beliefs about early education have sometimes been misinterpreted or unpopular. For example, people who favor a traditional approach to education that emphasizes basic skills may view Dewey's philosophy as giving children too much choice, and consequently the children do not acquire basic skills related to subject matter knowledge. Dewey did not oppose teaching basic skills and subject matter; rather, he believed that traditional educational strategies imposed knowledge on children (Weber, 1984; Wortham,1992). By the late 1940s, educational practices inspired by Dewey were coming under widespread attack. By the late 1950s, his philosophy was blamed for the perceived weak nature of American education (Wortham, 1992).

Early Childhood Education Practices

Early childhood educational practices continued to develop and change during the first half of the 20th century. Research in child growth and development influenced both the way teachers viewed the learning process and the types of experiences that were provided in kindergarten and nursery school classes (Spodek, 1991). For example, Gesell's theory of maturation and Thorndike's proposition that young children's behavior could be modified were considered by early childhood educators who implemented changes in the early childhood curriculum such as Patty Smith Hill (Weber, 1984).

In the 1900s, another philosophy and curriculum for teaching young children was developed in Italy by a doctor named Maria Montessori. Although the Montessori approach will be discussed in more detail in Chapter 10, a description is provided here to show how early childhood education continued to evolve as different programs were developed during this time.

Maria Montessori (1879–1952).   Montessori began her program when she was asked to organize schools for young children who lived in a large tenement project in Rome in the early 1900s (Goffin, 1994; Weber, 1969, 1984). Montessori originally began her work in medicine and subsequently served as an instructor in the psychiatric clinic at the University of Rome. While working in the clinic, she became interested in educating children with handicaps such as mental retardation, deafness, and paralysis. While planning the educational curriculum for the tenement program, Montessori studied the works of Rousseau, Pestalozzi, Froebel, and Seguin (Goffin, 1994; Weber, 1984). Seguin had previously developed an educational system for mentally retarded children in France.

Montessori's first school, *Casa dei Bambini,* or Children's House, opened in Rome in 1907. Through the process of planning the first *Casa dei Bambini,* Montessori was able to test her ideas and began to develop a system of "didactic materials" (Boyd, 1914). These materials were designed to provide practice in activities that focused on concepts such as form, color, texture, and quantity (Goffin, 1994; Weber, 1969). Montessori experimented with her activities and materials in her first school and subsequently demonstrated that the handicapped children could succeed on tests of reading and handwriting as well as nonhandicapped children (Weber, 1984; Wortham, 1992).

Additional opportunities were then presented to Montessori to extend and perfect her methods when she was asked to begin a day-care center for nonhandicapped children in a new housing project. There are a number of characteristics of the Children's House that were unique during the early part of the 20th century. For example, activities were organized for individuals rather than for groups, children were allowed to choose how they wanted to use the materials, and the children moved freely throughout the classroom (Boyd, 1914; Goffin, 1994; Montessori, 1949). Children were also placed in mixed-age groups and engaged in what Montessori called "practical life exercises," which involved activities such as games, manual work, gymnastics, and assisting with meals (Goffin, 1994; Montessori, 1949). Educators interested in learning about the Montessori method traveled to Italy, and Montessori schools began to appear in other countries including the United States.

A number of educators in the United States began to criticize Montessori's methods because they were perceived to be too structured, with little creativity and individual expression allowed (Goffin, 1994; Wortham, 1992). During the 1920s, Montessori schools almost disappeared in the United States because of what was perceived to be an over emphasis on academics. Montessori schools reappeared in the 1950s and continue to survive in the United States.

Kindergarten, Nursery Schools, and Child Care

During the late 19th and early 20th centuries, early childhood education involved education and care of young children by kindergartens, nursery schools, churches, philanthropic agencies, parent groups, public schools, and colleges and universities

(Weber, 1984; Wortham, 1992). The resources and methods that were developed were continuously exchanged and used by each of the different groups (Wortham, 1992). During the Depression, there was a general decline in kindergarten programs because of budget cuts in public schools. As kindergartens tended to decline during the Depression, nursery schools expanded (Hewes, 1995; Weber, 1969; Wortham, 1992).

The nursery school concept began in England through the efforts of Rachel and Margaret McMillan, who wanted to provide physical care under healthful conditions (Osborn, 1991; Weber, 1984). In the United States, nursery schools began as a result of the child study movement and research in child development (Weber, 1984). A number of child development research centers established nursery classrooms at colleges and universities in the early part of the 20th century (Osborn, 1991; Weber, 1984).

During the Depression, the federal government funded child care through nursery schools and day care in a number of ways. For example, by 1937, the Workers Progress Administration (WPA) supported up to 1,472 nursery schools in settings such as colleges and universities, high-school home economics departments, and local community agencies (Hewes, 1995; Osborn, 1991; Weber, 1984). A primary purpose of the WPA nursery schools was to provide jobs for people who were qualified to work with younger children, such as teachers (Wortham, 1992). During World War II, federal funding was provided through the Lanham Community Facilities Act, which supported nursery schools and other child-care facilities for children of working mothers (Hewes, 1995). At the end of World War II, Lanham Act nursery schools were no longer funded. Early childhood education experienced a great deal of expansion and change during the first half of the 20th century. The changes that occurred during this time period set the stage for more prominent changes during the 1950s, 1960s, and 1970s.

1950–1980:
DEVELOPMENT AND EXPANSION OF EARLY CHILDHOOD EDUCATION

Time line

1950   Erik Erikson published his writings on the "eight ages," or "stages" of personality growth and development and identified "tasks" for each stage of development. The information, known as "Personality in the Making," formed the basis for the 1950 White House Conference on Children and Youth.

1952   Jean Piaget's *The Origins of Intelligence in Children* was published in English translation.

1952   The Bureau of Indian Affairs established the Voluntary Relocation Program, which included vocational and academic training for Native Americans relocating to urban areas.

1954 The U.S. Supreme Court decided in the *Brown v. Topeka Board of Education* case that "separate but equal" doctrine was invalid in education.

1955 Rosa Parks was arrested for refusing to give up her seat to a white man on a Montgomery, Alabama bus.

1955 Rudolph Flesch's *Why Johnny Can't Read* criticized schools for their methodology in teaching reading and other basic skills.

1957 Dr. Martin Luther King, Jr. organized the Southern Christian Leadership Conference.

1957 The Soviet Union launched the Sputnik missile.

1958 The National Defense Education Act was passed to provide federal funds for improving education in the sciences, mathematics, and foreign languages.

1960 The Day Care and Child Development Council of America was formed to publicize the need for quality services for children.

1962 James Meredith fought to enter the University of Mississippi; federal troops were ordered to protect him.

1963 Cesar Chavez began his farm labor movement in the central valley of California.

1964 The Economic Opportunity Act of 1964 was passed, marking the beginning of the war on poverty and the foundation for Head Start.

1964 The Civil Rights Act of 1964 was passed.

1965 The Elementary and Secondary Education Act was passed to provide federal money for programs for educationally deprived children.

1965 The Head Start Program began with federal money allocated for preschool education; the early programs were known as child development centers.

1965 President Johnson signed a new law that repealed the National Origins Act of 1924 and established a new policy to enable large numbers of immigrants from many Asian countries to come to the United States.

1966 The Bureau of Education for the Handicapped was established.

1966 The Rough Rock Demonstrations School, the first modern school administered and controlled by a tribe, was established by the Navajo in cooperation with the Bureau of Indian Affairs.

1967 The Follow Through Program was initiated to extend the Head Start Program into the primary grades.

1968 B. F. Skinner wrote *The Technology of Teaching*, which outlined a programmed approach to learning.

1968 Dr. Martin Luther King, Jr. was assassinated in Memphis, Tennessee.

1968 The American Indian Movement was founded by Native Americans to improve social services in urban neighborhoods.

1969 The National Indian Education Association was organized in Minneapolis, Minnesota.

1970 The White House Conference on Children and Youth took place.

1971 The Stride-Rite Corporation in Boston was the first to start a corporate-supported child-care program.

1972 The National Home Start Program began with the purpose of involving parents in their children's education.

1974 The U.S. Supreme Court ruled on the case of *Lau v. Nichols*, declaring that bilingual education has to be provided to nonEnglish-speaking students.

1975 Public Law 94-142, The Education for All Handicapped Children Act, was passed, mandating a free and appropriate education for all handicapped children and extending many rights to parents of handicapped children.

1977 Congress passed the Indian Self-Determination and Education Assistance Act, which expanded tribal control over reservation programs and authorized federal funds to build public school facilities on or near reservations.

1978 Congress passed a 5-year extension of the Elementary and Secondary Education Act of 1965. This legislation continued the basic intent of the original act—federal assistance to schools with large enrollments of children from low-income families—and added funds to support the "back to basics" movement.

1979 The Department of Education was approved. Some 152 federal education programs were consolidated into the new agency; Shirley M. Hufstedler became the nation's first secretary of education.

From 1950 to 1980, the United States experienced a number of political, social, and economic changes that changed both the scope and focus of early childhood education. The launching of Sputnik in 1957 was a key event that accelerated interest in space exploration and focused the public's attention on the importance of science and mathematics education. Consequently, there was an increase in federal funding for research and education. The allocation of federal funds was based on the belief that technological and scientific innovations, along with improved schooling, would enhance American students' academic achievements and ability to compete internationally (Wortham, 1992).

There were also significant social changes as a result of the Civil Rights Movement of the 1960s. The movement focused attention on the needs of ethnic minorities and also influenced the women's movement (Crabtree et al., 1992). For African Americans, the Civil Rights Movement acquired momentum after the 1954 *Brown v. Board of Education of Topeka* Supreme Court decision that racial segregation in public schools was unconstitutional. As a result of this decision, African Americans in particular continued to seek civil rights. In 1964, the Civil Rights Act was passed, outlawing discrimination in public accommodations or employment based on race, religion, national origin, or gender (Crabtree et al., 1991). An additional piece of legislation, The Voting Rights Act of 1965, outlawed literacy tests as a requirement for African Americans to register to vote.

During the 1950s the Hispanic population began to grow in the United States.

During the 1960s, President Kennedy called for a "new frontier," which led to the establishment of programs such as space exploration and the Peace Corps. The Department of Health, Education, and Welfare was also established during Kennedy's administration. Following President Kennedy's call for social change, President Johnson continued to focus on improving American life by working with Congress to pass comprehensive legislation (Wortham, 1992). President Johnson's "Great Society" legislation also included the Elementary and Secondary Education Act of 1965. This legislation encouraged educational equity by funding programs to assist low-income, minority, and low-achieving students in school (Wortham, 1992).

By 1968, the interest and motivation for social change by means of federal legislation began to decline (Wortham, 1992). The United States was heavily involved in the war in Vietnam, and interest in social conditions and change was replaced by domestic dissent over the war (Crabtree et al., 1992). During the early 1970s, as the United States pulled out of the war, there was a large federal deficit. Public trust in the federal government deteriorated further as a result of events associated with "Watergate." By 1977, when Jimmy Carter assumed the presidency, the nation was in the midst of a recession. Inflation and rising prices impacted wages and salaries, which went up in response to inflation. The federal government also spent more in response to inflation, which resulted in larger deficits. Ronald Reagan became President in 1980 and adopted policies that focused on cutting federal spending and taxes to encourage investment and saving.

BOX 2.5 | *Hispanic Americans in the Late 20th Century*

For Hispanic Americans, family tradition is an important value. Family unity, respect, and loyalty to the family are viewed as important. Cooperation rather than competition among family members is stressed and interpersonal relationships are maintained within a large network of family and friends. The extended family includes not only blood relatives but also nonblood relatives such as the godfather and godmother, who are included as family members (Padilla & DeSnyder, 1985). Traditionally, large families have been valued in Hispanic culture.

While the family structure is generally hierarchical, with authority maintained by the father and elderly males, Hispanic mothers also exert a strong influence on their children, especially girls. Gender roles are clearly delineated and children are expected to be obedient and compliant. Male children are afforded more freedom to come and go as they wish. The concept of *machismo,* loosely translated from Spanish as "maleness," is a strong cultural value in Hispanic society. Machismo means that men should defend and honor their families and that women should defer to men's wishes at the sacrifice of their own desires and the best interest of the family (Mejia, 1983; Mizio, 1983; Sue, 1981).

Conflicts arise in Hispanic families when traditional family values and more mainstream American values meet, especially when the family's socioeconomic status has improved. Hispanic children often want to emulate mainstream American values, particularly in dating practices, which is usually met with resistance from more traditional Hispanic parents. As Hispanics become more acculturated into American society, traditional Hispanic values, such as family unity and loyalty, also undergo changes as women often acquire more independence and authority in the family (Sue, 1981).

Despite the generally optimistic economic conditions of the 1950s and early 1960s, children growing up in minority groups and/or at the poverty level did not live the comfortable lives we often associate with the middle class (Wortham, 1992). During the early 1950s, the Hispanic population began to grow as Mexican nationals entered the country as migrant workers. In addition, the Puerto Rican population grew rapidly because they could enter the United States freely as American citizens. A description of Hispanic family life during this time period is provided in Box 2.5.

As African Americans made progress in attaining equal rights, the Civil Rights Movement spread to other minority groups. For example, Native Americans organized the American Indian Movement, which focused attention on issues such as lawsuits to reclaim lands that had been illegally seized in violation of treaties. Hispanics organized into such groups as the political party "La Raza Unida" and the United Farm Workers, which represented the interests of migrant farm workers (Wortham, 1992). The Immigration Act of 1965 ended immigration quotas and opened America's doors to people from everywhere in the world (Crabtree et al., 1992).

During the 1960s, social concerns converged with new theories of child development as the basis for early childhood education (Spodek, 1991). As a result, federal policies were enacted that dramatically influenced the field. In the following sections, we discuss specific events, programs, and policies that continue to affect early childhood education.

Beliefs About Children

At the end of World War II, there was an escalation of the birthrate that is commonly referred to as the "baby boom." However, by the early 1970s, the birthrate dropped significantly as parents reduced the sizes of their families and working mothers postponed childbearing in favor of career advancement (Wortham, 1992). Other social changes began to evolve, resulting in changed family structures, lifestyles, and economics. The divorce rate rose steadily and mothers entered the workforce in increasing numbers. Many women from intact families chose to work because of economic necessity, to add to the family income, or to fulfill personal goals. By 1980, more than half of all American women were working (Hymes, 1991). The emergence of more single-parent families led to an increased need for child care. A number of advances were made in health care during this period, resulting in a lowered infant mortality rate and advances in the control of communicable diseases.

Interest in early childhood education continued to expand as beliefs about the critical nature of the early childhood years to intellectual development and learning emerged. Benjamin Bloom's work, *Stability and Change* (1964), reported longitudinal research indicating that the early years are significant to cognitive development. Bloom proposed that the environment influences development during the first 5 years of life. This research was in conflict with prevailing assumptions that intelligence was fixed at birth. According to Bloom, any type of deprivation during these years could impact cognitive and affective development. Consequently, Bloom proposed that preschool experiences could affect young children's learning (Elkind, 1987).

Hunt (1961) also provided additional support for early educational experiences. In his work *Intelligence and Experience* (1961), he questioned the assumption that intelligence was fixed and proposed that early educational experiences were critical to intellectual development. Hunt also reported that a higher level of adult intellectual capacity could be attained by providing quality educational experiences during the early years (Elkind, 1987). Hunt expanded upon the work of Piaget and focused attention on Piaget's theories of cognitive development. Piaget's work provided additional support for concentrating on children's experiences with the environment as a key element of cognitive development. Because Piaget's works have had such a tremendous impact on our ideas about children's intellectual development, we discuss his work in several parts of this text. In this chapter, we provide a brief summary of Piaget and his theories and then discuss his theories of cognitive development in Chapter 5. A curricular approach based on his theories is presented in Chapter 10.

Jean Piaget (1896–1980). Piaget was a Swiss biologist who became interested in children's thinking when he worked with French psychologist Alfred Binet in the development of intelligence tests. While working with intelligence tests, Piaget became intrigued with children's thinking in relation to the wrong answers they gave on the tests. His training in biology was influential in the development of his ideas about learning, thinking, and his theory of intelligence. Piaget conducted research at the Institute Jean Jacques Rousseau in Switzerland and developed a clinical method of interviewing and observing children.

Piaget's work was focused mainly on cognitive development, although he did publish one study of children's moral development. Many of his original studies were published in the 1920s and 1930s in Europe, but it was not until the 1960s that his work was translated and published in the United States. His work became influential, in part, because Americans were looking for ways to enhance the intellectual capabilities of the poor. Piaget's work suggested that infants and young children were active rather than passive initiators of their own learning.

Piaget is widely recognized for his contribution to a developmental perspective of the intellect. He delineated four stages of cognitive development: sensorimotor, preoperational, concrete operational, and formal operational. According to Piaget, knowledge is constructed through the organizational processes of assimilation, accommodation, and equilibration (Piaget, 1963). Currently, Piaget's work is often associated with the term "constructivism" since Piaget believed that children construct their own knowledge. In terms of curriculum and programs for young children, Piaget's theories suggest that children should be given the freedom to play, experiment, and participate in guided learning activities.

Other theorists interested in the enhancement of early learning and development contributed research demonstrating that young children's academic performance could be influenced. For example, in the 1950s and 1960s, B. F. Skinner extended the early works of Thorndike with his work in behaviorist psychology. Skinner's work focused on the shaping of behavior through operant conditioning (Weber, 1984). Operant conditioning used reinforcement strategies to increase the rate of occurrence of desired responses and to decrease the rate of undesirable behaviors through the absence of reinforcement (Todd, 1994). Skinner believed that all human behavior is externally caused and can be externally controlled. Skinner's work in behaviorism began to influence curriculum and teaching through his work on programmed instruction (Weber, 1984). We discuss more about applications of Skinner's work in Chapter 10 when we examine different early childhood curricular approaches.

During the 1960s and 1970s, attention was also focused on educational equity for children with different abilities. The segregation and isolation of handicapped children were viewed as similar to the segregation of minority children

(Wortham, 1992). In 1975, Public Law 94-142 was enacted by the U.S. Congress. This law, which is known as the Education for All Handicapped Children Act, was passed with the intent of providing special-needs children with opportunities to be educated alongside their peers. This law mandated that children with special needs be integrated, or mainstreamed, into regular classrooms. Rather than segregating children who are identified as having special needs, PL 94-142 states that children should be separated into a special school or class only if education in regular classes cannot be achieved satisfactorily due to the nature or severity of the handicap (Brewer, 1998). However, a major problem with PL 94-142 was that the law did not require states to serve children under age 6 (Mallory, 1994). Related legislation that required states to provide services to special-needs children under age 6 was not enacted until the late 1980s.

Early Childhood Programs and Practices

The federal legislation that occurred in the 1960s had a far-reaching impact on early childhood programs and curriculum. Early childhood education was linked with social reform—the early education of poor and minority children was viewed as a way to break the cycle of poverty. The improvement of school achievement for poor and minority children was approached by developing and implementing *intervention* and *compensatory* programs. Intervention programs were based on the idea that low-income children could benefit from early educational experiences prior to entering public school. Compensatory programs were based on the belief that poor and minority children need specialized educational experiences beyond the "regular" curriculum found in public schools. The philosophies of both intervention and compensatory programs were originally based on values and beliefs associated with the European American middle-class population.

Head Start and Follow Through.   The most widely recognized intervention and compensatory program in early childhood education is Project Head Start. Head Start originally began as a summer program and soon became a year-long program that was designed to encourage learning patterns, express emotions, and develop skills and attitudes that would help poor children be successful in school (McCarthy & Houston, 1980; Osborn, 1991; Spodek, Saracho, & Davis, 1991; Wortham, 1992). The following key aspects of Project Head Start have had a lasting impact on programs for young children:

- Project Head Start provides an educational program that includes comprehensive services to children from low-income families. In addition to appropriate educational experiences in a preschool setting, children and their families receive medical and dental care, meals, access to social and psychological services, and parent education.
- A social services coordinator assists families in locating community agencies when social and psychological services are needed.

- Parents are encouraged to become involved in the program by volunteering in classrooms, serving on policy advisory committees, and attending parent education classes.

A companion program, The Follow Through Project, was developed in 1967 to provide services similar to those found in Head Start. The program targeted low-income children and their families by furnishing services in kindergarten through third grade. The Follow Through Project was created because of concerns that the gains children attained academically and socially were not maintained when they began kindergarten and proceeded through the early grades in public school. Both Head Start and Follow Through are examples of federally funded programs that seek to enhance the intellectual performance and development of low-income children.

Planned variation. In the 1960s, the development of curriculum models began as psychologists concluded that the curriculum of traditional middle-class nursery schools could not effectively help children from low-income families to develop needed academic competencies (Goffin, 1994). There was a consensus among psychologists that an emphasis on cognitive and academic development was more appropriate for low-income children than a traditional social-emotional approach. A variety of experimental preschool programs or models were created, mainly by psychologists who based their curricula on theories of learning and development (Goffin, 1994; Wortham, 1992). Many times, the preschool programs were based on differing theoretical interpretations of child learning and development (Goffin, 1994).

The newer approaches, or models, became popular in the late 1960s and 1970s; however, few of these approaches were ever implemented on a large scale in public schools or private preschool settings (Spodek, 1991). Few public schools or private early childhood centers had the additional resources needed to fund these approaches. One approach that has endured and can be found in Head Start and public and private early childhood settings is the High/Scope Model (Hohmann, Banet, & Weikart, 1979). High/Scope is most often thought of as a Piagetian-based model.

For early childhood education, the late 1960s and early 1970s was a period of innovation and change. The field reflected the federal and social policies that were designed to address a high incidence of poverty and the problem of disadvantaged children's lack of school success. "Never before had a variety of philosophies and approaches to early childhood education been developed simultaneously and disseminated so widely" (Wortham, 1992, p. 51). By the middle 1970s, funding for model development was subsiding as research reports on the success of Head Start were discouraging (Wortham, 1992). Early research reports indicated that initial gains in learning appeared to be lost in the early grades. The general enthusiasm for early intervention and compensatory programs waned as federal funding declined. Head Start did continue to provide services even though the numbers of children needing the program far exceeded the capacity of Head Start programs (Wortham, 1992).

One of the legacies of this time period has been the lasting influence of child development theory and research on early childhood curriculum and practices. Theories of child development served as a primary foundation for curriculum model development. Many early childhood programs, especially those implemented outside of public schools, have reflected the belief that early childhood education should be directly derived from child development research and theory (Goffin, 1994). The optimistic spirit of the 1960s and 1970s was reflected in the establishment of new programs, a search for new knowledge, and an acceptance of many different ways of developing effective programs (Spodek, 1991).

1980–PRESENT:
CONTEMPORARY EARLY CHILDHOOD EDUCATION

Time line

1980 The White House Conference on Families was held.

1980 A preliminary U.S. Census count showed approximately 9,000,000 Mexican-descent Americans and 3,726,000 Asians and Pacific Islanders.

1981 The Coleman Report, a comparison of private and public education conducted for the National Center for Education Statistics, concluded that private schools provided better training and were more racially integrated than their public counterparts.

1981 Public Law 97-35, The Head Start Act of 1981, was passed to extend Head Start and provide for effective delivery of comprehensive services to economically disadvantaged children and their families.

1982 The Department of Education sought to remove many of the requirements placed on local schools for handicapped children; no action was taken.

1984 Congress passed a record $17.7 billion appropriation for the Department of Education in fiscal 1985. This marked the first time since taking office that President Reagan had not recommended cutting Education Department funding.

1984 Two education programs that were slated to be eliminated were extended: impact aid to school districts and Follow Through.

1984 Child-support enforcement legislation, PL 98-378, strengthened the collection of delinquent child-support payments.

1984 Congress approved aid to bilingual education.

1984 The High/Scope Educational Foundation released a study that documented the value of high-quality preschool programs for low-income children.

1986 U.S. Surgeon General C. Everett Koop called for AIDS education efforts in the early grades. By 1988, a majority of states had mandated some type of AIDS education.

1986 Congress approved PL 99-457, reauthorizing handicapped education programs for 3 years, with emphasis on preschool children.

1988 Congress reauthorized federal programs aiding elementary, secondary, and adult education. The bill authorized a total of $8.3 billion for fiscal year 1989 with few major changes in compensatory education programs.

1990 The Omnibus Human Services Reauthorization Bill increased the budget for Head Start, which in 1990 served approximately 20% of eligible children, to be sufficient by 1994 to serve all preschoolers who qualified. Budget constraints did not allow the program to reach the authorization levels.

1990 Head Start celebrated its 25th anniversary.

1991 The Carnegie Foundation issued "Ready to Learn," a plan to ensure children's readiness for school.

1992 Congress enacted the Ready to Learn Act, which provided grants to develop and distribute video programs focused on school readiness for children, parents, child-care providers, and educators.

1992 The Higher Education Act was passed by Congress, enabling more middle-class students to receive financial aid through the creation of an unsubsidized loan program, regardless of family income.

1992 The Welfare to Work Act permitted former welfare recipients to obtain federal assistance for transitioning from welfare to paid jobs in the workforce.

1993 The Goals 2000 Bill was passed by Congress, which laid the framework for academic achievement expected of all American students and schools through voluntary national standards, tests, and goals.

1993 Chapter I compensatory education program was restructured and renamed Title I, in order to provide more federal funding to states and local school districts for educating disadvantaged children.

1994 Congress passed a revised Head Start bill, restructuring the original legislation to provide more federal funding to assist preschoolers and their families as well as infants and toddlers under the age of 3.

1995 "Contract with America" proposed welfare overhaul. It ended entitlements for cash welfare benefits, converting them to other programs and individual state goals for encouraging people to move out of the welfare system.

1996 Individuals with Disabilities Education Act was reauthorized by Congress, allowing schools to distribute funds toward programs for disabled students. The principle of "the least restrictive environment" for individuals with disabilities was upheld.

1997   The Charter School concept was accepted by Congress and federal funding for such private schools was doubled, allowing them more autonomy in budgets and spending.

1997   The HELP (Helping Empower Low Income Parents) School voucher program was established to provide financial aid to allow low-income parents to send their children to private schools.

In this section we provide only a brief overview of the most recent time period and discuss one person, Lev Vygotsky. Since the remainder of this text focuses on contemporary issues, theories, and research related to child development, families, policy, and curriculum, we will discuss these topics in the context of people and events that have influenced early childhood education in the past 10 to 15 years. It is important to remember that many of the social, political, and economic factors that influence today's early childhood practices need to be considered in light of our most recent history.

During the early 1980s, the economy dominated the agendas of President Reagan and Congress with what is perceived as the greatest shift in federal spending priorities since the New Deal (Congressional Quarterly Service, 1985). By the late 1980s and early 1990s, the nation experienced the worst recession since the Great Depression and the federal deficit more than doubled. The role of federal education policies changed dramatically during the Reagan and Bush administrations. Since the large amounts of money invested in the compensatory and intervention programs of the 1960s had not eliminated the achievement differences between higher income and lower income students, there was a shift from federal interest and support in early childhood programs to state involvement (Wortham, 1992). During the Reagan and Bush administrations, there continued to be concerns with the growing number of students who were not succeeding in school. Consequently, there was a strong emphasis on raising the standards for both teachers and students and reforming and restructuring schools.

There were numerous changing social circumstances during the 1980s that continue to influence early childhood education. The rising number of single-parent households, the increase in the number of women working outside the home, an increase in homeless families with children, and an increase in births by teenage mothers have all provided federal and state governments with a rationale for examining programs and policies focused on young children. Since the mid-1980s, early childhood education has been perceived by many legislators, business people, and educators as a means for addressing social and economic problems (Goffin, 1994). The current interest in early childhood education reflects not only the success of early intervention programs begun in the 1960s, but also contemporary demographics and social and economic circumstances. In Chapter 3 we discuss how contemporary social forces, policies influencing

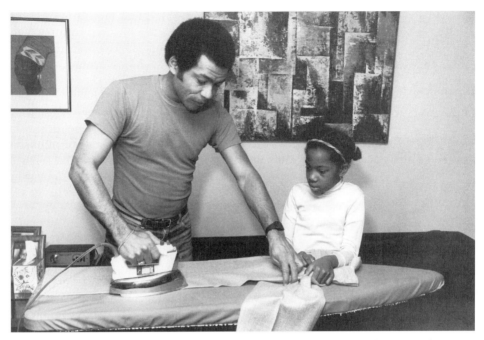

Single-parent households are one of the numerous social changes from the 1980s that continue to influence early childhood education.

school operations and teaching practices, and school programs impact early childhood education.

We have chosen to include in our discussion a final influential person, Lev Vygotsky. Vygotsky's theories about young children's development, the influence of adults on development, and how curriculum should be formulated have influenced early childhood programs and practices for the last 10 to 15 years.

Lev S. Vygotsky (1896–1934).   Lev Vygotsky was a Russian who is usually considered to be a developmental or educational psychologist. He helped reformulate psychology in the USSR in the 1920s and 1930s by seeking to make psychology more a part of a unified social science (Wertsch, 1985). Vygotsky considered how culture—the values, beliefs, customs, and skills of a social group—are transmitted to the next generation (Berk & Winsler, 1995; Bodrova & Leong, 1996). Vygotsky's perspective is called "sociocultural theory." According to Vygotsky, social interaction, in particular cooperative dialogues between children and more knowledgeable members of society, is necessary for children to acquire the ways of thinking and behaving that make up a community's culture.

Vygotsky entered adulthood just as his country was experiencing one of the greatest social upheavals of the 20th century, the Russian revolution of 1917

(Berk & Winsler, 1995; Wertsch, 1985). It was largely because of this setting that his ideas had such a significant impact in his own country. Vygotsky wanted to reformulate psychological theory along Marxist lines to develop concrete ways for dealing with practical problems such as illiteracy and cultural differences among the people of the former Soviet Union (Berk & Winsler, 1995). He was specifically concerned with children who were hearing impaired, mentally retarded, or learning disabled.

Much of Vygotsky's writings were banned for political reasons in the Soviet Union until Stalin's death in 1953. His works began to be published in 1956 and began to receive more attention in the United States in the 1970s, 1980s, and 1990s. Vygotsky believed that social interaction leads to continuous step-by-step changes in children's thought and behavior. We will discuss Vygotsky's theories on cognitive development in more detail in Chapter 5.

CHAPTER SUMMARY

Early childhood education has a unique and rich history that reflects changing social, economic, and demographic conditions. Influential people who have contributed to contemporary beliefs and practices in early childhood education include Luther, Comenius, Locke, Rousseau, Pestalozzi, Froebel, Dewey, Montessori, Piaget, and Vygotsky. As the field of early childhood education has evolved over time, many programs and curricula that were originally established to address the needs of certain groups of children have been extended to other groups and applied in different contexts. For example, Froebel's original "children's garden" was established for German children, yet today we find many of his ideas in public and private early childhood programs for children who come from upper and lower income families. It is important to remember that not all children have had equal access to early childhood programs over time. Up until the mid-20th century, ethnic minorities such as African Americans and Native Americans had few opportunities to participate in early childhood programs or they attended segregated programs.

Theories and research in child development began to strongly influence early childhood programs at the end of the 19th century and continue to guide curriculum development today. Early childhood programs and curriculum development expanded dramatically during the 1960s as early childhood compensatory and intervention programs were seen as a way to improve academic achievement of low-income and minority group children. Since the early 1980s, changing social circumstances have caused educators and policy makers to examine why there are children who are not succeeding in school.

ACTIVITIES

1. Using the philosophy you developed in Chapter 1, identify an influential person discussed in this chapter who best fits with your philosophy. Write a brief description of this person's contributions and then explain why this person's philosophy fits with your own.

2. Think about any of the activities you experienced as a young child in a preschool, a play group, kindergarten, or in the early elementary grades. Identify an influential person from this chapter whose ideas contributed to the creation and application of these activities. In small groups, discuss your experiences and the influential people who are responsible for these contributions.

3. Observe the activities that take place in a kindergarten classroom and in a first- or second-grade classroom. List any activities that can be associated with Froebel, Comenius, and Piaget. In small groups, compare your list with the lists of your classmates.

4. Locate the book *Early Childhood Education in Historical Perspective* by D. K. Osborn. Construct a time line that focuses on educational opportunities available to African Americans during the 17th and 18th centuries. How do these opportunities compare with the opportunities available to Native Americans or European Americans during the same time period?

5. Ask several teachers who work with young children to talk about their own teaching history. How long have they been working with young children? Who are the people that have influenced how they teach? Are they familiar with any of the influential people discussed in this chapter? Do they believe that they have been influenced by any one particular person discussed in the chapter? Is there anything they have learned about the history of early childhood education that affects their philosophy of teaching?

6. In small groups, discuss how federal legislation and policies have influenced early childhood education during the 20th century. What policies continue to be practiced today? Has the role of the federal government changed in the past 20 years? What predictions does your group have about the role of the federal government in early childhood education during the next 20 years?

chapter 3

Social Trends, Policies, and Programs in Early Childhood Education:

Strategies for Integration

After reading this chapter you should be able to discuss the following questions:

❖ In what ways are social forces changing early childhood education?
❖ What are the defining characteristics of different school governance approaches?
❖ What does the phrase "full-service school" mean?
❖ What types of school programs are being implemented to address social forces?
❖ In what ways are teachers both specialists and generalists?
❖ What are some strategies for pursuing child advocacy?

CHAPTER OVERVIEW

As society attempts to adjust to changing social forces, it looks to education as part of the solution to many current problems. This is especially true in regard to the preparation of children for changing job markets, work environments, and employer expectations (Johnston, 1993; Pallas, 1993; Smith, 1995). Some of the ways in which social forces are changing early childhood education include the following (Campbell & Taylor, 1996; Garcia, 1997; Morrison & Rodgers, 1996; National Commission on Children, 1991; Peters & Klinzing, 1990; Swick & Graves, 1993; Thompson, 1998):

• **Working parents.** More infants, toddlers, and preschool children are being placed in early childhood programs by working parents. As a result, greater attention is being given to raising early childhood programming standards.
• **Diversity.** Early childhood classrooms are becoming more diverse due to a widening economic gap between more affluent and poorer families, changing family structures and lifestyles, health threats like environmental pollution, alcohol and illegal drug use, a lack of universal health insurance, and diseases like AIDS. Teachers are subsequently challenged to accommodate the differences in developmental skills and life experiences represented in their classrooms.
• **Demographic patterns.** Changing demographic and immigration patterns are resulting in a wider range of languages and cultures found in schools. Teachers are subsequently challenged to understand and be responsive to varied cultural backgrounds.
• **Community services.** Early childhood programs are providing a wide range of social and health services to children and families to address multiple problems like poverty, family disorganization, health threats, and family stress. Teachers are therefore no longer limited to classroom concerns. They also must consider the impact of families and communities upon children's early development and education.

The importance of these social forces is reflected in the *educational reform movement,* a movement whose goal is to advance children's learning through changes in the educational system. In this chapter, we examine selected elements of educational reform. We begin with a review of policies and movements that are influencing school operations and teaching practices. Next, we examine the characteristics of full-service schools. Then we review school programs for a changing society. We conclude with an examination of teacher expectations that are associated with changing social forces and educational trends.

POLICIES INFLUENCING SCHOOL OPERATIONS AND TEACHING PRACTICES

Educational reform begins with a change in educational policies. A *policy* is defined as " . . . a series of interrelated choices aimed at achieving agreed-upon goals. . . " (Zimmerman, 1995, pp. 17–18). In the case of education, a number of policy choices are being examined as possible solutions to the social forces just discussed. In this section, we examine three such policies: a) school governance; b) the quality, compensation, and affordability movement; and c) developmentally appropriate practices.

School Governance

Some Americans contend that the educational system has failed to meet the needs of children, families, and society and that a change in the management of schools is needed. This argument raises an important question that, as a teacher, you will help to answer: Who should govern schools? Four approaches to school governance have been offered in response to this question: a) centralization of governance; b) governance by experts; c) decentralization of governance; and d) governance through marketplace forces (Plank & Boyd, 1994). Each approach has potential advantages and disadvantages, and there is no consensus as to which approach is most appropriate.

Consider the following reflective questions as you read about each approach. The questions are provided to help you begin to understand the challenges facing schools as they attempt to respond to changing social forces and expectations.

- What might the daily life of a teacher be like under each of the different approaches?
- What might parent-teacher, teacher-child, and teacher-administrator relationships be like under each of the different approaches?
- Which approach would you like to see schools adopt? Why do you like this approach?
- Which approach would you like to see schools reject? Why do you dislike this approach?

Centralization of school governance.

Those who advocate this position believe that a centralized authority can best ensure that educational standards are uniformly enforced. Calls for a national curriculum and a national examination system represent two examples by which a centralized approach to education might operate (Whitson, 1998).

Others are searching for a national early childhood agenda to lead us into the 21st century. A number of such agendas that were published during the early and mid-1990s continue to reflect our discussion about the goals of early childhood education in America (Boyer, 1992; Jennings, 1995; National Commission on Children, 1991). A sampling of the recommendations represented in one national agenda follows. Note how the recommendations extend outside the classroom, reflecting a focus on the "whole child," which we discussed in Chapter 1.

- **School readiness.** All children in America will start school ready to learn.
- **Safe, disciplined, and alcohol- and drug-free schools.** Every school in America will be free of drugs, violence, and the unauthorized presence of firearms and alcohol and will offer a disciplined environment conducive to learning.
- **Parental participation.** Every school will promote partnerships that will increase parental involvement and participation in promoting the social, emotional, and academic growth of children.*

Supporters of centralized school governance argue that this approach reinforces a sense of national cohesiveness and ensures that resources are equally shared between economically advantaged and disadvantaged school districts. Those who argue against this approach note that it places too much control in a central authority and downplays the unique interests, resources, and pressures of individual school districts (Spillane, 1998).

School governance by experts.

The goal of this approach is to remove the influence of personal interests from school governance by replacing them with the objective advice of disinterested experts who typically come from universities or private educational firms. It is hoped that the skills, knowledge, and objectivity of such experts will improve school operations and academic achievement.

Those who argue against this approach note that there are no "expert" solutions to school governance. In addition, experts may place too much emphasis on the cost-effectiveness of implementing new school programs while giving insufficient attention to community educational interests or to thoughtful discussions of individual school goals.

Decentralization of school governance.

This approach places decision-making responsibilities within the local community or the school itself. Advocates argue that in a democratic society decisions about educational goals and priorities

*Adapted from *National issues in education: Goals 2000 and school-to-work,* by J. F. Jennings. Copyright © 1995 by Phi Delta Kappa International.

Charter schools represent a move toward decentralization of school governance.

should be made by those who are most directly affected by them. Local communities, rather than large government departments, universities, or private firms are seen as better able to resolve local conflicts and competing interests while remaining accountable to the educational needs of children.

Charter schools represent perhaps the best example of the decentralization philosophy. *Charter schools* originate from community "entities" that are made up of individuals from educational and/or noneducational backgrounds (e.g., parents, community leaders, university faculty or staff, business leaders, cultural institution staff, educators). These entities in turn petition the state for a charter or contract to design and implement a school curriculum that is free of all or most state regulations and mandates. Subject-matter material, pedagogy, staffing patterns, and administrative and budgetary decision making are determined by those who are part of the charter. Charter schools continue to receive state funding, and their charter is reviewed every few years to determine if they are accomplishing their goals (Ellis & Fouts, 1994). One purpose of charter schools is to allow local communities to create educational environments that reflect a shared philosophy of education (Gelberg, 1997, p. 233).

Those who argue against decentralization contend that it leads to a weakening of educational standards due to pressures from influential groups and individuals within the community. For example, leaders of a charter school may be pressured to incorporate the views of special interest groups into the school curriculum. Likewise, the leaders themselves may be biased in their selection of individuals who are asked to design and implement the educational program under which the charter school will operate.

Governance through market forces.

This approach is based on the assumption that schools should operate as a "marketplace" in which parents freely choose the schools that they want their children to attend. Competition between schools is seen as reducing the influence of the "education establishment" while increasing the influence of parents. *School choice,* in which parents themselves choose the schools they want their children to attend, is a hallmark of this approach. Supporters contend that treating schools as competitors in an open marketplace will force the improvement of ineffective schools, an expansion of effective schools, and the encouragement of educational innovations.

Although it is a popular approach to school governance, a number of issues have been raised over the merits of a market approach. Some, for example, question if parents are prepared to devote the time and energy needed to make informed decisions about schools in open-market conditions (Holloway & Fuller, 1992). A listing of some of the difficult questions associated with such an approach follows:

- What criteria should be used to evaluate teachers and schools?
- How might the performance of school administrators and teachers change when their school is forced to compete with other schools for children?
- How does school choice influence family involvement in children's education?
- What happens when too many parents choose the same school for their children?
- What strategies should be used to strengthen those schools that are judged by parents to be ineffective?

Another educational issue that has attracted the attention of policymakers is the relationship between the delivery of quality child care and educational services, compensation for the professionals who deliver those services, and the affordability of those services for families and communities. Like school governance, this issue also has raised a number of questions that continue to be discussed by educators and government leaders.

The Quality, Compensation, and Affordability Movement

Families naturally expect child care and educational programs to promote their children's intellectual, social, and emotional development, their language and communication skills, and their physical development (National Association for the Education of Young Children [NAEYC], 1995). Over the past 20 years, researchers have found that the quality of early childhood programs is in fact related to children's cognitive and social development (Bryant, Peisner-Feinberg, & Clifford, 1993; Galinsky, Howes, Kontos, & Shinn, 1994; Goelman & Pence, 1987; Hayes, Palmer, & Zaslow, 1990; Helburn, 1995; Whitebrook, Phillips, & Howes, 1989). The quality, compensation, and affordability movement emerged in the 1980s when professional organizations such as the National Association for the Education of Young Children (NAEYC) began to issue policy statements that communicated the relationship between high-quality programs for young children, equitable compensation for staff, and affordable services for families or other consumers (NAEYC, 1995).

The focus on quality, compensation, and affordability increased during the 1990s as studies of licensed, full-day child-care centers and family-based care found quality to be minimally acceptable in most instances (Galinsky et al., 1994; Helburn, 1995). Quality of care was especially unacceptable for infants and toddlers (Cryer & Phillipsen, 1997), and licensing standards varied widely between states (Snow, Teleki, & Reguero-de-Atiles, 1996).

In fact, the level of quality in many U. S. child-care centers does not meet children's needs for health, safety, warm relationships, and learning (Helburn, 1995). Compensation has also been found to be inadequate since child-care teachers earn an average wage that is $5,000 less per year than the average wage for any role with comparable educational qualifications (Helburn, 1995). For example, in 1990, teachers in centers earned on the average approximately $11,500 per year (Willer, Hofferth, Kisker, Divine-Hawkins, Farquhar, & Glantz, 1991). More recent research indicates that salaries have not risen substantially since that time (Helburn, 1995). Affordability of child care is also an issue because lack of affordable child care is considered to be a serious barrier to employment or education, especially for low-income mothers (Shonkoff, 1995). To address this barrier, researchers are beginning to present evidence of the family and social economic returns that are associated with government-sponsored child-care subsidies for working families (Rohacek & Russell, 1998).

Today, a central goal of the quality, compensation, and affordability movement is to promote policies and practices that will influence the delivery of quality early childhood care and education services. Specific policies and practices that have been targeted for improvement include the following (NAEYC, 1995):

- Allowing large numbers of children to be cared for by one adult;
- Requiring minimal or no professional preparation;
- Restricting public payments for service to rates that fail to reflect actual costs of service provision;
- Exempting certain types of providers from regulation; and
- Failing to adequately enforce existing regulatory requirements.

A final important issue that is being addressed in the quality, compensation, and affordability movement relates to families and other purchasers of care (Helburn, 1995). Simply put, many families need more information about the importance of children's early years in shaping their later development and learning. Such information can help families to better understand how to distinguish good from mediocre and poor-quality centers. This is important since child-care centers cannot necessarily increase their fees to cover the increased costs of providing better care until families understand what is required to provide high-quality care and services (Helburn, 1995).

As reform in public education continues to evolve, providing quality child care and educational services to families of young children will continue to be a challenge for early childhood educators, families, and policymakers. A number of questions need to be addressed as professionals in the field consider the relationships between more qualified staff, high staff-to-child ratios, equitable compensation, and the affordability of high-quality services for all families:

- How can the public be informed about how to differentiate between high- and low-quality child care?
- Can a price-sensitive market financed primarily by fees from families and supplemented by public and private contributions be regulated to monitor quality, compensation, and affordability?
- Will child-care staff and administrators be willing to participate in ongoing training efforts?
- In periods of economic decline, how can child-care centers that depend upon donations or public funding be expected to upgrade staff qualifications, facilities, and staff-to-child ratios without dramatically raising fees?

A final policy-related issue that continues to receive a great deal of attention is "developmentally appropriate practices" (Bredekamp, 1987; Bredekamp & Copple, 1997). As you will see, this document has shaped the professional activities of early childhood educators in a number of ways.

Developmentally Appropriate Practices

Developmentally appropriate practice refers to the early childhood profession's longstanding belief that knowledge about child development should be the basis for making decisions about early childhood programs and practices. NAEYC has published guidelines reflecting the early childhood profession's definition of developmentally appropriate practice (DAP) in programs serving children from birth through age 8 (Bredekamp & Copple, 1997). These guidelines were developed following a lengthy and thoughtful process that involved the solicitation of input and feedback from thousands of early childhood practitioners (New & Mallory, 1994). The DAP document provides guidelines on curriculum, adult-child interaction, relations between the home and school, and developmental assessments of young children.

The importance of DAP became evident in the 1980s when early childhood researchers and practitioners began to note the need for a document to address a number of troubling trends, including: a) a growing emphasis on instruction in academic skills in early childhood programs; b) growth in the number of early childhood programs due to increased demand for out-of-home care; c) an increase in the enrollment of very young children in early childhood programs; d) an increasing length of the program day to accommodate a need for extended hours of care for children of employed families; and e) an increased involvement of public schools in providing prekindergarten programs and before- and after-school care (Bredekamp, 1987). There were also concerns with the use of readiness testing

Developmentally Appropriate Practices represent a set of guidelines for the care and education of children from birth through age 8.

(NAEYC, 1988) and the instructional practices required to prepare young children for standardized testing (Bredekamp & Shepard, 1989).

In order to address these challenges, the DAP document was divided into separate sections for infants and toddlers, 3-year-olds, 4- and 5-year-olds, and the primary grades serving 5- through 8-year-olds. A primary focus of DAP was to present a common philosophical approach to caring for and educating all children from birth to age 8. For example, emphasis is given to an integrated curriculum in which physical, cognitive, and social-emotional objectives are represented in all activities. Learning is promoted through free play that provides opportunities for children to choose from different materials and activities (Bryant, Clifford, & Peisner, 1991). Classrooms are child centered and well organized with the teacher playing the role of facilitator rather than director. All teachers are highly trained and interact with children in a responsive way. There is ongoing communication with families, and children are assessed using a variety of techniques rather than through the use of formal instruments.

Today, these philosophical characteristics of high-quality early childhood programs are widely accepted among early childhood educators. The importance of the DAP philosophy in defining early educational practices is perhaps best reflected in a movement by NAEYC to accredit early childhood programs that voluntarily meet DAP standards (Eisenberg & Rafanello, 1998; Talley, 1997).

A recent survey suggests a growing network of states that provide support and special recognition to those programs that seek to improve their quality through accreditation (Warman, 1998). This is significant, as research on the impact of DAP suggests that although teachers endorse DAP principles, as few as one-third to one-fifth of early childhood programs actually reflect developmentally appropriate practices (Dunn & Kontos, 1997). Likewise, gaps continue to exist in state licensing systems that regulate the care and education of young children in private (and sometimes public) centers and homes (NAEYC, 1998).

As a dominant reference point for most early childhood programs, it is important that you be familiar with DAP. It is also important to remember that DAP is not a prescription for how or what to teach. " . . . rather, it is a framework, a philosophy, or an approach to working with young children" (Bredekamp & Rosegrant, 1992, p. 4). Indeed, the usefulness of DAP as an educational guide is reflected in the success with which educators have used it to justify various instructional strategies (Burchfield, 1996).

Since the DAP document has had a significant impact on early childhood programs and practices, we will refer to it and the theories on which it is based in most of the remaining chapters of this textbook. We describe and discuss specific aspects of a developmentally appropriate philosophy and approach in greater detail in Chapter 10.

One of the realities reflected in DAP is that schools are becoming increasingly complex as administrators and teachers attempt to address the varied needs of children and families. In the following section, we review some of the steps that educators are taking as schools become full-service institutions.

FULL-SERVICE SCHOOLS

A number of characteristics make full-service schools an attractive alternative to our traditional ideas about the purpose and goals of early childhood education. However, as you will see, not everyone agrees with all aspects of full-service schools.

Characteristics of Full-Service Schools

Full-service schools go by a number of labels, including school-linked services, services integration, interprofessional collaboration, comprehensive services, collaborative services, coordinated services for children, and family support services (Knapp, 1995). As the phrase implies, the goal of full-service schools is to merge educational services with human services as a means of meeting the multiple needs of children and their families (Knapp, 1995; Stallings, 1995). An overview of services provided by full-service schools is presented in Checklist 3.1. The key characteristics of full-service schools, along with program examples, follow (see Lightburn & Kemp, 1994; Melaville & Blank, 1991, 1993).

Wide range of services.   A wide range of prevention, treatment, and support services is used to meet the multiple needs of children and families. For example, unemployment, family violence, child neglect, and school failure may have interrelated causes that require the expertise of different community professionals.

CHECKLIST 3.1

Is This a Full-Service School?

When observing a school in your community, or getting to know your own school, check to see how many of the following services are available.

Quality Education Provided by Schools

_____ Individualized instruction   _____ Healthy school climate

_____ Team teaching   _____ Alternatives to tracking

_____ Cooperative learning   _____ Parent involvement

_____ Effective discipline   _____ School-based management

Services Provided by Schools or Community Agencies

_____ Comprehensive health education   _____ Health promotion

_____ Social skills training   _____ Preparation for the world of work

Support Services Provided by Community Agencies

_____ Health-screening services   _____ Dental services

_____ Family planning   _____ Individual counseling

_____ Substance abuse treatment   _____ Mental health services

_____ Nutrition/weight management   _____ Housing/food/clothing assistance

_____ Recreation/sports/culture   _____ Mentoring

_____ Parent education/literacy   _____ Legal aid

_____ Child care   _____ Employment training

_____ Crisis intervention   _____ Community policing

Adapted from *Full-service schools* by J. G. Dryfoos. Copyright © 1994 by Jossey-Bass. Reprinted by permission.
Adapted from J. G. Dryfoos. Full-service schools. *Educational Leadership, 53,* 7:21, Figure 1. Used by permission of the Association for Supervision and Curriculum Development. Copyright © 1996 by ASCD. All rights reserved.

Arkansas: enhanced school health services.   Clinics operate in elementary, middle, and high schools to provide a wide range of services including health screening, counseling, immunizations, family planning, prenatal care, and health and family education classes. Staff includes nurses, social workers, nutritionists, and health educators (Dryfoos, 1994).

Efficient and flexible delivery of services.

Adequate resources and logistical support are used to ensure that children and families receive the range of services they need. For example, verbal referral from the school to a community service agency is not always an efficient strategy. Parents may lack the financial means, transportation, or time to follow up on such referrals. Some parents may fail to take such referrals seriously. In contrast, the delivery of such services within the schools themselves provides a more efficient way to ensure that families receive the services they need.

Communities are experimenting with a number of ways to coordinate educational and social services. Some communities are relocating social service representatives near or within schools to provide easy service access to teachers and families. Other communities are expanding school facilities for the purpose of locating human service agencies on school grounds. Still other communities are training community case managers to work across educational, human service, and health settings. Efficient and flexible service delivery is reflected in the following program example.

New Jersey: school-based youth services program.   Schools provide core services that include mental health and family counseling, drug and alcohol counseling, educational remediation, recreation, and employment services at one site. Health services are available on site or by referral. Flexibility is allowed for local programs to add additional services like child care, teen parenting classes, and hot lines. All centers are open after school, on weekends, and during summer vacation (Dryfoos, 1994).

Focus on the total family.

Total family well-being must be addressed if children are to benefit from early educational programs. This may include identifying employment opportunities for an unemployed parent, enrolling an older sibling who is addicted to drugs in a counseling program, or finding quality child care for a younger sibling whose parents must work or who want to further their own education. Kentucky is one state in which government leaders and educators have acknowledged the importance of focusing on the total family.

Kentucky: Kentucky Education Reform Act of 1990.   Among other things, this act created family resource centers and youth service centers as a means of addressing students' academic performance from a family perspective. Family resource centers provide full-time child care for 2- and 3-year-olds, after-school care, summer programs, parent education, and health services. Youth service centers provide health and human service referrals, employment counseling, drug and alcohol abuse counseling, and family crisis and mental health counseling (Dryfoos, 1994).

Empowerment of families.   Families are empowered when they are able to assert their needs and actively participate in decisions involving their members. Unfortunately, some families may feel they have little in common with teachers and human service workers. Others may mistrust schools and community agencies due to past negative experiences. Building family-school partnerships that are based on mutual respect, shared power, and a sensitivity to cultural, gender, and racial issues is therefore central to empowering families. The following example reflects one strategy used to empower families. We focus on specific family empowerment strategies in Chapter 8.

Michigan: teen health centers.   These centers are located in middle schools, high schools, or community-based centers. Information that can be used to help empower families is collected before communities receive state financial support, including community assessments of adolescent health status, needs, and attitudes. The assessments also include surveys of parents, students, and community members to determine if a center is needed and, if so, where it should be located. Each center designs its own services and policies (Dryfoos, 1994).

Outcome-based evaluation.   Simply keeping count of the number of family contacts or referrals made has no meaning in terms of outcomes. Short-term and long-term behavioral objectives must be set and assessed to determine if positive behavioral changes are being made and, if not, the adjustments needed to achieve them. The information that can result from outcome-based evaluation is reflected in the following program.

Missouri: parents as teachers program.   This program is based on a home-school partnership to give children under age 3 the best possible start in life and to support parents in their role as their child's first teachers. All socioeconomic groups are served. Families receive information on child growth and development. Health, developmental, hearing, and vision screenings are conducted on a routine basis. Parent educators make home visits to help parents learn appropriate strategies for supporting their child's development and to assist families in gaining access to needed social services. Families also serve as a support group, attending monthly group meetings.

Criteria for Creating Full-Service Schools

At the heart of all the programs summarized in this section is one goal—the creation of "pro-family schools" (Melaville & Blank, 1993). Various criteria have been suggested for assessing pro-family policies and programs. Some are specific to schools (Melaville & Blank, 1993) and others are more generic (Consortium of Family Organizations, 1990). While useful as general guides, communities also need to consider their own criteria for establishing and guiding local collaborative services. Although studies of collaborative services are limited, there are a number of factors that many professionals agree must be addressed in order to achieve family-school-community collaboration. Some of these are listed in Figure 3.1.

FIGURE 3.1 Factors that Facilitate Family-School-Community Collaboration

The following actions can help to create a cooperative environment among families, schools, and communities that will contribute to their collaboration:

- Define teacher roles to include responsibilities that go beyond teaching and learning within a classroom setting.
- Do away with mind-sets that establish rigid boundaries among home, school, and community.
- Establish a mind-set that the collaborative relationship will be equitable and productive for all concerned.
- Identify goals that are realistic.
- Allow families, schools, and social service agencies to share control in the planning and implementation of all services.
- Involve personnel from all levels of the school and social service agencies actively.
- Involve parents actively.
- Understand and value the work roles and responsibilities of all professionals involved in the delivery of educational and social services.
- Understand and value the contributions that families, schools, and social service agencies make to the total welfare of children.
- Reconcile policies and operational procedures between schools and social service agencies so that cooperative efforts, like reporting child abuse, can occur with ease.
- Provide adequate resources to support collaboration, including time, space, funds, personnel, and materials.
- Establish clear lines of communication between families, administrators, teachers, and social service professionals.

Adapted from "Coordinated services for children: Designing arks for storms and seas unknown" by Crowson, R. L., & Boyd, W. L., from *American Journal of Education* (February, 1993). Copyright © 1993 by American Educational Research Association. Reprinted by permission.

Adapted from "Components of early childhood interagency collaboration: Results of a statewide study" by Steglin, D. A., & Jones, S. D., from *Early Education and Development* (January, 1991). Copyright © 1991 by Psychology Press. Reprinted by permission.

Adapted from "Community coalitions for prevention and health promotion" by Butterfoss, F. D., Goodman, R. M., & Wandersman, A., from *Health Education Research* (September, 1993). Copyright © by Oxford University Press. Reprinted by permission.

SCHOOL PROGRAMS FOR A CHANGING SOCIETY

Another approach of the educational reform movement involves innovations in classroom instructional practices and school programs. Although often labeled as "innovative," some of the following practices and programs (Ellis & Fouts, 1994;

Greenawalt, 1994) can be traced back to educational ideas introduced as early as the 18th century (Block, Everson, & Guskey, 1995).

- **Cooperative learning.** Children of different abilities work together on projects. Projects are structured so that each child makes a contribution. Cooperation is emphasized over competition for the mutual benefit of all group members.
- **Peer tutoring.** Children who have advanced skills in a subject matter help peers who need assistance.
- **Conflict mediation.** Children are taught how to resolve conflicts between themselves peacefully. Children themselves sometimes serve as mediators in disputes.
- **Inclusion.** Children with special educational needs are taught alongside other children. Special education teachers develop lesson plans to compliment those of the classroom teacher. We discuss strategies for the inclusion of children with diverse abilities in Chapter 4.
- **Mastery learning.** Children demonstrate mastery of subject-matter material before they advance to more advanced material. The purpose of this instructional approach is to provide feedback and corrective support to students so that they are not left behind in their understanding of subject-matter material.
- **Bilingual education.** Children learn academic concepts in their own language as well as in English. The degree to which children are immersed in English varies. Some children receive instruction in their native language and then switch to English. Others receive separate lessons in English as a second language from the very beginning of school. Still others are expected to learn English from their daily interactions with teachers and peers.
- **Multicultural education.** Children are taught to understand and appreciate all racial, ethnic, and cultural groups. Educational activities reinforce diversity, social justice, acceptance of differences, and alternative life choices.
- **Distance learning.** Computer and other audiovisual technologies are used to supplement classroom instruction with educational materials and people located at distant sites.
- **Service learning.** Hands-on public service activities are performed by students within and outside schools to reinforce classroom experiences. Peer tutoring and conflict mediation are examples of possible service learning activities within schools. Community environmental and hunger relief projects are examples of service learning outside schools.
- **Looping.** Students and their teachers stay together for more than 1 year (prekindergarten-kindergarten; first grade-second grade). At the end of this period, the teacher "loops back" to pick up another class of students.
- **Multi-age classrooms.** Students from two grade levels are taught together in the same classroom. Two or more teachers may share teaching duties.
- **Family grouping.** Students in two or more grades are housed in adjacent classrooms. Although each class has its own classroom and teacher, the classrooms take part in group activities like school projects, lunch, recess, and field trips.

- **Pay for performance.** Teachers receive merit pay based upon educational goals and outcomes set by themselves or state leaders.
- **Year-round schools.** Year-round schools operate throughout the year using different calendar options. Supporters argue that year-round schools: a) break the antiquated 9-month calendar that is based on the needs of an agrarian society; b) reflect international trends in adopting a lengthened school year; c) provide disadvantaged children with additional schooling; d) save money, especially in school construction; and e) lessen school crowding. Opponents contend that: a) there is insufficient evidence to demonstrate that students learn more on year-round schedules; b) school staff experiences burnout; c) family summer vacations are disrupted; d) difficulties arise regarding the scheduling of major school repairs; and e) financial savings are minimal.
- **School choice.** Also referred to as *parental choice,* this program allows parents to decide where they send their children to school. Although usually limited to public school choice, some states are recognizing home schooling and private schools as educational alternatives. Those who favor school choice argue that: a) competition between schools leads to educational improvements; b) parental involvement in children's education increases; c) the individual needs of children are better met; and d) bureaucracy and waste in education are reduced. Those who oppose school choice contend that: a) public money used to support private schools drains resources from public schools; b) a lack of consistency in educational regulations reduces the quality of educational services; c) school choice benefits families with higher incomes more than those with lower incomes due to logistics like transportation; and d) using public money to support private religious schools violates the constitutional principle of separation of church and state.
- **Outcome-based education (OBE).** OBE is a philosophy of education that focuses on identifying educational outcomes so that instructional programs can be designed to reach those outcomes. A simple question is asked: What should every child know and be able to do by the time he or she graduates from high school? Two themes guide the response to this question. First, the curriculum should be designed backward from where teachers want students to end up. Second, focus is maintained on two types of outcomes. "Enabling outcomes" are benchmarks that are assessed as precursors to ultimate "exit outcomes." "Exit outcomes" are defined as complex capabilities and understandings that result from the mastery of specific skills and the acquisition of information over time. Exit outcomes subsequently reflect children's total time in a school system and not just the outcome at the end of the week or year.
- **Total quality management (TQM).** TQM is based on the belief that a quality educational process leads to a quality outcome. Emphasis is placed on altering school administrative practices to make educational leadership more inclusive of school staff, thereby increasing professional motivation and accountability. Some characteristics of the TQM philosophy of inclusion include: a) empowering school staff through continuous leadership and training programs rather than through standard merit system evaluations; b) abandoning externally imposed educational targets and focusing instead on

concerns and expectations of teachers themselves; c) encouraging teachers to monitor themselves by reflecting upon their teaching methods and materials; and d) abandoning the traditional "boss-management" administrative structure in favor of a facilitative "lead-management" structure that creates a more cooperative and motivating school environment.

- **Site-based management.**   The purpose of site-based management is to decentralize school governance. Control is taken away from states and is given to local communities. Directing decision making and power to localities is viewed as a means of making schools a more integral part of the community and a more efficient means of allowing schools to respond quickly and realistically to the needs of students. The charter school concept that we discussed earlier in this chapter is one example of site-based management.
- **Magnet schools.**   Originally used in the United States to desegregate schools during the 1970s, magnet schools are designed to attract students, thereby negating the sometimes difficult task of school assignment. The attraction of magnet schools is that they concentrate on certain topics like research, international studies, and the creative and performing arts. Students with interests in a particular area are often motivated to attend a magnet school even though it is not in their neighborhood. Opponents of magnet schools argue that they are not held to the same standards as other schools, that they remove the most motivated and talented students from "regular" schools, and that they cannot accommodate all students who seek admission to them.
- **Home schooling.**   Thirteen presidents received at least some home schooling, reflecting the history of this educational strategy in which parents educate children at home. In states that regulate home schooling, regulations typically address: a) parental qualifications; b) subject matter; c) required days or hours of instruction; d) purpose or intent of home schooling; and e) standardized testing. At least one state, Alaska, fully finances home schooling. Other states allow home-schooled children to participate in the extracurricular activities of public schools. Although still unresolved, one of the most important debates about home schooling is the socialization of children. While some argue that home-schooled children miss out on socializing with other children, others argue that home-school socialization may be superior to that found in schools since children have more contact with adults and children who are of different ages.

Public acceptance of these instructional approaches and school programs has been mixed. Consider one parent's reaction upon learning that conflict mediation was being implemented in his daughter's school:

> (My daughter) is not qualified to be a mediator. She's in third grade, for crying out loud ("Curriculum changes stir debate," 1994).

This reaction reflects the concern and controversy that new educational programs can create, especially when they represent a departure from parents' own educational experiences. As a teacher, you will be expected to respond to such concerns. How would you justify these instructional approaches and school programs? Use the following questions as reflective guides in considering the challenges that you and your colleagues will face as you are asked to plan and implement new educational programs:

- What social forces are creating the need for new educational approaches?
- What are the educational and social goals of new educational approaches?
- What arguments might be made by families in support of and against new educational approaches?
- How might you respond to these arguments?

CHANGING EXPECTATIONS OF TEACHERS

Although teachers' primary responsibility remains the education of children, it is clear from our discussion that, directly or indirectly, teachers are also addressing children's total life circumstances as part of their daily work. Such a comprehensive perspective creates a number of stated and unstated professional expectations for teachers. In this section, we review two of the more important professional expectations that community leaders and school administrators have of teachers.

Teachers Have Multiple Roles

As Checklist 3.2 shows, teachers carry out a number of professional roles. Even a quick review of these roles suggests that the professional life of teachers can be

Teachers carry out a number of professional roles within and outside the classroom.

CHECKLIST 3.2

What Are a Teacher's Roles?

A teacher wears many hats. Check to see how many roles you are prepared for.

Curriculum Designer

_____ Construct an attractive and interesting educational environment.

_____ Plan and implement learning activities.

_____ Select scope and sequence of subject-matter material.

_____ Adapt subject-matter content and teaching methods to individual needs.

_____ Use different teaching methods to meet individual needs.

_____ Plan short- and long-term goals for children and classroom.

_____ Match goals, subject matter, teaching techniques, and resources.

_____ Justify curriculum based on integration of developmental norms and educational theories.

Organizer of Instruction

_____ Integrate information in planning educational programs.

_____ Develop materials and search for new resources to enrich the learning environment.

_____ Organize the classroom.

Diagnostician

_____ Make use of assessment scales, observation techniques, interviews, portfolios, and other methods to assess children's educational and developmental advances.

_____ Consider the ways in which different teaching methods affect children.

_____ Offer a range of learning alternatives based on individual differences in skills, abilities, and interests.

Manager of Learning

_____ Guide children's behavior in carrying out classroom activities.

_____ Listen to children and demonstrate empathy with their feelings.

_____ Establish a daily classroom routine.

_____ Present subject matter in an interesting format.

_____ Schedule and implement transitions between activities.

continues

CHECKLIST 3.2 *Continued*

_____ Prevent behavioral problems through classroom design and curriculum implementation.

_____ Respond appropriately to behavior problems as they arise.

Protector

_____ Be aware of safety hazards within and outside the classroom.

_____ Assess children's physical well-being, including their hygiene, clothing, alertness, motor coordination, and general physical condition.

_____ Check condition of materials and equipment on a regular basis.

_____ Help children to resolve disagreements and to cooperate.

_____ Monitor children's rest and activity needs.

_____ Follow school health policies to prevent the spread of communicable diseases.

Advocate

_____ Help families identify and access community services.

_____ Keep school administrators, families, community leaders, and government representatives aware of children's educational successes and challenges.

Community Educator

_____ Provide educational workshops for parents.

_____ Write educational newsletter for parents.

Learner

_____ Reflect upon your successes and shortcomings in meeting multiple teacher roles.

_____ Weigh the advantages and disadvantages of trying new educational programs and approaches.

_____ Seek out new educational experiences for professional growth.

Adapted from "Comparing teachers' work with work in other occupations: Notes on the professional status of teaching," by B. Rowan, from *Educational Researcher* (August–September 1994). Copyright © 1994 by American Education Research Association. Reprinted by permission.

Adaptation reprinted by permission of the publisher from Spodek, B., & Saracho, O. N. (Eds.), *Yearbook in early childhood education, volume 1: Early childhood teacher preparation.* (New York: Teachers College Press, © 1990 by Teachers College, Columbia University. All rights reserved.) pp 32–35 (Table 2.1).

overwhelming. Reflection about one's strengths and challenges in carrying out multiple teacher roles is an important professional skill to develop. Thoughtful reflection about your reaction to various school situations can help you to assess your comfort with different roles. The role challenges that you identify can be addressed through educational readings, professional conferences, school in-service sessions, discussions with colleagues, and direction from experienced teachers.

Teachers Are Advocates

Some feel that only by becoming child advocates can teachers really impact the lives of children. In some cases, this may mean advocating for children and also their families. In still other cases, advocacy may become an educational citizenship objective within the classroom itself (McCall & Ford, 1998).

As you will see, child advocacy has many dimensions. For our purpose, we define *child advocacy* as a "state of mind" that leads to action (Fennimore, 1989). Unfortunately, making a decision to act is not always easy, as demonstrated in the following situation:

> For the last month David has masturbated quite actively all day long. Because he is a small child, his hand being in his pants has gone unnoticed by most of the children. I have not notified David's mother of her son's problem because she is extremely confrontational toward authority. If I advocate for her son, she is quite likely to make a fuss with the administration. What course of action should I take?*

Fortunately, child advocacy does not usually involve such dramatic situations. Rather, it is perhaps best characterized by simple and practical activities that over time have a cumulative effect. Some general advocacy strategies that you might choose to pursue are presented in Tips for Teachers 3.1.

Note how the state of California used advocacy activities to set a parent involvement policy in motion (see Solomon, 1991). Which activities reflect your personal interests and skills?

- **Announcement of policy.**   The superintendent of public instruction announced the adoption of a policy regarding a parent involvement initiative to the media.
- **Regional workshops.**   Regional workshops were conducted for school personnel and parents to introduce the policy and to collect information about successful parent involvement practices.
- **Informational booklets.**   The state department of public instruction developed booklets that included information on how parents might help students succeed in their studies.

*Adapted from Jacqueline Berner Hasson, How far should I go in advocating for one of my first-graders?, in *Young Children* (September 1998). Copyright © by Jacqueline Berner Hasson, Babylon Village, NY. Reprinted by permission.

TIPS FOR TEACHERS 3.1

Generating Teacher Advocacy

- Share your knowledge about early childhood education with the media, community task forces, and government leaders. Good policies are dependent upon quality information.
- Share your personal classroom experiences at school workshops or professional conferences, in local newspapers or professional newsletters, and with representatives regarding pending legislation.
- Join with other professionals who are working to develop issue papers, revamp community programs, or create new community initiatives to benefit children and families.
- Participate in professional organizations by presenting workshops, serving on committees, and assisting with organizational management.
- Assist parents in their efforts to speak for their children by providing reading materials that are relevant to their concerns, and by helping parents get involved in community advocacy activities.
- Be an active community citizen. Join community civic groups; serve as a member of a "telephone tree" to help mobilize others to quickly respond to events or legislation that may impact children and families.
- Keep up to date. Attend continuing education workshops and professional conferences to learn about new educational practices and child development issues.
- Understand opposing viewpoints. Keep an open mind to the opinions of others. Justifying your position requires that you understand the viewpoints of others.
- Use the internet. The internet allows us easily to keep track of cutting-edge issues related to children and education, as well as communicate with our representatives about these issues. Make it a practice to use the internet as an advocacy tool.

Adapted from Goffin, S. G., & Lombardi, J. (1988). *Speaking out: Early childhood advocacy.* Washington, DC: National Association for the Education of Young Children.

- **Reviews.**   The department also issued summaries of research findings and promising practices to school districts to support their parent involvement programs.
- **Assistance to local schools.**   The department assisted local education agencies in developing and implementing local parent involvement policies that provided families with multiple opportunities to take part in their children's educational experiences at home and at school.
- **Media collaboration.**   The department joined with a consortium of local cable television companies and state universities to produce a series of 1-hour

television programs aimed at educating parents on how to help their children with academic subjects within the home.

- **Legislative activities.**   The department worked with the state legislature to write, sponsor, and pass a law that required school districts to establish parent involvement programs.
- **Interdepartmental coordination.**   The department established an interdepartmental committee of professionals to review parent involvement activities, coordinate services to school districts, plan staff development activities, and plan evaluation studies to ensure that all activities supported the state policy on parent involvement.
- **Interagency coordination.**   The department established an interagency committee of professionals representing education and social service agencies to design ways to collaborate more effectively with each other and with families to pursue family support and family involvement activities.

CHAPTER SUMMARY

A number of social forces outside education are impacting the design and delivery of educational services. The phrase "educational reform movement" is often used to refer to the changes being made in the educational system. Three of the most important aspects of the educational reform movement include 1) school governance (How should we administer educational services?); 2) the quality, compensation, and affordability movement (What is the relationship between the cost and quality of educational services?); and 3) developmentally appropriate practices (How should we design and implement a developmentally appropriate curriculum for young children?).

The educational reform movement and the resulting move to full-service schools are resulting in a number of new educational programs and practices. Teachers must be prepared to explain and justify such new programs and practices to families and community leaders. Likewise, just as communities hold a number of expectations of schools, school and communities hold a number of expectations of teachers. In fact, teachers fulfill a number of roles throughout the school day, including child advocacy. Activity 1 provides you with an opportunity to develop your own philosophy of teacher roles and responsibilities.

ACTIVITIES

1. Review the teacher roles listed in Checklist 3.2. Write your personal philosophy of teacher roles and responsibilities in early childhood education. Use at least three roles to write your philosophy. You may find the

following questions helpful in prioritizing your selection of roles:
- Which roles are most important for a beginning teacher?
- What challenges are associated with different roles?

- With which roles do I personally feel the most comfortable?
- What types of support exist for helping me with roles with which I feel uncomfortable?

Divide into small groups and compare your respective philosophies. Discuss their possible implications for the classroom. Remember to keep your philosophy. You will refer to it as you read upcoming chapters.

2. As a class, interview teachers, school administrators, and parents about their views on the new educational strategies and school programs presented in this chapter. Discuss your results with your peers. Some possible questions to ask are:
   - Which strategies and programs were endorsed most frequently? Why?
   - Were the responses of teachers different from those of school administrators and parents?

3. Divide into small groups. Identify one social issue (e.g., child abuse, poverty, AIDS, drug abuse, immigration, etc.) that impacts education. Make three lists of your knowledge and skills related to this social issue. First, list the knowledge and skills that teachers themselves can address. Make a second list of knowledge and skills that teachers may need to acquire by consulting with school or community professionals. Make a final list of knowledge and skills that teachers may need to acquire by consulting with children's families. Which list is longer? Is there information and skills that belong in two or all three lists? What do the lists suggest about the importance of collaboration between teachers, other child professionals, and families in the education of young children?

4. Divide into small groups. Spend a few days developing a full-service school. Address the following points:
   - Identify your target audience or community (real or hypothetical).
   - State the goal of your full-service school.
   - Explain how your goal reflects the needs of families represented in your school.
   - List the services that you will provide.
   - Describe the qualifications and responsibilities of the staff who will deliver services.
   - Explain how the staff will coordinate their respective duties.
   - Identify the community location of your school.
   - Describe the methods used to deliver and evaluate the success of services.

5. As a class, collect newspaper articles related to early childhood issues. Divide into small groups. Identify specific advocacy tasks that your group might pursue to promote a particular position related to one childhood issue. Compare the different strategies used by different groups. In some cases, it might be possible to carry out one or more of your advocacy strategies.

chapter 4

Early Childhood Physical Development

After reading this chapter you should be able to discuss the following questions:

❖ Why are principles and trends of physical development important to early childhood teachers?
❖ How can teachers best meet the needs of children with diverse abilities?
❖ How can teachers help children to remain healthy?

CHAPTER OVERVIEW

The early childhood years are characterized by a period of dynamic physical development. As children move from painting with brushes to printing with pencils, they must learn to master small and large motor skills. As their games become more active, children must learn to eat properly and balance their rest and activity needs. In this chapter, we provide information to help you create an environment that is supportive of children's physical growth and development. We begin by examining the principles of physical development. Next, we review trends associated with growth and development, including perceptual-motor development. We then discuss the physical activity needs of children with diverse abilities. We conclude with a discussion of children's health. Activity 1 at the end of the chapter provides you with an opportunity to relate children's physical development to your evolving philosophy of early childhood education.

PRINCIPLES OF PHYSICAL GROWTH AND DEVELOPMENT

As we noted in Chapter 1, children's growth and development follow an orderly sequence. The early work of Gessell (1946), his colleagues (Ames, 1989), and more contemporary developmentalists like Illingworth (1987) and Tanner (1990) provide much of our knowledge about this sequence. In this section, we review the principles associated with children's growth and development as well as their implications for early childhood education.

General-to-Specific Movements

Children's movements progress from general, often poorly coordinated, movements involving the total body, to specialized and better coordinated movements involving specific body parts. This principle is seen in children's level of control over their bodies when communicating their thoughts. For example, young infants often use their entire body when reaching for an object.

Older infants display more intentional behavior by pointing to and picking up small objects. Preschoolers and school-age children manipulate a range of drawing and writing materials to express their thoughts.

Body awareness.   Children become aware of their whole body before they become aware of their body parts. Movement activities for very young children are most successful when they are planned with the whole body in mind. Teachers can gradually draw children's attention to separate body parts as they mature and their movements become more refined.

Directional Growth

The physical growth and development of children proceeds in two directions. *Cephalocaudal development* refers to physical growth and development that extends downward from the head to the feet. The cephalocaudal principle is reflected in children's motor skills. Infants first gain control over their head, then their shoulders and trunk, and finally their legs. The result is that the act of standing proceeds in a cephalocaudal direction from head to feet. Preschool and school-age children likewise have better control over their upper bodies than their legs. They subsequently find it easier to throw a ball while remaining in one spot. Throwing a ball while running is a skill that school-age children develop as they learn to coordinate their upper and lower bodies.

Proximodistal development refers to physical growth and development that extends outward from the center of the body to the extremities. Children gain control over their trunk and shoulders before controlling their arms, and they gain control over their arms before controlling their fingers. It is for this reason that preschoolers and young school-age children must first learn to control large brushes and crayons before they are introduced to pencils and pens. Painting with brushes and drawing with large crayons involve large sweeping movements made with the shoulders and arms. Printing and detailed drawings involve small, controlled movements made with the hand and fingers. This progression of physical development influences the materials that teachers provide to children. Large sheets of paper best support the large sweeping movements made by young children as they learn to gain control over their shoulders and arms. Smaller sheets of paper can be introduced as children begin to gain control over their hands and fingers.

Directional growth influences children's ability, and therefore their interest, in learning and performing different activities. For example, it is often easier to get children's cooperation in undressing themselves than in dressing. The small motor movements involved in taking off clothes are for the most part more simple than those involved in putting on clothes. Pulling a shoelace to release a tied shoe requires less skill than learning to tie shoelaces.

Reflexive-to-Voluntary Movement

A number of involuntary, primitive reflexes are present at birth that help newborns adapt to their environment. Some of these are described in Table 4.1. Primitive reflexes disappear over time and are replaced by voluntary and more complex movements. For example, very young infants display an involuntary, strong grasping reflex when a finger is inserted inside their palm. As the finger is drawn gently upward, the grasp becomes stronger. This reflex disappears at about 3 to 4 months of age and is gradually replaced by the voluntary movements of grasping and releasing. Grasping and releasing in turn form the foundation for later skills like holding a crayon, printing and writing, and throwing and catching. The disappearance of newborn primitive reflexes like the grasping reflex indicates that the nervous system, including the areas of the brain that control voluntary movements, is maturing.

Most reflexes disappear by 12 months of age, allowing children to display more voluntary movement. Teachers should note the age at which children began

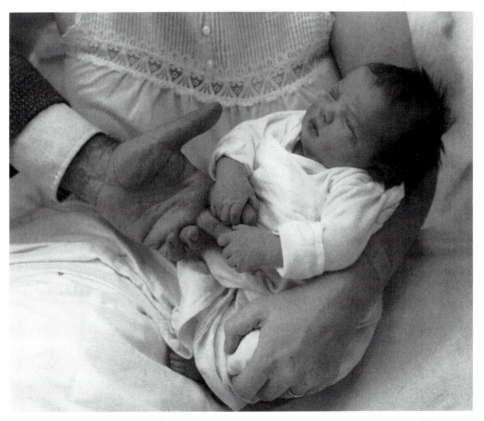

Primitive reflexes present at birth form the foundation for voluntary movements like drawing and writing.

TABLE 4.1 Newborn Reflexes

Reflex	Description	Age of Disappearance	Importance
Babinski	When the soles of infants' feet are stroked, the toes spread out and the foot curls.	After 8–12 months	Disappearance indicates nervous system is maturing
Grasping or palmer	When a finger or any other graspable object is placed in the palm of a hand, infants grasp it tightly.	After first 3 or 4 months.	Precursor of voluntary grasp and release movements that lead to manipulative motor skills
Moro	Infants held upside down or in another unnatural position throw out their arms and clench their hands.	After 4 or 5 months	May facilitate bonding; protective response
Stepping	When infants are held upright with their feet against a flat surface, they move their feet as if walking.	After 2 or 3 months	Precursor to walking
Rooting	When infants are lightly touched on the cheek with a finger, they turn their heads toward the finger and open their mouths in an attempt to suck the finger.	After 2 or 3 months	Facilitates nursing and bonding

Rooting (Rathus)

Stepping

Moro reflex (Fogel)

Babinski

Grasping

Adapted from *Children in a changing world: Development and social issues (2d ed),* by E. F. Zigler, & M. F. Stevenson. Copyright © 1993 by Wadsworth. Reprinted by permission.

Adapted from *Child development: Risk and opportunity,* by M. Krantz. Copyright © 1994 by Wadsworth. Reprinted by permission.

to display voluntary movements like walking and holding a spoon, as this information may help to put children's current motor skills into proper developmental perspective.

The Secular Trend

Demographic data indicate that children have been getting larger and growing to maturity more rapidly in industrialized countries over the past 100 years (Tanner, 1990). This phenomenon is referred to as the *secular trend*, and it is in large part due to better nutrition and disease prevention (Tanner, 1990). Although there is some evidence that the secular trend may be gradually ceasing in industrialized countries, it is continuing in poorer communities (Tanner, 1990).

Healthy environments.   Guidelines for creating healthy environments help to ensure that children meet their physical growth and development potentials. Some of the health factors that early childhood teachers are responsible for addressing include: a) adequate classroom space; b) a clean and sanitary environment; c) a safe environment that has age-appropriate materials and furnishings; d) close supervision of children's activities; and e) a diet that maximizes children's growth and development (Black, Puckett, & Michael, 1992).

Catch-Up Growth

Even after a delay in growth, due for example to malnutrition, young children have the potential to catch up with their peers if they receive proper care. Catch-up growth may occur in one of three ways. The speed of growth may increase, growth may continue for a longer period of time, or there may be a mixture of these two responses (Tanner, 1990).

Prevention versus intervention.   It is more economical and easier to prevent growth and developmental delays that it is to intervene. Today, schools are working closely with families and community agencies to identify and address problems that may interfere with children's physical growth and development.

The principles just discussed do not operate in isolation, but instead work together in directing children's physical growth and development. The cumulative influence of these principles underlies the trends in growth and development that we observe as children mature.

PHYSICAL GROWTH AND DEVELOPMENT TRENDS

In this section we first review general growth and development trends. We then review perceptual-motor trends.

Physical Growth Trends

The following trends are often considered by health professionals when assessing children's growth and development. As we have done previously, we address the implications of each trend for early childhood education.

Overall growth.   The most rapid growth during human development occurs during the *prenatal* (before birth) *period* (Rosenblith, 1992). The next most rapid period of growth occurs during infancy, surpassing even the adolescent growth spurt. Rapid growth in height and weight continues until about age 3 when growth begins to proceed at a steady, but slower, rate until around age 10 (Adams, 1991). Height and weight are most frequently tracked to assess the continuity of children's growth over time.

Teachers can work more cooperatively with health professionals in tracking children's growth if they are able to interpret growth curves. School nurses can help teachers to understand the possible consequences associated with different growth curves and their health and educational implications.

Body proportions and the center of gravity.   The proportion of body parts to total body size changes dramatically from birth to maturity (Nichols, 1990). At birth, the head makes up about one-fourth of the total body length. Although the head doubles in size by maturity, it makes up only about one-eighth of the total adult body length. In contrast, the legs increase five times their length at birth to make up about one-half the adult body length. The arms increase four times their length by adulthood, and the trunk triples in length by adulthood.

As body proportions change, so too does the body's center of gravity (Nichols, 1990). The center of gravity is located higher in the bodies of children than in adults, since children carry a higher proportion of their weight in their upper body. During the school-age years, body proportions become more adultlike and the center of gravity gradually moves to the pelvic area. This gradual shift in the center of gravity in part explains the difficulty that preschool and young school-age children have in maintaining their balance during movement activities, especially when balls or other objects are used.

Activities for body parts.   Young children are most successful when participating in activities that reflect their ability to control different body parts. For example, children's fingers begin to accelerate in growth during the preschool years so that by age 6 or 7, children are better able to grasp and manipulate objects. Attempts at teaching children to print neatly before age 6 or 7 will prove unsuccessful. Likewise, since the legs do not begin to accelerate in growth until puberty, preschool and younger school-age children perform better when participating in outdoor games that do not involve overly strenuous or sudden movements.

Activities involving balance.   The shift in children's center of gravity influences their ability to balance themselves. In particular, young children experience problems in coming to a quick stop, and they may fall when catching or throwing a ball (Nichols, 1990). Monitoring children's movement activities, as well as providing opportunities for children to practice and refine new and old movements, can help to reduce their falls.

Fat and muscle tissue.   There is an increase in the rate at which fatty tissue is deposited in the body during the first 6 months of life (Nichols, 1990). The rate then gradually decreases until age 6 to 8, only to accelerate once again just before the adolescent growth spurt.

Muscles increase in length, breadth, and width during childhood. Muscle weight increases about 40 times from birth to adulthood, making up from one-fifth to one-fourth of body weight at birth, one-third of body weight at adolescence, and two-fifths of body weight by early adulthood (Nichols, 1990).

Although we often attempt to do so, it is not possible to determine children's strength based solely upon their physical size, since children may grow taller and heavier before they grow stronger. Also, muscle strength is dependent upon environmental forces like practice, conditioning, and nutrition.

Strength activities.   Since the strength of children does not perfectly correspond to their physical size, expecting children of the same size to have equal strength or to perform the same activities with the same skill level is unrealistic. It is best to base expectations about strength on the individual skill levels of each child. We will return to this theme later in this chapter when discussing children with diverse abilities.

Sex differences.   Although boys and girls display similar height and weight patterns through late childhood, some gender differences are present in early childhood (Adams, 1991). Boys tend to outperform girls in gross motor movements like running, jumping, and throwing while girls perform better in skills requiring flexibility and fine motor coordination (Adams, 1991). It should be noted that these differences vary among children, and they may be influenced by gender-role socialization.

There is no reason to segregate young girls and boys during movement activities. Providing girls and boys with the same types of movement opportunities and encouragement helps to promote similar performance between the sexes.

Perceptual-Motor Milestones and Trends

Children's perceptual-motor skills are as important as their physical growth and development. In this section we first lay the foundation for perceptual-motor skill development by distinguishing among sensations, perceptions, and action. We then discuss the developmental trends that are associated with children's small and large perceptual-motor life skills. Implications for early childhood education are again presented.

Sensations.   "Sensation" refers to the brain's reception of information from sensory receptors in the eyes, ear, nose, tongue, skin, and muscles. Sensations carry no meaning in and of themselves. It is only when nerve impulses reach the brain, are recognized, and are assigned meaning that they become useful information to be acted upon. Teachers can stimulate young children's sensory development by providing experiences like those that follow:

- **Seasons.** Different sensations occur during the winter, spring, summer, and fall. Take advantage of changes in the weather to expose children to different temperatures, smells, and colors.
- **Community life.** The community provides a rich source of sensations. Take a short walk in the neighborhood to expose children to different sights and sounds.
- **Cooking.** Prepare a simple snack or meal to expose children to different tastes and textures.
- **Feeling.** Stimulate children's touch receptors by encouraging them to feel different textures.
- **Movement.** Stimulate children's kinesthetic receptors that monitor the body's position and movement by walking, jumping in place, and slowly turning around.

Perceptions. "Perception" refers to the process by which sensations from sensory receptors are processed in the brain so that they have meaning and provide the basis for action. Perceptions can be divided into three subprocesses (Sherrill, 1993). The first subprocess is *awareness* that a sensation has occurred. Failure to become aware of a sensation can indicate a problem with sensory receptors, nerves between receptors and the brain, or the brain itself. Awareness is promoted by experiences like the following that encourage children to use their senses to identify and label events and objects:

- Ask children to reach inside a "feel bag" and, using only their sense of touch, identify household objects as "hard" or "soft."
- Ask children to identify the colors of shirts, food, flags, and flowers.
- Ask children to identify odors by smelling cotton balls that have been dipped in familiar fragrances (e.g., fruit juices).
- Ask children to perform and identify simple movements like walking, running, jumping, and crawling.
- Ask children to close their eyes and identify by taste simple foods like apples and carrots.

The second perceptual subprocess is *discrimination,* or the ability to differentiate between different aspects of objects (e.g., color, size, and shape). For example, children learn to discriminate between colors before they learn to discriminate between shades of the same color. Discrimination is a higher-order cognitive activity that depends upon an intact nervous system, as well as experience and instruction. Discrimination is encouraged by educational games like the following that involve matching and classification:

- After children have identified the object inside the "feel bag" as hard or soft, ask them to classify it according to a set of instructions (e.g., "Is it smooth or rough?" "Can you get your hand around it?" "Have you ever felt anything else like it before?").

- Ask children to classify colors by placing fruit of the same color in the same basket. The fruit can then be further categorized based on odor or touch.
- Ask children to close their eyes and categorize odors as coming from fruit, flowers, or vegetables.
- Ask children to classify movements as slow or fast, high or low.
- Ask children to close their eyes and classify fruits and vegetables by taste alone.

Organization is the third perceptual subprocess, and it refers to children's ability to bring different pieces of sensory information into a conceptual whole (e.g., "My body is made up of different parts that do and feel different things.") and to break down the whole into its different sensory parts (e.g., "My hands are used for drawing, and my legs are used for walking"). The ability of children to organize their perceptions in creative ways is encouraged by educational activities like the following:

- Ask children to use objects in the "feel bag" to make a collage of household objects according to their use (e.g., "We use hard objects like spoons and cups when eating." "We use soft objects like sponges and napkins to keep things clean").
- Ask children to experiment with mixing different colors.
- Ask children to close their eyes and attempt to identify through smell the different fruits in a mixed fruit drink.
- Ask children to identify the parts of their body that are involved in hopping, throwing, crawling, and jumping. Children may be invited to hop or jump using one leg or to throw a small ball with their foot. Comparisons can then be made with the way they usually hop, jump, and throw.
- Ask children to experiment with new tastes and then discuss their likes and dislikes. They may choose to make "fruit faces" using different pieces of fruit. A follow-up discussion can explore the reasons why they chose different fruits to construct their fruit faces.

Action. "Action" refers to voluntary movements that result from the integration of sensations and perceptions. In order to carry out a movement, children must be aware of (sensations) and understand how to react to (perception) stimuli. It is through action that teachers are able to assess children's ability to draw conclusions based upon their sensations and perceptions. The appropriateness of children's action is facilitated by helping them to reflect upon their actions and plan accordingly.

Ms. Johnson:	"Tell me about your drawing."
Tamika:	"It's my dog, Charlie."
Ms. Johnson:	"You have used a lot of colors."
Tamika:	"Yeah. I like these colors."
Ms. Johnson:	"Charlie is a great looking dog. Is there some other way you could draw Charlie?"
Tamika:	"I don't know—no."
Ms. Johnson:	"Let's think. Do you remember the big painting that we saw yesterday?"

Tamika:	"Yeah, a picture of whales!"
Ms. Johnson:	"Could you make a big picture of Charlie?"
Tamika:	"How?"
Ms. Johnson:	"Well, you could use chalk to draw on the sidewalk. Remember, we did that a few weeks ago."
Tamika:	"Yeah. Could I draw Charlie's picture on the sidewalk?"
Ms. Johnson:	"Yes. Later, we'll compare your sidewalk picture with the one you have here."

Perceptual-motor skills.   The integration of sensations, perceptions, and action are revealed in perceptual-motor life skills like those described in Table 4.2. It is these life skills that guide teachers in their planning and facilitation of educational activities. For example, as children's perceptual-motor skills advance, so too does their manipulation of objects. Prior to age 2, children learn to reach, grasp, and release objects. During their preschool and school-age years, children refine and expand their use of objects. Consequently, the products that result from their artwork become increasingly more sophisticated, and the range of equipment they use in games increases.

As we noted earlier in this chapter and in Chapter 1, children's abilities are not always equal, even though all children follow the same physical growth and development trends. Children with diverse abilities may face different types of challenges.

CHILDREN WITH DIVERSE ABILITIES

As a teacher, you will encounter children with many different abilities. Some children may have difficulty controlling their emotions, while others may have difficulty learning new concepts. Some children may have orthopedic impairments, including a deformed or missing body part, while others may have perceptual-motor or speech impairments. Meeting the needs of all of these children need not be difficult. In this section, we address strategies for planning and facilitating the educational activities of children with diverse abilities.

Legislation Addressing Children with Diverse Abilities

During the past three decades, a number of laws were enacted establishing the right of access to federally funded programs by children and adults with diverse abilities. In 1990, the Individuals With Disabilities Education Act (IDEA, Public Law 101-476) was enacted, consolidating previous disability laws. Four concepts associated with Public Law 101-476 are especially important. These are adapted physical activity, least restrictive environment, the Individualized Education Plan (IEP), and the Individualized Family Service Plan (IFSP).

TABLE 4.2   Small Perceptual-Motor Life Skills

	Use of Writing Utensils	Object Manipulation	Manipulation of Self-Care Activities	Perceptual Skills
1 Year	Explores new objects by poking with one finger. Uses deliberate finger and thumb movement (pincer grasp) to pick up small objects.	Stacks a few objects. Places objects inside one another. Releases objects by dropping or throwing; cannot intentionally put down an object.	Manipulates objects, moving them from one hand to the other. Holds own cup; cooperates to some degree in being dressed.	Shows interest in opening and closing doors and cupboards. Imitates simple sounds. Follows simple verbal requests: come, no, bye. Points toward distant objects. Puts block in cup and takes it out when requested to do so.
2 Years	Holds crayon with gross grasp. Copies vertical and horizontal lines. Copies circular lines. Imitates a cross. Scribbles spontaneously.	Places small objects into small containers. Builds a tower of six cubes. Imitates a three-block train. Strings three large beads. Unwraps a piece of candy. Manipulates stacking rings. Pulls apart and tries to connect large pop beads. Folds paper in half imprecisely. Snips with scissors.	Feeds self with spoon. Pulls off socks. Pulls pants down with assistance. Assists with washing and drying hands. Assists with tooth brushing.	Matches two simple shapes. Matches toy animals. Matches one color.

continues

97

TABLE 4.2 Small Perceptual-Motor Life Skills *continued*

	Use of Writing Utensils	Object Manipulation	Manipulation of Self-Care Activities	Perceptual Skills
3 Years	Paints pictures with large brush. Differentiates between vertical and horizontal strokes easily. Copies a square and a cross. Traces a diamond.	Builds a 9- or 10-block tower. Places six round and six square pegs in pegboard holes. Cuts with scissors.	Feeds self with little spilling. Undresses self. Pulls pants on and off, but cannot fasten independently. Washes own hands. Brushes teeth. Zips zippers. Holds plastic cup in one hand. Wipes up spills. Approximates lacing shoes. Pours liquid into cup. Unbuttons own clothing. Pulls on socks and shoes. Washes and dries hands and face.	Matches primary colors. Sorts round and square pegs into correct holes. Works a four-piece puzzle. Tells which stimulus is missing from a previously viewed set.
4 Years	Holds brush with adult pattern. Draws crude pictures of familiar things. Copies diagonal lines. Draws large circle on chalkboard (15–20 inches). Begins to hold paper with supper hand when writing.	Manipulates lacing card to place thread through hole. Builds a six-block pyramid. Picks up scissors correctly. Cuts through paper strips. Cuts between the lines.	Screws and unscrews jar lids. Dresses self. Zips and buttons coats, shirts. Begins to cut with a knife.	Matches colored shape to colored outline on paper. Works 8–10 piece puzzles. Remembers up to three visual stimuli. Identifies common objects by feeling them (e.g., ball, block, crayon).

continues

	Use of Writing Utensils	Object Manipulation	Manipulation of Self-Care Activities	Perceptual Skills
TABLE 4.2	**Small Perceptual-Motor Life Skills** *continued*			
5 Years	Draws a triangle. Draws a recognizable human figure with head, trunk, legs, arms, and features. Draws a simple house with door, windows, roof, and chimney. Prints first name with large, irregular letters, and has frequent reversals.	Runs a small car on 1-inch-wide path without violating the boundaries. Builds a six-block step. Buttons two buttons on a button strip. Cuts 2-inch strips from larger piece of paper. Cuts on lines of increasing length (6–12 inches). Begins to cut curved lines. Folds triangle from 6-inch square.	Learns to lace shoes. Uses knife and fork together. Brushes and combs hair. Dresses and undresses alone except for tiny or hard-to-reach fasteners.	Manipulates variable size/shape puzzle pieces. Places 10 forms into formboard. Puts together two cut pieces of simple shapes (e.g., circle, rectangle). Chooses named object from group by feeling without vision. Constructs designs with blocks. Sequences four visual stimuli. Copies dot-to-dot designs.
6 Years	Draws human figure with several details and clothing. Imitates an inverted triangle. Imitates horizontal diamond. Writes upper- and lowercase letters from memory. Uses pincer grasp to manipulate writing utensils.	Cuts squares on heavy lines from construction paper. Cuts triangles on heavy lines from construction paper. Cuts circles on heavy lines from construction paper. Cuts pictures from magazines.	Blows own nose. Learns to tie own shoes. Spreads with a knife.	Places lines, circles in correct order by size. Finds matching picture from memory. Recognizes left and right sides.

continues

TABLE 4.2 Small Perceptual-Motor Life Skills *continued*

	Use of Writing Utensils	Object Manipulation	Manipulation of Self-Care Activities	Perceptual Skills
7–8 Years	Maintains tight hold on pencil. Produces letters and numbers in a deliberate fashion. Writes characters in increasingly uniform size and shape. Runs out of room on line or page on occasion when writing.	Uses knife and fork to cut food. Practices new skills in order to perfect them. Ties shoes with skill, but sometimes can't be bothered. Dresses self.	Takes pride in using good table manners. Has good control of bowel and bladder control when not stressed. Attends to tasks for longer periods of time. Assumes responsibility for personal care.	Collects and organizes objects. Reverses letters on occasion. Recalls details from stories with considerable accuracy. Enjoys reading books and stories independently.

Reproduced by permission. *Developmental profiles: Pre-birth through eight,* 2nd Ed. K. Eileen Allen., & Lynn Marotz. Delmar Publishers, Albany, New York, Copyright 1994.

From W. Dunn, "Assessment of sensorimotor and perceptual development" in *Assessing and screening preschoolers: Psychological and educational dimensions* by Nuttall, E. V., Romero, I., & Kalesnik, J. Copyright © 1992 by Allyn & Bacon. Adapted by permission.

Adapted Physical Activity

IDEA stipulates that physical education must be provided to every child who receives a public education. The phrase "adapted physical activity" reflects a philosophy of meeting the physical activity needs of individual children. The key to this philosophy is individual differences.

Individual differences can be "developmental," as in the case of children who display delayed or advanced motor coordination, or "acquired," as in the case of children who have head injuries or amputations (Sherrill, 1993). In either case, attention should be directed to including all children in all aspects of the learning environment without making a value judgement about what is normal and abnormal. As noted by one special education teacher, "inclusion is a recognition that all children have special needs" (Soriano-Nagurski, 1998, p. 41), reinforcing the idea that we should attend to the unique needs of every child regardless of his or her physical appearance or abilities. As noted by other special education specialists, "individual differences arising from disabling conditions (should be) seen as part of a general range of differences related to age, ability, ethnicity, social class and individual history" (Hanson et al., 1998, p. 195). In a study of inclusion, these specialists found the following classroom practices were most supportive in accommodating children with diverse abilities:

- Every child was assessed in each developmental domain so that individual learning plans and educational goals could be developed.
- The goals for each child were incorporated into weekly lesson plans.
- All children participated in all aspects of the daily classroom routine, including cleaning up after themselves.
- All adults in the classroom shared responsibility for all children, rather than one adult being assigned to a "special" child.
- Teachers created and extended opportunities for cooperation among children around common themes and interests.
- Teachers attached meaning to children's subtle and unconventional communication practices by "interpreting" for other children.
- Teachers provided "scaffolding" for children's interactions by first being directive and then withdrawing as children began to display more self-support in their interactions and activities.
- Teachers mediated peer entry into activities and conflict between children.

Least Restrictive Environment

The application of adapting physical activities to individual needs is reflected in the concept of least restrictive environment. IDEA stipulates that all children must be given equal opportunity to participate in the regular physical education program of a school, unless a team of individuals (including the parents) makes an informed decision that a specially designed program is more appropriate.

A least restrictive environment accommodates children with diverse abilities.

Defining a least restrictive environment depends upon the child, the nature of the physical activity, and the availability of qualified professionals (Sherrill, 1993). Consider, for example, a child in a wheelchair. A swimming pool would represent the least restrictive environment when teaching the child to swim. In contrast, a soccer field would represent a more restrictive environment in which to teach the child to play soccer. A gym or parking lot would represent least restrictive environments for this type of lesson, since they would allow the child to more easily steer the wheelchair.

Similarly, using a competitive and commanding environment when teaching a relay game would represent a restrictive environment for children with emotional problems. For example, children with Attention Deficit Hyperactivity Disorder (ADHD) have difficulty maintaining directed attention and controlling their level of activity. Providing children with ADHD the flexibility to pursue activities at their own pace and in their own way can help them adapt to group situations (Hogan, 1997). Subsequently, placing children with ADHD in a competitive situation such as that just described would restrict the ability of all to carry out the relay game. Think creatively! How might you modify the relay game to successfully include a child with ADHD so that everyone has a good time? You might find it helpful to review the strategies in Tips for Teachers 4.1 and 4.2 for creating a least restrictive environment before responding to this question.

TIPS FOR TEACHERS 4.1

Creating a Least Restrictive Physical Environment

Modifications for Youngsters Lacking Strength and Endurance

- Lower or enlarge the goal. In basketball, the goal can be lowered; in soccer the goal might be enlarged.
- Modify the tempo of the game. Use a brisk walk rather than run, or stop the game regularly for substitutions.
- Reduce the weight and/or modify the size of the projectile. A lighter object moves more slowly and inflicts less damage upon impact. A larger object is easier for children to track visually and catch.
- Reduce the distance that a ball must be thrown or served. Reduce the dimensions of the playing area or add more players to the game.
- Modify striking implements by shortening and reducing their weight. Rackets are much easier to control when they are shortened; bats are easier to control when they are lighter.
- Slow the ball down by letting some of the air out of it. This reduces the speed of rebound and makes the ball easier to control in a restricted area.
- Play the games in a different position. Some games can be played in a sitting or lying position, which is easier and less demanding than standing or running.
- Provide matching or substitution. Match a child on borrowed crutches with a child on braces. Two players can be combined to play one position.

Modifications for Youngsters Lacking Coordination

- Increase the size of goal or target. Another alternative is to offer points for hitting the backboard or getting near a goal.
- Offer protection (e.g., glasses, chest protectors, face masks, etc.). The lack of coordination makes the youngsters more susceptible to injury.
- Allow opportunity to throw at maximum velocity without concern for accuracy. Use small balls that can be grasped easily.
- Use a soft, lightweight, and slow-moving object for catching. Balloons and beach balls are excellent for beginning catching skills since they allow youngsters to track their movements visually.

Modifications for Youngsters Lacking Balance and Agility

- Increase the width of rails, lines, and beams when practicing balance. Carrying a long pole helps to minimize rapid shifts of balance and is a useful lead-up activity.
- Increase the width of the base support. Youngsters should be taught to keep their feet spread at least to shoulder width.
- Increase the surface area of the body parts in contact with the floor or beam. For example, walking flat-footed is easier than walking on tiptoes.
- Lower the center of gravity. Emphasis should be placed on bending the knees and leaning slightly forward.

continues

TIPS FOR TEACHERS **4.1**   *continued*

- Assure that surfaces offer good friction. Using carpets or tumbling mats increase a child's traction.
- Practice learning how to fall. This way children with balance problems will gradually learn how to absorb the force of the fall.

From Robert Pangrazi, *Dynamic physical education for elementary school children* (12th ed). Copyright © 1998 by Allyn & Bacon. Reprinted by permission.

Finally, it is important to note that arranging a least restrictive environment depends not only upon the diverse abilities of individual children but also on the cooperation of families, community professionals, and neighborhoods (Allred, Briem, & Black, 1998; Buysse, Wesley, & Keyes, 1998). Community-wide cooperation helps to build a sense of "connection to others," which in turn redefines inclusion as going beyond a narrow focus on "activities" and instead extends to building relationships and social networks for children with disabilities (Amado, 1993). Consider the following description of how one father described his son's connection to their neighborhood:

> Even when we walk around (a local market) . . . kids are constantly saying "hi Henry, hi Henry, . . . Even adults I don't know, know Henry. Of all the years I have lived here, I've gotten to know everybody that walks around the street. But Henry is becoming as popular as I am. He gets to know so many people. It really amazes me.*

The IEP and IFSP

IDEA-Part B mandates that individualized education programs (IEP) be developed for individuals with professionally diagnosed disabilities who are between 3 and 21 years of age. IDEA-Part H mandates that individualized family service plans (IFSP) be developed for disabled children between birth and age 2. The IEP and the IFSP represent the means by which children with disabilities are assessed, strategies are identified for addressing their needs, and evaluations are made of their progress. Both the IEP and IFSP must be developed by a multidisciplinary team that includes parents or guardians. Some of the issues that should be addressed in the IEP and IFSP are summarized in Figure 4.1.

The comprehensive approach used in developing the IEP and IFSP benefits children, families, teachers, and society (Auxter & Pyfer, 1989):

*Beckman, P. J., Barnwell, D., Horn, E., Hanson, M. J., Gutierrez, S., & Lieber, J. (1998). Communities, families, and inclusion. *Early Childhood Research Quarterly*, volume 13, number 1, 125–150. Reprinted by permission.

TIPS FOR TEACHERS 4.2

Inclusive and Encouraging Environments

- Plan activities using a positive mind-set. Create an atmosphere of encouragement.
- Selectively choose activities in which to involve the children. Pay attention to the abilities of children with disabilities, not just their disabilities.
- Help children in the regular school program to understand, accept, and feel comfortable with disabled children. Help them recognize the similarities (e.g., feelings, needs, goals, rights) between themselves and their peers with disabilities.
- Help children with disabilities develop positive coping skills. Do not allow them to use their disability to avoid self-responsibility.
- Assess children's progress on a continual basis. Use this information to make informed decisions about their progress and make plans for their future involvement in activities.
- Provide encouragement and remain sensitive to children's feelings. Reassure and reinforce children's efforts.
- Provide individual assistance. Assist children when they are experiencing difficulties performing in a group situation.
- Equalize rules. Modify rules so that everyone can contribute equally to a game.

- Encourage cooperation. Avoid games that involve elimination, instead emphasizing games that encourage groups of two or more to cooperate in order to accomplish a goal.
- Allow children to solve their own problems. Intervene only in the case of potential fighting or to facilitate the negotiation process.
- Make objectives clear. Ask children to repeat rules of play and brainstorm play strategies.
- Use a variety of activities. Challenge children to adapt their movements to new situations.

From Robert Pangrazi, *Dynamic physical education for elementary school children* (12th ed.). Copyright © 1998 by Allyn & Bacon. Reprinted by permission.
From D. Auxter el al., *Principles and methods of adapted physical education* (7th ed.) Copyright © 1992 by The McGraw-Hill Companies. Reproduced by permission.
From B. Nichols, *Moving and learning: The elementary school physical education experience* (3rd ed.). Copyright © 1994 by The McGraw-Hill Companies. Reproduced by permission.

- Children benefit by receiving a quality education.
- Parents are empowered by their involvement in helping to plan the services that their children receive.
- Teachers benefit from having a plan from which to conduct activities that build toward achievable goals.
- Society benefits as a result of children meeting educational goals that promote self-sufficiency, thereby reducing dependency on societal resources.

Regardless of their physical abilities, all children face health challenges. In the following section, we examine the role of teachers in keeping children healthy.

FIGURE 4.1   The IEP and IFSP

The IEP addresses the following issues:

- The child's level of educational performance.
- The instructional objectives for meeting educational goals.
- The services that will be provided to the child and the ways in which the child will participate in the regular school program.
- The dates for beginning services and an estimation of their duration.
- An evaluation plan for determining if objectives are being met.
- A transition plan to ensure that the needs and rights of children continue to be met once they leave school.

The IFSP addresses the following issues:

- The status of the child's development.
- Information about family strengths and needs.
- Projected goals, along with objectives and a time line for meeting those goals.
- The dates for beginning services and an estimation of their duration.
- Identification of the case manager who will coordinate interagency services for the child and family.
- A transition plan to ensure that the rights and needs of the child and family continue to be met when they move between programs or schools.

From Robert Pangrazi, *Dynamic physical education for elementary school children* (12th ed.). Copyright © 1998 by Allyn & Bacon. Reprinted by permission.

From B. Nichols, *Moving and learning: The elementary school physical education experience* (3rd ed.). Copyright © 1994 by The McGraw-Hill Companies. Reproduced by permission.

PLANNING FOR CHILDREN'S HEALTH

Childhood health involves all three domains of development that we referred to in Chapter 1, thus making it possible for children to be "healthy" in one domain but not in other domains (Pollock, 1994). Health education is one means by which teachers assist children to make life choices (e.g., exercise, diet, safety) that will lead to a total state of well-being. In this section, we focus on three aspects of health for which teachers have been given responsibility. These include the control of environmental toxins, the prevention of communicable diseases, and the facilitation of children's nutritional habits.

Environmental Toxins

Children are susceptible to a range of environmental toxins like cleaners, smoke, gases, and other air-borne or solid pollutants. Chemicals used for daily cleaning and those in building and classroom paints may not be detectable even by teachers. In addition, some urban areas now have "ozone alert days" during which high levels of ozone can irritate eyes and cause breathing difficulty in young children and the elderly.

Such widespread environmental toxins can be especially threatening to the health of young children because of their immature body systems and rapid growth (Marotz, Cross, & Rush, 1993; Noyes, 1987). Some common health effects of environmental toxins include a chronic cough, headaches, dizziness, fatigue, eye irritation, skin irritation, nausea, and shortness of breath (Marotz et al., 1993). Fortunately, there are steps that teachers can take to minimize the threat of environmental toxins, including the following (Marotz et al., 1993; Noyes, 1987):

- Increase ventilation by opening doors and windows.
- Learn to identify common toxic materials and make appropriate substitutions.
- Reduce the use of toxic pesticides, cleaners, carpet shampoos, and personal care products (e.g., perfumes).
- Avoid aerosols when possible.
- Do not use any chemical product in higher concentrations than is necessary.
- Regularly clean air filters.
- Store paints, varnishes, and cleaners in a locked closet or in a room away from children.
- Control dampness and dust.

Communicable Diseases

Children are also susceptible to a number of communicable diseases like chicken-pox, measles, influenza, mumps, smallpox, and whooping cough. The transmission of communicable diseases can occur in a number of ways (Kendrick, Kaufmann, & Messenger, 1991). Some are transmitted through the respiratory tract via fluids from the eyes, nose, mouth, or lungs (e.g., coughing or sneezing). Others are transmitted through the intestinal tract (e.g., stool). Some communicable diseases are transmitted through direct contact or touching, and others through blood contact. Communicable diseases can also occur indirectly through contaminated water, milk, food, and eating utensils (Newman, 1993).

Of all the "commandments" followed by health specialists in controlling infectious diseases (Kendrick et al., 1991), the first and most important step is to prevent illnesses from spreading. This is also the area where teachers have the most control, as indicated in the following preventive actions:

- Include periods of rest and exercise during the day.
- Instruct children in preventive health practices like handwashing and the control of bodily functions. Allow children to practice what they are taught.
- Incorporate health practices into all aspects of the day, including drama (doctor's office), art (drawings of healthy food), science (listening to heart rates before and after exercise), and reading (books about wellness).
- Ask community health professionals to visit the classroom to deliver educational programs on different aspects of wellness (e.g., nutrition, stress, taking care of colds, visiting the health department).

Handwashing is one of the most effective ways to prevent the spread of communicable diseases.

- Provide children with sufficient space to support their learning activities.

    Teachers can further control the spread of communicable diseases by remaining alert to potential signs of illness and taking appropriate actions. The following symptoms are widely used as general indicators of a potentially impending childhood illness (Marotz et al., 1993):

- Unusually pale or flushed skin
- Red or sore throat
- Enlarged lymph glands
- Nausea, vomiting, or diarrhea
- Rash
- Watery or red eyes
- Headache or dizziness
- Chills, fever, or achiness
- Fatigue or loss of appetite

    Note that many of these symptoms are the same as those for exposure to environment toxins, indicating their value as early warning signs of illness. Teachers who are ever-vigilant for such symptoms, and who monitor the learning environment for environmental toxins, will be less likely to encounter sick children than those who do not. Finally, attention to nutrition can also help to reduce the number of absences due to illness.

Early Childhood Nutrition

The diet of children and adults can be divided into three functional categories: a) protein for growth, b) carbohydrates for energy, and c) vitamins, fats, minerals, and water to support growth and body processes (Williams & Caliendo, 1984). Put another way, the nutrients that we consume provide us with a source of energy, help to maintain our body tissues, and help to regulate our body processes (Marotz et al., 1993). This means that children must learn to eat both the right amounts and the right kinds of foods.

In 1992, the federal government altered its nutritional guidelines for daily dietary intake, replacing the traditional four food groups with the food pyramid. As shown in Figure 4.2, a greater number of servings per day come from items at the bottom of the pyramid (bread, cereal, rice, and pasta), while fewer servings come from foods at the top of the pyramid (fats, oil, and sweets).

The food pyramid is especially important when considering the diet of young children, since their nutritional needs are not exactly the same as those for adults. Some of the considerations associated with children's nutritional needs follow (Lifshitz, Finch, & Lifshitz, 1991; Marotz et al., 1993):

- **Food intake.** Changes in growth rates and unpredictable whims lead to daily alterations in the appetites of young children. Even so, children have been shown to take in about the same number of calories each day (Birch, Johnson, Andresen, Peters, & Schulte, 1991). Severely restricting the diet of children can lead to malnutrition, and insisting that children eat when they are not hungry can lead to obesity. Children, like adults, should eat a variety of foods. New foods should be introduced one at a time.
- **Sugar intake.** Children should limit their consumption of sugar to avoid tooth decay and a diet that is void of nutritional value. However, severely limiting children's sugar intake may lead to a diet that does not include enough calories. It is more practical to provide substitutes for sugar like fruits and carbohydrates.
- **Fat intake.** Severely limiting the fat intake of young children can interfere with their growth, since fat provides a rich source of calories. Just as young children should not eat only fatty foods, neither should they be denied foods simply because they are high in fat.
- **Cholesterol intake.** Severely reducing foods like red meat and eggs that are high in cholesterol can lead to insufficient mineral intake by young children. For example, red meat and eggs are excellent sources of essential minerals that are needed for growth. As with fat, cholesterol should not always be considered bad for children. Rather, it should be considered within the context of children's growth and health needs.

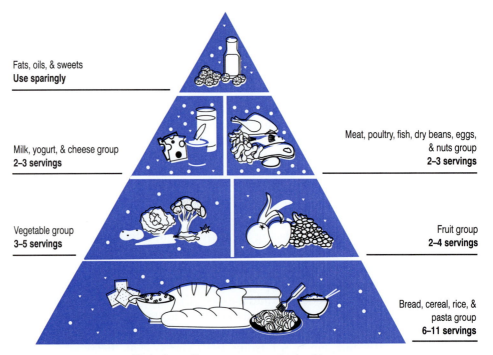

Fats, oils, & sweets
Use sparingly

Milk, yogurt, & cheese group
2–3 servings

Meat, poultry, fish, dry beans, eggs,
& nuts group
2–3 servings

Vegetable group
3–5 servings

Fruit group
2–4 servings

Bread, cereal, rice, &
pasta group
6–11 servings

The food pyramid encourages more grains, less fat.

FIGURE 4.2   U. S. Department of Agriculture Food Pyramid

Source: U.S. Department of Agriculture. *Human Nutrition*, 1992. Information service, Hyattsville, MD.

- **Fiber intake.**   Adding too much fiber to the diet of young children may cause gastrointestinal problems like abdominal pain, gas, and bowel movement irregularities. Children can get the fiber they need from eating fruits and vegetables.
- **Salt intake.**   Children's preference for salt is more an acquired than inborn taste (Columbia University College of Physicians and Surgeons, 1990). On the other hand, severely limiting children's salt intake may result in an insufficient sodium intake. Sodium is required for the body to carry out its functions. An appropriate goal is to restrict, not eliminate, salt intake.
- **Dietary supplements.**   Healthy children should meet their vitamin and mineral needs through the consumption of foods, not supplements. Supplements should be given to children only under the advice of physicians.

- **Facilitating children's appreciation of a healthy diet.** Young children have a reputation for being selective in their food choices. Teachers can help to facilitate children's appreciation of a healthy diet by attending to the way in which food is served and eaten (Fuhr & Barclay, 1998). Food can also be used as a strategy for introducing or reinforcing concepts like counting, sequencing, distinguishing patterns, and learning fractions (Meriwether, 1997). Some suggestions for encouraging children to appreciate food and develop healthy eating habits are presented in Checklist 4.1.

CHECKLIST 4.1

What Do They Like to Eat?

When observing meal and snacktime in an early childhood classroom, or when preparing food for your own class, make sure your choices are:

_____ **At room temperature:** Allow time for hot soup or cold milk to come to room temperature.

_____ **Soft:** Soft foods like bagels are easier for young children to chew and swallow than are hard foods like toast.

_____ **Appealing in color:** Placing a few raisins or orange slices on top of oatmeal can improve the chances of children accepting what might otherwise be considered an unappealing food.

_____ **Mild in flavor:** Children are especially sensitive to flavors and are most accepting of fresh and rather bland foods.

_____ **Familiar:** Children prefer familiar foods and should never be forced to try a new food.

_____ **Varied:** It can be as simple as choosing between apple or grape juice, peas or beans, yogurt or fruit.

CHAPTER SUMMARY

The orderly nature of children's physical development is directed by a number of maturational growth principles and trends. Even after a delay in growth, the power of these principles and trends can be seen in children's ability to catch up with their peers.

Children with diverse abilities need not represent a challenge to teachers who are aware of strategies for adapting physical activities to meet the needs of individual children. An emphasis on the needs of each child best contributes to arranging a "least restrictive environment" that is supportive of all skill levels.

Although children are susceptible to a number of environmental toxins and communicable diseases, steps can be taken to prevent serious health problems. Likewise, understanding the unique nutritional needs and preferences of children can help teachers to guide them toward healthy eating habits.

ACTIVITIES

1. Reflect back on the principles and trends of growth and development reviewed in this chapter. Use this information to write your philosophy of a least restrictive environment. Consider the following reflective questions:
   - Which principles and trends are most important in the construction of a least restrictive environment?
   - Which inclusion strategies best reflect these principles and trends?
   - In what ways is my philosophy of a least restrictive environment supported by the philosophy of early childhood education that I drafted in Chapter 1?
2. Visit a preschool classroom, child-care center, mall, playground, theme park, or some other early childhood environment. Observe children of different ages, noting examples of the cephalocaudal and proximodistal principles.
3. Ask the significant adults in your life about your own development. At what age did you begin to talk and walk? At what age were you potty trained? Did you achieve these developmental milestones quickly or gradually? What types of support did the adults in your life provide to help you meet these milestones?
4. Develop an activity that involves sensations, perceptions, and action. Demonstrate the activity in class. After receiving feedback from your peers, conduct the activity with one or two children. Note the children's responses. Did they seem interested in the activity? How did they perform? What aspects of the activity would you change?
5. Develop an activity to reinforce a small or large perceptual-motor skill (see Table 4.2). Demonstrate the activity in class. After receiving feedback from your peers, conduct the activity with one or two children. Note the children's responses. Did they seem interested in the activity? How

did they perform? What aspects of the activity would you change?

6. As a class, list the different types of diverse abilities that you have encountered. Divide the class into small groups. As a small group, develop or modify a group game in which two children with diverse abilities are represented. Share your group games. Role-play the games in class or outside of class. Ask local teachers to comment upon your games.

7. Visit your local cooperative extension office, health department, school, or other agency that deals with childhood nutrition. Ask for copies of menus and other information related to childhood nutrition. Develop a snack for a target group of young children. Share your menus in class. Ask a local nutritionist who specializes in childhood nutrition to assess the menus and to demonstrate other healthy snacks for young children.

chapter 5

Cognitive and
Language Development

After reading this chapter you should be able to discuss the following questions:

❖ How is cognitive ability defined?
❖ What makes up language ability?
❖ What factors contribute to cognitive and language development in young children?
❖ How can teachers promote cognitive and language development?

CHAPTER OVERVIEW

Teachers, along with parents and families, have the primary responsibility for helping children develop cognitive and language abilities to their fullest potential. In this chapter, we provide theoretical and applied strategies for fulfilling your responsibility to help children learn and communicate. We begin with recent research on the brain, discuss three specific theories of cognitive development that you will find in most applied early childhood settings, and then address language development. As usual, we embed issues related to educational practices throughout the chapter.

RECENT FINDINGS FROM BRAIN RESEARCH

We begin this chapter with a summary of recent findings from brain research because of the connection to young children's interactions with others and the environment. The findings from brain research also show how *all* areas of human development are interconnected. As we learn more about research on the brain, our beliefs about the intellectual capabilities of young children continue to change.

Recent breakthroughs in neuroscience have come about because of new research tools and devices that allow for examination of the brain. Magnetic resonance imaging (MRI) has given neuroscientists a much more detailed picture of the brain. Positron emission tomography, or PET scan, allows scientists to observe, record, and measure activity levels of various parts of the brain. For example, scientists can now use PET scans of infants and toddlers to determine which parts of the brain are particularly active and observe the parts of the brain associated with particular activities or affected by different types of stimulation. This information can be used to compare similarities and differences in brain development and neurological functioning between individuals (Shore, 1997).

A critical finding of recent brain research is that although there are certain genetic characteristics of individual brain growth, environmental conditions such as the kind of nourishment, care, and stimulation an individual receives influence brain development.

The brain is made up of a complex network of "wiring" or "circuitry" in which there is a rapid, efficient passage of signals from one part of the brain to another. These signals are sent through a network made up of brain cells (neurons) and the connections (synapses) that they form. The synapses are critical to healthy development because they connect to form neural pathways. Signals move along neural pathways as an infant interacts with the environment (reacts to stimuli). Before a baby is born, the developing brain produces many times more neurons and synapses than it will actually need. Most of the excess neurons and synapses are shed by birth. However, as each neuron expands, the brain continues to grow in size. The number of synapses increases dramatically in the first three years, while the number of neurons remains the same. The brain development that occurs during a baby's first year is more rapid and extensive than researchers have previously believed (Shore, 1997).

The neural pathways that are formed during the early years carry signals in the brain and facilitate the processing of information throughout our lives. How well we think and learn as children and as adults depends on the extent and nature of these connections. Recent brain research findings show that:

- The ways that families and care givers negotiate their child's contact with the environment directly affect the formation of neural pathways (Dawson, Hessl, & Frey, 1994).
- Children's capacity to control emotions appears to depend on the biological systems formed by their early experiences.
- Infants and babies need warm, consistent care so that they can form secure attachments to those who care for them.
- The first 10 years of a child's life are critical for language development and cognitive functioning.
- There are *critical periods* of opportunity for learning during the first five years of life. During a critical period, neurons create synapses most easily and efficiently. Once the critical period has passed, opportunities for shaping certain types of neural pathways lessen (Kraemer, 1992). Language development is strongly associated with critical periods.
- Young children (up to age 10) can easily acquire a new language because the brain cells that process language are in the process of being wired, and are especially responsive to experience (Shore, 1997).

Other cognitive functions, such as visual processing, also require particular types of stimulation during a child's first 10 years. If damage does occur to the brain during critical periods of growth, certain types of intervention can help the brain compensate for problems caused by a stroke or other injuries to the brain.

However, we must remember that as the brain grows over time, it is less susceptible to outside influence or intervention. The adaptability of the brain also means
that negative experiences or the lack of stimulation can have serious and sustained
effects on all areas of development. Risk factors such as trauma, emotional neglect,
social deprivation, and lack of proper nutrition can endanger development.
Detrimental experiences throughout critical periods of brain growth can damage
children's emotional, social, physical, and cognitive functioning. In summary, important findings of brain research indicate that:

- Human development depends on the interplay between genetics (nature) and
  the environment (nurture).
- Early care and nurturing have a definite and long-lasting impact on how
  people develop, their ability to learn, and their capacity to regulate their
  emotions.
- The human brain has the capacity to be changed, but timing is significant.
- There are critical periods of brain growth when both positive and negative
  experiences are more likely to have sustained effects (Shore, 1997).

In Tips for Teachers 5.1, we provide guidelines from brain research for care of
young children.

In the following sections we describe three theories of cognitive development: Piagetian, information processing, and Vygotskyian. Each of these three theories conveys the notion that there are levels or stages of development that all children experience in some particular sequence. Although teachers need to have a
common framework from which they can observe all children, we know that teachers must also deal with cognitive differences in children at all ages. For this reason,
we summarize the theories of Howard Gardner and Robert Sternberg. These theories provide unique ways to consider differences in children's cognitive development. Many teachers use a theory such as Gardner's multiple intelligences in planning for and teaching to the cognitive differences in young children.

PIAGET'S COGNITIVE DEVELOPMENTAL THEORY

Jean Piaget's (1896–1980) theory of cognitive development is characterized by the
belief that children construct their own knowledge and understanding of the
world through active exploration of their environments. Piaget is recognized for
his ideas about how knowledge is organized and how children construct knowledge in a series of stages. He is famous for his belief that children pass through a
series of stages of thinking that are qualitatively different from each other
(Sutherland, 1992). Piaget's theory is one of the most often used theories to explain
how children learn and develop their thought processes. We begin with his principles on how thinking is organized. Keep these principles in mind as you read about
his stages of cognitive development.

TIPS FOR TEACHERS 5.1

Guidelines from Brain Research for Caring for Young Children

- **Ensure health, safety, and good nutrition.** Safety-proof the places where children play; use a car seat whenever a child is traveling in a car.
- **Develop a warm, caring relationship with children.** Express joy in who they are; help them feel safe and secure.
- **Respond to children's cues and clues.** Notice their rhythms and moods; respond to them when they are upset as well as when they are happy.
- **Recognize that each child is unique.** Keep in mind that from birth, children have different temperaments, they grow at their own pace, and this pace varies from child to child.
- **Have positive expectations about what children can do.** Hold onto the belief that every child can succeed.
- **Talk to children.** Maintain an ongoing conversation with them about what you and they are doing; play word games; ask toddlers and preschoolers questions that require more than a yes or no answer.
- **Read to children.** Tell stories and read books; ask toddlers and preschoolers to guess what will come next in a story.

- **Sing to children.** Play music and surround them with rhythm, melody, and language.
- **Encourage safe exploration and play.** Give children opportunities to move around, explore, and play.
- **Allow children to explore relationships.** Arrange for children to spend time with other children of their own age and other ages.
- **Use discipline to teach.** Talk to children about what they seem to be feeling and teach them words to describe those feelings; tell them what you want them to do, not just what you don't want them to do.
- **Establish routines.** Create rituals for special times during the day like meal time, nap time, and bed time; try to be predictable so the children know that they can count on you.

From Shore, R. (1997). *Rethinking the Brain: New Insights into Early Development*. Families and Work Institute: New York.

The Organizing Processes of Cognition

Schemes and adaptation.   Piaget believed that children adapt to the world around them. He called the techniques of adaptation *schemes*. A scheme (or schema) in Piaget's words is:

> . . . the structure or organization of actions as they are transferred or gener-alized by repetition in similar or analogous circumstances (Piaget & Inhelder, 1969, p. 4).

Schemes are important because they provide a way for infants and young children to organize the knowledge that they are always acquiring. A scheme, according to Piaget, is the action of categorizing the information that is coming into the child through different senses. When you are shopping for groceries in a grocery store you are using your "grocery-shopping scheme," or when eating in a restaurant, you are using your "restaurant scheme." A newborn's schemes are very limited to reflex-action patterns such as crying out, sneezing, or flexing limbs (Santrock, 1997; Thomas, 1985). Eventually, toddlers and young children develop mental schemes such as categorizing or classifying objects. As children get older, they add complex mental schemes. What are some schemes that you use to balance your checkbook or calculate bowling or golf scores?

According to Piaget, there are **three adaptation processes** that help infants move from simple reflex-action patterns to more complex mental schemes. These processes are assimilation, accommodation, and equilibration:

1. **Assimilation.**   Assimilation means that a child is taking in or understanding events in the environment. According to Piaget, when you assimilate you are incorporating new information into your existing knowledge (Santrock, 1997; Trawick-Smith, 1997). When a baby looks at a rattle and then reaches for it and shakes it, Piaget would say that the baby has assimilated the rattle into his or her looking, reaching, and shaking scheme. When a young child who thinks that all four-legged animals are dogs sees a cow and calls out "doggie," her teacher may say, "No that is a cow." According to Piaget, when the child comes across this strange, new animal, she makes sense of this experience based on her previous understandings. When confronted with a cow, the child fits this large animal with horns into her mental category "dog" (Trawick-Smith, 1997). The child has assimilated this new phenomenon into her existing scheme for animals. According to Piaget, assimilation is necessary for learning.

2. **Accommodation.**   Accommodation is a process that is complementary to assimilation. In accommodation, a scheme is changed to fit the new information that is taken in. In other words, we reorganize our thoughts, improve our skills, and change our thinking strategies (Bee, 1997). A child takes in or assimilates new information (sees a cow for the first time and thinks it is a dog) and then changes her scheme to fit the new information (Trawick-Smith, 1997). If a child's scheme for four-legged animals consists of only one mental category such as a dog, she may gradually change her concepts and categories to include other four-legged animals such as cows, pigs, tigers, and lions. She adds new mental categories for several different types of four-legged animals as she assimilates the new types of animals. Since no new event is perfectly identical with those past events that were used in the formation of schemes, there is always some degree of mismatch of schemes with new events. However, this mismatch, or cognitive conflict, is adjusted by the counterplay between assimilation and accommodation. Assimilation reshapes the new information coming into the child to fit

existing schemes. Accommodation revises or adds to the schemes to readjust for the new information that cannot be ignored.

3. **Equilibration.**   Equilibration is the balance between the adaptation processes of assimilation and accommodation. During the adaptation process, equilibration helps the child create an understanding of the environment that makes sense. According to Piaget, equilibration helps the child regulate his or her cognitive growth. Think back to our example of a child seeing a cow for the first time:

- If the child believes that all four-legged animals are dogs, and new information comes along when she sees a cow, she assimilates this information into the existing scheme.
- The information may not fit; she might simply ignore the idea of a cow being a four-legged animal or she may change her scheme so that she thinks that cows *and* dogs are four-legged animals.
- After seeing a number of other four-legged animals, such as horses, cows, tigers, and lions, she may change her scheme so that she understands that *any* animal that has four legs fits this concept or category.
- The process of equilibration has facilitated the change in her scheme by balancing assimilation and accommodation.

Piaget's Stages of Development

Piaget believed that cognitive growth proceeds continuously and advances in stages (Trawick-Smith, 1997; Thomas, 1985). Cognitive growth, according to Piaget, develops in a series of time periods or stages. These stages of growth are commonly divided into: 1) the sensorimotor stage, 2) the preoperational thought stage, 3) the concrete operations stage, and 4) the formal operations stage. According to Piaget, the corresponding ages for each period can vary from one society to another (Piaget, 1973). Table 5.1 summarizes Piaget's four stages of development.

Piaget believed that there are four additional characteristics of each stage of development. These characteristics are universality, invariant sequence, transformation and irreversibility, and gradual evolution:

- **Universality.**   Stages are the same for all children. In order for a pattern of behavior to be recognized as a stage, the pattern must be found in all children.
- **Invariant sequence.**   Everyone goes through the patterns of behaviors in exactly the same sequence. All children must pass through all of the stages in the same order.
- **Transformation and irreversibility.**   Once children enter a new stage, they interpret all future experiences through the lens of the new stage. Once children reach a more sophisticated stage of thinking, they seldom, if ever, go back to thinking the way they did in a less sophisticated stage.

TABLE 5.1	Piaget's Stages of Development	
Stage	**Age**	**Description**
Sensorimotor	0 to 18 months	Infants rely solely on action and the senses to "know" things. Intelligence is an ability to get what one needs through movement and perception.
Preoperational	18 months to 6–7 years	Preschool children can use symbols and internal thought to solve problems. Their thinking is still tied to concrete objects and to the here and now. They are fooled by the appearance of things.
Concrete operational	8 years to 12 years	Elementary school children are more abstract in their thinking. They can use early logic to solve some problems and are less fooled by perception. They still require the support of concrete objects to learn.
Formal operational	12 years to adulthood	Adolescents and adults can think abstractly and hypothetically. They can contemplate the long ago and far away. Their thinking is free from the immediate physical context.

- **Gradual evolution.** The movement from one stage to another does not occur all of a sudden, or even within a period of a month or a year. Rather, according to Piaget, movement occurs in rather small segments until transformation to the next stage is complete.

As you read about each of the different stages of development, think about children you have seen or played with. Do these stages apply to any interactions you have had with children?

The sensorimotor stage. During the sensorimotor stage of development, infants rely upon sensory and motor schemes to grow intellectually. Piaget specified six substages through which infants develop (Piaget & Inhelder, 1969). A summary of these six stages is presented in Table 5.2. During these stages, the baby: 1) adapts to his environment through unlearned reflexes such as sucking, crying, and breathing; 2) engages in repetitive activity, such as

TABLE 5.2	Piaget's Stages of Sensorimotor Development	
Stage (and Approximate Age Range)	**Description**	**Example**
1 (birth–1 month)	Reflexes (the first schemes)	Sucking on the mother's breast
2 (1–3 months)	The first acquired adaptations and the primary circular reaction	Thumb sucking
3 (4–8 months)	Secondary circular reactions and procedures to make interesting sights last	Using leg kicks to make a crib mobile move
4 (8–12 months)	The coordination of secondary schemes and their application to new situations	Pushing an obstacle away and then grabbing the toy behind it
5 (12–18 months)	Tertiary circular reactions and the discovery of new means through active experimentation	Experimenting with dropping foods or other objects off a highchair tray
6 (above 18 months)	The invention of new means through mental combinations	Thinking of a way to get a watch chain out of a matchbox

From Berndt, Thomas J. *Child Development,* 2d edition. © 1997 by The McGraw-Hill Companies. Reproduced with permission of The McGraw-Hill Companies.

grasping and letting go of an object which, according to Piaget, is purposeful and designed to either preserve or rediscover an act or skill; 3) acts intentionally to consciously attain a goal, demonstrating awareness of the environment as the intentional acts are directed toward repeating the achievement of a goal; 4) anticipates people and objects and searches for objects that are out of sight, demonstrating that a quality of permanence has been attained; 5) reproduces through experimentation an original object or event in modified form—"a discovery of new means through experimentation" (Piaget, 1963, p. 267); and 6) represents objects to solve problems mentally and can cognitively combine and manipulate them. There is no longer the need to experiment with objects themselves to solve problems (Piaget, 1963). By the end of the sensorimotor stage, the child can both form and manipulate mental images and use symbols. At this point, the child is beginning to shift into the preoperational stage.

The preoperational stage.   Generally, in the preoperational stage, Piaget believed that children are limited in their ability to think and reason abstractly. Young children in the preoperational stage are said to be *egocentric*. That is, children are self-centered, view life from their own perspectives, and have difficulty seeing

Piaget believed that young children learn through interaction with objects.

things from the perspective of others. When talking and listening to others, children use egocentric speech, which is characterized by a running oral commentary that accompanies what the child is doing at the moment and is not intended to communicate anything to anyone else (Berk, 1996).

In terms of preoperational children's thinking, Piaget believed that children base their problem solving on what they can see and hear directly rather than on what they remember about objects and events. An aspect of their cognitive development at this stage is *centration*. Children at this age center on one aspect of an object and believe that this aspect completely characterizes the object. Two dimensions of an object, such as size and shape, cannot be considered at the same time. Similarly, Piaget contended that children at this age cannot demonstrate an understanding of *conservation*. A classic experiment that Piaget used to characterize children's lack of reasoning and logical thought involves the same amount of water poured into two glasses—one glass is tall and thin and the other is short and fat. A young child may center on the height dimension only and conclude that the tall glass contains more water. Consequently, a child in this stage cannot conserve or understand that the amount of water has been conserved (it is the same amount even if poured into different sized containers).

At the end of the preoperational stage, children become less self-centered and begin to recognize the permanence of an object's substance when its size or shape has been changed. Children are better able to solve problems intuitively when the objects involved are not in front of them. However, Piaget believed that by age 7, children still depend highly upon how events appear concretely.

The concrete operations stage.

According to Piaget, children in the stage of concrete operations are capable of performing actions on objects, however, they are not able to perform more abstract operations. Consequently, concrete operational children cannot deal with problems that do not involve particular objects. During the concrete operations stage, children demonstrate a more sophisticated understanding of *conservation* and *reversibility.* When two lumps of clay of the same size and shape are shown to children during this stage, they discover that the substance has been conserved when one lump of clay is rolled into a snake. In terms of *centering,* the child can now consider different dimensions of an object simultaneously rather than attend to only one attribute. For example, when presented with a rectangular block that is large and red, the child now recognizes that color, shape, and size are three different classifications and does not focus only on color or only on shape.

When interacting with objects and others in the environment, the child begins to see things from the viewpoint or perspective of others. Children are no longer as egocentric as they were in earlier stages of cognitive development. They are able to socialize more with other children and increase their language facility. Similarly, children begin to understand causation.

The formal operations stage.

During adolescence, children can solve more abstract problems and envision different conditions of a problem such as the past, present, or future (Piaget, 1963). For example, one of Piaget's favorite examples involves *transitivity.* Transitivity means that a relationship between two elements or objects is carried over to other elements logically related to the first two. The child has solved the problem of transitivity if he recognizes that when A = B and B = C, then A = C. Consider the following question: "Jennifer is fairer than Sarah; Jennifer is darker than Katie. Who is the darkest of the three?" Piaget asserted that only after age 12 could children solve this question because they comprehend the transitivity it involves. During the formal operations stage, adolescents can engage in thought that is independent of action, hypothesize and draw deductions from the hypotheses, and understand general theories (Piaget, 1950). The type of thinking that adults use is within the repertoire of an adolescent's thinking processes. According to Piaget, the adolescent is capable of all the forms of logic that the adult commands. Checklist 5.1 can help you look for different implications of Piaget's theory when you are working in an early childhood classroom.

CHECKLIST 5.1

Is This a Piagetian Classroom?

When considering your own early childhood classroom work, check for the following implications of Piaget's theory.

Do You

_____ Provide opportunities for children to play an active role in their own cognitive development?

_____ Provide both mental and physical activities?

_____ Provide opportunities to freely explore objects and interact with those objects in the immediate environment?

_____ Recognize that cognitive development is a continuous process?

_____ Provide situations in which children have to solve problems independently without being told the answers?

INFORMATION-PROCESSING THEORY

Information processing is not a single theory of cognitive development; rather, it is a combination of work that has evolved from a number of researchers in the field of cognitive psychology. These researchers have focused on how information enters the mind, how it is stored, and how it is retrieved to perform such complex activities as problem solving and reasoning (Santrock, 1997). According to information-processing theorists, children's cognitive skills develop as their memories expand.

Like Piaget's theory, the information-processing approach considers children as active sense-makers who modify their own thinking in response to what occurs in their environment (Klahr, 1992). Unlike Piaget's theory, there are no stages of development; rather the processes that have been studied such as perception, attention, memory, planning strategies, and problem solving are assumed to be similar at all ages but less sophisticated in children. While Piaget focused on the acquisition of concepts and their organization with other concepts, information-processing theorists focus on how information enters and is stored in the mind. Since our purpose in this chapter is to provide you with an overview of information processing, we discuss three areas of cognition: (1) attention, (2) memory, and (3) metacognition.

Attention

If you have ever spent time with preschool children, you have probably noticed that they spend only short periods of time involved in a task. Similarly, preschoolers are easily distracted and have difficulty concentrating on details. For example, when given detailed pictures or written materials, preschoolers fail to search thoroughly (Enns, 1990). In contrast, school-age children know what to pay attention to and can focus on an essential learning task while ignoring stimuli that distract younger children (Hagen, 1967; Maccoby & Hagen, 1965; Steinberg & Meyer, 1995). As children become older they also become more strategic in focusing their attention. When 4- to 8-year-olds are asked to find similarities among groups of pictures, older children approach the task more systematically and efficiently than do younger children (Vurpillot, 1968). One explanation for increased attention is that older children understand the consequences of paying attention (Steinberg & Meyer, 1995). However, even in the primary grades, children can only be expected to typically attend to one task for no more than 30 minutes. When early childhood teachers plan for experiences that will capture the attention of young children because the activities are interesting and meaningful, they are applying information-processing theory to their practice.

Memory

Preschoolers have few strategies for recalling information, but between the ages of 5 and 11, memory improves dramatically. Two possible reasons for this improvement involve: 1) children's increased and more organized knowledge, and 2) their growing use of strategies or techniques for remembering (Berk, 1996). However, preschool children can notice a simple, familiar shape just about as quickly as do older children when the object is flashed on a screen for a fraction of a second (Steinberg & Meyer, 1995). What does change during the preschool years is how much information can be processed at once. For example, 6- or 8-year-olds can repeat more random digits immediately after hearing them than can 3-year-olds. Many information-processing psychologists believe that there are changes in the speed and efficiency of processing information (Santrock, 1997). As the brain and nervous system develop (the formation of synapses followed by the pruning of redundant ones), the capacity, speed, and efficiency of the processing system possibly increase. Researchers have found that young children remember fewer items in lists of numbers, letters, or words than do older children (Berk, 1996). Research has also determined that the organization of memory is important. When information can be grouped and organized meaningfully, even young children can show considerable memory abilities. Primary-grade teachers who use charts and figures, such as a Venn diagram to organize the characters and plot of a story, are applying information-processing theory on memory.

Memory strategies. In information-processing theory, the development of memory is closely tied to the acquisition of knowledge (Santrock, 1997). Strategies that help us remember are useful because they may convert the information that is to be learned into a more lasting "chunk" of material. Consequently, children are more likely to remember material that is meaningful to them. A way to help young children remember is to introduce new ideas and information by connecting the material to their previous knowledge. When teachers take children on a field trip to a farm to actually see animals such as horses, cows, chickens, and pigs, children are more likely to remember what is the same and different about these animals than if an adult merely explains it to them.

The most basic memory strategy is *verbal rehearsal*—simply repeating information over and over (Flavell, 1985). When studying a list, children who rehearse the most recent word along with other words in a cumulative way tend to recall more words later than children who just repeat isolated words (Steinberg & Meyer, 1995). Linking words creates a more active and larger set for memory (Ornstein, Baker-Ward, & Naus, 1975). In the primary grades, teachers often try to teach students how to connect words in their mind to help them remember.

Young children may have appropriate strategies for remembering, but are deficient in knowing when, where, and how to use them effectively. This is commonly referred to as a *production deficiency* by information-processing theorists (Berk, 1996; Santrock, 1997). Some strategies for remembering improve as we age. During the childhood years, children learn to use associations, inferences, and cues to recall information. To recall a former classmate's name, a child may try to visualize the seating arrangement in the old classroom and retrieve the name by associating the child with a specific location in the class (Steinberg & Meyer, 1995). Some researchers claim that greater efficiency in processing information is gained as a result of the child's acquisition of new strategies for solving problems or remembering. For example, children often experiment with different rules or strategies for remembering and understanding events of daily life.

Metacognition

Metacognition, a third area that information-processing researchers have studied, concentrates on how children come to know what they know. *Metacognition* is the awareness that children develop about their own knowledge and abilities (Flavell, 1988). Metacognitive knowledge is knowledge that a child has about cognition (Berk, 1996). When you have to decide how to remember something, metacognitive knowledge helps you decide what memory strategies work best for you (Kail, 1984). For example, Kreutzer, Leonard, & Flavell (1975) found that kindergartners and first-graders knew that remembering a phone number would be easier immediately after being told the number rather than after getting a drink of water.

Metamemory is thinking about the process of remembering. Metamemory is important because what children believe about memory strategies influences whether they use them (Berndt, 1997; Santrock, 1997). If young children are unaware of various strategies or believe that they are not useful or necessary, then they are unlikely to use them. For example, preschool children do not seem to realize that when listening to one message, they may not fully understand another simultaneous message. By kindergarten age, children do seem to understand that what they know and understand depends on what they pay attention to (Pillow, 1989). Can you think of an instance when two or three people tried to explain something to you at once and you had trouble remembering what each person said?

Metamemory and metacognition are part of a larger category of skills that information-processing theorists refer to as *executive processes* (Berk, 1996; Santrock, 1997). Examples of executive processes include planning what to do and considering different strategies for solving problems. Information-processing theorists contend that metacognitive or executive process skills emerge with age. Four- and five-year old children do demonstrate some beginning indications of monitoring their own performance or recognizing the need to use a particular strategy, but these abilities are seldom found in children younger than age 4. These metacognitive or executive skills may serve as the foundation for many of the age changes described by Piaget (Berk, 1996).

Another aspect of metacognition is *cognitive monitoring,* which includes self-appraisal and self-management (Paris & Winograd, 1990). When you evaluate your own knowledge and then choose suitable plans to strengthen it, you are using self-appraisal. Self-appraisal helps children to distinguish what they know from what they don't know. For example, when a child realizes that she needs more information to answer a question or complete a written report, she is using self-appraisal. Younger children in preschool, kindergarten, and the primary grades are not as good at self-appraisal as older children are. When nonsense words appear in a story or when words are scrambled, young children tend to miss these misrepresentations (Markman & Gorin, 1981; Paris & Myers, 1981).

A second aspect of cognitive monitoring that is important to the management of thinking is *self-management.* Self-management enables us to select appropriate strategies for solving a problem and to change those plans if they do not work. When children are able to shift gears in solving problems, they persist longer and are ultimately more successful (Brown, Bransford, Ferrara, & Campione, 1983). Self-management does not really appear in children until the end of the primary grades. In Checklist 5.2, you can examine these implications of information-processing theory for your own classroom practice.

In summary, there are several general changes in the development of information processing in preschool and primary-grade children:

- There is greater speed in the processing of information as children move into the primary grades.
- The amount of knowledge increases and leads to better remembering and problem solving.
- Metacognitive abilities related to memory and planning develop during the end of the primary grades.
- Memory strategies begin to transfer to new tasks.
- Different strategies can be applied to the same problem during the primary grades.

CHECKLIST 5.2

Is This an Information-Processing Classroom?

When considering your own early childhood classroom work, check for the following implications of the information-processing theory.

Do You

_____ Allow children to explore and examine materials such as objects or pictures over a period of time?

_____ Not expect young children to sit and attend to one activity for a long period of time?

_____ Make the classroom as free of unnecessary or distracting stimuli as possible?

_____ Model strategies for memorizing (such as verbal rehearsal) information?

_____ Introduce new ideas and information by referring to what the students already know and understand?

VYGOTSKY'S SOCIOCULTURAL THEORY

As you may recall from Chapter 2, Vygotsky (1896–1934) outlined a theory of cognitive development that is different from Piaget's ages and stages theory of development. Vygotsky's theory is based on the premise that cognitive development takes place as a result of mutual interaction between children and those people with whom they have regular social contact (Berk & Winsler, 1995; Sutherland, 1992). Vygotsky contributed the idea that a child's intellectual development involves social interactions with others. According to Vygotsky, social interactions or cooperative dialogues between children and more knowledgeable members of society are necessary for children to acquire the ways of thinking and behaving that make up a community's culture (Wertsch & Tulviste, 1992).

As adults and more competent peers help children master culturally meaningful activities, the communication between these partners—both adults and peers—becomes part of children's thinking (Berk & Winsler, 1995). Once children internalize the essential features of these dialogues, they can use the language within them to guide their actions and accomplish skills on their own (Berk & Winsler, 1995; Van der Veer & Valsiner, 1991). Research indicates that children's problem solving seems to improve most when their partner is an expert who can provide new ways of approaching the situation that are not already familiar to the child (Azmitia, 1988; Radziszewska & Rogoff, 1988). When a young child instructs herself while working a puzzle or tying her shoes, she has started to produce the same type of guiding comments that an adult previously used to help her master important tasks (Berk, 1992).

A central idea of Vygotsky's theory is that cognition is always situated in activity and that people learn best when they are working with others while actively engaged in a problem (Brown, Collins, & Duguid, 1989; Lave & Wenger, 1991). It is important to remember that Vygotsky's sociocultural theory is in opposition to the idea that thinking and problem solving develop in the same ways for all children. Rather, thinking and problem solving are much more a product of specific contexts and cultural conditions (Berk & Winsler, 1995). Although Vygotksy's theory has not historically been as widely used as Piaget's, more and more educators are thinking about how the basic premises can be used in different instructional settings with young children. In this section, we focus on three important components of Vygotsky's theory: the zone of proximal development, scaffolding, and private speech.

Zone of Proximal Development

Vygotsky's ideas on the *zone of proximal development* have had an impact on how we view the role of the teacher and the child in cognitive development. The zone of proximal development is an application of Vygotsky's belief that children learn best with the help of others. The zone of proximal development also explains how children learn through joint activities with more mature members of their society and think in ways that have meaning in their culture (Berk, 1996). When trying to assess what children know or can do, Vygotsky suggested that we should measure what children can do with the help of another person, rather than measure what children can do by themselves or what they already know (Berk & Winsler, 1995). By measuring what children can do with the help of another person, we are measuring their *potential* to learn (Berk & Winsler, 1995). The region in which the child develops new capacities during collaboration with adults and more competent peers and then internalizes is called the zone of proximal development, or the ZPD.

Vygotsky (1978) described the ZPD as the distance between the actual developmental level, as determined by independent problem solving, and the level of potential development, as determined through problem solving under adult guidance or in collaboration with more capable peers. The ZPD is the dynamic zone of sensitivity in which learning and cognitive development occur (Berk & Winsler, 1995). When we consider tasks that children cannot do individually but can do with help from others, we are focusing on the cognitive mechanisms that are currently in the process of developing rather than those that have already matured.

According to Vygotsky, the role of education is to provide children with experiences that are in their ZPD. These experiences should include activities that challenge children and can be accomplished with sensitive adult guidance. Consider the following example:

Five-year-old Natalie and her teacher Mr. Foster are working together on sorting blocks by color and shape. Natalie begins by picking up and looking at each block.

Mr. Foster:	"OK, Natalie, you need to put these shapes in groups so that each group has the same color and same shape."
Natalie:	"This is easy, I know how to do this."
Mr. Foster:	"Good, now, remember, you need to put the blocks in groups that go together because they are the same color and same shape."
Natalie:	(Places the triangles in one group, the rectangles in another group, the squares in a group, and the circles in a group.) "There, I did it."
Mr. Foster:	"You put all of the same shapes in groups. Now you need to make sure that all of the shapes are the same color."
Natalie:	"Oh, like we did at group time yesterday?"
Mr. Foster:	"That's right, remember that when we put the blocks in groups we looked at both the color and the shape, not just the shape."
Natalie:	(Places all of the red circles together, all of green triangles together, but mixes colors when grouping the squares and rectangles.)
Mr. Foster:	"OK, Natalie, you put the red circles and green triangles together so that we have groups that are all the same shape and same color. Now, are the squares and rectangles the same shape and color?"
Natalie:	"I don't know. I guess not."
Mr. Foster:	"Why aren't they the same shape and color?"
Natalie:	"Cause there are yellow, red, and blue squares here (pointing to the squares) and red and blue rectangles here (pointing to the rectangles)."
Mr. Foster:	"That's right. How can you make these groups have the same color and shape?"
Natalie:	"By taking away the red ones?"
Mr. Foster:	"Yes, taking away the red ones will leave yellow and blue squares and blue rectangles. So, we will have a group of red circles, green triangles, and blue rectangles. The circles, triangles, and rectangles are all the same shape and color. What about the squares?"
Natalie:	"They have four sides that are the same."
Mr. Foster:	"Yes, they do. But they are not the same shape and same color (Mr. Foster takes away the yellow squares). If I take away the yellow squares we have only blue squares and the group is now all the same shape; they are squares, and the same color; they are all blue."

In Vygotsky's theory, adults carry much responsibility for making sure that children's learning is maximized by actively leading them along the developmental pathway. The teacher's role is to keep tasks in children's ZPD or slightly above their level of functioning rather than giving them tasks for which they have already acquired the necessary mental operations (Berk, 1996). In other words, the ZPD refers to a range of tasks that a child cannot yet handle alone but can accomplish with the help of a more skilled partner.

Scaffolding

A common metaphor that is used to explain scaffolding is the idea that a scaffold or support system is constructed around a building when it is being constructed. As the building nears completion, the scaffolding is gradually removed. In Vygotsky's theory, adults scaffold children's problem solving as they adjust the communication they provide to children's immediate ability, and offer help for mastery while prompting children to take more responsibility for the task as their skill increases (Berk & Winsler, 1995). Scaffolding provides a support system that is focused on the specific needs of children as they attempt to solve a problem or complete a task.

A crucial part of scaffolding is the context in which it occurs. Vygotsky believed that adults transmit cultural knowledge when they scaffold a child. Consequently, an important part of scaffolding is the engagement of children in an interesting and culturally meaningful, collaborative problem-solving activity (Berk, 1996). As a learner, you have most likely experienced a problem or situation in which you have needed the support or scaffold from someone more skillful or knowledgeable. Many adults need scaffolding when they encounter a problem that is unfamiliar to them, such as learning how to use new computer software.

When children are learning by means of a scaffold, the participants can either be adult-child or child-child. The child receives support, guidance, and challenge during the transmission of knowledge and skills via scaffolding. Research has shown that even though young children benefit from working on tasks with same-age peers, their planning and problem solving show more improvement when their partner is a peer who is especially accomplished at the task (Azmitia, 1988; Radziszewska & Rogoff, 1988). The critical aspect of scaffolding is that a child interacts with someone while the two are jointly trying to reach a goal. The communication with the child provides necessary assistance for mastery while prompting her to take more responsibility for the task as her skill increases (Berk & Winsler, 1995).

According to Vygotsky, children's learning cannot be separated from the task in which it takes place, and people learn best when they are working with others while actively engaged in a problem (Berk & Winsler, 1995; Brown, Collins, & Dugiud, 1989; Lave & Wenger, 1991). To establish a scaffolding situation, there needs to be true collaboration in which the child is communicating with the more competent partner and both participants are working toward the same goal. Can you think of a scaffolding situation in which you learned a new concept or skill because of collaboration with another?

Private Speech

Many preschoolers talk to themselves as they go about their daily activities. For example, as Sam played with blocks one day, he said, "Where is the big one? I need a big one to build a bridge. Now, a little one. Oops, that doesn't fit." Vygotsky

According to Vygotsky, children can learn to solve problems from the scaffolding provided by an adult.

believed that young children speak to themselves for self-guidance and self-direction (Berk & Winsler, 1995). Speech to self, or *private speech,* helps children think about their own behavior and select courses of action. Vygotsky believed that private speech plays a critical and special role in cognitive development. Private speech serves as the foundation for all higher cognitive processes, such as sustained attention, deliberate memorization and recall, categorization, planning, problem solving, and self-reflection (Berk, 1996). The primary goal of private speech is not communication with others, but communication with the self for the purpose of self-regulation or guiding one's own thought processes and actions.

Vygotsky (1986) contended that the most significant moment in cognitive development occurs when the preschool child begins to use language not only for communication with others but also as a tool for thought. According to Vygotsky, this use of language occurs when a child internalizes language to direct his or her own attention and behavior. While language is first used for social communication, it then turns inward and becomes a tool of the mind for speaking to the self and guiding behavior (Berk & Winsler, 1995). The process of internalizing language is an example of Vygotsky's belief about cultural development that mental functions are first shared between people and then become part of an individual's psychological functioning (Berk, 1996). Private speech is regarded by Vygotsky as the primary means through which children transfer the regulatory role from others to self. With private speech, children do for themselves what caregivers did for them during joint problem solving through scaffolding.

Vygotsky and his followers provide a developmental sequence of private speech. Private speech, or self-regulatory language, is first overt (spoken out loud) and then gradually becomes covert (inner speech or verbal thinking). As young children mature, private speech goes underground, changing from utterances spoken out loud to whispers and silent lip movement (Berk & Landau, 1993; Frauenglass & Diaz, 1985). With age, the frequency of private speech shows an inverted U-shaped pattern. It peaks during the middle to the end of the preschool years and then declines as children's overt private speech is replaced by whispers and inaudible muttering. Children's private speech also undergoes structural grammatical changes as it is abbreviated and internalized. With development, the timing of children's self-speech, with respect to their ongoing behavior, changes. Private speech moves from following behavior to preceding behavior as it takes on a planning and regulating function.

Private speech does not increase with age, as Piaget suggested. Instead, it becomes less understandable to others as it is abbreviated and internalized. The more opportunities there are for social interaction, the more private speech occurs. According to Vygotsky, private speech does not give way to social speech, as Piaget suggested. Rather, social and private speech seem to go together. Research shows that children use more private speech while working on difficult tasks, after they make errors, or when they are confused about how to proceed (Berk, 1992). In addition, children who use private speech freely when faced with difficult tasks are more attentive and involved and show greater improvement in their performance than their less talkative peers (Berk & Spuhl, 1995; Bivens & Berk, 1990). As you think about how you can apply Vygotsky's theory to your own classroom, examine Checklist 5.3.

CHECKLIST 5.3

Is This a Vygotskian Classroom?

When considering your own early childhood classroom work, check for the following implications of Vygotsky's theory.

Do You

_____ Guide students in paying attention and concentrating?

_____ Jointly participate in classroom tasks by modeling and then providing cues to the student (scaffolding the task)?

_____ Encourage students to go beyond their independent level of performance?

_____ Allow children to work together (and talk about what they are doing) to solve problems and complete tasks?

_____ Encourage children to use cues such as concrete objects or pictures to complete tasks or solve problems before expecting children to work independently?

ALTERNATIVE VIEWS OF INTELLIGENCE AND COGNITION

We have focused on how the three theories—Piagetian, information processing, and Vygotskian—provide us with some general guidelines of how children develop cognitively. Although teachers of young children apply different parts of each theory in the classroom, many teachers rely on recent theories that help to accommodate for differences in abilities and talents. As you read the next section, think about how these different ideas about intelligence might apply to yourself, members of your family, or children that you may work with in a classroom.

Sternberg's Triarchic Theory of Intelligence

Sternberg's Triarchic Theory of Intelligence has evolved from Sternberg's interest and work on the complexity of intelligent behavior and different types of human mental skills. His theory about intelligence questions the widely accepted view that intelligence is hierarchial with a general ability at the top and more specific abilities at lower levels (Sternberg, 1996). Rather than viewing intelligence as the only thing that is measured on IQ tests, Sternberg believes that there are other aspects of intelligence, such as creative, practical, and analytical abilities, that are not measured on conventional intelligence tests (Sternberg, 1996). Sternberg's theory includes three types of intelligences: componential, experiential, and contextual.

The first type of intelligence, *componential intelligence*, involves what is typically measured on IQ and achievement tests. Skills and abilities that Sternberg includes in componential intelligence are information-processing skills such as remembering, thinking, and attending (Trawick-Smith, 1997). Sternberg believes that the use of these skills and abilities is not just a matter of internal capability, but also the conditions under which intelligence is assessed (Sternberg, 1986).

The second type of intelligence is called *experiential intelligence*. A person who is well developed in experiential intelligence is creative, sees new connections between things, and can relate to experiences in unusual and insightful ways. When given a new task such as an experiment, a person with experiential intelligence can generate unique ways to conduct the experiment, is able to see how a theory could be applied to a totally different situation, or can learn a large number of new facts rapidly and organize the facts in new ways (Sternberg & Davidson, 1986).

The third type of intelligence is called *contextual intelligence*. Contextual intelligence is sometimes referred to as "street smarts," or the ability to adapt one's desires and requirements to the everyday environment. People with contextual intelligence are able to see how they can fit in best. They establish relationships with the "right" people and can adapt themselves to their setting or the setting to themselves (Sternberg, 1986). A student who is good at figuring out what the teacher wants in a given course, who talks to the teacher informally, and who expresses interest in topics she knows the teacher is interested in is demonstrating contextual intelligence (Bee, 1997). This type of intelligence involves tuning into a variety of subtle signals and then acting on the information (Bee, 1997). People who are able to modify their presentation or "sales pitch" based on the subtle cues of the audience or customer have contextual intelligence.

Sternberg contends that the most common view of intelligence is restricted to information about componential intelligence, which is the type of intelligence demanded in school. Sternberg's work has shown that measures of intelligence that predict success in school and measures of practical intelligence that predict performance on the job do not meaningfully relate to traditional psychometric intelligence measures (Sternberg, 1996). He points out that in the world beyond the school walls, experiential or contextual intelligence may be required as much or more than the type of skill measured on an IQ test (Sternberg & Wagner, 1993).

Gardner's Theory of Multiple Intelligences

Gardner (1983) provides another theory of intelligence that dismisses the idea that there is one general intelligence focusing primarily on linguistic and logical-mathematical abilities. Like Sternberg's theory, Gardner's theory questions measures of intelligence that only assess how well an individual can problem solve, see patterns, read, write, and compute. Instead, Gardner has proposed eight independent intelligences, which are described in Table 5.3.

Gardner believes that intelligence is a dynamic entity within each individual and is related to an individual's cultural setting. In addition, each intelligence has a unique biological basis, a distinct course of development, and different levels of expertise (Berk, 1996). According to Gardner, a lengthy process of education is required to transform any raw potential into a mature social role. This means that cultural values and learning opportunities have a great deal to do with the extent to which a child's intellectual strengths are realized and the ways in which they are expressed. Gardner (1983) also contends that: 1) each individual has each intelligence in varying degrees; 2) each intelligence is modifiable; 3) each intelligence can be developed to adequate levels even though each individual is born with different capacities; and 4) intelligences often work together in complex ways.

Gardner's multiple intelligences can be applied to early childhood curriculum and some educators have developed different methods to assess the different intelligences. It is important to note that Gardner's multiple intelligences have not been examined extensively through research. There is no clear evidence for the independence of the different abilities. Feldman (1991) points out that there are exceptionally gifted individuals whose abilities are broad, rather than being limited to a particular domain. Many teachers find that understanding and nurturing special talents in children can be challenging.

LANGUAGE DEVELOPMENT

Infants and children use language to express a number of cognitive skills and many believe that language and cognition go hand in hand. Language is not merely a collection of sounds for infants and young children. Rather, language involves communication and is: 1) an arbitrary system of symbols; 2) rule-governed; and

TABLE 5.3   Gardner's Multiple Intelligences

Intelligence	Processing Operations	End-State Performance Possibilities
Linguistic	Sensitivity to the sounds, rhythms, and meanings of words and the different functions of language	Poet, journalist
Logico-mathematical	Sensitivity to, and capacity to detect, logical or numerical patterns; ability to handle long chains of logical reasoning	Mathematician, scientist
Musical	Ability to produce and appreciate pitch, rhythm (or melody), and aesthetic-sounding tones; understanding of the forms of musical expressiveness	Violinist, composer
Spatial	Ability to perceive the visual-spatial world accurately, to perform transformations on those perceptions, and to recreate aspects of visual experience in the absence of relevant stimuli	Sculptor, navigator
Bodily-kinesthetic	Ability to use the body skillfully for expressive as well as goal-directed purposes; ability to handle objects skillfully	Dancer, athlete
Interpersonal	Ability to detect and respond appropriately to the moods, temperaments, motivations, and intentions of others	Therapist, salesperson
Intrapersonal	Ability to discriminate complex inner feelings and to use them to guide one's own behavior; knowledge of one's own strengths, weaknesses, desires, and intelligences	Person with detailed, accurate self-knowledge
Naturalistic	Ability to recognize, discriminate and classify living things as well as sensitivity to other features of the natural world	Botanist, farmer

The first seven intelligences from "Gardner's Multiple Intelligences" adapted from *Frames of Mind* by Howard Gardner. Copyright © 1983 by Howard Gardner. Reprinted by permission of BasicBooks, a division of HarperCollins Publishers, Inc. The eighth intelligence from K. Checkley, "The First Seven . . . and the Eighth," *Educational Leadership* 55, 1: 8–13. (excerpt p. 12). Used by permission of the Association for Supervision and Curriculum Development. Copyright © 1997 by ASCD. All rights reserved.

3) creative. The process of language development begins before words appear, as infants and adults communicate through sounds, gestures, and social cues during the first year. This process begins with *prelinguistic communication.* Even though babies do not use sounds to refer to objects and events and do not combine individual sounds to make sentences, they are still communicating. The importance of experience and interaction with others is evident when we think about how young babies respond and react to the environment around them.

Prelinguistic Communication

Sounds, facial expressions, and imitation are types of prelinguistic communication. It appears that babies are either born with or develop very quickly the ability to discriminate speech sounds. Games such as "pattycake" and "peek-a-boo" are similar to conversation because they require give and take, or turn taking, as parents make sounds of gaiety, pause for the baby's response, and then make another sound or movement in response (Bloom, Beckith, & Capatides, 1988; Tronick, 1989). By 1 to 2 months, through what is called a "behavioral dialogue," infants demonstrate that they can clearly discriminate sounds and are sensitive to the intonation and patterns of speech they listen to. Infants grow in their ability to use language intentionally, which is an essential part of communicating with others. This ability is nurtured by adults who respond to infants' sounds as if they had meaning (Bates, Camaioni, & Volterra, 1975; Snow, 1977).

As infants grow and move toward real language, they rely less on physical effort to get what they want (Baldwin & Markman, 1989; Steinberg & Meyer, 1995). At around 2 months, infants begin to make vowel-like noises called *cooing*. As consonants are added at around 6 months, infants string the sounds together ("ba-ba-ba-ba," "na-na-na-na-na") into sound combinations called *babbling*. The presence of babbling is universal and occurs around 6 months. Even deaf children babble. Since all infants babble at about the same time and produce the same sounds, there appears to be a series of stages that are linked to mature spoken language. However, infants must be able to hear human speech for development to continue. When infants who are hearing-impaired are exposed to sign language, they appear to be babbling silently as they repeat motions with their hands (Petitto & Marentette, 1991).

Adults often imitate the coos and babbles a baby makes, which is also part of prelinguistic communication. As infants hear adults' imitations and reactions to babbling, such as "What a big boy, are you having fun in your stroller?" in spoken language, their babbling increases. The turn-taking games such as "peek-a-boo" help babies practice the turn-taking of human conversation. These simple games help facilitate infants' ability to attain the function and meaning of spoken words (Ratner & Bruner, 1978). At the end of the first year, infants elicit responses in adults by using physical gestures such as pointing to a toy such as a doll. An adult may respond by saying, "Doll, doll, Oh, you want the doll." Infants learn quickly to communicate intentionally and they begin to use their first words. Milestones of language development during the first two years are summarized in Table 5.4.

First words.   Vocabulary increases rapidly after babies begin speaking their first words. The first words that infants use are those associated with objects that are important to them ("mama," "baw" [ball]) as well as cognitive achievements such as disappearance words like "all gone." Initially, infants use words narrowly. For example, a toddler may use a word such as "ball" to refer only to the beach ball he has played with every day rather than to other balls such as the basketball or little red ball that his brother plays with. Using words too narrowly is referred to as *underextension*. Fairly soon, the opposite occurs. Words that are used too broadly are re-

TABLE 5.4	Milestones of Language Development During the First Two Years

Approximate Age	Milestone
2 months	Infants coo, making pleasurable vowel sounds.
4 months on	Infants and parents establish joint attention, and parents often verbally label what the baby is looking at.
6–14 months	Infants babble, adding consonants to the sounds of the cooing period and repeating syllables. By 7 months, babbling of hearing infants starts to include many sounds of mature spoken languages. Deaf babies exposed to sign language babble with their hands.
6–14 months	Infants become capable of playing simple games, such as pat-a-cake and peekaboo. These provide practice in conversational turn-taking and also highlight the meaning and function of spoken words.
8–12 months	Infants begin using preverbal gestures, such as showing and pointing, to influence the behavior of others. Word comprehension first appears.
12 months	Infants say their first recognizable word.
18–24 months	Vocabulary expands from about 50 to 200 words.
20–26 months	Toddlers combine two words.

From Berk, L. E. (1996). *Infants, Children and Adolescents,* 2nd Ed. Allyn & Bacon: Boston, MA. Reprinted by permission.

ferred to as *overextensions.* When a toddler uses the word "cat" to refer to all four-legged animals, she is overextending. Toddlers' overextensions show that they are forming conceptual categories. By forming relations in categories, toddlers are applying a familiar word to new experiences, an important cognitive advance. Overextensions begin to disappear as children's vocabularies increase and they make distinctions in their comprehension. It is important to remember that both speaking and understanding influence children's language development. Children understand many more words than they can say. Comprehension vocabulary may be 5 to 10 times greater than speaking vocabulary (Reznick & Goldfield, 1992).

Two-word utterances.   By 24 months, children use two-word utterances such as "more cookie" and "play again." At this point, children's vocabulary has increased dramatically. Between 18 and 24 months, many children add 10 to 20 new words a week to their vocabulary (Reznick & Goldfield, 1992). These two-word utterances are typically referred to as *telegraphic speech.* The most common types of utterances are requests and observations of the world (Steinberg & Meyer, 1995). Although toddlers are making a number of grammatical errors at this stage, they are figuring out meanings of words and trying to convey their thoughts to others despite their limited vocabulary.

Parents' use of motherese reinforces language learning.

Differences in language development.   We have described the common stages that children follow as they learn to comprehend and use language. Many infants have a 50-word vocabulary by the age of 24 months; some reach that level earlier and some later. Some infants begin using two-word utterances at 1 year of age. There are immense differences in how children acquire language. Theorists and researchers believe that both heredity and experience contribute to the differences that we see in children's language development.

Researchers such as Nelson (1973; 1981) have identified differences in the words and phrases that toddlers produce. Children who use nouns—many children use words that refer to objects rather than to people—use a *referential* style. These children think that words are used mainly for naming objects ("dog," "house," "toy"). Children who use their vocabulary to express their involvement with people and social routines use an *expressive* style. These children believe that words are for talking about the feelings and needs of themselves and other people ("stop," "thank you," "want"). Nelson (1981) says that the different language styles come from how a child's parents use language. Referential children have parents who respond to their child's interest in exploring objects by naming things. Expressive children have parents who speak to them more conversationally and use language to support social relationships.

There are several factors that researchers have identified as influences on language development. For example, studies show that girls are slightly ahead of boys in early vocabulary growth (Jacklin & Maccoby, 1983), and that family and social differences are linked to referential and expressive children (Nelson, 1973). Referential children are often firstborns in middle-class homes, while expressive children are often later-borns to less-educated parents. Nelson (1973) accounted for these differences by positing that middle-class firstborns get their educated mothers' full attention while later-borns may receive less direct teaching because the mother's time is more divided. As we have discussed earlier in this chapter, a family's intellectual and emotional environment, as well as heredity, influence language learning. Another significant influence on a child's language development is a form of language made up of short sentences and slow, high-pitched speech with exaggerated expression called *motherese*. Motherese captures and holds babies' attention even in infants as young as 1 month old (Fernald & Mazzie, 1991; Newport, Gleitman, & Gleitman, 1977). Parents' use of motherese reinforces language learning by exaggerating the differences between sounds and keeping infants' attention. Box 5.1 provides an example of a parent communicating with an infant in motherese.

Language Development in the Preschool Years

Language development during the preschool years can be characterized by the impressive advances that are accomplished. Young children's vocabularies are increasing at a dramatic rate, they are learning and using the rules of language, and they are better able to communicate. As children experiment with their growing verbal skills, they are using rule-oriented strategies. Preschool children learn as many as five new words daily (Anglin, 1993) so that by age 6 they will have acquired around 10,000 words. Preschoolers may continue to use overextension as they use vocabulary words to refer to things that are similar, but not identical, to the object that the word actually refers to (Clark, 1983). Young children also use a strategy called *fast mapping*, which occurs when a child relates a new word to a general domain of meaning immediately after hearing the word for the first time (Steinberg & Meyer, 1995). For example, a child may hear the word "triangle" and understand that it refers to a shape before she actually knows what the word means explicitly. Younger preschoolers appear to acquire labels for objects rapidly because of their concrete experiences with the objects. The words they learn are from many grammatical categories, however, they tend to use *who, what, when, where,* and *why* words frequently.

Preschool children can figure out the meanings of new words by comparing them to words they already know. They also follow the *principle of mutual exclusivity,* which means that they assume that words can refer to only one object. For example, when preschoolers hear a new word, they tend to associate it with a unique object rather than with an object they already know. Preschoolers use cues in adults' speech and behavior to learn names for objects and categories of objects

| BOX 5.1 | *Example of Parent Communicating in Motherese* |

Here is an example of Felicia speaking motherese to 18-month-old April as they get ready to leave for home.

Felicia: "Time to go, April."

April: "Go car."

Felicia: "Yes, time to go in the car. Where's your jacket?"

April: (looks around, walks to the closet) "Dacket!" (pointing to her jacket)

Felicia: "There's the jacket! Let's put it on. (She helps April into the jacket.) On it goes! Let's zip up (zips up the jacket). Now, say bye-bye to Byron and Rachel."

April: "Bye-bye, By-on."

Felicia: "What about Rachel? Bye to Rachel?"

April: "Bye, bye, Ta-tel (Rachel)."

Felicia: "Where's your doll? Don't forget your doll."

April: (Looks around)

Felicia: "Look by the sofa. See? Go get the doll. By the sofa."

(April gets the doll).

From Berk, L. E. (1996) p. 241. *Infants, Children and Adolescents,* 2nd Ed. Allyn & Bacon, Boston, MA. Reproduced by permission.

such as size and color. At the same time, they are learning complex relations among objects, people, situations, and time periods. They are also learning words that express these relationships such as prepositions like *in, on, under, before,* and *after,* and comparative adjectives such as *more, less, bigger, smaller, younger,* and *older.* If you have ever spent time with 2- and 3-year-olds, you have probably heard their creative use of words such as "plant man" for gardener or "crayoner" for a child using crayons (Berk, 1996; Clark & Hecht, 1982). Preschoolers also use comparisons such as metaphors to extend language meanings. Metaphors that involve concrete, sensory comparisons such as "clouds are pillows" or "leaves are dancers" are used as preschoolers learn to communicate and make sense of the world around them (Berk, 1996).

Development of grammar.   *Grammar* simply refers to the set of rules that governs the use of words and how words are combined or changed to create meaningful phrases and sentences. Young children learn rules about word order and apply the many rules that govern the basic structure of sentences by hearing others speak. For example, they learn to build on the basic structure of English sentences (subject-verb-object) by adding "s" to express plurals, applying prepositions such as "in" and "on," negating statements by adding "no," and later inserting negatives within a sentence, such as "dog not chase ball." The mastery of grammatical markers occurs in a regular sequence (de Villiers & de Villiers, 1973), beginning with the simplest meanings and fewest structural changes (mastering the plural form of "s" before learning tense of the verb "to be"). However, because the English language has many irregularities, preschoolers follow grammatical rules too regularly and make the type of error called *overregulation*. Errors such as "My brother *runned* away" and "She *holded* the puppy by herself" are examples of overregularization.

Preschoolers continue to master more complex forms of grammar although they can be confused by complex sentences that involve time relations. They also adhere to a consistent word order. Passive sentences such as "The cat was chased by the dog" can be troublesome to preschool children. A preschooler might be confused and think that the cat chased the dog because of the passive verb "was chased," and the grammatical subject of the sentence "cat," which is the object of the action described. Five-year-olds understand sentences like this, but proficiency in understanding the passive form does not occur until the end of the elementary school years (Horgan, 1978; Lempert, 1989). As we discussed earlier in this chapter, there is evidence from recent brain research that maturational changes in the brain create critical periods of development in which language is learned more quickly and efficiently (Newport, 1990). Consequently, some researchers believe that language is learned more easily and fluently in early or middle childhood. It is also important to remember that language acquisition is also influenced by experience, especially in the family. For example, parents who regularly repeat a child's ungrammatical statements and fill in missing words to make the statements grammatical have children who display more complex grammar at an earlier age than children whose parents ignore grammatical mistakes (Bohannon & Stanowicz, 1988; Nelson, 1973).

Communicating with others.

Children need to learn to use language successfully in different social contexts. Conversations with others involve turn-taking, staying on the same topic, stating a message clearly, and conforming to cultural rules that regulate how individuals are supposed to interact (Berk, 1996). This useful aspect of language is known as *pragmatics*. Preschoolers can take turns, say what they want, bargain, manipulate, and maintain a topic over time (Garvey, 1975; Podrouzek & Furrow, 1988). As we have discussed previously, these pragmatic aspects of language emerge from early interactive experiences with adults, other children, and family members.

As you recall from our discussion earlier in this chapter, Piaget considered preschoolers to be limited in their ability to communicate with others because of their egocentric viewpoint and limited perspective-taking abilities. Recent research has shown that preschoolers are more capable in communicating with language than Piaget assumed. Four-year-olds are aware of how to adjust their speech to fit the age, sex, and social status of their listeners. For example, they can take another's perspective and communicate effectively when speaking to younger children (Steinberg & Meyer, 1995). Shatz and Gelman (1973) found that when 4-year-olds showed a new toy to adults and to 2-year-olds, they used simple, short sentences and attention-grabbing language with the 2-year-olds while they were more polite and asked for more information with adults. It has also been found that older preschoolers give fuller explanations to a stranger than to someone with whom they share common experiences, such as a friend (Menig-Peterson, 1975). These findings demonstrate that preschoolers' communication with others is less egocentric than Piaget (1963) believed.

There are still limitations to preschoolers' communication skills. Research supports the idea that preschoolers' communication difficulties may be due to information processing because they are always egocentric (Menyuk, 1977). Information-processing research indicates that preschoolers have difficulty coordinating the skills used in conversations such as gaining and keeping a listeners' attention, paying attention to someone else, giving or asking for information, considering another person's point of view, and adjusting language accordingly (Schmidt & Paris, 1984). We also know that the social context has a major influence on their communication skills. When preschoolers talk face-to-face with familiar people about topics they know well, they make more sophisticated language adjustments (Berk, 1996). In contrast, when they cannot use gestures and other concrete support to help overcome the limits of their current knowledge, vocabulary, and memory, their communication with others appears less mature (Berk, 1996; Warren-Leubecker & Bohannon, 1989).

Language Development in 5- to 8-Year Olds

Although changes in vocabulary, grammar, and communication skills are not as dramatic during the 5- to 8-year-old period when compared to earlier language development, vocabulary, grammar, and communication abilities become extended and refined. At the beginning of the elementary school years, children continue to expand their vocabulary by learning 20 new words each day (Berk, 1996). Children in kindergarten and the primary grades expand their vocabularies through their ability to analyze the structure of complex words and derive meaning from context, especially while reading (Miller, 1991). During the primary grades, synonyms and explanations of categorical relationships appear (Litowitz, 1977; Wehren, DeLisi, & Arnold, 1981). Children at this age are also beginning to value the multiple meanings of words.

During the primary grades, children improve in the use of more complex grammatical constructions. For example, an understanding of the passive voice is applied to a wider range of nouns and verbs. Children at this age are also able to understand infinitive phrases, such as the difference between "Luis is eager to please" and "Luis is easy to please" (Berk, 1996; Chomsky, 1969). Primary-grade children improve in their ability to analyze and reflect on language and begin to evaluate the grammatical correctness of a sentence. In terms of communication skills, children in the primary grades become increasingly able to adapt to the needs of listeners. They also can pick up on more inferential statements and understand subtle inferences. For example, when a third-grade teacher says "The art center looks like a garbage dump," an 8-year-old knows that the teacher is really saying "Clean up the art center."

CHAPTER SUMMARY

We hope that our discussion of cognitive and language development has helped you understand both the similarities and the differences that may be apparent in young children at different ages. When you interact with young children, it is important to remember that they do have specific language and cognitive limitations. However, it is also important to consider recent research on the brain in the areas of cognition and language. Teachers will be challenged more and more to address a wider range of cognitive and language abilities as we learn more about what young children are truly capable of. We hope that we have provided you with examples of how theoretical frameworks and recent research can result in practical applications for your classroom. In Activity 1, we ask you to refer back to the philosophy you developed in Chapter 1. Try to identify theories of cognitive development that "fit" with your beliefs about how young children develop and learn.

ACTIVITIES

1. Using the philosophy that you developed in Chapter 1, think about your beliefs about how children develop and learn. Do any of your beliefs match with the three central theories (Piagetian, information processing, and Vygotskian) that were discussed in this chapter? Identify one theory, or aspects of different theories, that best fit with your philosophy. Develop a simple chart. In one column, list your basic beliefs about how young children learn and develop. In another column, identify a theory or combination of theories that matches each belief.

2. Observe an infant and parent interacting. Is the parent using "motherese"? Write down several of the verbal expressions that the parent uses and describe how the infant responds. Share your notes and observations with your peers.

3. Engage a 4- or 5-year-old in a Piagetian conservation activity. For example, using a ball of clay, change the shape or form of the clay (from a ball into a snake) and ask the child if there is the same amount of clay. Ask the child why it is the same or why it changed. Share your findings with your peers. You could also try pouring the same amount of water from a short glass into a tall glass and ask the child if the amount of water has changed or stayed the same.

4. Interview a teacher about intelligence. How does he or she define intelligence? Do the tests he or she uses to assess cognitive abilities accurately assess his or her children's "true" abilities? Does the teacher use any of Gardner's multiple intelligences in planning activities for different children in his or her class?

5. Visit a preschool or kindergarten class. Sit behind children who are seated at a table while they are working on a task such as a puzzle or game. Tell them that you are there to do some work of your own. Listen to see if any of the children uses private speech. What are they saying to themselves?

6. Observe children when they are talking to their peers and with adults. Do they use the same gestures, vocabulary, and sentence structure? If there are differences in how they communicate with other children and with adults, write them down. Share your findings with your peers.

chapter 6

Early Childhood Social-Emotional Development

After reading this chapter you should be able to discuss the following questions:

❖ What factors are essential to healthy social-emotional development?
❖ How do parents contribute to children's social-emotional development?
❖ In what ways can teachers support children's social-emotional development?
❖ What instructional strategies contribute to children's moral reasoning?

CHAPTER OVERVIEW

Socialization is the process by which children internalize the behavioral standards and social customs of their culture. Teachers, along with parents and youth leaders, have the responsibility of helping children to learn social rules of behavior, develop positive self-concepts, and practice appropriate interpersonal skills. In this chapter, we provide you with theoretical and applied strategies for fulfilling your responsibility to help socialize children. We begin with a review of children's social-emotional development and then address their moral development. As usual, we embed issues related to educational practices throughout the chapter.

ERIK ERIKSON'S SOCIAL-EMOTIONAL THEORY

Erik Erikson's (1902–1994) theory of social-emotional development is characterized by a series of life "crises" whose resolution shapes our social adjustment. Like all developmental theorists, Erikson (1963, 1964, 1980, 1994) relied upon certain assumptions to explain his views of development. It is important that you understand these assumptions before reading about the specific stages of social-emotional development.

Social-Emotional Development Across the Lifespan

Erikson divided social-emotional development into eight stages that extend across the lifespan. In this chapter, we consider the four stages that relate to the early childhood period between birth and age 8 (Table 6.1, Column A).

As we enter a new stage of social-emotional development, we encounter a different developmental "crisis" that challenges us to make adjustments in the way we see ourselves and others (Table 6.1, Column B). Erikson considered that all stages and their associated "crises" apply to all cultures.

TABLE 6.1   Erikson's Early Childhood Social-Emotional Stages

A Developmental Stage	B Crisis and Associated Developmental Challenges	C Significant Others in Helping Child to Resolve Crisis	D Virtues Forming Positive Ego-Identity	E Applied Implications
Birth– 12/18 Mos.	Trust vs. mistrust • Trust in parents • Trust in others • Trust in self	Primary caregivers (e.g., parents)	Hope • For positive relationships • For positive outcomes	Attachment; temperament
12/18 Mos.– 3 Years	Autonomy vs. shame and doubt • Independence • Self-restraint	Parents Child caregivers	Will • To undertake new challenges • To control impulses	Parenting styles
3–6 Years	Initiative vs. guilt • Self-expression • Personal responsibility for one's behavior	Parents Child caregivers Teachers	Purpose • To achieve goals • To overcome obstacles	Gender; play
6 Years– Adolescence	Industry vs. inferiority • Productive behavior that is valued by others • Mastery of tasks	Family Teachers Youth leaders	Competence • Self-motivation • Self-confidence	Role-taking and friendships; stress and resiliency

Adapted from *Identity: Youth and Crisis* by Erik H. Erikson. Copyright © 1968 by W. W. Norton & Company, Inc. Reprinted by permission of W. W. Norton & Company, Inc.
Adapted from *Insight and Responsibility* by Erik H. Erikson. Copyright © 1964 by Erik H. Erikson. Reprinted by permission of W. W. Norton & Company, Inc.
Adapted from *Identity and the Life Cycle* by Erik H. Erikson. Copyright © 1980 by W. W. Norton & Company, Inc. Copyright © 1959 by International Universities Press, Inc. Reprinted by permission of W. W. Norton & Company.

An Interactionist Perspective

Erikson took an interactionist perspective of development. He began by noting that the stages of social-emotional development are genetically driven by innate "inner laws" that set the timetable and define the significance of our social interactions (Erikson, 1994). For example, during the first social-emotional stage, infants have an innate need to develop a sense of "trust" in their parents. During the third social-emotional stage, preschoolers and young school-age children have an innate need to demonstrate their developing cognitive and motor skills through displays of "initiative."

Although the ordering of the social-emotional stages may be guided by "inner laws," the social environment is important in determining the nature of our life experiences. For example, children from inner-city neighborhoods are exposed to different family demands, economic conditions, and safety concerns than their peers from rural areas. Although both children may live in two-parent families, have the same family incomes, and receive the same quality of education, their social environments create different realities that force them to structure their lives in different ways.

Perhaps more than any other factor, children's social environments are defined by their interactions with significant others. As noted in Table 6.1, Column C, children's social interactions extend outward over time to include parents, peers, teachers, youth leaders, and social institutions. Parents are the first and most important agents in children's social environment, introducing basic social rules like when to say "thank you" and "excuse me." Teachers and peer groups introduce social roles like leader versus follower. They also reinforce group social skills like cooperative problem solving. Youth clubs reinforce civic pride, perseverance, and loyalty through the use of oaths and community projects.

Social-Emotional Development and Ego Identity

Erikson viewed *ego identity* as a balance between a positive self-image (i.e., knowing and accepting ourselves) and acceptance of social standards. Individuals who are able to function within the boundaries of society while maintaining a healthy self-image have a positive ego identity.

This balancing act is achieved through successful resolution of each social-emotional "crisis." The result is an internalization of personal strengths, or "virtues." Collectively, the virtues listed in Table 6.1, Column D can be said to define a positive ego identity. For example, during the first social-emotional stage, infants' sense of "hope" evolves out of the trust that they place in their parents, along with a healthy sense of "mistrust" when confronted with new, and potentially dangerous, experiences. A toddler's healthy sense of "will" is dependent upon both a sense of personal "autonomy" as well as recognition that violation of social rules can lead to disapproval and "shame."

Invariant Stages of Social-Emotional Development

The ordering of the stages in Table 6.1 is invariant in that we move through them in a sequential order. The first stage must be addressed before we can move on to the second stage, and the second stage must be addressed before we can move on to the third stage. The manner in which we resolve each crisis influences our handling of all subsequent crises. A preschooler's lack of initiative (stage 3) may reflect a failure to have successfully established a sense of trust (stage 1) or autonomy (stage 2).

This does not mean that we cannot revisit earlier stages. Positive experiences later in life can help us to compensate for problems encountered during earlier social-emotional crises. Likewise, a series of ongoing or traumatic life difficulties have the potential to challenge the positive ego identity that we may have established earlier in our lives.

ERIKSON'S STAGES OF SOCIAL-EMOTIONAL DEVELOPMENT

As discussed earlier, only the first four stages of Erikson's theory address young children from birth through age 8. We therefore limit our narrative to these four stages.

As you read about the following four stages, think about their implications. To assist you, we include specific examples of research and practice in this section to highlight the developmental significance of the first four stages (Table 6.1, Column E). Infant attachment and temperament are reviewed as examples of concern during the first stage of children's social-emotional development. We address parenting styles in relation to the second stage. In the third stage we address issues of gender and play. Finally, we discuss perspective role-taking and childhood stress in relationship to the fourth stage of social-emotional development.

Stage 1. Trust Versus Mistrust (Birth to 12–18 Months)

The relationship between infants and their primary caregivers (most often parents) sets the stage for the first social-emotional stage. As noted by Erikson, infants' sense of trust is based on "an essential trustfulness of others as well as a fundamental sense of one's own trustworthiness" (1994, p. 96). Infants develop a sense of trust when their parents are nurturing and consistently responsive to their needs. In turn, infants begin to see themselves as trustworthy, and they recognize that their needs and feelings are worthy of the attention they receive from others.

Children who establish a sense of trust in self and others internalize the virtue of hope (Erikson, 1964; 1994). And it is the sense of hope that allows children to withstand daily frustrations while maintaining a positive attitude toward life. Children who are unable to develop a trusting relationship with their parents fail to develop the virtue of hope. They become mistrustful of others, lack self-confidence in themselves, and have difficulty withstanding the frustrations that accompany life challenges.

Helping infants establish a sense of trust presents a number of challenges for parents. Feeding and sleeping schedules must be adjusted during the first year of life. Parents must also learn to interpret and respond appropriately to their infant's cries and other forms of verbal and nonverbal communication. Even play time can be demanding if parents are tired, lack self-confidence, or lack knowledge about the types of toys or activities that are appropriate for establishing a trusting infant-parent relationship.

Infants develop a sense of trust when their parents and caregivers are nurturing and consistently responsive to their needs.

Two factors that influence the way in which parents meet these demands are the quality of infant-parent attachment and an infant's temperament. An infant's attachment to his or her parents forms the foundation for a healthy sense of trust in both self and others. Infant temperament can influence the nature of the infant-parent relationship in general, and the quality of infant-parent attachment in particular.

Attachment and trust.   You can probably think back to your own early childhood to identify individuals to whom you turned for emotional support and guidance. Chances are that your parents served as your earliest and most important adult figures. One of the very first tasks for infants and parents is to establish a sense of mutual attachment. *Attachment* can be defined as the affectionate and reciprocal relationship between infants and parents that reinforces their emotional bond. Attachment is important to ensure that infants and parents remain emotionally connected and responsive to one another. Without attachment, an infant's cries may go unheard and parents may fail to adequately stimulate their infant through verbal and physical play.

Infants may not immediately attach themselves to their parents. Rather, infant attachment tends to take place in stages. Although Erikson did not himself attempt to describe the stages of attachment, others have done so. A detailed study conducted in the 1960s resulted in four general stages of attachment that developmentalists often refer to when summarizing infant-parent attachment (Schaffer & Emerson, 1964):

Asocial stage.   Newborns respond about equally to social (e.g., parents) and nonsocial (e.g., puppets) stimuli during the first few weeks of life. This is quite normal. Cognitively, infants are still unable to assign a great deal of personal meaning to individuals, objects, or events. This soon changes as they become more cognizant of their surroundings.

Indiscriminate attachments.   Between 6 weeks and 6 months of age, infants begin to clearly prefer social over nonsocial stimulation. Although they may show a preference for familiar adults, they also show a willingness to respond to any adult who displays nurturing behavior.

Specific attachments.   Beginning around 6 to 9 months of age, infants begin to form a close relationship with their parents and reject, or at least become wary of, strangers. This specificity of attachment is again the result of cognitive advances. As we noted in Chapter 5, infants begin to develop a sense of *object permanence* at around 6 to 9 months of age, as reflected in their ability to retain a mental image of individuals and objects that are no longer directly observable. *Separation anxiety,* the anxiety and fearfulness that infants display when they are separated from their parents, is one indication of object permanence and is a hallmark of the specific attachment stage. The infant's ability to retain a mental image of the parent creates anxiety when the parent is not readily available. *Stranger anxiety,* the anxiety and fearfulness that infants display when they are first introduced to nonfamiliar adults, is another indicator of object permanence and the specific attachment stage. Faces and voices that do not correspond to familiar mental images and sounds create anxiety in infants.

Specificity of attachment marks still another important social-emotional milestone. Infants begin to use their parents and other significant caregivers as a *secure base* (Ainsworth, Blehar, Waters, & Wall, 1978). That is, infants use parents as a source of emotional support from which to explore their surroundings.

You can easily observe infants' use of parents as a secure base in public places. Note an infant's behavior the next time you are in a waiting room. In a typical case, you will first observe that the infant remains close to the parent, visually checking out the surroundings. After a while, the infant will move slightly away from the parent to investigate a toy or object, all the while glancing back to make sure that the parent is still available. If startled, the infant will immediately return to the parent's side.

Parents who allow themselves to be used as a secure base reinforce their infant's first feelings of independence and confidence. In contrast, overprotective parents thwart their infant's attempts to explore, while neglectful parents fail to provide the emotional support needed for infants to feel safe in their explorations.

Multiple attachments.   By 18 months of age, toddlers begin to associate specific activities or functions with different individuals. For example, infants often prefer mothers as a "secure base" for emotional comfort while fathers are preferred as more active and interesting playmates (Lamb, 1981; Lamb & Oppenheim, 1989).

As you no doubt have already noticed, the ease with which infants move through the attachment stages is in large part dependent upon the behavior of their parents and other significant caregivers. Some parents are more responsive to their infant's attachment needs than are others. Likewise, some parents are better able to match their expectations and behavior to their infant's temperament.

Temperament and trust.   As we just noted, the manner is which infants move through the attachment stages can be influenced by a number of factors. One of the most important factors is infant temperament. Erikson did not specifically address infant temperament, but its importance to defining the quality of the infant-parent relationship has been clearly established through research.

Temperament can be defined as an inborn response pattern to social and environmental stimuli that is first observable during infancy. You may have heard parents talk about the behavioral or emotional differences that exist between their children. You may even have a sibling who is "just the opposite" of yourself. The behavioral and emotional differences that are sometimes observed between children, even those from the same family, can in part be attributed to different inborn temperament styles.

In a now famous study, nine categories of temperament were identified through interviews with parents and teachers, as well as through observations of children themselves (Thomas & Chess, 1977). When used in research studies, the nine categories resulted in the three temperament styles that are summarized in the following section. As you read these summaries, keep in mind that most children cannot be neatly classified under any one temperament category. Also, there is variation in the degree to which children may display a particular temperament style across situations (Thomas & Chess, 1981).

Easy-going temperament.   The characteristics of this temperament include biological regularity (e.g., predictable routine of sleeping and eating), an interest in new events and objects, an ability to adapt quickly to changes in the immediate environment, a general positive mood, and only mild reactions to daily frustrations. Common terms that describe easy-going infants include "predictable," "sociable," "adaptable," and "even-tempered."

Difficult or irritable temperament.   Characteristics associated with irritable temperaments include biological irregularity (e.g., unpredictable eating and sleeping schedules), withdrawal from new experiences, slow adaptation to changes in the immediate environment, more frequent negative moods, and a low threshold for frustration. Common terms sometimes used to describe infants with irritable temperaments include "moody," "unpredictable," and "overreactive."

Slow-to-warm-up temperament. Characteristics associated with this temperament include mildly unpredictable eating and sleeping schedules, a hesitant but gradual interest in exploring new objects and events, a gradual ability to adapt to changes in the immediate environment, and mild to moderate reactions to daily frustrations. Common descriptions sometimes associated with this temperament include "mostly positive," "usually predictable," and "likes to take everything in before responding."

A number of longitudinal reports published since the 1970s indicate that early childhood temperaments are predictive of later child, adolescent, and adult adjustment (see Bates, 1989; Garrison & Earls, 1987; Prior, 1992). More recent research reinforces and expands this theme. For example, young children with easy-going temperaments are judged to be well adjusted by parents and teachers following their transition to preschool (Jewsuwan, Luster, & Kostelnik, 1993). Children with easy-going temperaments also display fewer negative adjustment behaviors to family conflict than do children with difficult temperaments (Tschann, Kaiser, Chesney, Alkon, & Boyce, 1996). In contrast, children who display difficult temperaments experience greater behavioral problems in adolescence (Caspi, Henry, McGee, Moffitt, & Silva, 1995) and early adulthood (Caspi & Silva, 1995). Given these findings, it is nevertheless important to note that temperament in and of itself is not a risk factor (Sanson, Oberklaid, Pedlow, & Prior, 1991). Other factors must be considered, especially the response patterns of parents.

It should come as no surprise that not all parents respond equally well to different infant temperaments. Parents' own personality characteristics, their particular life stressors, sources of support, as well as their expectations regarding infant behavior can influence their response to different infant temperaments. The phrase *goodness of fit* is used to characterize the appropriateness of parents' expectations and responses to their infant's particular temperament (Lerner & Lerner, 1983). An appropriate goodness of fit between parent expectations and infant temperament is necessary to establish a trusting infant-parent attachment.

For example, parents who remain calm and reassuring can help infants with difficult temperaments to better regulate their behavior. The infant-parent relationship is in turn more harmonious, creating an environment in which infants can develop a healthy sense of trust in their parents. Parents with slow-to-warm-up infants are often advised to allow for extra time during daily routines as well as when introducing new toys or situations. In order to create a trusting environment, these infants need parents who recognize the need for a goodness of fit response pattern characterized by patience. What goodness of fit expectations and response patterns would help irritable infants to develop a healthy sense of trust in their parents?

The importance of attachment and temperament to infants' sense of trust becomes even more evident as children enter into Erikson's second stage of social-emotional development. Infants who successfully establish a sense of trust in their parents are better able to meet their next challenge—establishing a sense of personal autonomy.

Stage 2. Autonomy Versus Shame and Doubt (12/18 Months to 3 Years)

As children's neurological and muscular systems mature, they are able to do more things on their own. Toddlers and young school-age children are constantly on the move, exploring their physical world. Likewise, preschoolers' improved communication skills allow them to more clearly and forcefully express their thoughts and feelings. Food, clothes, daily routines, and play activities now become areas of potential disagreement between preschoolers and their parents. While often described as a "battle of wills" or the "terrible twos," the negativity that is associated with this period of development actually reflects the beginning of childhood independence, or autonomy.

Helping young children achieve a healthy sense of autonomy is dependent upon adults providing the right amount of protection and guidance, especially since young children do not yet have an adequate level of experience, skill, or knowledge to always make informed and safe decisions. Adults who recognize and support children's need to assert their independence in socially appropriate ways reinforce children's healthy sense of autonomy. In contrast, adults who are overly protective or who issue rigid commandments can disrupt children's emerging sense of autonomy. Children who are prevented from demonstrating their cognitive skills, expressing their emotions, and exercising their physical skills may develop feelings of shame or doubt about their abilities.

These responses to the crisis of "autonomy versus shame and doubt" influence the degree to which children ultimately achieve the virtue of will described by Erikson (1994) as ". . . the unbroken determination to exercise free choice as well as self-restraint" (p. 119). In Erikson's words, it is the virtue of will that gives children "a sense of self-control without loss of self-esteem. . ." (Erikson, 1994, p. 109). A successful resolution of this second stage of social-emotional development thus results in a healthy balance between a sense of autonomy, the ability to realistically assess a situation, and the ability to restrain one's impulses when it is necessary to do so.

Although numerous factors influence children's successful adaptation of autonomy, perhaps none are more important than the parenting styles under which children are reared.

Parenting styles and autonomy.   How would you describe the parenting behavior of your parents or other significant caregivers? Were they demanding or flexible, controlling or permissive? *Parenting style* is a descriptive phrase that characterizes parents' child-guidance strategies. Three parenting styles are typically discussed (Baumrind, 1967; 1971), although a fourth and more extreme parenting style is sometimes included (Maccoby & Martin, 1983). As you read about each parenting style, think about its potential influence on children's sense of autonomy.

Authoritarian parenting.   This is an autocratic style of parenting. Although they are accepting and mean well, parents demand strict obedience from their children. Rules are imposed without explanation and children's views are ignored. Discipline strategies are forceful and punitive.

Authoritative parenting.   This is a democratic style of parenting. Parents respect children's views and feelings, and they in turn expect respect from their children. Parents are flexible, allowing children the freedom to make their own decisions. At the same time, they provide guidance by establishing rules of conduct and explaining the consequences for breaking them. Obedience is valued, but so is children's sense of independence.

Permissive parenting.   This style of parenting is characterized by what might be described as anarchy, in that there is a lack of consistent guidance from parents. Parents are warm, but they fail to monitor their children's behavior. Instead, children are allowed to freely follow their own interests, and they are excused from assuming personal responsibility for their behavior.

Which parenting style do you believe is the most effective in supporting children's sense of autonomy? Baumrind (1967; 1971; 1991a,b) and her followers found the authoritative style of parenting to be most closely associated with a positive childhood adjustment. For example, children of authoritative parents were found to display greater sociability and a greater achievement orientation than children of authoritarian and permissive parents. These positive characteristics extended into middle childhood and adolescence with continued displays of socially competent, self-confident, and achievement-oriented behaviors (Baumrind, 1991a,b; Steinberg, Lamborn, Darling, Mounts, & Dornbusch, 1994; Steinberg, Lamborn, Dornbusch, & Darling, 1992; Steinberg, Mounts, Lamborn, & Dornbusch, 1991), along with an absence or infrequent display of behavioral problems like alcohol or drug abuse (Barnes & Farrell, 1992; Baumrind, 1991a,b).

Uninvolved parenting.   In all three of the cases just described, parents assumed responsibility for their parenting role. In extreme cases, however, parents may reject or even abuse their children. Some parents may be so overwhelmed with their own problems that they are emotionally and/or physically unresponsive to their children's needs.

For example, maternal depression and emotional stress can prevent some mothers from forming a close emotional attachment with their infants (Ainsworth, Blehar, Waters, & Wall, 1978; Main & Hesse, 1990; Main & Solomon, 1990; Teti,

Messinger, Gelfand, & Issabella, 1995). This situation in turn has the potential to contribute to *learned helplessness,* a response pattern in which children become easily frustrated when presented with a problem-solving situation (Nolen-Hocksema, Wolfson, Mumme, & Guskin, 1995). Children who display learned helplessness also fail to show enthusiasm for new situations or persistence in pursuing a task. They often give up without ever really trying. Such behavior is associated with lower competency and higher ratings of helpless behavior by teachers (Nolen-Hocksema et al., 1995) that can extend across the childhood years (Nolen-Hocksema, Girgus, & Seligman, 1992).

Similarly, children of uninvolved parents exhibit a number of adjustment problems that extend across time. During the school-age years, they have more absences, lower grades, lower test scores, more grade retentions, and more discipline problems than their peers who are not maltreated (Eckenrode, Laird, & Doris, 1993; Leiter & Johnsen, 1994). During adolescence, they are more prone to rebellious and antisocial behavior such as alcohol and drug abuse (Barber, 1992; Lamborn, Mounts, Steinberg, & Dornbusch, 1991; Maccoby & Martin, 1983).

In closing, it is important to note that these parenting styles also have relevance for the classroom. Teachers themselves employ their own parenting style when responding to children's behavior, as we see in Checklist 6.1. What parenting/teaching style might you use in the following situations?

- Hassan, a 4-year-old, refuses your request to remain silent while his peers are speaking. When you give him the option of remaining silent or leaving the group, he stands up, yells an obscenity at you, and runs out of the room.
- Mary, a 5-year-old, has returned to the classroom following a week-long absence due to illness. She appears timid and anxious. When asked to share her work with a small group of peers, she begins to cry. She tearfully asks if she can go home.
- It is your first week as a first-grade teacher. One of your first responsibilities is to establish classroom rules of conduct. How will you do this?
- Carlos and Jack, two 7-year-olds, are best friends. You are thus surprised to find them fighting on the playground. Neither is willing to talk about the fight. In fact, neither is willing to talk at all. Recess is ending and you must gather the other children together. You hear a scream and turn around to see Carlos swinging a baseball bat at Jack.

Stage 3. Initiative Versus Guilt (3 to 6 Years)

As children enter into the third stage of social-emotional development, they use their sense of autonomy as a basis for acting upon their more advanced physical and cognitive skills. Children are now able to plan ahead and carry out more complex sequences of behavior. For example, rather than responding to a one-step directive from their parents, children are now able to remember and carry out tasks involving two or more steps. Children at this stage also seek out new experiences.

CHECKLIST 6.1

What's Your Teaching Style?

What is your teaching style? Check the statements that sound most like you and find out.

Authoritarian

_____ Introduces numerous rules.

_____ Emphasizes "don'ts" over "dos."

_____ Withdraws emotional support to punish children on occasion.

_____ Believes in the use of corporal punishment.

_____ Follows a structured instructional style, telling children exactly how to carry out tasks.

_____ Establishes a rigid seating plan and schedule; sets strict limits on all tasks.

_____ Makes use of the statement, "Do as I say, not as I do."

Authoritative

_____ Sets an example by modeling appropriate behavior for children.

_____ Takes time to listen to children's concerns, interests, and explanations.

_____ Allows children to help set classroom rules of conduct.

_____ Consistently enforces rules, but is also willing to take into account unusual situations.

_____ Focuses more on reinforcing children's positive behavior than on punishing their misbehavior.

_____ Focuses more on children's efforts and accomplishments than on their failures.

_____ Encourages children to think through tasks on their own, providing support and guidance as needed.

_____ Remains flexible, giving children extra time and material to complete or extend projects that are of obvious interest to them.

_____ Allows children some freedom in choosing their seating arrangement and work partners.

_____ Encourages students to provide feedback about classroom rules and activities.

_____ Makes use of the statement, "If at first you don't succeed, try, try again."

Permissive

_____ Introduces few classroom rules of conduct, which tend to be vague ("Be kind") rather than specific ("We call each other by our names").

continues

CHECKLIST 6.1 *Continued*

_____ Allows children to freely follow their own initiatives; provides little support or guidance.

_____ Warmly receives children who ask for help and encourages them to follow their own instincts.

_____ Provides little classroom planning or scheduling.

_____ Allows children to forego an activity that does not interest them or to engage in another activity of their choosing.

_____ Enforces few consequences following children's disruptive behavior.

_____ Allows students to choose their work partners, and to decide how to carry out a project.

_____ Makes use of the statement, "Each child knows best."

They are curious, imaginative, and are better able to focus their attention. All of these skills prepare children to take the initiative by engaging in creative work that they find interesting and by completing tasks on their own.

Children's sense of initiative can also become troublesome. For example, children's attempts to solve problems on their own may result in failure or even physical harm if they are not properly supervised. Yet children at this age often resist, and may even resent, adult guidance. A balance must therefore be reached between guiding children's behavior to protect them from failure or harm while supporting their emerging sense of initiative.

Children who are prevented from exercising their imagination and creativity, as well as those whose efforts result in criticism or who are allowed to consistently fail, can develop a sense of "guilt" over what they perceive as their own personal failings. The result may be an identity that is characterized by self-monitoring and self-punishment. Children may also fail to apply themselves, fail to give themselves credit for their efforts, and even fail to recognize and appreciate their successes.

In contrast, children who are encouraged and guided in their creative efforts are able to succeed and receive the approval they seek from significant adults. The resulting sense of initiative leads to the virtue of "purpose." As described by Erikson (1964), the virtue of purpose instills in children the "courage to envisage and pursue valued goals" (p. 122). The virtue of purpose also provides children with a "sense of purpose for adult tasks which promise (but cannot guarantee) a fulfillment of one's range of capacities" (Erikson, 1994, p. 122). In short, a child begins to develop a life philosophy that "I am what I can imagine I will be" (Erikson, 1994, p. 122).

In the remainder of this section, we discuss two factors that are important at this stage of children's social-emotional development. The first factor involves children learning the social norms associated with male/female behavioral initiatives. The second factor involves the value of play as a mechanism for children's expression of initiative.

Children between the ages of 3 and 6 take the initiative in carrying out creative activities that they find interesting.

Gender and initiative.
It should come as no surprise that gender plays an important role in defining the nature of children's initiative. All children are faced with the task of adapting socially appropriate gender roles, and it is through gender roles that society defines the appropriate behavioral initiatives for girls and boys.

Before proceeding, we first need to make a distinction between two terms. Although sometimes used interchangeably, "gender" and "sex" are not synonymous. *Sex* refers to the biological characteristics (e.g., genitals) that define one as male or female. *Gender* refers to the roles that society assigns to the different sexes. Sex is thus a biological given, while gender involves socialization. Gender socialization begins at birth as parents dress their newborn in blue or pink and begin to formulate different expectations about their child's life experiences. The process continues throughout early childhood as children are exposed to media gender portrayals, peer expectations, and even school policies regarding gender dress codes and behaviors. The gender socialization process involves three components:

- **Gender identity.**   *Gender identity* is established around age 3 when young children learn to label themselves as boys or girls (Beal, 1994). At this age, children make stereotyped decisions about what is male and female based upon superficial appearances like clothing, hairstyles, and games.
- **Gender stability.**   *Gender stability* is established during the preschool years as children come to recognize that their gender is permanent, and that their sex will remain the same across time (Beal, 1994). Boys grow up to become men, and girls grow up to become women.
- **Gender constancy.**   *Gender constancy* is established between 5 and 7 years of age as children come to recognize that their gender remains the same despite alterations in their appearance or behavior (Beal, 1994). This is a radical change from the preschool years when children are more apt to believe that a change in gender is associated with changes in wardrobe or play activities. In contrast, young school-age children realize that gender remains constant regardless of one's dress or activity.

Parents and teachers often see these gender concepts in action during their daily interactions with young children. A 3- or 4-year-old may be inconsistent in labeling herself as a girl. She may tell you that she is a girl when she puts on an apron and adopts the mommy role during dramatic play, or that she is a boy when she adopts the daddy role during outdoor play. In contrast, 6-year-olds display much more rigid sex roles, reflecting their need to consistently display their male and female identities. *Gender-role stereotyping* occurs when children display a rigid preference for same-sex playmates, gender-typed toys, same-sex activities, and same-sex role models. Parents and teachers are sometimes frustrated in their attempts to help children be less gender-role stereotyped. It may help to know that there is a developmental reason behind this behavior.

The development of gender constancy is progressive and begins with a highly selective mindset. Researchers refer to this selective mindset as the *gender schema,* which is characterized by children seeking out, organizing, and giving meaning to everyday experiences based on socially approved gender roles (Martin, 1993; Martin & Halverson, 1983; Serbin, Powlishta, & Gulko, 1993). At first, children tend to use their gender schema in a rigid manner. For example, a toy or behavior may be defined as being male or female, but not both. Boys prefer to play with boys, and girls prefer to play with girls. Such early rigidity reflects children's initial attempts at understanding and adopting socially approved gender roles. Fortunately, children's gender schema becomes less rigid with time and experience. Some of the ways in which teachers can respond to young children's rigid gender-role stereotyping follow:

- **Talk about children's similarities.**   Both girls and boys (men and women) have feelings, must follow rules, need exercise, have a desire to do their best, are creative and expressive, and need to eat healthy meals. What other gender-role similarities exist between the two sexes?
- **Encourage children to share gender-typed toys and games.**   Boys may find they enjoy playing the role of a dancer or helping to prepare snacks or test new

recipes. Girls may find they enjoy playing first base or helping to mount insects collected during a field trip.

- **Plan time to share feelings and ideas.**   Ask children to share their feelings and ideas while planning a project or immediately upon its completion. Note the similarities in feelings and ideas expressed by boys and girls.
- **Invite adults in nontraditional roles to talk about their activities.**   Some nontraditional roles might include stay-at-home fathers, executive mothers, female firefighters, male nurses, female construction workers, and male secretaries. Ask the visitors to talk about their duties and share what they enjoy about their jobs.
- **Talk with children about gender images seen on TV.**   What types of gender-roles do children see on TV? Do they match the gender-roles that children see in their everyday lives? How would children change the way in which gender-roles are presented on TV?

Regardless of their gender, all children view play as an important activity. As you will discover in the following section, there are many dimensions of play. Teachers who understand the importance of play in relationship to children's sense of initiative are better able to plan and facilitate meaningful learning experiences.

Play and initiative.   Early childhood teachers have long noted that "play is a child's work"—and for good reason. Play is the most important reflection of children's development. It is through play that children practice coordinating their movements, make discoveries about their work, challenge themselves, learn to communicate with others, and develop cooperative social skills.

The nature of children's play activities evolves over time, making it necessary for teachers to plan and facilitate activities that match children's interests and abilities. The first two nonplay stages in the following list reflect Parten's (1932) original classification of play that has been followed for decades. The remaining stages reflect an updated classification scheme developed by Howes and Matheson (1992).

- **Nonplay (unoccupied).**   Rather than engaging in active play, very young children simply observe the play of others. This type of behavior is often not sustained for very long periods of time. Children may redirect their attention to whatever interests them at the moment.
- **Nonplay (onlooker).**   Children display a sustained interest in observing a particular play activity, but they do not join the play. Instead, they may ask questions or make comments about their peers' play.
- **Parallel play (6–12 months).**   Children at this stage play alone, ignoring their peers. They seem to be self-absorbed in their own play and uninterested in what others might be doing. Parten (1932) placed this stage of play at a later age (2–3 years) and labeled it *solitary play.*
- **Parallel aware play (around 1 year).**   This is the first step that children take in playing together. Although children play by themselves, they play close to their peers and engage in the same type of play with similar toys. Children's play thus remains parallel in that there is no attempt to coordinate play activities. Parten (1932) also described this stage as occurring at a later age (2–3 years).

- **Simple pretend play (1–1 1/2 years).** Children begin to show the first signs of cooperation. They talk with each other and may even share toys while engaged in similar activities. However, their play is simple, momentary, and does not yet reflect a well-developed theme. Parten (1932) did not describe a similar play stage, although her stage of "associative play" contained elements of this stage.
- **Reciprocal play (1 1/2–2 years).** Children begin to engage in simple give-and-take type activities that last for longer periods of time. Chase, peek-a-boo, and mimicking someone's behavior or language involve a reciprocal type of social exchange. Parten (1932) did not describe this stage in her classification scheme, although it too has elements of what she labeled "associative play."
- **Cooperative social pretend play (2 1/2–3 years).** At this stage, children begin to coordinate their play activities. They share toys, cooperate in playing out adult roles, and may even attempt to control who is allowed to play along. However, no attempts are made to organize play activities. Each child follows his or her own script, and there is no consultation as the play theme progresses. Parten (1932) labeled this type of play *associative play* and associated it with somewhat older children (3–4 years).
- **Complex social pretend play (3 1/2–4 years).** Children's play is organized and directed toward a goal. Children take on different roles and clearly cooperate in carrying out their play theme. They may even stop their play to discuss disagreements about how the theme of their play is being interpreted. This stage forms the foundation for children's involvement in more sophisticated and demanding school projects and plays, team sports, and club activities. Parten (1932) used the label *cooperative play* to describe this play stage. As with the other stages, she associated it with somewhat older children (4–5 years).

In addition to these stages of play, teachers must also understand the different functions of play. A review of the major functional types of play that teachers use to facilitate children's play initiatives follows:

- **Sensory play.** Children and adults alike enjoy pleasurable sensory experiences. Young children especially are excited by new odors, tastes, sights, smells, and touches. How might you engage children in sensory play using the following items: cotton balls, fruits, finger paint, or items collected during a field trip to a nature park? What types of dangerous sensory play might teachers need to consider as they monitor children's play activities?
- **Movement play.** Young children especially enjoy free movements like running and hopping. Older children prefer to combine these movements into more structured games like t-ball and hopscotch. How might you structure a movement activity to make it possible for children to play together even though they display different levels of motor development?
- **Symbolic play.** Symbolic play, sometimes referred to as dramatic or pretend play, involves the use of symbols to represent reality. Toys and make-believe props are used to represent real-life objects. Family roles (e.g., mother and father) and community roles (e.g., postal workers, shop owners) are adopted

and carefully scripted to reflect the adult world. These symbolic activities develop over time and are dependent upon the support of parents and teachers.

- **Language play.** Young children love to play with sounds and words, even making up words of their own. Teachers can build upon language play to reinforce children's reading and writing skills. What types of reading or writing activities might you introduce to a second-grade class that involve community symbols (e.g., fast-food symbols, advertising jingles and figures, transportation symbols, safety symbols)? How might these same symbols be used with preschoolers?
- **Games.** Games are a more structured form of play. They involve rules of conduct and the awarding of points. Unlike play, games are usually competitive and result in winners and losers. However, some parents and teachers have turned to a unique type of game to de-emphasize competition and to emphasize cooperation. *Noncompetitive games* require cooperation and do not result in individual winners and losers. Rather, everyone wins. Children must work as a collective team to move an object, score points, locate an object, or hit a target. Teachers have different views on competitive and noncompetitive games. What are your views? Is it possible to keep competition out of children's games? How might children's sense of initiative change if noncompetitive games are emphasized over competitive games? How might you turn a competitive game that you played as a child into a noncompetitive game?
- **Playful routines.** Daily classroom routines like going to lunch, changing clothes, transitioning between activities, cleaning up, and resting can become boring. And, as every teacher knows, boredom sets the stage for disruptive behavior as children look for ways to entertain themselves. Teachers therefore strive to make classroom routines playful as a means of keeping children focused and to reinforce their sense of initiative. For example, children may sing a song while going to lunch. Groups of children may accumulate points for displaying responsible behavior while transitioning between classroom activities. Secret signals may be used to communicate quietly during cleanup. Think of ways in which you might alter any one aspect of a daily routine to keep it playful, interesting, and reinforcing of children's initiative.

Play not only reflects preschool and young school-age children's concern with initiative, it also lays the foundation for the next stage of development. As you will discover, school-age children are more focused in their pursuit of activities. In particular, they focus their efforts on activities that have an end purpose or result in an end product. In short, their concern shifts from displays of initiative to displays of industriousness.

Stage 4. Industry Versus Inferiority (6 Years to Adolescence)

As children enter school they encounter new challenges and opportunities. It is during the primary grades that children begin to receive detailed instruction in the use of tools associated with the adult world (e.g., books, maps, and computers), as well as various artistic and technical materials. Children's cognitive and motor skills allow them to make use of these tools to demonstrate their growing sense of competence, or "industry." New challenges are eagerly sought and attempts are made to master them. Outcomes or products like homework, class projects, school grades, athletic awards, achievement pins and stickers, and artwork become important symbols of school-age children's accomplishments. Each new grade or sticker reinforces children's sense of competence and industriousness.

The previous three social-emotional stages establish the groundwork for this extended period of social-emotional development. Children who achieve a sense of trust, autonomy, and initiative are more likely to view their broadening social world as one that presents opportunities to be experienced and mastered. And as children master new opportunities, they acquire the virtue of "competence," defined by Erikson (1994, p. 234) as the ability to appreciate and make effective use of the "tools and weapons, symbols and concepts . . . and roles" associated with one's culture. In short, the virtue of competence in childhood leads to "workmanship" in adulthood (Erikson, 1964). In contrast, children who have feelings of mistrust, shame, doubt, or guilt are more likely to be timid and hesitant to take advantage of academic, athletic, or artistic opportunities. Children who fail to engage in, or to be rewarded for, industrious behavior during the early and middle-school

School-age children display industrious behavior as they seek out and attempt to master new learning experiences.

years develop a sense of "inferiority" that is characterized by feelings of inadequacy and a lack of competence.

Although parents and youth leaders are important figures in helping children to acquire a healthy sense of industry and competence, Erikson (1994) made special mention of teachers. You yourself may have been fortunate enough to experience the following type of student-teacher relationship:

> For nothing less is at stake than the development and maintenance in children of a positive identification with those who know things and know how to do things. Again and again in interviews with especially gifted and inspired people, one is told spontaneously and with a special glow that *one* teacher can be credited with having kindled the flame of hidden talent (Erikson, 1994, p. 125).

In this section, we discuss two factors that can help you in guiding and supporting children's emerging sense of industry and competence. We first examine the importance of perspective role-taking and friendships. We then examine the various sources of childhood stress that threaten children's sense of industry. We conclude with a review of strategies that teachers can use to help children cope with stress.

Social perspective-taking, friendships, and industry.

Many school and community experiences are designed to advance school-age children's empathy, cooperation, and communication with others. Teachers often ask children to work together on classroom tasks. Sport activities involve team work. Youth groups work on community projects that require a group identity and the coordination of group activities. All of these activities require that children understand the perspectives of those around them in order to achieve a goal. Children also develop a better understanding of themselves as they reflect on how others respond to their behavior. Finally, the achievement of shared goals reinforces children's sense of industriousness, which is essential to their adopting adult roles related to parenting, marital relations, and employment.

In order to accomplish these tasks, children must be able to not only communicate their own thoughts and feelings, they must also be able to understand and appreciate the thoughts and feelings of others. This process is referred to as *social perspective-taking*. As described by its originator, "Social perspective-taking refers to the process by which a child is able to take the perspective of another and relate it to his or her own".*

Like other areas of development, perspective role-taking is a gradual process that takes place over time. Selman* notes that, "developmentally, social perspective-taking is viewed as beginning at the level at which the child fails to distinguish the social viewpoints of self and other. It then develops in a series of qualitative steps: first,

---

*From Selman, R. L. (1981). "The child as a friendship philosopher." In Asher, S. R. and Gottman, J. M. (eds.) *Children's Friendships*. Copyright © 1981 by Cambridge University Press. Reprinted by permission.

distinguishing the social viewpoints of self and other, and then relating them to each other in progressively more complex and integrated ways." Altogether, Selman (1980; 1981) identified five stages of perspective role-taking, each of which is accompanied by five stages of friendship. A summary of the first three stages related to the early childhood years follows. Note the wide range of ages associated with each stage and the age overlaps between stages, highlighting the individual variations among children as they gradually progress toward more sophisticated levels of role-taking.

Stage 0: Egocentric perspectives and momentary playmates (3–7 years).
The "0" indicates that there is in fact little role-taking during the preschool years. Children see only their own viewpoints. They assume that their views are equally shared by others (example: "I like cake better than candy. Dad will like cake better than candy"). Because children at this stage are unable to consider the motives or intentions of others, friendships are defined in egocentric terms. Friends are those who live in close proximity, attend the same school, or possess a valued toy (example: "Liz is my friend. She lives in my apartment building").

Stage 1: Subjective perspectives and one-way assistance (4–9 years).
At this stage, children recognize that everyone has his or her own viewpoints, but they continue to interpret events and behaviors in unilateral terms. They still cannot think simultaneously about their own viewpoint and that of someone else. They are also unable to take another person's perspective, and they are not aware of how others might see them (example: "Dad does not like cake better than candy! I'll tell him why cake is better than candy"). Likewise, although children begin to use themes of sharing and support as indicators of friendship, that support is one-way, superficial, and tenuous. Friends are those who do what you want them to do when you want them to do it (example: "Tyrone is not my friend anymore. He didn't let me have a turn").

Stage 2: Self-reflective perspectives and two-way cooperation (6–12 years).
Sometime during primary school, children first begin to understand that individuals hold different values and beliefs, and this is why there are differences in viewpoint. They also appreciate the importance of two-way communication. They subsequently begin to reflect upon their own thoughts and behaviors in an attempt to anticipate how others will respond to their actions (example: "I like cake, but dad likes candy. Maybe we should give him candy for his birthday"). The reflective quality of role-taking is reflected in children's definition of friendship. Reciprocity and negotiation begin to characterize children's social exchanges. There is a sense of sharing, although children's explanations of friendship still have a self-serving theme. Friendships also tend to be "fair-weather" in that an argument may result in an end to the relationship rather than an opportunity for building a stronger friendship bond (example: "We had an argument last night. She's not my friend anymore").

Although friendships are important to the social-emotional development of school-age children, even friends cannot protect children from the stressors that accompany contemporary life. We next examine the sources and symptoms of childhood stress, in addition to the characteristics that make some children resilient to stress.

Stress, resiliency, and industry. Parents and teachers frequently express concern over the pressures associated with childhood today. Concern about physical safety include child abuse, drugs, and street crime. Parents and teachers also express concern over the "hurried child" who is pushed to grow up too fast and too early (Elkind, 1981). All of these concerns, plus others, are justified in that they represent potential sources of childhood stress that can interfere with school-age children's emerging sense of industry.

Each of us experiences stress in different ways. You may experience stress as an emotional reaction (e.g., crying), a physiological reaction (e.g., headaches), or a cognitive reaction (e.g., problems with concentration). For our purpose, we define *stress* simply as the body's reaction to perceived life demands (Selye, 1974). The important thing to remember about this classic definition is that only those life demands that we perceive as threatening become stressful. This is why different children may respond to similar situations in very different ways. The meaning that children give to a potential stressful situation is based on a number of factors, including their level of cognitive development, their personality, and their support system.

When making an assessment of childhood stress, several questions are typically asked. How many stress symptoms are displayed by the child? Are the symptoms temporary or are they displayed over a period of time? Is the behavior uncharacteristic of the child? Does the behavior coincide with changes in the child's life? The following symptoms may indicate a childhood stress reaction (Barton & Zeanah, 1990; Sears & Milburn, 1990):

- Regression to more immature behavior like bed wetting, thumb sucking, separation anxiety, attention seeking behavior, or unusually emotional behavior
- Difficulty going to sleep or staying asleep
- An unexplained loss of appetite
- Unusual withdrawal from significant others
- Unusual gloomy mood
- Unexplained irritability
- Trouble getting along with peers, including an unexplained increase in aggressiveness
- Unexplained loss of motivation
- Inability to concentrate or think clearly
- Unexplained and repeated physical complaints like headaches and stomachaches

Teachers also need to understand the sources of childhood stress. *Situational stressors,* those situations or events that create stress symptoms, can be negative (e.g., death in family) or positive (e.g., winning an award). A sampling of potential stressors follows (Blom, Cheney, & Snoddy, 1986). Although developed over a decade ago, these stressors remain very much a part of children's lives today. What other stressors might you add to these lists?

- **Stressors at home.** Divorce of parents; birth of brother or sister; change in parents' employment status; family arguments; family illness; brother or sister leaving home; sibling competition; holidays

- **Stressors at school.**   Move to a new school; beginning school; giving a class report; ridicule or criticism; tests; new teacher; homework; relations between parents and teacher; being labeled
- **Neighborhood and world stressors.**   Loss of playmates; unsupervised after-school care; going to the dentist; not feeling a part of the community; fear of war or violence; discrimination; pollution

Of course, not all stressors are situational. Some are associated with normal developmental challenges. A sample of common developmental stressors found in children is summarized in the following section (Silverman, La Greca, & Wasserstein, 1995). Can you find an example of how a developmental stressor might be linked to a situational stressor? Here is one question to think about: In what types of situations might giving a class report (situational stressor) contribute to a fear of failure (developmental stressor)?

Preschool developmental stressors include:

- **Egocentrism.**   Preschoolers' inability to take others' perspective can lead to communication problems.
- **Autonomy and initiative.**   Feelings of frustration and aggression can arise when parents impose safety rules that restrict preschoolers' emerging sense of autonomy and initiative.
- **Consistency.**   Young children do not handle change well. They often become upset when their daily routines are altered.
- **Overstimulation.**   The high activity level and curiosity of preschool children can lead to overstimulation. Children often become emotional (e.g., tearful, argumentative) when they are tired or overstimulated.
- **Active imagination.**   Children make use of fantasy to gain a sense of control over their world. Their play themes often involve situations that they fear (e.g., slaying storybook beasts) or have little control over (e.g., directing family activities). However, they are not always able to separate their imaginative world from reality. Children may believe that an imaginary beast has suddenly appeared in a darkened bedroom. The holiday characters that children read about in books can become frightening when they suddenly appear in an oversized form during classroom holiday celebrations.
- **Curiosity.**   Preschool children's natural curiosity can lead them to engage in unsafe behaviors that result in harm, failure, criticism, or discipline.
- **Self-awareness.**   As children become aware of the differences between themselves and others, they also become more aware of who receives attention from others. Children may subsequently exaggerate their behavior to gain the attention of significant adults.

School-age developmental stressors include:

- **School-related stress.**   As noted previously, school is a potential source of stress for school-age children. In particular, school-age children worry most frequently about school performance issues (e.g., tests, being disliked by teachers), health issues (e.g., someone else's health and their own), and especially personal harm (e.g., getting robbed, stabbed, shot, etc.) (Silverman et al., 1995). In fact, personal harm remains a top worry even for children who do not live in high-crime areas and have never experienced personal harm (Silverman et al. 1995).

- **Fear of success.**   School-age children's sense of industry can be seriously challenged if they feel that they are being closely scrutinized by parents and teachers. Failure is one way to lessen the stress associated with the scrutiny and high expectations of others.
- **Fear of failure.**   Children may avoid activities or tasks that they believe will result in feelings of inferiority. This may be especially true among children who feel that they are unprepared or unable to meet the demands of a task. Criticism or lack of support of children's efforts and successes can result in a fear of failure and children's subsequent resistance to attempt new challenges.
- **Peer pressure.**   The peer group is an important part of school-age children's lives, influencing their attitudes, behaviors, and even their dress. As noted earlier, children use their peers to practice perspective role-taking. Peers also are the source of children's first meaningful relationships outside the family. Children can therefore find it stressful when their attitudes or beliefs run counter to those of their peer group. Children may sometimes even engage in behaviors that they disagree with to gain the approval of their peers.
- **Separation from family.**   As children become more involved with peers and school, they begin to separate from their families. At the same time, their families remain a vital source of financial and emotional support. At one time or another, most children experience conflict involving separation from family. They may express embarrassment over their parents' behavior but still see their parents as important confidants who provide valuable guidance. They may request that their parents not attend a music recital or athletic event but still seek their parents' support and approval.
- **Role models.**   School-age children model their dress and behaviors after television characters, rock bands, athletes, and movie heroes. Rules of conduct and dress in the home and school sometimes run counter to the behaviors displayed by children's role models. These conflicts set the stage for arguments and for the testing of limits.

Regardless of their origin—situational or developmental—once stress occurs it can interfere with children's industriousness. We only have to reflect upon our own childhood to understand the negative effect that stress can have on our self-esteem and our motivation to carry through with even simple daily routines. Fortunately, researchers have identified one group of children who seem resistant to stress.

As the label implies, *resilient children* are those who are able to ward off stress even when confronted with extreme life stressors (Zimmerman & Arunkumar, 1994). Pioneering longitudinal work in this area found resilient children among families living in poverty, families experiencing instability or discord, and families with parents experiencing psychopathology (Garmezy, 1991, 1993; Garmezy, Masten, & Tellegen, 1984; Rutter, Maughan, Mortimore, & Ouston, 1979; Werner, 1993; Werner & Smith, 1977, 1989, 1992).

Some characteristics of childhood resiliency include an achievement orientation, a sense of autonomy, problem-solving skills, a positive self-concept, a sense of personal control, a high tolerance for frustration, sensitivity to the needs of others, good "impulse" control, a willingness and ability to express personal feelings, and a support base within or outside the family (Blom et al., 1986; Garmezy et al., 1984; Zimmerman & Arunkumar, 1994).

You may think that these characteristics make resilient children invulnerable. They do not. *Resiliency* is a relative, not an absolute, term. It simply denotes the potential capacity of children to adapt to stressful life experiences. Therefore, it is also important to keep the following two factors in mind when assessing children's resiliency:

- **Children's total life context must be considered in assessing resiliency.** Children may be resilient when faced with certain life stressors but vulnerable to other life stressors. Some factors that can mediate children's reactions to stressors include their family structure and support, their school and peer group, and their own stage of development. For example, although we might think of temperament as an important mediator in children's adjustment to life stressors, it has been found to have limited value in predicting young children's social-emotional adjustment by itself (Sanson et al., 1991). How might the concept of goodness of fit determine whether or not a child's particular temperament represents a resilient strength? You may find it helpful to review the section of this chapter dealing with goodness of fit before responding to this question.
- **Children play an active role in demonstrating their resiliency.** Children who possess resilient strengths may nevertheless succumb to stress if they are not able or willing to exercise those strengths. A listing of instructional strategies for helping children to identify and use their resilient characteristics is presented in Tips for Teaching 6.1. After reviewing these tips, read the case study presented in Box 6.1. What strategies did Mr. Carr and Chang's parents use to help strengthen Chang's resiliency?

Consideration of children's social-emotional development would not be complete without a discussion of their moral development. In fact, Erikson's social-emotional stages reflect a series of moral crises to which children must respond. With this in mind, we now turn to Lawrence Kohlberg's (1927–1987) theory of moral development to examine the progression of children's moral reasoning.

KOHLBERG'S THEORY OF MORAL DEVELOPMENT

Morality, equality, justice, fairness, and reciprocity—these are concepts that are hotly debated in our nation. They are not, however, new to parents and teachers who have always faced the daunting challenge of teaching children to act responsibly; to treat others with respect and kindness; to take turns, share, and cooperate with others; and to be honest and reliable. Today, the challenge of instilling these social behaviors is sometimes made more difficult by differing opinions about the

TIPS FOR TEACHERS 6.1

Addressing Childhood Stress

Cognitive Understanding

- Label feelings. Young children may not always possess the vocabulary needed to express their feelings about a situation.
- Explain and clarify. Help children to understand a stressful situation by providing factual explanations. Children may also need help in clarifying their interpretation of a situation.
- Gather and provide information. Help children to frame a stressful situation by listing questions that need answers. Steps can then be taken to gather the information needed to provide appropriate answers.

Emotional Expression

- Listen to children's views and concerns. This will send the message that you care and provide you with information about children's interpretation of a situation.
- Permit and channel feelings. Children can become more resilient by learning appropriate strategies for expressing and channeling their feelings.
- Connect events and feelings. This can be accomplished through personal discussions, art projects, reflective journals, role-plays, and books that are related to stressful situations.

Emotional Support

- Display empathy. Acknowledge the importance of children's concerns.
- Plan for peer support when appropriate. For example, the school counselor might arrange for a small group of children whose families have lost their homes due to a flood to meet together during the school day.

- Involve parents. Meet with parents to plan strategies for providing emotional support in the home and school.

Structure and Control

- Provide daily structure. All children need structure so that they develop a sense of control over their lives. When children's home lives are disrupted due to death, divorce, or disaster it is especially important that their school lives remain structured.
- Provide limits. Limits do more than keep children safe; they send the message that the teacher cares about the safety of children and help children feel in control of their lives.
- Be flexible. Children who are experiencing stress may display behaviors that are atypical and classroom rules may not always apply.

Skill Development

- Recall past successes. Children may lose sight of their strengths when under stress. Help them to assess their personal strengths and ways that they might use them to respond to a stressful situation.
- Model appropriate stress-management behaviors. Invite children to spend a few moments in reflective thought each day; introduce breathing or stretching exercises; lead children in daily exercise; provide opportunities to discuss the connection between nutrition and health.

Adaption reprinted by permission of the publisher from Blom, G. E., Cheney, B. D., & Snoddy, J. E. *Stress in Childhood: An Intervention Model for Teachers and Other Professionals.* (New York: Teachers College Press, © 1986 by Teachers College, Columbia University. All rights reserved.), pp. 85–86 (Table 9.1); p. 153 (Table 14.1).

BOX 6.1	*Chang's New Life*

Chang, a 6-year-old, was moving to a new city. He was not happy. It wasn't just that he was moving away from his home, school, best friend, t-ball team, and his treehouse and secret spot in the woods. He was also moving away from his mother. Chang's mother and father were recently divorced. His father was awarded custody, and they were moving to another state. Fortunately, Chang's mother and father had agreed to a generous visitation plan, and both held good jobs that would allow them to remain in close contact. It was also fortunate that the city to which Chang and his father were moving was the same city that his mother visited on business every few weeks. Yes, these were all fortunate arrangements, but not for Chang. He didn't care that everyone was pleased to be starting their "new life." And he couldn't understand why everyone was so happy about how well his mother and father had worked things out so they could remain "friends." Chang did not want a "new life" and he did not need his parents to be "friends." He needed his "old life."

The first day of Chang's "new life" was not what he expected. His teacher, Mr. Carr, met him in the front office. After speaking with his father, Mr. Carr escorted Chang to his new classroom. He introduced Chang to his new classmates and helped him to get acquainted with the classroom. Chang thought it strange that the first thing Mr. Carr asked him to do was to draw a picture of his new house. Chang enjoyed drawing, although he had to think very hard about his new house. Mr. Carr told him not to worry about the details and to just draw whatever he could remember. He presented his drawing to Mr. Carr, who commented on Chang's good memory and creative use of colors. He asked Chang to tell him a little about his house. Chang began talking about his room, since this is what he knew best, but before long he was also including information about his former house, school, and t-ball team. He also told Mr. Carr about his parents' divorce. Mr. Carr listened quietly. All this drawing and talking was tiring. Chang was glad that it was time for lunch.

The afternoon went as well as the morning. Mr. Carr asked Chang to spend time observing his classmates at work before deciding which group he would join. Chang decided to work on the class butterfly collection. Ajie and George were already busy at work deciding how best to mount a big butterfly they had caught that morning. Mr. Carr listened to the concerns expressed by Ajie and George about the big butterfly. He then asked Chang if he had any ideas. Chang didn't have any ideas. Mr. Carr said that he had confidence that together Chang, Ajie, and George could come up with an excellent solution. They talked for a little while, even trying to gently make the big butterfly fit onto the board with the other butterflies. They finally decided that there was no solution. The big butterfly would need to be mounted on a separate board. They told Mr. Carr the bad news. But it wasn't bad news. Mr. Carr said that he thought their solution was excellent, and he promised to bring in a suitable board the next day. Chang felt good about having helped to solve a class problem. He was also pleased that Ajie and George had asked him to work with them again tomorrow.

One week passed, and Chang was feeling more at home . . . at least at school. He liked the

continues

BOX 6.1	*Chang's New Life* continued

way Mr. Carr asked children to help make class decisions. Ajie, George, and Chang were becoming good friends. Home, however, was another matter. Chang still missed his mother. It was thus with great surprise that he found her waiting for him when he got home from school. They had a good visit. That night, Chang's father and mother talked alone for a little while. They then asked if Chang would come into the dining room for a snack. Chang's mother asked if she could visit his school. Chang was pleased. The next day, he proudly introduced his mother to Mr. Carr. Mr. Carr again spent some time alone with Chang's mother. Mr. Carr then asked Chang to join them. Chang was surprised to find all his art work (even the first drawing he did for Mr. Carr) laid out on a table. Even the big butterfly was on the table, proudly mounted on its own individual board. Chang's mother was beaming. She spoke highly of Chang's accomplishments, and said, "I bet you're glad that Mr. Carr is your new teacher." Chang was glad. And, maybe he was wrong. Maybe his "new life" would be filled with new and old friends!

types of "values" that children should be taught in school . . . or not taught in school. In this section, we discuss the stages of moral development as a means of providing a framework for thinking about the guidance of children's moral reasoning. We begin with a review of Kohlberg's levels and stages of moral reasoning (Colby & Kohlberg, 1987; Colby, Kohlberg, Gibbs, & Lieberman, 1983; Kohlberg, 1969; Kohlberg & Kramer, 1969).

Stages of Moral Reasoning

As a teacher, you will be confronted with many situations that raise questions about children's moral reasoning. How do children define fairness and honesty? Does their behavior really reflect their belief system? Why do children argue about certain issues while ignoring others? Your response to these questions will be made easier by considering the stages of children's moral reasoning. Kohlberg identified three levels of moral reasoning: preconventional, conventional, and postconventional. Only the first two levels, which are related to the early childhood years, are discussed in this chapter. Note that both of the following levels are associated with general grade levels, again reflecting the individual differences associated with children's gradual increase in moral reasoning.

Preconventional level (preschool to middle school years). At this level, moral reasoning is imposed from the outside. Children judge an act as right or wrong based on the resulting consequences. At *stage 1,* an act is judged to be good or bad based on a *punishment and obedience orientation* (e.g., "He was punished because he misbehaved"). Children follow rules to avoid punishment or to gain a reward. Personal standards have little relevance. At *stage 2,* an *instrumental orientation* is followed whereby children's primary concern is to take care of personal needs or interests. The rationale for doing something nice is to have something nice done for you in return. Interactions are thus based upon an exchange of rewards (e.g., "I'll stick up for you, if you will stick up for me") or instrumental rewards (e.g., "I let you borrow my bike. I need to borrow your CD").

Conventional level (middle school to junior high years). Moral reasoning at the conventional level is based on social conformity. It is at this level that we begin to clearly see an internationalization of social standards, as decisions about right and wrong are based on the rules of conduct established by society (e.g., "He has to do it. It's the law").

At *stage 3,* children follow a *good boy-nice girl orientation.* Children expect behavior to conform to social expectations, and they strive to follow the Golden Rule—treating others as they wish to be treated. Children at stage 3 are also able to take into account the intentions that may accompany behavior. For example, a child might excuse the inappropriate behavior of someone with the statement, "Well, her intentions were good." At *stage 4,* there is an even stronger sense of social conformity as children begin to talk about duty and responsibility (e.g., "Rules are meant to be followed"). This *law-and-order orientation* is characterized by respect for authority and rules. Conformity is viewed as essential to maintaining social order (e.g., "If everyone did as he pleased, we wouldn't be able to get anything done").

Application of Kohlberg's Theory

Kohlberg's theory has implications for education beyond providing us with an understanding of children's moral reasoning. Thomas (1996) and Crain (1992), two authors who write about developmental theory, have discussed the ways in which Kohlberg and his followers have translated Kohlberg's theory for educational use. Their work again highlights the importance of developmental theories in guiding educational practices.

Challenging dilemmas. In Piagetian terms (we discussed Piaget in Chapter 5), children should be challenged to reach higher levels of equilibrium in their moral reasoning. The challenges should not be too difficult, as children may become overwhelmed if presented with dilemmas that are too advanced. Rather, moral dilemmas (real or hypothetical) that challenge children to use reasoning skills characteristic of the stage just beyond their current stage of reasoning should be presented. For example, if children are currently using skills characteristic of stage 2, then they should be encouraged to use skills characteristic of stage 3.

Timing. Children should be presented with developmentally appropriate moral challenges that meet their level of experience. Developmentally, children should possess the appropriate level of cognitive reasoning. Experientially, they should have had sufficient opportunities at role-taking to appreciate and respond to others' perspectives. Likewise, they should have had adequate exposure to appropriate social justice experiences and structures.

TIPS FOR TEACHERS 6.2

Creating a Just Community Environment

- Employ cooperative decision making. Children can help to make rules of conduct for the class.
- Use cooperative learning groups. Encourage children to work together in solving class projects. Ideally, more advanced students should be paired with students who need assistance.
- Ask for feedback from students about classroom rules and practices. Their feedback should be discussed so that misperceptions and school policies can be clarified.
- Utilize reflective learning. Allow children time for reflection at the beginning of the day to think about upcoming tasks and

events, or at the end of the day to reflect on activities and share thoughts and feelings through group discussion, personal diary entries, art, or literary experiences.
- Use peer mediation. Help children learn to reason through disputes and reach a compromise.
- Challenge students to think in alternative ways. Brainstorm as many responses to a dilemma (real or hypothetical) as possible. Promote further reasoning by allowing a pair of children to discuss the issue further while they walk around the school building, or divide the class into small discussion groups.

Active engagement of children.   Lectures and other teacher-centered instructional strategies are less effective in teaching moral reasoning than are child-centered strategies. In Vygotskian terms (we discussed Vygotsky in Chapter 5), teachers should provide a "scaffolding" for children's moral reasoning by helping them to think through hypothetical or real-life dilemmas. Teachers might ask questions, clarify issues, or suggest alternative views to guide children's moral reasoning. Teachers might even provide what they view as an appropriate response to a moral dilemma to further stimulate discussion or redirect the moral reasoning process.

The just community.   This concept represents another way to provide "scaffolding" to support children's active engagement in moral reasoning. The *just community* involves children collectively practicing moral reasoning on a daily basis to overcome disagreements, negotiate conflict, and resolve fears and biases (Logan, 1998). For example, children themselves may assume responsibility for daily dilemmas that occur in the classroom and decide upon the consequences for disruptive behaviors. They may even have a say in the formulation of school policies. Some other strategies for creating a just community within the classroom are presented in Tips for Teachers 6.2. All of the tips can help children to practice moral reasoning by considering the views of others as well as learning to express and defend their own views (McClurg, 1998).

CHAPTER SUMMARY

Parents and teachers sometimes feel frustrated when discussing children's social-emotional adjustment. They note that children seem to change their behavior overnight, making it difficult to build a consistent interpersonal relationship. We hope that our discussion of social-emotional development has helped you to better understand the sometimes unpredictable behavior of young children. Above all, we hope that we have provided you with examples of how theoretical models and research-based information can result in practical applications for your classroom.

Activity 1 provides you with a series of questions for further development of your philosophy of education. In this case, we ask you to reflect upon the moral responsibilities associated with your role as an educator of young children.

ACTIVITIES

1. As a teacher, you will face many professional dilemmas that require moral reasoning. Consider the following questions prior to writing a philosophy of your moral responsibilities to children and their education:
   - Are there limits to my responsibilities as a teacher?
   - Are all educational needs equal or should I reserve the right to selectively attend to such needs?
   - How might I respond to school policies that conflict with my moral values? The following dilemma may prove especially helpful in formulating a response to this question:

   > **Dilemma.** You have at least one child in your classroom who you know comes from an illegal immigrant family. A law in your state requires teachers to report such children and their families to the authorities. Your report will result in the child being dismissed from school and the denial of medical and social services for the family. You can be fired or even prosecuted if you knowingly fail to report the child.

   - What conflicts are involved in this dilemma?
   - What are your moral responsibilities in this situation?

2. Observe two children of different ages at play. Classify their respective stages of play. Share your observations with your peers. Do your peers agree with your assessment?

3. Interview a teacher about common classroom stressors. What actions do teachers take to reduce classroom stress? As a group, discuss how teachers themselves might serve as potential childhood stressors.

4. Write a moral dilemma and administer it to two children of different ages. What level and stage of moral reasoning are reflected in their responses?

5. Teachers often note that children operate under three justice structures: (a) family; (b) school; and (c) peer group. In what ways might the home, school, and peer group fail to provide consistent justice structures for children? As a teacher, what strategies can you use to make the home, classroom, and peer group justice structures more consistent?

chapter 7

Principles of Family Development

After reading this chapter you should be able to discuss the following questions:

❖ Why is it difficult to define "family"?
❖ What forces have shaped American family lives in the 20th century?
❖ Why is it important to separate family myths from family facts?
❖ How can family theoretical perspectives be used to address family-school relations?

CHAPTER OVERVIEW

Families are a popular topic of debate today. Some contend that the family is in decline, arguing that as a society we no longer value children or marriage (Popenoe, 1993). Others contend that such concern is unwarranted and ignores the historical context of family lives (Cowan, 1993; Stacey, 1993). These scholars argue that families, like other social institutions, are in constant flux, both creating change and adapting to larger social forces. Such discussions characterize what some define as the "family wars" (Skolnick, 1997).

Schools are increasingly drawn into the family debate, and for good reason. The family and school represent two of the most important social institutions in which children are socialized and educated. Just as children and their families must adapt to different school environments, schools must adapt to different families. In this chapter, we set the stage for helping teachers understand the challenges and opportunities associated with family involvement that are addressed in Chapter 8. We begin with a definition of family. Then we examine the social context of contemporary family lives. Next, we review family myths and facts. We conclude with a review of family theoretical perspectives, as well as guides for helping you to use the perspectives when working with families. You will have an opportunity to develop your own philosophy of family life in activities 1 and 2 at the end of the chapter.

DEFINING FAMILIES

Because the concept of family is not easily defined, we routinely ask our students to define "family" for themselves. Our students often find that their individual definitions vary considerably. This should not be surprising, since family life is as much a personal experience as a public one (Cherlin, 1996). For better or worse, families today have no uniform structure or lifestyle, and their social functions continue to change. One commentator addressed the status of contemporary families in the following way:

The American family does not exist. Rather, we are creating many American families, of diverse styles and shapes. In unprecedented numbers, our families are unalike: We have fathers working while mothers keep house; fathers and mothers both working away from home; single parents; second marriages bringing children together from unrelated backgrounds; childless couples; unmarried couples, with or without children; gay and lesbian parents. We are living through a period of historic change in American life.*

No doubt, you can identify other family arrangements. Some traditional and emerging family definitions are given in Figure 7.1. Your personal feelings about families may reflect some of these definitions better than others. You may even find some terms offensive. For example, some of you may view the term "stepfamily" as outdated and negative, while others may view the term "reconstituted family" as too technical and cold. Whatever your feelings, as teachers you will have the responsibility of treating all families with equal respect. It is for this reason that we adopt an inclusive definition of family.

A *family* is two or more persons who are committed to each other and who share intimacy, resources, decisions, and values (Olson & DeFrain, 1994, p. 9).

This is a broad definition that a majority of Americans seem to feel comfortable with (Footlick, 1990), although it certainly does not meet everyone's definition (Cherlin, 1997; Glenn, 1997, Scanzoni, 1997; Skolnick, 1997) and may not resemble your own. Nevertheless, it is a realistic definition in that it reflects the idea that although families may differ in their structures and lifestyles, they all are bound together through a sense of mutual closeness and commitment (Scanzoni, 1987; Schwartz & Scott, 1994; Strong, DeVault, & Sayad; Zimmerman, 1992). It is this sense of family closeness and commitment that frames the challenges associated with contemporary family lives.

THE SOCIAL CONTEXT OF CONTEMPORARY FAMILY LIVES

American families are similar in at least one respect—they value their privacy. The separation of family and work life that began during the industrial period is today a value shared by families at all income levels (Hareven, 1984). Two 20th-century forces that are in part responsible for the emphasis we give to family privacy include the family-consumer economy and the companionate family.

The Family-Consumer Economy

As the technological advances of the industrial period expanded during the 20th century, so too did the mass production and marketing of products. American society gradually changed from a family-wage economy, where family members

*From *Newsweek,* Winter/Spring 1990 and © 1990 Newsweek, Inc. All rights reserved. Reprinted by permission.

FIGURE 7.1   Family Definitions

The different terms that we use to describe families and their relationships reflect the diversity of family life in the United States.

Structural Definitions

The following definitions are used to describe family structures:

Family of origin.   This is the family into which you are born and raised. It is made up of your parents and siblings.

Family of procreation.   This is the family that you form by having children of your own. It is made up of your marriage partner and your children.

Nuclear family.   This is a family that consists of parents and their children.

Extended family.   This family includes relatives who are related to the nuclear family. Grandparents, aunts, uncles, and cousins are all part of the extended family.

Blended family.   Also referred to as reconstituted, this is a generic term for all families that are formed when divorced or widowed individuals, with or without children, remarry.

Stepfamily.   This is a particular type of blended family in that both marriage partners have children from a previous marriage.

Life Cycle Definitions

The following definitions are used to describe changes in family structures:

Remarriage.   Remarriage occurs when a man or woman who is widowed or divorced marries another person of the opposite sex.

Recoupling.   Recoupling is similar to remarriage except that it is not legally recognized. Cohabitating heterosexual, gay, or lesbian individuals recouple when they leave one partner and enter into a relationship with another partner.

Serial marriage.   This term refers to multiple marriages. It is sometimes reserved for individuals who divorce and remarry three or more times.

Serial monogamy.   This term is related to serial marriage. It refers to the series of monogamous relationships that individuals enter into as they remarry. In most cultures today, we assume that serial marriages are characterized by serial monogamous relationships.

Emerging Definitions

The following definitions are used to describe the growing number of emerging family structures and relationships:

Fictive kin.   Fictive kin, sometimes also referred to as affiliated kin (Strong et al., 1998), are individuals who are not legally or biologically related to a family but who nevertheless have status and role responsibilities within a family (Crosbie-Burnett & Lewis, 1993). Immigrant families, poor families, homeless families, single-parent families, African American families, and gay and lesbian families are examples of family groups who at one point or another in their history have relied upon fictive kin as sources of support. Middle-class families also rely upon fictive kin when they ask neighbors to assume child-care responsibilities for their school-age children during afterschool hours.

continues

FIGURE 7.1 *continued*

Partner.   This term is sometimes used by married and cohabitating heterosexuals, as well as gay and lesbian couples, to refer to their "spouse" or "significant other."

Gay and lesbian families.   These families are made up of same-sex couples living in committed relationships. Children may or may not be present.

Domestic partners.   Domestic partners are two people of the opposite or same sex who have a committed relationship. Heterosexual cohabitators, as well as gay and lesbian couples, are considered domestic partners. Although not recognized by law, domestic partnerships are increasingly being recognized by local governments and businesses. More than two dozen U.S. counties, cities, and local jurisdictions recognize some type of domestic partnership benefits for government employees (Congressional Quarterly Research, 1992). A number of private organizations (companies, unions, advocacy groups) also extend benefits to domestic partners. The range of benefits varies. Some organizations offer health and dental health benefits. Others offer extended sick and bereavement leave.

Network families.   Network families, also called friendship families, are made up of a network of unrelated close friends who provide emotional support for one another. Friendship families are becoming increasingly important for single adults of all ages who, due to their work or life circumstances, do not have direct access to relatives.

Homeless families.   These are families who have no stable living environment. Homeless families with young children face a number of logistical challenges when attempting to ensure that their children attend school on a regular basis. One such challenge is transportation. What are some other challenges?

Working poor families.   These are families whose members work full- or part-time, but do not earn enough to raise the family's income above the poverty level.

Foster families.   These families care for children whose families are unable to do so. Foster families are approved by and receive support from social service agencies.

Domestic partners. (1992, September 4). *Congressional Quarterly Research 2*, 761–874.
Crosbie-Burnett, M., & Lewis, E. A. (1993). Use of African-American family structures and functioning to address the challenges of European-American postdivorce families. *Family Relations 42*, 243–248.
Strong, B., DeVault, C., & Sayad, B. W. (1998). *The marriage and family experience: Intimate relationships in a changing society.* Belmont, CA: Wadsworth.

worked in factories that were heavily dependent upon people, to a *family-consumer economy,* where families became units of economic consumption, purchasing new products made by industries that are today heavily dependent upon technology and marketing forces (Zinn & Eitzen, 1990).

Early in the 20th century, the salaries of most middle-income husbands were sufficient to purchase the new products sought by families. This changed over

American families are diverse.

time, with the economic well-being of most families becoming increasingly dependent upon two wage earners (Ferber & O'Farrell, 1991). Wives and mothers subsequently began to work outside the home. By the mid-1990s, well over half of mothers with young children had entered the labor force (U.S. Bureau of the Census, 1996).

Most families today continue in their struggle to balance family privacy with work demands. Parents must decide on the type of child-care arrangement to use while they are away at work. They also must overcome the guilt they may feel about leaving their children in the care of others. Families must develop strategies for managing competing household and work demands. Recreation and meals must be scheduled around work schedules. Time and energy must be devoted to maintaining a stable and harmonious family life. These are the types of 20th-century challenges that have led to the creation of the companionate family.

The Companionate Family

The concept of the *companionate family* was introduced by psychologists, educators, and legal scholars who felt that the industrial family, with its focus on sexual repression and patriarchal authority, was not in keeping with more permissive, liberal, and technological lifestyles of the 20th century (Mintz & Kellogg, 1988). Changes in husband-wife and parent-child relations accompanied the introduction of the companionate family. Husbands and wives became both "friends and lovers" (Coontz, 1988) as they sought to counterbalance the impersonal work environment with a more humane family environment. At the same time, more permissive child-rearing techniques were introduced, emphasizing, for example, a greater focus on children's self-expression. Obedience to parental authority was moderated by concern that children be allowed to freely express their own ideas and to pursue their own interests.

Although the companionate family represents the ideal for most families, we must be careful not to use any one "norm" for judging how well families are living up to this ideal. Different families face different types of challenges in maintaining a companionate family environment. When considering the different types of companionate families represented in your classroom, we suggest that you keep the following points in mind.

Diversity.   Family diversity has always been a part of American life reflecting the cultural, racial, socioeconomic, ethnic, and geographic differences of the time. America has been less a "melting pot" of sameness and more a "salad bowl" of differences (Bowman & Brady, 1982).

What types of family diversity are represented in your hometown?

Ideal family.   No one family type is ideal. Even families from the same socioeconomic group often face different challenges. Families must organize their lives in response to their particular living situation.

In what ways does your family represent an ideal family?

Family types.   Family lives have always been in flux (Coontz, 1992). Likewise, change and tradition in family lives have always coexisted. Even today, "new" and "traditional" families coexist in every city and town throughout the country.

What are some strengths and challenges associated with the different families that you have encountered?

Social forces.   Although we sometimes think of the challenges facing families as being unique to contemporary society, family lives have always been intertwined with larger social forces (Coontz, 1992).

How might social forces today have different influences on different types of families?

Social change and family well-being.   Social changes have always proven more beneficial for some families than for others. For example, computer technology has presented new job opportunities for some families while it has forced other families into lower-paying jobs.

What current social changes benefit some families while hurting others?

Family resources. The challenges facing families of past eras were as difficult to resolve at the time as those facing families today. Although families today face multiple challenges, they also have more social resources by which to resolve them.

> What resources do contemporary families have available to help them meet the challenges accompanying social change?

Myths. Many of our beliefs about families are based upon myths or half-truths (Coontz, 1992). For example, some consider the "father knows best" family of the 1950s as the standard by which to evaluate family lives today (Ganong, Coleman, & Mapes, 1990). However, the idea of such a *nuclear family,* consisting of an employed father, stay-at-home mother, and their children, is only about 50 years old (Levin, 1993 as cited in Strong et al., 1998). It was not the standard upon which previous generations operated, and it is not the norm for families today.

> What are the most common myths that we hold about families? How did we develop these myths?

CONTEMPORARY FAMILY MYTHS AND FACTS

Myths and half-truths about contemporary families are in large part based on our lack of understanding and our idealization of family history (Coontz, 1992), as well as our inability to appreciate the diverse circumstances that lead families to adopt different life priorities and lifestyles. Separating family myths from fact is not just an academic exercise, it also has implications for how we view and work with families. Some of the advantages of separating family myths from facts include the following:

- We resist romanticizing past family lives and thereby avoid using false standards by which to assess contemporary families.
- We examine more closely our own beliefs and values about families in their past and present forms.
- We appreciate the many choices and challenges that are associated with such family issues as parenthood, work, child care, sex, finances, household tasks, gender-roles, and leisure time.
- We begin to search for potential relationships between family functioning and larger social forces.
- We appreciate the uniqueness of each family and avoid the temptation to group families into categories.

As you read this section, you may be able to identify other myths, either from your own family or the families of your friends.

The Myth that Families Are Self-Sufficient

Families have never been totally self-sufficient. They have always been dependent upon the assistance of relatives, neighbors, colleagues, religious institutions, civic groups, and government agencies (Coontz, 1992). The survival of the early colonists was dependent upon the help of Native Americans and the community at large. Industrial families were dependent upon neighbors, civic organizations, and their employers. Families of the western American frontier were dependent upon government land grants. In one way or another, most families today are dependent upon government programs, nonprofit social organizations, community civic groups, and work unions for economic support, food, shelter, medical assistance, or housing.

Fact.   The United States is undergoing a dramatic change in government-sponsored programs for families. Health-care reform, education reform, welfare reform, child-care support for working parents, and family leave from work to care for family members are some of the areas in which the federal government is intervening on behalf of families.

The Myth that Children Strengthen Unhappy Marriages

Even though our views toward children have changed over time, many myths about parenthood remain. Among others, these include the belief that rearing children is fun; children are always sweet and cute; "good" children result from "good" parents; parenthood receives top priority in our society; parenting ends when children leave home; and only biological parents can successfully rear children (LeMasters & DeFrain, 1989).

Fact.   There are many reasons why individuals choose to become parents. Some people become parents because of their own positive family experiences as a child. Others view parenthood as an opportunity to form a close emotional bond with another human being and to experience the rewards and challenges of guiding children's development. Still others feel obligated to continue their family name, to follow religious teachings, or to fulfill what they perceive to be their social obligations as adults. And still others may have children in an attempt to end their sense of loneliness or to relive their own childhood.

Fact.   Parent-child relations today have been described as "supportive detachment" (Demo, 1992). Although parents and children are spending less time together, they remain close due to a growing network of child-care, educational, and recreational programs that provide "detached" parental support. Supportive detachment allows parents to fulfill their career responsibilities while providing for the supervised care and education that their children need in order to become independent and self-reliant. Individualism, self-reliance, and self-fulfillment are becoming increasingly important as societal norms (Bellah, Sullivan, Swidler, & Tipton, 1985; Thornton, 1989). In particular, schools and after-school programs are responsible for helping children to acquire these skills (Coleman, Wallinga, & Toledo, 1998).

Families have never been totally self-sufficient.

The Myth that Conflict Is a Sign of a Dysfunctional Family

Conflict is a part of any relationship. Families are made up of individuals with different values, personalities, expectations, interests, and communication styles.

These differences naturally form the basis for interpersonal conflict. It is not conflict itself that makes for an unhappy family, but the way in which conflict is handled.

Fact.   The sharing of power is important in resolving conflict. We all have different sources of power; some are granted to us by our gender and cultural or socioeconomic status, and others are due to our unique skills or educational status. Regardless of our level of power, it is important that we learn to use it in responsible ways. This involves respect and empathy for others, as well as the willingness and ability to practice good communication skills. Some of the themes to keep in mind in order to equalize power between yourself and families include the following (U.S. Department of Agriculture, 1998):

- **Become a student.**   Learn as much as you can about families by introducing yourself to community leaders who can provide you with information about community needs and customs.
- **Become part of the community.**   Ask your community contacts to introduce you to families and community activities. Your presence within the community will increase your credibility among community members.
- **Encourage active communication.**   Provide multiple opportunities for families to communicate with you. Some families may communicate best through interactive methods like visual aids and hands-on activities. Other families may require an interpreter.
- **Be realistic.**   Be patient and realistic in your expectations of families. Remember that the life experiences that have defined your life priorities may be quite different from those of other families.

We will return to these themes at different points in this textbook. In particular, we have more to say about empowering families in Chapter 8.

These myths highlight some of the difficulties involved in making sense out of diverse family lives. Even though it is impossible to establish a "norm" for family development, family scholars have developed a number of theoretical perspectives that can help us to better understand and work with families.

THEORETICAL PERSPECTIVES OF FAMILY DEVELOPMENT

Just as developmentalists use different theoretical perspectives to understand the complexities of child development, family scientists use different perspectives to understand the complexities of family development. In this section, we review the family development perspective, the structure-functional perspective, the social exchange perspective, and the systems perspective. Following each perspective, we provide a few questions that a teacher might ask when considering the linkages between family and school environments.

Family Development Perspective

The family development perspective is based on the assumption that families, like individuals, proceed through a series of life stages. The first stage in family development begins with marriage and the last stage ends with the death of both spouses. Taken together, these stages of family development are referred to as the *family life cycle* or *family life career.*

One of the ways in which families adapt to change over time is by altering their expectations of family members. For example, parents learn to alter their expectations of preschool children by giving them more independence, although the ways in which they do so may vary. One case in point is the strategies used by families from different socioeconomic groups to guide their children's emerging sense of self-expression and autonomy. A recent study of working- and middle-class families found that parents from the former group held their preschoolers more accountable for their views and opinions than did middle-class families (Wiley, Rose, Burger, & Miller, 1998), suggesting that self-expression is viewed as a "natural right" for middle-class families but something to "be earned and defended" for working-class families.

Strong families, those families who successfully make family life transitions and adapt to normal (e.g., death of family member) and abnormal (e.g., natural disaster) life stressors, provide further insight into the usefulness of the developmental perspective in understanding the family lives of young children. Information resulting from studies of strong families suggests that the following characteristics are helpful in assisting these families meet their developmental tasks and make smooth transitions between stages of the family life cycle (Strong et al., 1998):

- **Communication.** Family members are able to share their feelings with one another in an open and supportive communication.
- **Commitment.** Strong families recognize that their health, like the health of individuals, requires time and work. Strong families are committed families. They monitor the status of their relationships, identify their strengths and challenges, and seek out information (e.g., parent education, financial counseling, time management) to help them remain healthy.
- **Crisis management.** Families are confident in their ability to meet challenges and control their own affairs. However, they are also willing and able to seek out and make use of support provided through relatives, friends, and community agencies.
- **Routines.** Families establish a schedule for family meals, chores, and recreation as a means of creating a sense of family stability and continuity.
- **Traditions.** Families honor important family experiences as a means of reinforcing stability and continuity.

When following a family development perspective, teachers might ask the following questions:

- What developmental tasks face this family in regard to parenting, education, finance, and leisure issues?
- What types of support does this family need to meet its developmental tasks?
- Are this family's expectations of this child realistic?

Structure-Functional Perspective

The structure-functional perspective helps us to understand the functions that families fulfill in society. As a social institution, families help to maintain social order by carrying out functions like those listed in Table 7.1. Note that many of these functions are also shared with other groups. Does this mean that families have no unique social function or purpose? It all depends upon your point of view.

A pessimistic point of view is that families are disintegrating because they must share functions for which they once had full responsibility. Consider, for example, how some families view educational and social service institutions. Some families see home schooling as the only means by which to reassert their rightful control over their children's education. Others view social and health agencies as a challenge to family self-sufficiency. As a result, they may refuse to use the services provided by these agencies, relying instead upon friends, neighbors, and extended family members.

TABLE 7.1   Family Functions

Families share many of their functions with other individuals, groups, and agencies.

The Function of Families Is to:	Families Share this Function with:
Reproduce children	Sperm banks, fertility clinics, and family planning programs
Socialize children	Schools, youth groups, churches, the media, and peer groups
Regulate sexual relations	Dating services and prostitutes
Give its members social status	Peer groups, social clubs, sports teams, civic groups, religious institutions, and educational institutions
Provide economic support	Government programs, religious institutions, civic groups, and neighborhood groups
Protect its members	Police departments, neighborhood groups, safety programs, child-care programs, and social service agencies
Provide emotional nurturance	Schools, religious institutions, child-care programs, youth groups, social groups, sports teams, and peer groups
Provide a common residence	Foster homes, group homes, homeless shelters, the justice system (for children in joint custody), and the social service system (for abused and neglected children)

Families share their social functions with other institutions.

An optimistic point of view is that in our complex society it is more efficient for families to share their functions with other institutions. In fact, families could be overwhelmed if they had sole responsibility for all the social functions listed in Table 7.1. Likewise, although families today share their functions with other institutions, they usually assume equal or primary responsibility in carrying out those functions. Reflect again on Table 7.1. For which functions do families assume the most responsibility?

Finally, it is important to note that, rather than losing roles, families are actually acquiring new ones. For example, families have major responsibility for identifying and coordinating the delivery of services provided by a growing number of specialized agencies that address the needs and interests of children (Ishwaran, 1989). It is to American families' credit that they are able to continually adapt to social changes by modifying and sharing their functions, as well as by creating new ones.

When following a structure-functional perspective, teachers might ask the following questions:

- How well is this family meeting its various social functions?
- In what ways are the social functions of this family being supported by community agencies?
- How can I best coordinate the educational and socialization functions of the classroom with those of the family?

Social Exchange Perspective

The social exchange perspective helps us to understand the motivation behind the behavior of family members. In short, attention is given to the social exchanges by which family members maintain fair and "equal" relationships while avoiding unfair and unequal ones. Tangible things (e.g., food, money, and property) and intangible things (e.g., love, power, admiration, respect, autonomy, security, and equality) are all part of the social exchange process. We are not necessarily conscious of these exchanges, nor are they necessarily assigned the same value in all families. For example, children who feel lonely or neglected might voluntarily share their lunch or personal belongings with other children in exchange for the attention that they receive. It is unlikely that such children are fully aware of the meaning of this exchange, and it is therefore the responsibility of teachers and parents to help these children identify other ways to meet their need for social attention.

The social exchange between parents and teachers is also important. For example, the quality of family-school relations is largely dependent upon the quality of family-school social exchanges. In particular, the education of young children is best advanced when parents and teachers both feel that their contributions to children's education are equally valued.

When following a social exchange perspective, teachers might ask the following questions:

- Are the social exchanges within this family equal or unbalanced?
- Who in this family seems to make most of the decisions about this child?
- How can I construct an equal parent-teacher partnership?

Systems Perspective

This perspective views the family as a system that is made up of subsystems (e.g., mother-father dyad, father-son dyad, sibling dyad, mother-father-daughter triad). Family life is interconnected. Everything that happens to one family member impacts the system as a whole. For example, a 7-year-old boy may have to assume adultlike responsibilities if his father's drug addiction prevents him from fulfilling his family responsibilities.

All systems have *boundaries*. As noted in Figure 7.2, families have *closed boundaries* when members only interact among themselves. A closed family system is characterized by the family's isolation from the community. A child living in a family with closed boundaries may not be permitted to visit or receive friends, participate in extracurricular school functions, or attend community events. This type of isolation is sometimes associated with abusive families (Williams, 1992) in that it allows both greater control over family members and helps to keep the family "secret" hidden from authorities.

Families have *open boundaries* when they interact with other social systems. A "healthy" open family system is characterized by individual members interacting freely with others in the community while maintaining a commitment to the family

Community

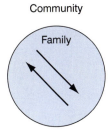

Family

Closed Family System.
Members interact only with themselves. The family is isolated from the community.

Community

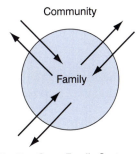

Family

Healthy, Open Family System.
Members interact with others in the community while maintaning a commitment to the family unit.

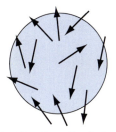

Unhealthy, Open Family System.
Members have only a few family rules. Family roles are undefined. There is little or no sense of family commitment.

FIGURE 7.2   Family Systems

unit. An "unhealthy" open family system has no mutually agreed-upon family rules or limits. There is no sense of family unity or commitment, and family roles are not clearly defined. In extreme cases, community agencies must intervene in order to protect children who are being neglected. Such intervention usually involves helping families to establish boundaries and limits. For example, neglectful parents may receive training in parenting skills to help them define their parenting roles and learn strategies for placing appropriate limits on their children's behavior.

BOX 7.1　　*Jason's Family*

Teachers often must piece together limited information about children's families when attempting to understand and address children's classroom behavior. The following passage is typical of a situation that you might face as a teacher. The theoretical questions at the end of the passage can guide you in developing hypotheses about Jason's home life and its possible link to his classroom behavior. The questions can also guide you in developing strategies for addressing Jason's behavior.

Diane is the 22-year-old mother of Jason, a 6-year-old who has just entered the first grade. It was during their very first meeting that Diane told Jason's teacher, Ms. Williams, that she "went from being a child to a mother" when she became pregnant with Jason at age 16. Diane never married Jason's father, who moved to another state shortly after Jason's birth. He has had no contact with Diane or Jason since his departure. Diane was honest with Ms. Williams about her feelings toward Jason's father—"I don't need him or any other man to take care of me or my son! We're doing just fine!"

Diane never completed high school, instead taking a cashier's job to help support herself and Jason. Currently, Diane and Jason live with Diane's mother, an arrangement that seems to be mutually beneficial. Diane (now a waitress) and her mother (a factory worker) earn just enough to pay their bills and buy groceries. Diane provides her mother with company and her mother serves as a babysitter for Jason. As Jason's grandmother once told Ms. Williams," I don't know what I would do without them. They keep my life interesting."

Despite a harmonious family life, both Diane and her mother admit that there are problems. They are most concerned that Jason is beginning to take care of himself during the week, due to his mother's and grandmother's work schedules. Jason's grandmother arrives home from work about 30 minutes after the school bus drops him off in front of his apartment building. During that 30 minutes, Jason is only allowed to watch television. Diane does not arrive home from work until close to midnight. This leaves very little time for Jason and his mother to interact. In fact, Jason usually turns to his grandmother for help with his school and household tasks. Jason's grandmother is supportive and loving, but she admits that between her job and her housework, she has very little time to "play those games" with Jason. She would like Diane to spend more time with Jason, even though she understands that Diane's work schedule leaves her exhausted.

Ms. Williams developed a better understanding of the stress in the family after Jason failed to return a parent-child project that was to be completed at home. Diane called Ms. Williams to apologize for not helping Jason

When taking a systems perspective, teachers might ask the following questions:

- Does this family keep to itself or is it actively involved in community life?
- Where is the strongest adult-child relationship in this family (e.g., mother-child, father-child, grandparent-child)?
- What rules does this family use to structure this child's life?

BOX 7.1   *Jason's Family* continued

with the project and to explain that even her weekends provide her with little time for "play." Diane works short shifts on Saturday and Sunday. She spends the rest of her weekend taking care of household tasks or, as she put it, "just getting myself together." Jason's grandmother usually takes Jason with her as she runs her Saturday errands. On Sunday afternoons, Jason, his mother, and grandmother usually relax by watching television.

Although Jason seems to be adapting to his home life, he is not doing as well at school. Ms. Williams has noticed that he becomes argumentative and anxious when his work is interrupted. Lately, he has begun to hit children who try to help him. Last week he would not even allow his best friend to help him put on his jacket. Jason's behavior has become disruptive and other children are now refusing to play with him. Some of the children seem to fear Jason. Equally upsetting to Ms. Williams is Jason's satisfaction with his isolation. He is increasingly avoiding his classroom peers and choosing to play alone. Ms. Williams feels that it is time to talk with Jason's mother and grandmother.

- Are Jason's mother and grandmother appropriately adapting their expectations to Jason's changing developmental needs and interests? Use the *family development* perspective to address this question.

- Use the *structure-functional* perspective to hypothesize the different ways in which Jason's family may be meeting its social functions of socialization, economic support, protection, and emotional nurturance. Might some functions be receiving higher priority than others?

- Use the *social exchange* perspective to describe how Jason's social exchanges at home with his mother and grandmother may be influencing his social exchanges at school with his peers and teachers. How might his social exchange environment at home differ from his social exchange environment at school?

- Use the *systems perspective* to describe the challenges that Jason's family might face in maintaining a healthy open system. Would you describe his family as more "closed" or "open"? Why?

- Reflect upon your responses to these questions to describe the mind-set that Ms. Williams should take when she meets with Jason's mother and grandmother. How cooperative will Jason's mother and grandmother be in addressing Jason's classroom behavior? What types of family issues might need to be considered in addressing Jason's classroom behavior? How should Ms. Williams approach these family issues?

Applying Theoretical Perspectives to the Classroom

Students sometimes state that they do not know how to apply theoretical perspectives to real classroom situations. It is true that their application to the classroom takes practice. On the other hand, even our brief review of theoretical perspectives should help you begin to formulate strategies for dealing with different types of family issues. In Box 7.1, we show how family perspectives can provide a basis for understanding and working with families.

CHAPTER SUMMARY

The concept of "the American family" has given way to recognition that we are a nation of many different "American families." Subsequently, there is no one family norm or standard by which to judge all families.

There are a number of myths and half-truths associated with contemporary American family lives. Becoming aware of these myths can help teachers to be more effective in working with families.

Although it takes practice, teachers can learn to use family theoretical perspectives to better understand and relate to families. Each perspective provides a different set of lenses from which to assess and plan for better family-school relations.

ACTIVITIES

1. Write your own philosophy of family life. What type of family structure do you seek? How do you feel about family issues like parenthood, work, finances, and sexual relations? Compare your philosophy with those of your peers. Consider the following questions:
   - What are the similarities and differences between your philosophies?
   - How does your philosophy compare to that of your parents?
   - How might your philosophy compare to those of families from different backgrounds?
   - What steps will you take to implement your family philosophy?
   - What activities might you plan for a target group of young children to allow them to explore their own meaning of family?
   - What steps will you take to respect the family philosophies of families represented within your classroom?
2. Construct a picture of your family history. How have your family experiences influenced your philosophy of family life? Compare your reflections with those of your peers.

3. If you choose to have children, what "family values" do you hope to pass on to them? What might be your reaction if your partner or child holds different values?
4. Identify a family myth in addition to those discussed in this chapter. Research reasons why this myth exists. What are the facts that should replace this myth?
5. Can you identify a family function other than those listed in Table 7.1? Do families have sole responsibility for this function or do they share it with another institution?
6. Would you describe your family as more "open" or "closed"? Refer to Figure 7.2 to draw the openness of your family system. Compare your drawing with those of your peers.
7. What one theoretical perspective do you find most useful for understanding families? Why? As a class, develop a scenario in which a teacher needs to understand a child's family life. You may choose to ask a local teacher to provide you with a real-life situation. Divide into small groups with each group using one theoretical perspective to brainstorm strategies for addressing this situation.

chapter 8

Family-School Relations:
Promoting Family Involvement

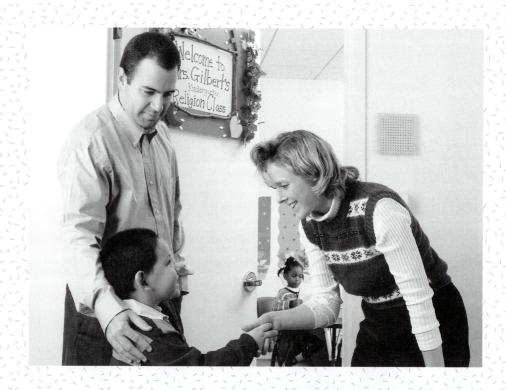

After reading this chapter you should be able to discuss the following questions:

❖ Why is it important to distinguish between "family involvement" and "parent involvement"?

❖ How can theoretical models be used to plan for family involvement?

❖ What challenges are associated with family involvement, and how can they be addressed?

❖ What roles do teachers and parents share?

❖ In what ways can teachers' understanding of ethnic and racial diversity be used to plan for family involvement?

CHAPTER OVERVIEW

Family-school relations has become a central theme of the educational reform movement, which we discussed in Chapter 3. One only has to read the preface of any educational report to find phrases like "parent involvement," "family-school collaboration," and "family-school partnership." In fact, a comprehensive study of past work on student learning concluded that "the home functions as the most salient out-of-school context for student learning, amplifying or diminishing the school's effect on learning" (Wang, Haertel, & Walberg, 1993, p. 278). Examples of home-related behaviors and activities that have been associated with student learning include the following (Ryan & Adams, 1995; Scott-Jones, 1995; Silvern, 1988; Wang et al., 1993):

• Expressions of interest in children's schoolwork
• Communicating expectations for children's academic success
• Monitoring completion of homework and school attendance
• Providing a variety of learning activities and experiences
• Engaging children in conversation at home
• Providing opportunities for children to try out new skills
• Participation in school conferences and other school activities
• A supportive and nurturing home environment

In this chapter, we address family involvement from a number of viewpoints. Following a short section on definitions, we turn to theoretical models for guiding family involvement practices. We then review the challenges associated with implementing a family involvement program and possible solutions to those challenges. At the end of the chapter you will have an opportunity to write your own family involvement philosophy.

DEFINITIONS

You may have already noticed that we use two phrases in the title of this chapter: family-school relations and family involvement. We use both phrases to emphasize their interrelationship. Schools cannot have quality family involvement programs without having quality family-school relations. Because these two phrases are so important, we will look at each one a little more closely before moving on.

Family-School Relations

As the phrases implies, *family-school relations* describes the nature of the relationship between families and schools. Just like other interpersonal relationships, the one between parents and teachers is complex, ever-changing, involves conflict, and is in need of constant care and attention. And just like other relationships, those involving parents and teachers are dependent upon a shared sense of trust, communication, and negotiation.

Family Involvement

Family involvement describes the strategies by which parents and teachers cooperate to support children's early education. Family involvement activities can take place in the school, at home, or in the community. It is also important to note that we use the phrase "family involvement" instead of "parent involvement" to reflect the diverse nature of contemporary family lives that we discussed in Chapter 7. Other educators, like Davies (1991, p. 377), have also noted the need for "new and broader definitions of parent involvement," such as the following.*

- **Family structural diversity.** The new definitions go beyond the term "parent," which is too narrow to describe today's reality. "Family" is a more encompassing term. The most significant adults in the lives of many children may be grandparents, aunts and uncles, brothers and sisters, or even neighbors who provide child care. (Davies, 1991, p. 377)
- **Family life experiences.** The new definitions include not only those parents who readily respond to teacher and school initiatives but also the families that schools consider "hard to reach." The latter group (which in some schools encompasses a majority of families) include those who lack the energy, time, self-confidence, or English-language proficiency to take part in traditional parent involvement activities, as well as those who are fearful of schools because of past experiences or cultural norms. (Davies, 1991, p. 378)
- **Family educational priorities.** The new definitions go beyond the agendas and priorities of educators and school administrators to include the priorities of families themselves, and they extend beyond specifically academic activities

*Adapted from "Schools reaching out: Family, school & community partnerships for student success," by D. Davies in *Phi Delta Kappan* (1991), 72. Copyright © Don Davies, Center on Families, Boston University. Reprinted by permission.

to include all the contributions that families make to the education of their children. (Davies, 1991, p. 378)

These definitions require all school personnel to assess their responsibility in supporting families. For example, teachers may not always be the best people to help families make positive contributions to their children's education. In some cases, a family might benefit more from working with a school counselor to learn positive child-guidance strategies. In other cases, a family might benefit from working with a school nurse to learn about child safety or hygiene.

As the definitions reflect, family involvement is an ongoing process rather than an end state. The connection between family relations and family involvement will become clearer as you consider the following theoretical models.

THEORETICAL MODELS OF FAMILY INVOLVEMENT

We have noted the importance of theories to teaching practices in previous chapters. In this section, we review additional theoretical models that serve as guides in the planning and implementation of family involvement programs.

Bronfenbrenner's Ecological Model: A Broad Perspective

In Chapter 3, we discussed the broad view of education adapted by teachers working in full-service schools. This view considers children's education within the context of their family, school, and community environments. Full-service schools thus arrange a variety of family involvement opportunities through which parents can contribute to their children's education. Urie Bronfenbrenner's (1979) ecological model provides a framework for structuring such opportunities.

Bronfenbrenner divides the "human ecology" into a "set of nested structures, each inside the next, like a set of Russian dolls" (1979, p. 22). These structures are referred to as "systems." Four ecological systems make up the human ecology: a) microsystems, b) mesosystems, c) exosystems, and d) macrosystems. Each system has developmental risks and opportunities (Garbarino & Abramowitz, 1992).

Microsystems. Microsystems involve those relationships in which children play an active role. Families, schools, peer groups, and religious institutions are the most important microsystems in children's lives. They define children's immediate world and provide the daily experiences that influence their life adjustment. Our discussion of family development in Chapter 7, as well as that of classroom organization in Chapter 11 and behavior management in Chapter 12, are examples of childhood microsystems that involve both risks and opportunities. Supportive family and classroom microsystems provide opportunities for children to develop their full potential. Nonsupportive or ineffective families and classrooms represent developmental risks that can prevent children from reaching their full potential. For example, the support unit represented by a single-parent family may represent a developmental and educational risk when the family has no ties to the community or to extended family members.

As individuals, single parents may be excellent caregivers. But as microsystems, their households may be insufficient, unless they are augmented from the outside to provide a fuller, richer range of roles, activities, and relationships for the child to use in his or her development.*

Schools can help address this risk by sponsoring single-parent support groups in which parents can share their family life experiences and learn from each other. What other situations might characterize family and classroom risks and opportunities for young children?

Mesosystems.   Mesosystems are defined by the quantity and quality of linkages between children's microsystems. The more families are connected to the social networks of their communities, the greater their social capital in advancing children's welfare (Coleman, 1988). *Social capital* is reflected in the degree to which families are involved with other families and community institutions in support of children's development and education—social service agencies, civic groups, boys and girls clubs, religious institutions, and schools. It may be helpful to view social capital as a human form of economic capital. In the latter case, families use their economic resources to provide for their children's welfare. In the former case, families use friendships, family ties, and educational and social services to provide for children's welfare. Two examples of social capital associated with children's positive academic and social adjustment include a strong family help network and parents' frequent interactions with their children's friends (Furstenberg & Hughes, 1995).

The topic of this chapter, family-school relations, is one of the most important mesosystems in children's lives. The amount of social capital generated through education is in part determined by the quality of the family-school mesosystem. The family involvement challenges that we discuss later in this chapter represent risks to the family-school mesosystem. The possible solutions to those challenges that we discuss represent opportunities for strengthening the family-school mesosystem.

Exosystems.   Exosystems involve settings that influence children's lives, but children have no direct participation in them. For example, children do not serve on school boards, but the policies made by school boards influence children's educational experiences. Children do not accompany their parents to work, but the policies set by their parents' employers influence parent-child relations in general, and family involvement opportunities in particular. For example, employment policies that allow parents leave time to attend school functions represent an opportunity for parents to support their children's education. Employers who maintain a strict work schedule limit parents' ability to support their children's school. This represents a risk for children's education. As a school board member, what school poli-

*From "Sociocultural risk and opportunity," by J. Garbarino and R. H. Ambramowitz (1992). In J. Garbarino (ed.), *Children and families in the social environment.* 2d ed. Copyright © 1992 by Walter de Gruyter, Inc. Reprinted by permission.

cies might you promote to advance children's education (e.g., funding priorities, school schedules, educational programs, relationships with community agencies)?

Macrosystems.   Macrosystems are the "blueprints" or broad ideological values that are shared by a society (Garbarino & Abramowitz, 1992). They encompass and influence exosystems, mesosystems, and microsystems. Some examples of American macrosystems include democracy, capitalism, freedom of speech, and the rights of individuals.

When considering a macrosystem, it is important to remember that values can change with time and historical events. For example, the civil unrest and technological advances that occurred during the 1960s created a shift in the American consciousness. American citizens began to challenge government authority while at the same time supporting government-sponsored research on technological innovations for use in education and business. What recent events might be influencing the American macrosystem "blueprint" for the new millennium? How are these events likely to influence our attitudes toward young children in general and early childhood education in particular?

A number of family involvement models follow an ecological perspective (see Comer & Haynes, 1991; Gordon, 1977; Powell, 1991; Swick, 1984). The best known model is that of Epstein (see Epstein 1987a, 1987b; Epstein & Dauber, 1991).

Epstein's Model of Family Involvement: Family-School Obligations

Epstein lists six types of family involvement obligations (Epstein, 1995; Epstein & Dauber, 1991; Sanders & Epstein, 1998). All six obligations remain equally important across grade levels, although accommodations are made in each as children's educational needs change. In this section, we address the applied implications for five of the six family involvement types: parenting, communicating, volunteering, learning at home, and decision making. We addressed the final obligation (family-school-community collaboration) in Chapter 3. Some of the suggestions that we share come from our own experience or from informal discussion with experienced teachers. Other suggestions come from professional articles related to family involvement (Coleman, 1991; Rosenthal & Sawyers, 1996).

Parenting.   Families have an obligation to provide for their children's health and safety. They have an obligation to acquire positive parenting skills. And, they have an obligation to provide a home environment that supports children's early education. The following school activities can assist families in protecting, nurturing, and educating young children:

- **Child-guidance workshops.**   Typically, these workshops begin with a description of typical childhood behavior and then progress to discussions of positive guidance strategies. Parents serve as the "experts," with a trained leader facilitating group discussions. Speakers are sometimes introduced to stimulate and focus discussions. Parents are encouraged to share their parenting experiences and to examine the intended and unintended results of their child-guidance strategies.

- **Family literacy programs.**   Trained volunteers or reading specialists tutor parents with limited reading proficiency. Activities for making literacy a family affair are often included in these programs, as well as emotional support for parents who may feel embarrassed about their limited reading skills.
- **Family enrichment workshops.**   The goal of these workshops is to help families maintain a stable environment through learning or practicing communication, money management, and time-management skills.
- **Child health and safety workshops.**   Working parents in particular often appreciate learning new strategies for "child-proofing" their homes and protecting their children from diseases, crime, and drugs.
- **Child and family nutrition workshops.**   School nutritionists or cooperative extension agents teach parents to prepare quick, inexpensive, and nutritional snacks and meals. Teachers themselves sometimes attend these workshops in order to apply the information to their own lives or to get ideas for classroom activities.

Communicating.   Schools have an obligation to communicate with families about school programs and children's progress in school. This means communicating in a form that family members understand. Opportunities are also provided for families to communicate with schools. A sampling of some traditional and more innovative communication strategies follows:

- **Parent bulletin boards.**   Parent bulletin boards are used to post messages for parents who bring their children to school. Interactive bulletin boards, in which parents and children add to or complete an activity, are sometimes used.
- **Classroom newsletters.**   Newsletters are used to communicate recent classroom accomplishments and provide information about upcoming events. Children typically decorate the newsletter.
- **Monthly calendars.**   Monthly calendars serve multiple purposes. They can be used to remind parents of upcoming school and community events. They can inform parents of school lunches and classroom activities. They also can provide parents with "daily tips" for reinforcing children's classroom learning activities.
- **Monthly flyers.**   Personalized, brightly colored flyers can be sent home each month to summarize each child's accomplishments. The tone of the flyer should be positive. Classroom art and writing projects can be tied to the flyers. For example, children might write short poems or stories about a field trip. They might also write personal notes to their parents.
- **Telephone contacts.**   Some parents may prefer to be contacted by telephone. This requires teachers to schedule calls so that their time, and that of parents, is not wasted.

- **E-mail.**   For those parents with home computers, e-mail provides an efficient means of staying in contact with teachers. Brief e-mail messages can be exchanged on a weekly basis. Parents likewise can e-mail teachers whenever they have questions or concerns.
- **An internet home page.**   Another communication strategy used by some schools is a school internet page. Daily announcements about school events can be posted, as well as more detailed information about changes in school operations. This communication strategy will no doubt become more common as personal computers continue to make their way into children's homes.
- **Homework hotlines.**   These can take many forms. In some cases, a prerecorded message provides parents with information about homework assignments. In other cases, volunteers are available to assist children and parents who have questions or concerns about homework assignments.
- **Transition days and activities.**   Special days can be set aside for preschool children and their parents to visit classrooms in preparation for their transition into school. Kindergarten children and their parents can likewise visit first-grade classrooms. This is a perfect time for teachers to learn a little about the children who will be in their classrooms, and to provide parents with information that they can use at home to prepare children for their upcoming transition.
- **Lists of useful questions.**   Teachers can help parents to prepare for parent-teacher meetings by providing them with a list of questions like: a) May I see examples of my child's work? b) How do you motivate my child to do well in her classroom work? c) What rules is my child expected to follow? How is he made aware of these rules? How well is he doing in following classroom rules? d) What guidance strategies are used in the classroom? How does my child respond to those strategies? e) What are my child's most and least favorite activities? f) How can I best support my child's education? (Coleman, 1997).

Volunteering.   Family members have an obligation to assist within their child's school. However, not all volunteer experiences need to be conducted directly within the classroom. Some examples of direct and indirect activities that support classroom activities and school operations include the following:

- **Support roles.**   Many parents still prefer to support their children's education in traditional ways. Cutting out materials for bulletin boards, conducting bake sales, assisting with field trips and classroom activities, volunteering as a substitute teacher, and assisting with school administrative duties represent some of the support roles that can help schools to operate effectively.
- **School functions.**   Parents' attendance at school athletic events, plays, and parent-teacher association meetings represent displays of school support. Some parents may choose to help plan and facilitate these school functions.
- **School-community relations.**   Volunteer outreach activities are also important. For example, parents sometimes assume responsibility for developing a community resource directory of health and social services,

Family resource centers contain educational materials that families check out for use at home.

recreational groups, athletic teams, and art education groups. These directories serve as useful guides for both parents and teachers.

- **Family resource centers.**   Family resource centers contain books, educational materials, and learning activities that parents check out for use at home. Parents often take responsibility for developing and staffing family resource centers, as well as for raising funds to add resources.
- **School facilities.**   Parents can help to coordinate a school "spring cleaning" in which school repairs are made, playgrounds are built, new equipment is installed, and the physical facility is given an overall cleaning. Parents themselves often have the expertise and skills to accomplish tasks that would otherwise prove costly. A spaghetti dinner, awards ceremony, or school fair can serve as a "thank-you."

Learning at home.   Family members have an obligation to support children's classroom education by providing learning activities at home. Teachers can help families to fulfill this obligation by facilitating the following activities:

- **Monitoring homework.** Children's homework receives a "quality check" when parents establish an in-home place and time for its completion. Teachers can help parents to monitor homework completion by providing them with suggestions for arranging a pleasant study environment (e.g., materials, lighting, noise level).
- **Discussing schoolwork.** Parents reinforce the importance of homework when they discuss it with their children. A general discussion of homework assignments and their relevance to home or community life will reflect parents' interest in their children's education. Teachers can facilitate such discussions by giving parents tips on how to talk with their children about homework assignments.
- **Practicing academic skills.** Parents can help their children to practice skills learned in the classroom through home activities. Math problems might be applied to a child's allowance or a family gardening project. Writing skills might be applied to food labels or road signs. As a teacher, you may choose to compile a listing of home activities for parents' consideration. For example, a simple lesson guide that is matched to the educational backgrounds of each family and that explains the educational significance of each activity might be prepared. Examples of a few in-home activities are presented in Figure 8.1.
- **Making school decisions.** Children sometimes need to make difficult school decisions. Will joining an athletic team jeopardize a child's school grades? Is there too much emphasis on academic work and not enough on extracurricular activities? Should a child attend a birthday party when she does not really like the child who has extended the invitation? Children appreciate the views of parents and teachers on such issues when they keep an open mind and help children to see the potential consequences associated with their various choices.

Decision making. Families and teachers have an obligation to contribute to parent-teacher associations and school advisory councils. They also have an obligation to network with community agencies and professional groups that share an interest in children's well-being. We discussed some advocacy strategies in Chapter 3. The following suggestions can further support the family-school decision-making process:

- **Planning workshops.** Planning workshops can be used to seek parents' input on school policies and events. For example, the questions we listed earlier for use by parents in preparing for parent-teacher conferences might be shared during planning workshops.
- **School committees.** A school policy stating that one or more parents are to serve on each school committee can be adapted. A position description should be developed that specifies parents' responsibilities on each committee. It is especially important that parents' views are respected. Otherwise, they will view themselves as merely token members of the committee.

FIGURE 8.1   In-Home Activities to Link Family-School Learning Environments

The "ABCs" of Labels

Home materials: Five canned or boxed grocery items

Purpose: To practice reading skills

Activity: Place the five grocery items on a table. Pick one grocery item and read the label. Ask your child to pick another grocery item and read its label.

Follow-up activity: Take your child grocery shopping. He may help you to write the grocery list or help you find the grocery items. For example, when you get to the cereal section, ask "What is the name of the cereal that we need to buy? Can you point it out to me?"

Paper Patterns

Home materials: Strips of paper

Purpose: To create and identify different patterns

Activity: Create a simple pattern (square). Ask your child to copy your pattern. Ask your child to create a pattern that you can copy.

Follow-up activity: Look around the room. How many patterns can your child identify that are the same as the one you created? How many patterns can your child identify that are the same as the one she created?

Yum: Home Cooking and Home Counting

Home chore: Setting the table

Purpose: To practice counting skills

Activity: Tell your child that you will play a counting game with her as you both set the table. Ask her to count out five plates and five cups, and to place each plate and cup on the table. After the meal, ask your child to remove each plate from the table one at a time. After removing each plate, ask her how many remain.

Follow-up activity: Ask your child to help you organize a construction project. Ask him to collect one hammer. Then ask him to collect 10 nails. Finally, ask him to collect four pieces of wood.

Let's Make Getting Ready for School Fun!

Home routine: Getting ready for school

Purpose: To practice planning and organizational skills

Activity: Make getting ready for school part of your child's evening routine. Ask him about his school routine for the following day. Will the class take a field trip? Will he be involved in a messy art or science project? Will he be making a class or school presentation? Ask him to lay out the clothes that he wants to wear the next morning taking into consideration the school activities that he just described. You may also ask him to help you set out the items that will be needed to prepare his breakfast or lunch for the following day.

Follow-up activity: Ask your child to help you plan a trip to a park. What will you need to take? What snacks will you need? What types of clothes should you wear? When should you leave the house and when should you return?

- **School report card.** Parents can provide an annual "report card" to summarize school-related strengths and challenges. The purpose of the report card should be to critique and not criticize. Each strength should be accompanied by suggestions for its maintenance, and each challenge should be accompanied by suggestions for improvements.
- **Feedback.** Parents can be provided with formal opportunities to provide feedback to teachers about their child's education. Teachers should routinely ask for feedback during parent-teacher conferences or during planning workshops. A more anonymous approach is to send questionnaires to parents.

As reflected in these suggestions, family involvement represents a continuum of options that can be adjusted to meet the needs of individual families (Coleman & Wallinga, 1998; Comer & Haynes, 1991; Powell, 1991). For example, Epstein and her colleague (Epstein & Dauber, 1991) found that "learning at home" activities were introduced earlier than usual when parents specifically requested assistance in supporting their children's education. Another group of researchers designed a family involvement program consisting of different levels of involvement (Comer & Haynes, 1991). This program allowed parents to choose activities that best fit their interests and life demands. Parents' role as teacher was reinforced at each level.

Although Epstein's model provides us with an understanding of family involvement obligations, it is less informative regarding the daily parent-teacher interactions that determine how such obligations are met. Family feminists provide guidance in this area.

Family Feminists: Empowering Families

Feminist thinking encompasses a variety of perspectives (Schwartz & Scott, 1994). In this section, we limit our discussion to family feminists' writings about social programming and educational practices that can empower parents (Walker, Martin, & Thompson, 1988). We define *family empowerment* as a process whereby parents acquire the self-confidence and motivation to actively mediate the forces that shape their children's lives (Cochran & Dean, 1991). Empowered families respect themselves and expect respect from others. They are able and willing to assert their views in an appropriate manner. They likewise view the assertiveness of others as the foundation for open and honest communication. In contrast, families that feel a lack of personal power to contribute to their children's education may relinquish their decision-making rights to schools. For example, families with lower levels of education may feel that they must trust their school as it represents the mechanism for ensuring their children's academic success and upward mobility (Johnson, 1990). However, such relinquishing of power weakens their role as their child's teacher. Providing families with evidence of their own in-home teaching skills can empower them to assume other family involvement roles that can in turn strengthen the family-school mesosystem.

Family empowerment provides the basis for open communication between parents and teachers.

Three characteristics form the foundation of family feminist programming (Walker et al., 1988). Each has implications for empowering parents:

Recognition of cultural context.   Teachers and other educators can best understand and appreciate the cultural backgrounds of families represented in their school by learning from parents themselves their beliefs, values, customs, and practices within their homes and communities (Neuman, Hagedorn, Celano, & Daly, 1995). Likewise, family backgrounds can be made evident in schools only if parents are empowered to take an active, collaborative role in creating culturally responsive classrooms (Neuman et al., 1995). Such understanding, appreciation, and inclusion is not easily accomplished. For example, one principal described his school as undergoing a transformation from a traditional grammar school to a "therapeutic community" in order to fully understand and implement changes in the school environment that would make it more culturally responsive (Powell, 1991). In Box 8.1, we provide you with an introduction to understanding some of the subtleties of family cultural lives that can help you to establish a similar thera-peutic community within your school.

BOX 8.1	*Understanding Family Cultures*

Culture is defined as a set of ". . . value systems that are transmitted from generation to generation and represent an integrated pattern of human knowledge, belief, and behavior" (Slonim, 1991, p. 3). Our culture influences our behavior, expectations, relationships, and interests. However, it is a mistake to homogenize any given culture. Just as the growth and development of individuals vary, so too do the behaviors and values of families within any culture. Some of the factors to consider when assessing the family cultures represented in your classroom follow (see Slonim, 1991). These factors are meant only as informal strategies for guiding your observations of and interactions with families, *not* as formal interview guides.

Child's Name

Significance. A child's name may reflect family expectations of the child's position within the family.

Reflective questions. What does this child's name mean? How was the child's name selected?

Family Immigration History

Significance. This is important in assessing the ability of recent immigrants to balance the cultural values of their native country with those of their new community and country.

Reflective questions. What are the most common misconceptions that people have about this family's country of origin? Is the family adapting?

Family Composition

Significance. Family structures, emotional closeness, and availability of support will vary.

Reflective questions. Who lives in the home? To whom does the family turn when in need?

Family Neighborhood

Significance. A family's level of comfort within its neighborhood will depend upon the family's ability to adapt to its new culture, as well as a welcoming and supportive neighborhood.

Reflective questions. How well does this family's neighborhood reflect the family's native culture? Is the neighborhood supportive of the family's native culture and its attempt to adapt to a new culture?

Language and Communication Style

Significance. A family's proficiency in the languages represented in its neighborhood will influence its interpersonal relations and ability to function within its community.

Reflective questions. What language is spoken in the home? What challenges does this family face in understanding and being understood in its neighborhood and school?

Parenting Practices

Significance. Parenting practices reflect a family's values regarding cooperation, competition, dependency, and individualism.

continues

BOX 8.1   *Understanding Family Cultures* continued

Reflective questions. What kind of person do these parents want their child to be? What kind of child guidance practices are used by the family?

Health Care

Significance. A family's concept of health may be influenced by religious and cultural values.

Reflective questions. What steps does this family take to remain healthy? How does the family respond to illness?

Dietary Practices

Significance. Dietary practices may be influenced by geography, lifestyle, socioeconomic status, and religious beliefs.

Reflective questions. Are some foods prohibited in this family? Why? How is food used by the family to socialize and celebrate?

Family Strengths and Challenges

Significance. A family's perceptions of its strengths and challenges often reflect its values regarding health, religion, child rearing, extended family, and community life.

Reflective questions. How does this family define its strengths and challenges? Does the school and neighborhood respect the family's attempts to remain strong and to address life challenges?

Consider Your Own Culture

Significance. Reflecting upon your own culture helps you to understand and appreciate other cultures.

Reflective questions. What family traditions and cultural events in your life are most important to you? How does your family make decisions? Which family members had the most impact on you? What family practices and beliefs have you adopted or rejected?

Adapted from *Children, culture, and ethnicity: Evaluating and understanding the impact* by M. B. Slonim. Copyright © (1991) by Garland Publishing. Reprinted by permission.

Responsiveness to the vulnerable. The "vulnerable" include families who historically have received discriminatory treatment or held little power: families of color, low-income families, families with disabled individuals, gay and lesbian families, and single-parent families. It is important to stress that membership in any one of these groups presents only the *potential* for vulnerability. Some families from these groups would no doubt feel insulted if they learned that they were considered vulnerable. It is therefore important that teachers remain sensitive to the life experiences of families when considering their degree of vulnerability.

Swick and Graves (1993) use the phrase "context indicators" to remind us that the lives of vulnerable families are permeated by numerous life stressors. In particular, they list eight family life indicators that can potentially create an "ecology of despair." These indicators are presented in Checklist 8.1.

We realize that this short list will not allow you to identify all vulnerable families. Such an assessment takes time and input from other professionals, as well as from families themselves. Therefore, we provide the following suggestions to help you create an environment in which potentially vulnerable families feel safe and valued:

- **Provide a sense of control.** Parents need to feel in control of their own lives and the lives of their children (Swick & Graves, 1993). Make parents active players in every aspect of the family involvement program. Acknowledge their contributions to their children's education, no matter how small.
- **Be consistent.** Provide consistent, positive feedback to all families regarding their support of their children's development and education (Swick & Graves, 1993).
- **Provide support and guidance.** Do more than just refer parents to appropriate social service agencies. Work with family service coordinators to meet the logistical and financial challenges that may prevent some parents from following up on your referral. However, avoid placing blame or making demands. Patience is one key to working with vulnerable families (Coleman & Wallinga, 1998).
- **Listen to families.** Avoid forming opinions about children's families until you have spent time listening to them. All families are capable of speaking for themselves when others are willing to listen. It is especially important to listen for the possible "sources" of feelings expressed by family members, not just their words (Coleman & Wallinga, 1998; Swick & Graves, 1993).
- **Provide safety rules.** Remind everyone of group safety rules (e.g., respect, confidentiality, agree to disagree, one speaker at a time, no bad ideas) at the beginning of each parent meeting. This will help to create an environment of tolerance while encouraging everyone to express their thoughts.

Participation and equality.

Parents are widely touted as the "experts" when it comes to their children. They, more than anyone else, understand the strengths and needs of their children. They also are best able to interpret their children's behavior and communication. The knowledge that parents possess about their children should be acknowledged and incorporated into family involvement programs. The same is true for parents' skills in guiding and teaching their children. For example, one high school made modifications in the organization of its preschool program as a result of suggestions made by teenage mothers whose children were enrolled in the center (Neuman et al., 1995). This "shift of power" was justified based upon the goals of empowering the teenage mothers to make informed decisions and to take control of their lives.

CHECKLIST 8.1

Is This Family Vulnerable?

When interacting with families, look for the following possible indicators of vulnerability. Which combination of indicators do you believe might reflect more serious vulnerability?

Family Context Indicators

The following indicators represent life stressors that, over time, may make some families vulnerable:

_____ Physical pathologies

_____ Drug impairments

_____ Extreme poverty

_____ Severe family dysfunction

_____ Illiteracy

_____ Malnutrition

_____ Chronic health problems

_____ Chronic isolation

_____ High-risk community

_____ Chronic unemployment

_____ Discrimination

_____ Poor social support network

Indicators of Despair

The following behaviors may suggest that families or family members, including children, are exhibiting signs of vulnerability:

_____ A fatalistic belief system

_____ A low sense of control

_____ A low self-esteem

_____ Closed and unresponsive interpersonal relationships

_____ Rigid family interactions

_____ A cognitive schema that promotes impulsive, nonreflective thinking

continues

CHECKLIST 8.1 *Continued*

_____ Poor problem-solving skills

_____ Abusive and antisocial behavior

As we have already noted, some families require greater support in the empowerment process than others. Some examples of how to create an environment of equality follow:

- **Prepare for parent-teacher interactions.** Workshops on communication, child guidance, and in-home educational practices can be made more meaningful by including parent-teacher role-plays of situations experienced by families themselves. Discussions can then be held to identify appropriate strategies for dealing with such situations (Cochran & Dean, 1991).
- **Reassess leader-follower role.** Continually reassess your role as facilitator or leader. Allow families themselves to facilitate and lead whenever possible. Remember, one goal of family involvement is to promote families as "experts" and leaders in their children's lives (Swick & Graves, 1993).
- **Provide mutual training.** Another way to establish a sense of parent-teacher equality is to arrange for workshops that are of interest to parents and teachers (Coleman & Wallinga, 1998). For example, both parents and teachers can benefit from workshops on assertiveness training, computer skills, child guidance, and communication skills.
- **Arrange collaborative projects.** Work with parents on collaborative school or community projects. The projects can range from constructing a reading loft for the classroom, to conducting a survey of the community, to developing a family recipe book. Make shared leadership and decision making the hallmarks of such projects (Coleman & Wallinga, 1998).

We have now introduced you to three models for addressing different aspects of family involvement. The ecological model provides a contextual mindset for addressing family involvement as a family-school-community issue. Epstein provides a specific set of obligations for structuring a family involvement program. Family feminists provide an interpersonal mindset for empowering parents. To put these models into further perspective, we next turn to challenges associated with implementation of family involvement programs. You will no doubt again notice that some challenges are interpersonal, involving family-school relationships, while others are logistical, involving family involvement practices.

CHALLENGES AND SOLUTIONS TO FAMILY INVOLVEMENT

As you may have already guessed, there is considerable debate regarding family involvement. The debate is not over whether schools should have family involvement. On this point most are in agreement, as reflected in the following justifications of family involvement programming:

- **Childhood benefits.**   Research on family involvement is still relatively new, and there are conceptual and methodological limitations to our understanding of family involvement (see Powell, 1991; White, Taylor, & Moss, 1992). Nevertheless, there is increasing evidence that family involvement can contribute to children's academic and social adjustment. Some of the potential benefits resulting from family involvement include: a) higher academic achievement; b) better student school attendance; c) positive student attitudes and behavior; d) student readiness to do homework; e) increased student time spent with parents; and f) higher educational aspirations among students and their parents (Greenwood & Hickman, 1991).
- **Family benefits.**   While also in need of further research, some potential benefits of family involvement programs for families include the following: a) improvement in parents' sense of self-esteem; b) improvement in parents' self-confidence; c) improvement in parents' self-sufficiency; and d) an increase in parents' active stance in dealing with their child's school (Powell, 1991; Sanders & Epstein, 1998).
- **School and community benefits.**   Teachers and school administrators note the following school and community benefits when justifying family involvement programs: a) parents increase their lobbying efforts for school resources to improve educational services for children; b) parents better understand and reinforce the philosophy and goals of the school; and c) business and government leaders look to schools to help provide a productive work force, as well as to help solve social problems like teenage pregnancy, poverty, and violence (Kelley-Laine, 1998; Powell, 1991; White et al., 1992).

It is this range of potential family involvement benefits that gives rise to debate over how best to pursue a family involvement program. In short, we continue to struggle in prioritizing family involvement objectives and the strategies for pursuing them. Greater insight into the nature of this debate can be gained by considering the challenges to family involvement. For each challenge, we provide possible solutions.

Institutional Resources

Although family involvement receives widespread verbal support, there is often a lack of resources to ensure its success (Epstein & Dauber, 1991; Greenberg, 1989; Powell, 1991). Consider the following family involvement services that might be provided by full-service schools. What financial, personnel, space, and material resources might be required to implement and maintain them?

- The development of before- and after-school enrichment programs for children of working parents.
- The delivery of school-based services like health screenings, dental services, counseling, and housing and food services.
- The delivery of family educational services like child-guidance classes, adult literacy classes, and employment training.
- The establishment of family resource centers with toys, books, and activity packets that can be checked out for home use.
- The establishment of family advisory councils to provide input to teachers regarding school policies.
- The hiring of family service coordinators to link children's classrooms and families.

Possible solutions.   Community collaboration, sharing of resources, and logistical planning are key to the success of family involvement services. It is especially important that school facilities, classroom materials and equipment, and the expertise of teachers be seen as potential sources of support and not as "givens." Most schools by themselves cannot implement or maintain the range of services just listed without family and community assistance.

True, school facilities stand empty when school is not in session. However, activities conducted in school facilities during nonschool hours require additional personnel to provide supervision and custodial services, as well as additional materials and equipment. Teachers spend many hours arranging their classrooms, and they are likely to resist having them disrupted in order to accommodate after-school programs or evening classes.

True, schools provide daily contact with children and their families, making them the ideal community hub for providing health and social services. However, some families require transportation, child care, and other types of support in order to make use of such services. In addition, school traffic flow, parking, and security need to be addressed before introducing additional services and personnel into school facilities.

True, teachers are well trained to address child development issues. However, they may not be the best choice for providing some family involvement or family support services. Their time schedules, training, and interests also must be considered. For example, many teachers use their nonschool hours to prepare for classroom activities. They may also be too tired at the end of a school day to facilitate after-school activities or evening child-guidance classes. For these reasons, school administrators sometimes hire community professionals or recruit volunteers to staff after-school and evening programs.

Schools may limit their family involvement program to certain services because of resource demands. Or they may begin small and gradually expand as more resources are made available. Other schools may seek grant money to support their family involvement goals. And still other schools may enter into a collaborative partnership with community agencies to share the costs of a family involvement program. For example, schools may provide space for health screenings while the health department provides the staff and materials needed to operate this service. Schools may hire family service coordinators to serve as contacts between children's classrooms and homes while a community agency provides transportation and in-service staff training.

Ambiguous Meaning

Parents and teachers often have different ideas about the meaning of family involvement. Confusion can therefore result when a family involvement program is not clearly defined. Some of the meanings that may be associated with family involvement include: a) the delivery of factual information regarding child development and early childhood education; b) the exchange of information between families and teachers; c) the enhancement of parenting skills; d) the development of a positive parent-teacher relationship; e) family empowerment; f) family needs assessment and referral; and g) childhood assessment.

Possible solutions.   Obviously, it is impossible for teachers to address all of these expectations at once. A philosophy of family involvement provides teachers with the structure needed to prioritize and pursue family involvement objectives in a realistic manner. You will have an opportunity to write your own family involvement philosophy in activity 1 at the end of this chapter. For now, consider the following benefits associated with a family involvement philosophy (Coleman, 1997):

- It sends a message throughout the school and community that family involvement is important.
- It provides a guide for identifying specific family involvement strategies and resources to support those strategies.
- It provides a guide for family involvement in-service training.
- It provides a guide for defining the roles that parents and teachers can play in supporting family involvement.
- It provides a guide for assessing the impact of family involvement.

Family-School Expectations

Despite what some may believe, parents and teachers have similar beliefs and expectations in regard to certain aspects of early childhood education (Chavkin,

1994; Epstein, 1991; Epstein & Dauber, 1991). The results of three national surveys of parents and teachers indicated that a majority of both groups agreed on three aspects of school readiness: (a) children's ability to communicate needs, wants, and thoughts verbally in the child's primary language; (b) children's enthusiasm and curiosity in approaching new activities; and (c) children's ability to take turns and share (Lewit & Baker, 1995). Another group of researchers found that the teenage mothers in their study shared the educational values of teachers when endorsing behaviors and activities that supported their children's educational achievement, security, and independence in learning; respect from and for teachers; and parental assistance in facilitating children's learning (Neuman et al., 1995).

Parent and teacher expectations about teaching strategies also sometimes match. For example, parents who follow an authoritarian parenting style approve of the uniform treatment of all children regardless of their particular life circumstances (Schaefer, 1991). They believe that the goal of education is to transmit information. In contrast, parents who follow an authoritative parenting style are more likely to believe that children are active learners and that the goal of education is learning how to learn. These parents are more likely to approve of instructional strategies that encourage children to verbalize their ideas, use their imagination, and engage in active play.

Now compare these parent expectations to those of two groups of teachers. "Participatory educators," those who encourage children to talk and ask questions during all classroom activities, are more tolerant of children's verbal interruptions than are "didactic educators," those who encourage children to talk only at certain times (Hadley, Wilcox, & Rice, 1994). Which parenting style best matches the participatory versus didactic teaching style?

It is also true that parents and teachers can hold different expectations about early childhood education. For example, parents, more than teachers, use specific skills like knowledge of the alphabet and the ability to count to 20 as indicators of school readiness (Lewit & Baker, 1995). Teachers, more than parents, tend to focus on physical health, following directions, and group social skills as indicators of school readiness (Lewit & Baker, 1995).

Finally, teachers' expectations about families can influence family involvement. For example, teachers sometimes view minority families and families of educationally disadvantaged students in terms of their deficiencies instead of their strengths (Epstein & Dauber, 1991). One benefit of the feminist approach to empowering families is that it helps to focus attention on family strengths rather than on weaknesses.

Possible solutions. As we mentioned earlier, the voices of parents themselves provide the best insight into how family involvement programs can best meet family expectations. A summary of parents' responses to questions about what they want from their schools follows (Wasley, 1993). Although the participants were parents of high school students, their responses are applicable to all grades. As a teacher, what specific family involvement strategies might you suggest to meet the following expectations?

- Parents want access to information about what the school is changing from and to so that they can provide support to their children.
- Parents want schools to challenge their children.
- Parents want to understand how the school works so that they know how to contact teachers, staff, and administrators.
- Parents want their children to be known and well cared for.
- Parents want their children to gain competence and confidence in school.
- Parents want their children to like school, to talk about it at night, and to demonstrate what it is they are learning.
- Parents want their children to feel that their active participation in school means something.
- Parents want to see their children engaged in work that reflects the real world and that has real consequences.
- Parents want opportunities to talk with teachers and school administrators about what they want for their children.
- Parents want to help in reaching out to gain the active involvement of other parents.
- Parents want the opportunity to express their views on instructional standards and practices.

Ambiguous Boundaries

The collaborative relationship between families and schools has been referred to as a "third institution" built on mutual support and reciprocal exchanges between parents and teachers (Stamp & Groves, 1994). However, we have already noted that this alliance is not a clearly defined one. Although families and schools share the social functions of educating, nurturing, and protecting children, the boundaries separating family and school responsibilities are ambiguous (Johnson, 1990). Such ambiguity can result in power struggles (Haseloff, 1990).

A number of factors have been suggested as contributing to the ambiguous boundaries between families and schools. For example, conflict can arise over issues of control (Powell, 1991). School administrators may knowingly or unknowingly create control boundaries by enacting policies to prevent "parental tampering" (e.g., membership on the school advisory board is limited to one parent; parent-teacher meetings must take place between 3 P.M. and 5 P.M.). Parents, too, are eager to exert their rights in controlling their children's education. They may subsequently insist on reviewing textbooks and dictating school discipline policies.

Finally, the nature of relationships within schools and families must be considered (Johnson, 1990). In families, relationships are "functionally diffused." All family members are intimately connected to one another and membership is a birthright. In schools, relationships are "functionally specific," with the assessment of children resulting in child-to-child comparisons. Parents have "particular expectations" of children (e.g., "I expect Carlos to excel in math. I'm not that concerned about his writing skills"). In contrast, teachers have "universal expectations" of children (e.g., "All the children in my classroom will learn correct punctuation by the end of the school year"). These differences in adult-child relationships can lead to conflict in the way parents and teachers view children's behavior and school performance, as well as their ideas about how best to approach children's education within the home and classroom.

Possible solutions.   A number of family involvement roles for parents have been suggested—helper, learner, teacher, and decision maker (Berger, 1991; Comer & Haynes, 1991; Greenwood & Hickman, 1991; Olmstead, 1991; Wasley, 1993). These roles are also shared by teachers. The sharing of parent-teacher roles represents one solution to establishing family-school boundaries that are flexible and supportive of reciprocal family-school relations. The four roles that follow are examples of the "common ground" that parents and teachers share in supporting children's education (Coleman, 1997).

Parents and teachers as cultural ambassadors.   Both parents and teachers serve as children's guides to the world. Both play an important role in helping children to understand the differences and similarities among cultures. And both can make use of similar opportunities to provide children with daily lessons in cultural diversity. For example, parents and teachers can expose children to art, music, and literature from different cultures that reveal common human feelings like love, hate, respect, and despair. Both parents and teachers can watch videos and television programs with children, noting positive cultural portrayals as well as examples of negative stereotypes.

Parents and teachers as educators.   Both parents and teachers serve as educators. For example, Gardner's (1983) framework of multiple intelligences provides a framework by which parents and teachers can work together to support the intellectual strengths of every child. As you recall from Chapter 5, Gardner describes eight types of intelligences. Figure 8.2 presents examples of in-home and classroom activities that might be pursued to support each type of intelligence.

Parents and teachers as community life teachers.   Both parents and teachers are responsible for helping children to understand the importance of community life. Teachers can assist in this endeavor by incorporating community life themes into classroom activities. Teachers can also use parents' work experiences to bring a sense of personal contact and reality to children's understanding of community life. Parents can assist by volunteering to talk about their jobs with

FIGURE 8.2 Supporting Multiple Intelligences at Home and School

Linguistic Learners

Parents. Read with your children. Listen to their questions, concerns, and experiences. Provide books, paper, pencils, and pens for reading and writing activities. Encourage children to tell you about their books and writing activities. Provide children with a tape recorder to record their experiences. Make visits to libraries and bookstores.

Teachers. Provide opportunities for children to express themselves through verbal communication. Develop activities that allow children to explore the meanings, sounds, and rhythms of words. Expose children to different types of language experiences like poetry, tongue twisters, humor, fiction, and riddles. Conduct reading/writing workshops, book sharing, storytelling workshops, dialogue writing, newspaper activities, and word-processing activities on personal computers.

Logical-Mathematical Learners

Parents. Allow children to assist you with in-home activities that require logical-mathematical skills like baking and cooking, home repairs, sorting clothes, setting the table, organizing the family workbench, bookkeeping, home construction, and gardening projects. Teach children how to budget their allowances. Provide opportunities for children to experiment with water, sand, and wind. Allow them to experiment with their own small gardening project (e.g., selection, planting, weeding, and harvesting of vegetables).

Teachers. Provide children with opportunities to express themselves through the use of problem solving and organizational skills. Introduce them to manipulatives and activities that involve patterns and sequence. Introduce them to activities that reinforce their interest in asking and solving questions. They may find computer programs, number games, and science activities of interest. Involve children in charting weather conditions throughout the school year. Compare their chart with that of another classroom in another part of the country. Children may also enjoy surveying and charting food or clothing preferences among their peers.

Spatial Learners

Parents. Provide opportunities for children to plan and organize the look of their bedroom. This may include rearranging furniture or choosing a color scheme. Provide children with materials that can be used to experiment with color and design like pens, paints, fingerpaints, clay, natural materials, pencils, chalk, and paper. Spatial learners may enjoy attending workshops on garden or landscape design, cake decorating, quilting, pottery, and drawing or painting. Provide them with an inexpensive camera or take them to photography classes that provide instruction on inexpensive ways to photograph nature. Make visits to art museums, garden shows, and home design shows.

Teachers. Provide children with opportunities to express themselves through artistic pursuits. Integrate art materials into science, math, and writing activities. Introduce them to different classroom tools involving visual patterns like maps, charts, diagrams, puzzles, and mazes. Provide plenty of manipulatives. These children may also respond well to activities that involve mental imagery.

continues

FIGURE 8.2 *continued*

Musical Learners

Parents. Surround children with music. They may enjoy playing with musical instruments, wind chimes, and recorders. Encourage them to discriminate between different sounds of nature (e.g., water, rain, wind) and those that are man-made (e.g., traffic, social conversations). Engage them in singing, clapping, vocal play, and other rhythmic activities. Take trips to community concerts, band rehearsals, and musicals.

Teachers. Provide children with opportunities to express themselves through music and sound. Introduce activities that engage children in mimicking sounds or making up sound patterns. Conduct sing-alongs. Encourage children to note the volume and pitch or their voices during different activities (e.g., arrival at school, group time, recess). Use a variety of music in the classroom during transitions. Establish listening and music centers. Provide tape-recorded story books. Tape recorders can be used to encourage children's interest in sound. Children may enjoy producing creative recordings of school sounds, voice patterns, music selections, or sounds of nature.

Kinesthetic Learners

Parents. Provide children with fine-motor manipulative toys. Introduce them to dances and games that involve large-motor activities. Kinesthetic learners enjoy family walks, jogging, hiking, bowling, and biking. Trips to parks can include opportunities to play on swings, riding toys, and slides. In-home chores might include sweeping, gardening, organizing and moving living room or deck furniture, and construction projects.

Teachers. Provide children with opportunities to express themselves through movement. Introduce them to folk dances, role-plays, action dramas, and cooperative and noncooperative games. Help children "walk through" mental problems using manipulatives or movements for demonstration. Introduce math and science activities that make use of movement (e.g., acceleration and deceleration, balance, force and counterforce) or that involve sensory materials (e.g., fabric, clay, manipulatives, materials from nature).

Interpersonal Learners

Parents. Make use of "family time" to talk about daily events. Engage children in discussions of upcoming family activities like vacation plans. Play listening games in which one player repeats what he hears another person saying. Provide opportunities for children to engage in group games and activities that involve interpersonal communication. Provide opportunities for children to assist others through volunteer work or youth clubs.

Teachers. Provide opportunities for children to express themselves throughout the day. Allow children to take turns leading an activity. Children can also serve as tutors for their peers or for younger children. Allow for the expression of feelings through class discussions or art and writing activities. Skits, group work, debates, and cooperative learning are activities that interpersonal learners sometimes enjoy.

continues

FIGURE 8.2   *continued*

Intrapersonal Learners

Parents.   Set aside time for children to play alone or engage in personal reflection. Provide children with personal and private materials for expressing their thoughts like diaries, writing journals, and or personal art pads. Ask children to think about an issue that their family has discussed, and ask them if they would like to provide the family with their personal opinion. Encourage children to think independently as well as to recognize the importance of their emotions. Community workshops that focus on self-expression through art and writing activities are sometimes offered.

Teachers.   Provide a quiet time each day for personal reflection. Provide opportunities for children to express their thoughts and feelings. For example, encourage the use of personal journals. Children may also use dance, art, or music to express their feelings. Introduce children to the different learning styles reviewed in this figure, encouraging them to think about the different ways in which they approach situations and express themselves.

Naturalistic Learners

Parents.   Introduce your child to the different types of animals found in your neighborhood, at a local farm, a nature park, or a zoo. Discuss the types of food that different animals eat, where they live, what they do during different seasons. Talk with your child about the differences and similarities between animals. For example, all birds have feathers, but not all birds fly. Ask your child to make similar comparisons between other animals (e.g., "How is your kitty different from the lion at the zoo?"). When possible, allow your child to adopt a pet. Check with a veterinarian to make sure the pet is appropriate for your living arrangement and the age of your child. Give your child age-appropriate responsibilities for the care of the pet.

Teachers.   Make nature a part of your integrated curriculum. Field trips can be used to explore animal habitats and seasonal behaviors. Natural materials can be collected during field trips for art projects. Asking children to listen to the sound of wind through trees can stimulate their creativity and interest in music. Counting and classifying different types of rocks and leaves involve mathematical skills. Also consider the adoption of a classroom pet. Use the classroom pet to teach lessons about personal responsibility, kindness, nutrition, and the life cycle.

Adapted from "Bridging home and school through multiple intelligences" by J. C. Reiff, from *Childhood Education* (Spring, 1996). Copyright © 1996 by Association for Childhood Education International. Reprinted by permission.

children or by demonstrating their job skills. Parents whose work schedules do not allow them to attend school might be videotaped or interviewed. Finally, community professionals can be invited to the classroom to share information about their work with children.

Parents and teachers as advocates.   Together, parents and teachers represent a formidable force in responding to family, educational, and community issues that impact children. We introduced the concept of advocacy in Chapter 3, and suggested further activities for facilitating joint decision making earlier in this chapter. We now provide the following questions as guides for helping parents and teachers to prioritize their advocacy efforts (National Association for the Education of Young Children [NAEYC], 1996):

- How many children in your town come to school hungry?
- Do all children have access to basic, preventive health care?
- Do all families have access to quality, affordable early childhood programs?
- Do all early childhood programs have sufficient resources and qualified staff?
- Do local schools adequately respond to individual learning needs?
- Are there sources of stress in local school environments that make learning difficult?
- What additional school services or programs are needed to support children's learning?
- Do local businesses support local schools?
- In what ways do local business policies support children and their families?
- Do local schools value multilingual/multicultural learning?
- Is the community committed to affordable housing and violence-free neighborhoods?

Family-School Discontinuities

A final challenge that parents and teachers face is to link children's home and school educational experiences (Silvern, 1988). Young children find it difficult to adjust to a school environment that involves schedules, spaces, materials, language, expectations, behaviors, and situations that are different from those in their homes. Home-school discontinuities can thus be especially troublesome for children from economically disadvantaged families (Coleman & Churchill, 1997), since school environments tend to reflect middle-class home environments.

Possible solutions. Linking children's home and school learning experiences requires a shift in thinking about the purpose of family involvement. Rather than viewing family involvement as a strategy for delivering information to families to prepare children for school, it can be viewed as a strategy for collecting information from families to help prepare teachers for children (Powell, 1991). The goal behind this shift in mindset is twofold. First, it helps parents to feel equal and competent in their interactions with teachers. Second, it helps teachers and family service coordinators to focus their collection of information about events, materials, people, and situations in children's families that can be used to link their educational experiences at home and school. Figure 8.3 lists themes that might be used by teachers and family service coordinators to provide this focus.

These themes are especially important in guiding home visits. Although traditionally thought of as a means of collecting information and delivering services, home visits do much more. Consider the comments from the following teacher:

Children learn best when their family and classroom learning experiences are linked.

The whole business of making a home visit is a statement of how much you care and respect this child. . . . You take that first step, you meet children on their territory. . . . It is scary to walk into so many homes you have absolutely no idea about. But it does make a statement; and if the child doesn't pick up on that caring, the parents do, and it is conveyed back to the child. Home visits are the best way I can think of to make an initial contact with a child and to say to that child, "You are important."*

As reflected in this teacher's comments, home visits can be scary for both teachers and families. With careful planning, such fear can be easily managed. Some practical tips on making home visits are presented in Tips for Teachers 8.1.

*Adapted from "Easing Children's Entry to School: Home Visits Help," by L. Johnston and J. Mermin in *Young Children* (July, 1994). Copyright © 1994 by National Association for the Education of Young Children. Reprinted by permission.

FIGURE 8.3 Themes for Conducting Parent-Teacher Discussions

The following themes can serve as guides for parent-teacher discussions and home visits. Plan carefully before addressing these themes. Some families may view them as personal matters. Develop a nonthreatening environment by limiting the number of questions asked, explaining why you are asking each question, and providing parents with examples of how they can use these themes to promote common family-school life experiences for their child. In short, give parents as much information and support as you ask them to give to you.

Home materials. What home materials (e.g., magazines, toys, household equipment, construction materials, cooking and gardening utensils) are found in the home? How does the child play or make use of these materials?

Home routines. What is the child's daily schedule? What activities does the child pursue on a daily basis?

Child's interests. What are the child's favorite toys, television programs, foods, games, books, etc.?

Behavior management. What types of encouragement, reinforcements, limits, and consequences are used by parents to guide the child's behavior?

Communication. What verbal and nonverbal communication strategies are used by parents to instruct the child, deliver explanations, and make requests of the child?

Child's fear. What objects, events, and situations does the child fear?

Community exposure. What community events, activities, and locations does the child routinely visit? What are the child's most and least favorite community outings?

Relationships. What are the child's most important interpersonal relations within and outside the home? Why are these relationships important to the child?

Self-help expectations. What self-help skills are taught to the child at home (e.g., personal hygiene, safety, home chores)?

Instructional strategies. What instructional strategies do the parents use with the child (e.g., instructions, demonstrations, play, self-exploration, explanations, labeling)?

Adapted from "Challenges to family involvement" by M. Coleman & S. Churchill in *Childhood Education* (Spring, 1997). Copyright © (1997) by Association for Childhood Education International. Reprinted by permission.

TIPS FOR TEACHERS 8.1

Making Home Visits

Preplanning

- Establish with parents a purpose for the visit and expectations you and parents hope to meet.
- Gather basic information about the family before your visit. Make sure you know the correct names of family members.

Scheduling

- Plan no more than three home visits in one day.
- Send a reminder note to families to confirm the date and time of your visit.
- Leave plenty of time between visits to find the next house and enough time during visits so you don't feel rushed.
- Tell parents how long your visit will last.

Visiting

- Work to alleviate parents' concerns about sending their child to your classroom.
- Encourage parents to express their beliefs about how home visits can help them to improve the lives of their children.
- Avoid taking even small gifts to the child on home visits. Instead, ask the child to share a personal belonging or activity with you.
- Let the parent and child know when your visit is almost over so that there is sufficient time for questions and closure.

Reflecting

- Explore your own expectations of home visitation and determine whether they are shared with families.
- Prioritize goals for each family. Focus first upon the family's self-stated immediate concerns.
- Remain flexible. Original goals and plans may be altered as family experiences change.
- Give relationships time to develop. Patience, sensitivity, and open communication are needed to establish trusting relationships.
- Request feedback from colleagues, families, and outside observers.
- Always consider the possibility that alternative programs, like group-based service or support sessions, may be needed to supplement home visits.

From "Home Visiting: Analysis and Recommendations." *The Future of Children* (Winter 1993) 3, 3:6–22. Adapted with permission of the David and Lucile Packard Foundation. *The Future of Children* journals and executive summaries are available free of charge by faxing mailing information to: Circulation Department (650) 948-6498.
Adapted from "Easing Children's Entry to School: Home Visits Help," by L. Johnston and J. Mermin in *Young Children* (July, 1994). Copyright © 1994 by National Association for the Education of Young Children. Reprinted by permission.

CHAPTER SUMMARY

Establishing positive family-school relations is a challenge for most teachers. We often talk to teachers who are frustrated in their attempts to reach out to parents. Likewise, we talk to parents who feel that their input is not well received by teachers. We hope that the information provided in this chapter helps you to see the perspectives of both teachers and parents. Although there are certainly many challenges to establishing a family involvement program that is inclusive of all families, teachers are meeting these challenges by joining with families and community professionals to search for innovative strategies in support of children's education within and outside the classroom.

ACTIVITIES

1. A philosophy of family involvement begins with a general statement of its importance. You may find it helpful to reflect upon the following questions as you write your own family involvement philosophy:
   - What meaning do I give to family involvement? Why is it important?
   - What roles should parents and teachers share in their support of children's education?
   - What types of family involvement activities might I pursue during my first year of teaching? Do these activities reflect a particular family involvement model (Bronfenbrenner, Epstein, feminism)?

   As a class, compare your respective philosophies. How are your philosophies similar and dissimilar?

2. Think back to your elementary school years. How did family involvement programs operate then? Can you identify classmates whose lives and education might have been made better if some of the family involvement ideas and strategies currently being implemented were in place during your school years?

3. Interview teachers about family involvement. How much attention is given to family involvement in their schools? What specific family involvement activities are used? What challenges do teachers face in gaining family involvement participation? What strategies do they use to communicate with families? Are there particular families who seem especially difficult to reach? Why is this the case?

4. Develop a 10-item checklist of family involvement activities or services that you consider important. Give your survey to teachers who occupy different positions in a local school (e.g., teachers, principals, family service coordinators, school advisory board members). Do all of them check the same activities and services as being important? If not, how do their responses differ?

5. Discuss with your classmates the questions and concerns that you would have in working with the following families: a) a child from a homeless family; b) a child whose father is gay and has a live-in partner; c) a child who at age 7 has run away from home on three separate occasions; d) a child whose parents insist that you supervise their child's "biblical worksheet" during his 20-minute free time each day; and e) parents who have clearly expressed their disinterest in any type of family involvement activity. List your concerns and questions about working with these families. Then, list the steps you would take to feel comfortable with these situations.

6. In Figure 8.1, we present examples of in-home activities for linking children's home and school learning experiences. Divide into pairs to develop your own in-home learning activities. Share your activities with teachers in a local school to gain feedback about their usefulness.

7. Develop a short list of "school readiness" skills that children in kindergarten should display. Interview teachers and parents regarding their own "top 10" readiness skills. How do the three lists compare? What steps would you take to reconcile the three lists?

chapter 9

Assessment of Young Children

After reading this chapter you should be able to discuss the following questions:

❖ What is assessment?
❖ What are the differences between formal and informal methods of assessment?
❖ What are some different assessment techniques that can be used with families and school personnel to address individual needs and differences?
❖ How should assessment be related to the instructional activities that teachers provide in an early childhood classroom?

CHAPTER OVERVIEW

Assessment is a critical part of planning instructional activities for evaluating the needs of each individual child. Classroom teachers, along with parents and other educational specialists, are responsible for determining whether or not children are making adequate developmental progress socially, emotionally, physically, and intellectually. In this chapter, we provide you with examples of different types of assessment techniques and strategies for use in the classroom. We begin with a definition and the purposes of assessment, discuss the use of formal methods for assessing young children, and then address informal ways using observational techniques. We integrate assessment issues related to instructional practices throughout the chapter.

Many times families and students concerned with ways to assess children ask, "What is meant by the term *assessment?*" We draw upon the National Association for the Education of Young Children (NAEYC) publication *Reaching potentials: Appropriate curriculum and assessment for young children (Vol. 1)* (1992) for a definition. According to this NAEYC publication, assessment is defined as "the process of observing, recording, and otherwise documenting the work children do and how they do it, as a basis for a variety of educational decisions that affect the child" (p. 10). Assessment needs to include information that is collected on children's development and learning. This information then needs to be used in planning for individuals and programs and in communicating the findings to parents and other involved parties (NAEYC, 1992).

Assessment in any instructional setting always involves a planned process designed to accomplish a specific educational purpose, with the primary beneficiary of the process being the child (Cizak, 1997). Our approach to assessment will adhere to developmentally appropriate practices by focusing on the integration of assessment with the curriculum and instructional experiences that teachers provide. As we will discuss in Chapter 10, we define curriculum as *all of the experiences children encounter in educational settings that take into consideration the child's cultural background, previous experience and knowledge, family, and developmental level.*

We believe that the assessment techniques used with young children must be matched to the child's cultural and family background, previous experience and knowledge, and the child's cognitive, social, and physical developmental level. To make this match, we use the purposes of assessment that have been developed by NAEYC. These purposes include assessment for: 1) instructional planning and communicating with parents; 2) identification of children with special needs; and 3) program and accountability (NAEYC, 1992). In this chapter, we focus primarily on instructional planning, communicating with parents, and identification of children with special needs.

FORMAL ASSESSMENT TECHNIQUES

Standardized tests are measures that typically include fixed administration and scoring procedures, empirical tryout of items, set apparatus or format, and tables of norms (Goodwin & Goodwin, 1997). That is, a standard has been set after the instruments are tried out on a large number of children by specialists in tests and measurement. The standard is established by using the test with children who are representative of the general population (Wortham, 1992).

A standardized assessment instrument provides a measure of a student's relative standing among peers on common educational content. Most standardized measures are published commercially, are produced for general use, and are based on common educational objectives that are widely accepted by practitioners and institutions in diverse settings. However, these common objectives rarely match exactly the specific objectives of an individual classroom teacher or a given early childhood project (Goodwin & Goodwin, 1997). Typical types of standardized measures include intelligence and aptitude tests, achievement tests, readiness tests, screening measures, diagnostic tests, psychometric measures, and personality and attitude measures.

During a child's infancy, toddler, and preschool years, developmental change is rapid and there is often a need to assess whether development is progressing normally. If development is not normal, the assessment procedures used are important in making decisions regarding appropriate intervention services during the years critical to development (Wortham, 1995). Consequently, during infancy and the toddler years, child development specialists such as obstetricians and pediatricians follow children's progress and initiate therapy when development is not normal. During the preschool years, developmental assessment can be used to evaluate and predict whether or not a child is likely to experience learning difficulties (Wortham, 1995). If development is not progressing in a typical manner, medical specialists and educators work with children from birth to minimize the effects of delays in growth that influence developmental progress. Formal standardized tests are usually used to evaluate developmental progress or lack of progress. Table 9.1 provides a sum-

TABLE 9.1 Neonatal and Infant Test Instruments

Name	Level	Type	Purpose
Apgar Scale	Neonate	Birth status	Assess health of the newborn infant
Brazelton Neonatal Assessment Scale	Neonate	Neonatal status	Locate mild neurological dysfunctions and variations in temperament
Neonate Behavioral Assessment Scale	First month		Identify the infant's ability to modulate its behavioral systems in response to external stimuli
Assessment of Preterm Infants' Behavior (APIB)	Preterm infants	Preterm development	Identify current status. Identify intervention targets
Bayley Scales of Infant Development	Infant	Intelligence	Diagnose developmental delays in infants
Gesell Developmental Schedules	Infant	Development	Detect developmental delays
Denver Developmental Screening Test–Revised	1 month– 6 years	Developmental screening	Identify significant developmental delays

Measurement and Evaluation in Early Childhood Education, by Wortham, © 1995. Reprinted by permission of Prentice-Hall, Inc. Upper Saddle River, NJ.

mary of several assessment instruments that are typically used with infants and toddlers to determine their progress in different developmental areas.

Standardized tests are used with preschool children to evaluate and predict whether a child may experience difficulties in learning or develop a learning disability that will affect his or her success in school. These tests are also used in most school settings to compare children's cognitive abilities and academic achievement. In preschool and primary grade settings, standardized tests are used for two purposes: 1) to evaluate achievement compared with that of a sample group of children and 2) to measure the child's achievement on specific test objectives (Wortham, 1995).

There are two types of standardized tests that teachers of young children will encounter: norm-referenced and criterion-referenced tests.

Norm-Referenced Tests

A *norm-referenced* test measures achievement by how the performance of an individual compares with that of others. In other words, an individual's achievement is compared with that of a group that is known by the establishment of norms. Norms are numerical descriptions of the test performance in which the raw score

Standardized tests are often used as a measure of a child's relative standing among peers on common educational content.

of an individual is converted into a derived score so that an individual test taker can be compared with the scores of others who took the test (Goodwin & Goodwin, 1993). At the preschool level, norm-referenced tests should be used to identify children who need special instruction or instruction that is adapted to their specific needs because they are not developing in a typical way. Table 9.2 provides a summary of standardized tests that can be used with preschool children.

In elementary schools, children may take norm-referenced tests as early as kindergarten. Norm-referenced tests can be used to measure school achievement, intelligence, or aptitude and personality. Typically, these tests may be used to assess children who are having difficulty in school or to assess the achievement of all children in certain subject areas, such as literacy and mathematics. Many states and individual school districts use norm-referenced tests to examine the achievement of a single class in a school, all classes of a certain grade level in a school, all schools with the grade level in the school district, and all schools within a state with that grade level (Wortham, 1995). We discuss objections to overuse, misuse, and abuse of formal standardized testing following our explanation of the second type of standardized tests: criterion-referenced tests.

Criterion-Referenced Tests

Criterion-referenced tests inform the teacher about how an individual performs in relation to a predetermined standard or objective. By using criterion-referenced tests, teachers can assess an individual's performance on specific behavioral or instructional objectives without comparing the individual to the performance of others. An individual child's strengths and weaknesses in the content area measured

TABLE 9.2		**Formal Assessment Instruments that Can be Used with Preschool Children**	
Name	**Level**	**Type**	**Purpose**
Stanford-Binet Intelligence Scale	Ages 2–adult	Global intelligence	To detect delays and mental retardation
McCarthy Scales of Children's Abilities	Ages 2½–8	Intelligence	To identify and diagnose delays in cognitive and noncognitive areas through subtests
Wechsler Preschool and Primary Scale of Intelligence	Ages 4–6	Intelligence	To identify signs of uneven development; to detect overall delay
Vineland Social Maturity Scale	Ages 1–25	Adaptive behavior	To assess whether the child mastered living skills expected for the age level in terms of everyday behavior
AAMD Adaptive Behavior Scale	Ages 3–16	Adaptive behavior	Assesses adaptive behavior in terms of personal independence and development; can be compared to norms for children developing normally, with retardation, and with severe retardation
Developmental Indicators for the Assessment of Learning–Revised	Ages 2–5	Developmental	Assesses motor, language, and cognitive development

Measurement and Evaluation in Early Childhood Education, by Wortham, © 1995. Reprinted by permission of Prentice-Hall, Inc. Upper Saddle River, NJ.

by the criterion-referenced test can be determined. These types of tests are designed to measure the results of instruction by determining the individual's performance on specific behavioral or instructional objectives (Wilson, 1980; Wortham, 1995). Criterion-referenced tests make no comparisons among test takers. Instead, an individual student passes the test if he or she has met the standards or objectives that are measured by the test.

At the preschool level, criterion-referenced tests are also used for developmental screening, diagnostic assessment, and planning for instruction (Wortham, 1995). Developmental screening tests are typically used to identify children who might profit from early education intervention or from special services before kindergarten or first grade. Many screening tests have been developed as a result of Public Law 94-142, the Individuals with Disabilities Education Act, to assess affective, cognitive,

TABLE 9.3   Standardized Tests that Are Typically Used in Kindergarten and the Primary Grades

Name	Level	Type	Purpose
Bilingual Syntax Measure	Kindergarten–grade 2	Language	To determine language dominance
Wechsler Intelligence Scale for Children–Revised	Ages 6½–16½	Intelligence	To diagnose mental retardation and learning disability; includes verbal and performance subscales
Bender Gestalt Test	Ages 4–10	Visual motor functioning	To assess perceptual skills and hand-eye coordination, identify learning disabilities
Peabody Picture Vocabulary Test–Revised	Ages 2½–18	Vocabulary	To measure receptive vocabulary for standard American English
Peabody Individual Achievement Test	Kindergarten–grade 12	Individual achievement	To assess achievement in mathematics, reading, spelling, and general information
Metropolitan Early School Inventory	Kindergarten	Development	To assess physical cognitive, language, and social-emotional development
Boehm Test of Basic Concepts–Revised	Kindergarten–grade 2	Cognitive ability	To screen for beginning school concepts
Circus	Preschool–grade 3	Achievement program evaluation	To assess developmental skills and knowledge
Brigance Diagnostic Inventory of Basic Skills	Kindergarten–grade 6	Academic achievement	To assess academic skills and diagnose learning difficulties in language, math, and reading
Spache Diagnostic Reading Scales	Grade 1–8 reading levels	Diagnostic reading test	To locate reading problems and plan remedial instruction
Battelle Developmental Inventory	Birth–8 years	Comprehensive developmental assessment	To identify child's strengths and weaknesses and plan for intervention or instruction

Measurement and Evaluation in Early Childhood Education, by Wortham, © 1995. Reprinted by permission of Prentice-Hall, Inc. Upper Saddle River, NJ.

and psychomotor characteristics. The test results are then used to decide whether further assessment is needed to identify disabilities and potential remediation techniques. Teachers use criterion-referenced tests in kindergarten and the primary grades to plan instruction and to describe individual performance. Criterion-referenced tests may also be used as diagnostic tests with students who exhibit learning difficulties. Table 9.3 provides a summary of standardized tests that are often used in kindergarten and the primary grades.

In the next section, we discuss numerous concerns and issues about the use and misuse of formal assessment instruments (mainly standardized tests) with young children that have been expressed by numerous educators and psychologists in the past 15 years.

CONCERNS ABOUT USING STANDARDIZED TESTING IN EARLY CHILDHOOD EDUCATION

Standardized tests may be used along with informal assessment measures in preschool, kindergarten, and first grade to determine whether children will be admitted to preschool programs, promoted to first grade, placed in transitional classrooms, or retained. The use of standardized tests for these purposes is considered to be developmentally inappropriate for this age by most early childhood educators. In fact, NAEYC (1997) reports that an unprecedented concern has been demonstrated about the extent of standardized testing, the prevalence of standardized testing, and an over-reliance on standardized testing by those who work with young children in developmentally appropriate situations. In this section, we discuss the reasons why standardized tests may be inappropriate for young children, examine when standardized tests should be used with young children, and provide a rationale for appropriate ways to assess young children.

Decisions about placing a child in a transition class or retaining a child in preschool, kindergarten, or first grade can have a powerful impact on the self-esteem of a young child and can influence the perception of whether the child is successful or a failure (Wortham, 1995). The use of standardized tests has been criticized by NAEYC (1992; 1997) and others (Kamii & Kamii, 1990; Shepard & Smith, 1988) because when teachers focus only on preparing their children to take standardized tests, children's construction of knowledge, thinking, and development of independence are ignored. Many early childhood educators believe that a consequence of focusing primarily on preparation for standardized tests has been an increased emphasis on academic skills measured by the test, rather than an emphasis on all areas of development. Similarly, when teachers only use standardized tests as measures of performance, they tend to lose sight of individual rates of development and may think that if any child performs poorly, the child is viewed as a failure. An additional concern with using standardized tests is that many "readiness" tests—some intelligence tests, developmental screening measures, and certain academic readiness tests—have not been used for their original purpose (Goodwin & Goodwin, 1997). That is, tests that were designed to determine if children had specific developmental delays or learning problems have been used to make decisions about retaining children in preschool or kindergarten or about placing them into specially funded or transitional kindergarten classes rather than into first grade. This practice continues in some school districts, despite the results of research showing that transitional classes and kindergarten retention do little to improve children's school achievement in later years (Dyson & Genishi, 1993; Shepard & Smith, 1988).

Many educators believe that standardized tests do not measure the true capabilities of young children because of children's developmental characteristics. According to Gullo (1997), young children are considered to be poor test takers because: 1) they may not understand the importance or significance of their performance in assessment situations (they may perform simply to complete the task so that they can move on to a more comfortable or appealing experience); 2) they are impulsive and may respond to the first thing that comes to mind without reflecting or considering alternative responses (often young children will circle the first picture on the sheet or the first one that "seems" right without looking to see if a subsequent picture is "more right"); 3) they may be required to use controlled fine motor movements (the inability of some children to demonstrate such movements may inhibit the child's ability to demonstrate that he or she really has acquired the knowledge or skill being assessed); and 4) the language that is used by the teacher to assess a child's performance may not be consistent with the child's own level of language (the teacher's language may not reflect content that is familiar to the child because he or she comes from a different social or cultural background).

There have also been concerns expressed about ethnic, cultural, and gender biases. These concerns are based on the idea of fairness. Because some children's ethnic background or cultural or language experiences may be different from the skills and content that a test is measuring, they may perform poorly. According to Gullo (1997), some children may have more experience with "assessment-like" situations and therefore be more motivated at earlier ages than others to perform. Typically, children who come from middle socioeconomic status backgrounds are likely to have engaged in these types of situations than children who come from homes of economic poverty (Gullo, 1997).

As we have discussed in previous chapters, young children's development can, at times, be uneven, with periods of rapid change and periods of little change. Consequently, their performance on standardized tests can be unstable and unreliable. Since young children are poor test takers, teachers and administrators who use standardized tests must be aware of typical developmental characteristics. Standardized tests should be administered following the established procedures outlined in the manual provided by the test publisher to assure that children's test scores actually reflect their knowledge and ability. Because of the developmental characteristics of younger children, teachers often find it difficult to follow these carefully prescribed procedures. For example, young children may react to prescribed testing conditions by calling out answers or crying. Consequently, there have been problems with consistency and validity of test scores when teachers allow interruptions during testing, repeat items, modify instructions, or cue correct answers.

The NAEYC (1992) recommends that standardized tests should only be used if it is clear that benefits to children will result. Standardized tests are required when it is necessary to assess young children in the process of determining eligibility for special education services. When this type of assessment occurs, there is a specific process that needs to be followed. For example, there is a brief assessment procedure, referred to as screening, which is designed to identify children who may have a learning problem or handicapping condition that requires more intensive diagnosis based on many sources of information, including that obtained from families and expert diagnosticians (NAEYC, 1992). The screening process may then be followed by a comprehensive diagnostic process. Whenever a child is recommended for screening or diagnosis, his or her family must be informed. For a more detailed description of guidelines for identifying children with special needs, see NAEYC's (1992) *Reaching potentials: Appropriate curriculum and assessment for young children* (Vol. 1).

You may be asking yourself, "How should I assess young children in my classroom?" In the remainder of this chapter, we focus on informal ways to assess the developmental progress, thinking, and learning of young children. We include these informal methods of assessment because they are considered by early childhood educators to be the most appropriate and meaningful ways to find out what you need to know when teaching young children. In the remaining chapters of this textbook, we explain and describe developmentally appropriate curriculum. A key component of planning and implementing a developmentally appropriate curriculum is assessment. Since we have focused on developmental theories up to this point, we emphasize informal methods of assessment that rely on observation as the predominant method for assessment of developmental progress. Before we describe different observational techniques, we discuss how assessment should be used when teaching young children.

According to Gullo (1997), assessment in early childhood classrooms should: 1) be a continuous process that occurs over a long period of time; 2) be a comprehensive process that acknowledges different aspects of learning and development; and 3) not be separate from the instructional experiences and activities that are planned in the curriculum. Children need to be assessed within the context of the classroom while engaged in meaningful activities that are provided in an environment that is interesting and engaging (Gullo, 1997). When assessing young children, teachers need to focus on the process of children's learning (how they are learning) as well as what they are learning.

In our discussion of curriculum in the next section, it is important to remember that assessment information should be a key part of planning and implementing learning experiences. The assessment practices that teachers use should directly reflect the curriculum that teachers teach. In a developmentally appropriate curriculum, assessment information should be used to understand in what stage of development children are performing so that changes in the curriculum can be made to address individual needs. Specific principles that should be used to guide assessment procedures for young children can also be found in the NAEYC (1992) publication *Reaching potentials: Appropriate curriculum and assessment for young children* (Vol. 1). In the next section, we provide you with descriptions of different ways to informally assess the progress of young children across different developmental areas. As we have discussed, most early childhood educators advocate the use of informal assessment instruments that can be used to plan for instructional activities for individuals and groups of young children.

INFORMAL ASSESSMENT METHODS

Informal assessment measures can be used to obtain specific information about each child's developmental level and knowledge about certain concepts or skills. These measures can also assist in making decisions about placement in particular programs such as special education services for an identified developmental delay or disability. When teachers use informal assessment measures, the goal is to encourage children to demonstrate what they know as they are engaged in active learning experiences that are interesting and relevant. Young children's knowledge can be assessed through performance of typical age-appropriate tasks or samples of work rather than through assessment instruments that are limited to mastery of discrete skills (Goodwin & Goodwin, 1993; Wortham, 1995).

Informal assessment measures provide a viable alternative to the use of standardized instruments, such as intelligence and achievement tests, readiness tests, and developmental screening instruments. In our discussion of specific informal assessment techniques, we begin with a general discussion of observation; describe the techniques of anecdotal records, running records, event sampling, time sampling, rating scales, checklists, work samples, interviews, audiotaping, and videotaping; and conclude with portfolio assessment.

Observation

Observation can be defined as a systematic way of viewing children to find out as much as possible about different areas of their development. One of the major purposes of observation is to help teachers make appropriate decisions about what to teach, based on their knowledge of each child's intellectual, physical, social, and emotional functioning as well as the child's cultural and family background and individual interests (Puckett & Black, 1994). Information derived from observations can also be shared with families, administrators, and other teachers. Documented information about children's development can be combined with other assessment measures to provide a comprehensive representation of each child's capabilities. In order for observations to be effective, teachers need to have a method for recording what they see. That is, teachers need to clearly remember and analyze what is observed in order to use this information to develop a comprehensive profile of children's developmental progress (Puckett & Black, 1994).

Teachers need to be familiar with specific terms when they use informal assessment methods based on observation. "Kidwatching" is a term that refers to finding out how children learn and what they are thinking. "Keeping track" and "documenting" are terms often used by teachers to refer to how observational information is used. That is, the information that is recorded during an observation helps teachers keep track of children's progress and provides evidence or documentation of a child's performance. For example, a teacher might track how a child is progressing in counting and grouping a number of objects, or document how a child interacts with other children while playing in the housekeeping cen-

Teacher observation can be used to help teachers make appropriate decisions about what to teach.

ter. "Naturalistic" or "authentic" assessment is believed to be a valid way to evaluate children by watching them behave in their typical home or school setting (Puckett & Black, 1994). An example of authentic assessment is observing and recording a child's responses to questions while he or she is reading a story under the guidance of an adult. "Performance assessments" are commonly used to determine how children perform on specific tasks that replicate real-life experiences (Billman & Sherman, 1996). Figure 9.1 provides a summary of the components of authentic assessment.

All of these assessment terms refer to methods that depend upon careful observation of children. By using different observational methods and techniques, teachers can use their knowledge of each child's physical, emotional, social, and cognitive performance in combination with the child's cultural and family background to:

- Plan and implement appropriate curriculum;
- Develop appropriate teaching strategies and interactions;
- Communicate children's progress to parents; and
- Refer children who need additional assessment for possible special education services (Billman & Sherman, 1996).

FIGURE 9.1   Components of Authentic Assessment

Authentic assessment:

- Is performance based
- Capitalizes on the strengths of the learner
- Is based on real-life events
- Emphasizes emerging skills
- Focuses on purposeful learning
- Relates to instruction
- Is ongoing in all contexts—home, school, community
- Provides a broad and general picture of student learning and capabilities
- Is based on authentic curriculums
- Celebrates, supports, and facilitates development and learning

Authentic Assessment of the Young Child by Puckett/Black, © 1994. Reprinted by permission of Prentice-Hall, Inc. Upper Saddle River, NJ.

Observation can also help the teacher identify children's interests for devising activities that are motivating and interesting to young children. We discuss the importance of children's interest in planning learning experiences in chapters 10 through 13.

To determine and document the developmental level of individual children through observation and then plan appropriate activities that address individual needs, teachers must be *skilled observers*. Being a skilled observer means that a teacher attends to a variety of cues or signals that children exhibit and is alert to behaviors across contexts (in the classroom, on the playground, with individuals, in groups, with parents and other adults, etc.). According to Puckett & Black (1994), a skilled observer is one who:

- Is informed by knowledge of child growth and development;
- Avoids jumping to conclusions;
- Is empathic and devoid of bias and preconceived ideas;
- Attends to details;
- Forms hypotheses and observes further for verification;
- Draws valid inferences;
- Generates a plan for further observation; and
- Uses information obtained from observations to make decisions about instruction (p. 179).

When observing children in any context, the observer must be aware of the appropriate way to use any information that is collected. The privacy of the children, their families, and other school personnel needs to be considered (Wortham, 1995). When reporting the results of the observation to others (such as families or other teachers), only the child should be discussed. Names and identifying characteristics of children should not be included in written materials unless they are specifically called for (Billman & Sherman, 1996). The child should not be discussed informally or in an unprofessional manner with other observers, school staff members, or outsiders (Billman & Sherman, 1996; Wortham, 1995).

The remainder of this chapter provides you with summaries of different informal assessment techniques that rely on observation. We have also included the use of audiotaping and videotaping as specific techniques that can be used separately or with other observational techniques. We conclude the chapter with an explanation of portfolios.

Anecdotal records.   An anecdote is a brief account, either short or very detailed, of an important event or incident in a child's day. The record can describe a specific behavior or can be used to track the development of an infant or toddler. Writing an anecdote about a child playing in the block area can reveal a great deal about the child's social, language, and problem-solving skills. A number of anecdotes recorded over time can not only increase the teacher's understandings of individual children as patterns of behavior emerge, but can also provide an extensive profile of a child's development in different areas. Many teachers use anecdotal records to help plan activities for individual children. Anecdotal records are usually recorded as an incident occurs or immediately thereafter. The record should report, in a factual way, the incident, its context, and what was said or done by the participants (Puckett & Black, 1994).

Teachers use different methods for writing and keeping anecdotal records to assure that all aspects of the event can be recalled. For example, some teachers keep notes on 3″ × 5″ index cards that can be carried in a pocket or placed in the classroom for easy access. Other teachers simply keep sheets of paper in file folders or use stick-on notes and then place them on a paper or in a folder. Writing one-word reminders or short phrases on a card or piece of paper as an incident unfolds can provide reminders for recording the complete anecdotal record later in the day (Puckett & Black, 1994). An anecdotal record can include the child's initials, antecedents to an incident, and the events of the beginning, middle, and end of the incident. An example of an anecdotal record is provided in Figure 9.2.

Running record.   A running record is a more detailed method of recording behavior. This type of record includes the sequence of events—everything that occurred over a period of time. A running record focuses on all behavior that is observed, as opposed to a specific incident that is used in anecdotal records. The behavior description is objective and everything that happened or was said during the observation period is recorded. Running records may be recorded over a period ranging from a few minutes to a few weeks or even months (Billman & Sherman, 1996).

Running records are typically used in connection with emergent literacy assessment. For example, a teacher may listen to a child read and record the errors and corrections that the child makes. Many teachers take detailed running records by using a systematic method of identifying errors that children make while reading a passage such as letter reversals, word substitutions, and word omissions. The

FIGURE 9.2 Sample Anecdotal Record

MA
Tuesday, 9/18

After large group circle time, MA ran to the science center and said (loudly) that he wanted to do the sink and float activity. LR, who had already started to drop objects in the water, said that she didn't want him to play with her. MA started to cry and went to sit at the work table by himself. After sitting alone for 2–3 minutes, MA went back over to the science center and asked LR if he could work with her. LR said that he could if he didn't grab things away from her. MA didn't respond; however, he began to pick up objects such as the clay, paper clips, and unifix cubes and dropped them into the water one at a time. LR asked if she could take a turn; MA said "sure." When LR began to drop different objects in the water, MA grabbed the clay and magnets away from LR. LR ran to Mrs. S and said that MA was not sharing. MA then threw all of the objects sitting on the table in the water and then ran across the room to the block center. Mrs. S then went over to the block center to talk to MA about his behavior in the science center.

intent of a running record while a child is actually reading is to informally assess the child's reading capabilities. The teacher may comment on the child's performance as he or she analyzes the record so that others who read the record later can actually visualize what behaviors occurred when the running record was recorded (Billman & Sherman, 1996).

Event sampling.   Event sampling can be used to record events or categories of events as they occur. A teacher may use event sampling to focus on a particular child's behavior during a particular activity or event, such as painting at the easel during free play, playing in the housekeeping center during free play, or engaging in a specific task such as matching objects to a numeral. Event sampling can be brief or as detailed as time allows. Teachers can easily develop an event sampling record. The more information that is included in the event sampling record, the more useful it can be later when interpretation and summarization are required (Puckett & Black, 1994). Event sampling is typically used when a behavior tends to occur in a particular setting. The observer decides when the behavior is likely to occur and waits for it to take place. However, if the event does not readily occur, the observer's time is wasted. An example of an event sampling record is shown in Figure 9.3.

Time sampling.   In the time sampling method, the teacher records the occurrence or nonoccurrence of selected behaviors during designated time frames. The teacher decides ahead of time what behaviors will be observed, what the time interval will be, and how to record the behaviors (Wortham, 1995). During the preset, uniform time frames, the teacher observes only the designated behaviors and records how many times the behaviors occur. After completing a

FIGURE 9.3   Event Sampling Record

Group observed: _____   Child(ren)'s age: _____

Date and time: _____   Observer: _____

Target behavior:

Recently Ms. W's class has been reported to be pushing and shoving at various transition points, such as preparation for lunch or recess.

Time	Antecedent Behavior	Behavior	Consequences

Interpretation:

Interventions to be made:

number of observations, the teacher can examine the observation data to determine when and why a behavior is occurring. The teacher can then think about how to use the data to develop a plan to assist the child, such as changing specific behaviors. An example of a time sampling chart is presented in Figure 9.4. Time sampling can be helpful in determining both the frequency with which certain behaviors occur and the situation in which the behaviors occur (Puckett & Black, 1994).

Rating scales.   There are different types of rating scales that can be used with young children to help teachers record observations quickly and efficiently. When using rating scales, teachers need to be sure that they are fair by representing the observed behavior without bias. According to Billman and Sherman (1996), many rating scales require the teacher to determine where a child's behavior fits on a numbered scale (such as a 3- to 7-point scale) or on a scale that has points that vary along a continuum from "almost always" to "almost never" or from "very quickly" to "very slowly" (a scale referred to as a *Likert Scale*). Another type of rating scale uses written categories of behavior and requires the teacher to choose the category most similar to the child's behavior. This type of rating scale can be used to measure how well or how often a child demonstrates certain predetermined behaviors (Billman & Sherman, 1996). Each teacher who uses a rating scale needs to have a common understanding of the key descriptors and numerical ratings that are used on each particular scale. Consequently, many teachers use rating scales that are commercially published or developed by a specific school district or education agency. An example of a rating scale can be found in Figure 9.5.

Checklists.   Checklists are typically used by teachers to gather specific information on individuals, a small group, or an entire classroom of young children. A checklist helps to focus the teacher's attention on the presence or absence of selected behaviors (Puckett & Black, 1994). There are different types of checklists that teachers of young children may encounter. Puckett & Black (1995) note that checklists may focus on: 1) indicators of growth and development; 2) specific learning objectives; 3) concepts, skills, behaviors, or interests; and 4) student performance or products. Checklists may be developed by an individual teacher or group of teachers or by researchers and theorists in a specific developmental area. It is important that the criteria found on checklists be well defined and sensitive to children's prior experiences and cultural background (Billman & Sherman, 1996).

Teachers can readily use checklists by focusing on a small group of three to four children per day. For example, during a small group counting activity, the teacher can observe and talk to children individually to see who can count to 10 or 20. Checklists can be used in a natural context without putting the child in a "testing" situation (Wortham, 1995). It is important to remember that checklists do not provide contextual cues about the observed behavior—they do not tell the duration of the behavior or situation in which the behavior occurred (Puckett & Black,

FIGURE 9.4 Time Sampling Record

Observer's name: _____

Observation setting (home, day-care center, family day-care home, etc.) _____

Date: _____ Time: _____ Activity: _____

Brief description of setting/situation:

Procedure: Observe for 10 seconds and note whether child is displaying any of the behaviors listed. Select six children to observe. Record the behavior code; give yourself 20 seconds to make the recording. Then move to the next child; stay in Column "1" until all six children have been observed once. Repeat the process until you have a total of six (6) separate recordings for each child.

Behavior Signs

Proximity-Seeking

FT Follows teacher
FC Follows child
CT Cries when teacher
  leaves area
RS Resists strangers
CT Clings to teacher

Positive Attention-Seeking

AT Seeks approval from teacher
  for specific acts done, work
  accomplished
AC Seeks approval from child
  for acts done, work
  accomplished
GT Seeks general
  acknowledgment from teacher—
  no specific focus of efforts
GC Seeks general
  acknowledgment from child—
  no specific focus of efforts

Negative Attention-Seeking

WA Whines for attention
CA Cries for attention
TT Temper tantrum for attention
DG Disrupts group activities to
  get attention

Child/Recording Intervals	1	2	3	4	5	6

FIGURE 9.5 Sample Rating Scale

Kindergarten Communication Skills

Teacher: _____   Date: _____

Use the following rating scale for each item: 1–Never, 2–Occasionally, 3–Always

Child's Name	Talks with adults	Talks with other children	Talks with animals, dolls, toys	Adults can understand him/her	Children can understand him/her	Uses whole sentences	Talks "baby talk"	Talks spontaneously when playing	Talks spontaneously at mealtime	Uses language props such as toy telephone	Starts conversations	Expresses his/her feelings in words
1.												
2.												
3.												
4.												
5.												
6.												
7.												
8.												
9.												
10.												
11.												
12.												
13.												
14.												

1994). Figure 9.6 provides an example of a checklist used to assess early mathematics concepts and skills.

Work samples.   Work samples are examples of children's work that can demonstrate their developmental progress or accomplishments (Puckett & Black, 1994). For preschool children, work samples can be paintings, scribbling, drawings, an animal they have made out of boxes, or dictated stories about pictures they've drawn. Primary-grade children can contribute creative writing, pictorial representations of addition or subtraction problems, drawings, or pages they have written in a mathematics or science journal. Some teachers have included photographs, videotapes, or audiotapes.

Interviews.   Through the use of interviews, teachers can gain insight into childrens' prior knowledge and experience, and current understanding of a concept or skill, interest, and motivation. In an interview, the teacher can observe and listen to the child's responses and reactions to questions without looking for one correct answer (Billman & Sherman, 1996). Interviews can be either informal or structured. An informal interview can occur when a teacher asks a child to explain an answer, a drawing, a written response, or a product such as a feeling picture with different textures. This could take place when children are playing, working in centers, or

Teachers can gain insight into children's knowledge and skills through interviews.

FIGURE 9.6 Sample Checklists

Math Concepts

Child: _____   Age: _____   Grade: _____

Observation 1.   Beginning of the year (date): _____

Observation 2.   Beginning of second semester (date): _____

Observation 3.   End of the year(date): _____

Concept	Obs. 1	Comments	Obs. 2	Comments	Obs. 3	Comments
Size: Big						
Bigger						
Biggest						
No. Concepts						
Counts objects up to 5						
Counts objects up to 10						
Counts objects beyond 20 (give #)						
Recognizes & identifies sets of: 1						
2 → 10						

continues

FIGURE 9.6 *continued*

Or for a class checklist:

Name	Size: Big	Bigger	Biggest	No. Concepts	Counts objects up to 5	Counts objects up to 10	Counts objects beyond 20 (give #)	Recognizes & identifies sets of: 1	2	3	4	5	6
1.													
2.													
3.													
4.													
5.													
6.													
7.													
8.													
9.													
10.													
11.													
12.													
13.													
14.													

engaged in other classroom activities. Structured interviews are pre-planned by the teacher and conducted to elicit responses to specific questions.

Concepts in mathematics can be assessed through a structured interview in which the teacher presents a counting task to a child. The teacher asks the child different questions about how many objects there are and how the child knows how many objects there are. In such an interview, the teacher is trying to find out how the child arrives at the solution to a particular problem. The rightness and wrongness of the answer is not as important as how the child arrives at the answer (Charlesworth & Lind, 1995). An interview can also help determine a child's zone of proximal development (which we discussed in Chapter 5) and provide an opportunity for the teacher to engage in scaffolding activities that enhance children's learning and understanding (Billman & Sherman, 1996).

Audiotaping.   Recording children's verbal responses can help a teacher assess young children's language skills. Tape recorders can be placed in different places in the room to capture children's conversations or child-child or teacher-child verbal exchanges. Since audiotapes are inexpensive to use, teachers can listen to tapes repeatedly in order to understand what is being said (Billman & Sherman, 1996). Some teachers record a child while he or she is reading or telling a story. The tapes can then be used in different ways to document and analyze progress. For example, the teacher can share the tape with a child's other teachers or his or her family.

Videotaping.   Videotaping children in different classroom contexts can be one of the most accurate ways to observe and record interaction. In addition to the visual moving picture, noises and spoken words are also included (Billman & Sherman, 1996). Some teachers set up a video recorder on a tripod in an unobtrusive spot or simply hold the video recorder to capture a specific event. Once children become used to being recorded by a video camera, they typically are unaware of its presence. There are a number of ways videotapes of children in the classroom can be used. Billman and Sherman (1996) suggest that teachers use videotapes to:

- Show each child playing or working with others during free time or in a teacher-directed group to share with families.
- Obtain information about the child's behavior or performance on different tasks.
- Assess different areas of the child's development. For example, a videotape of the child running, jumping, and hopping could provide examples of the child's physical–large motor skill.
- Examine a child's progress in different developmental areas across time over the school year.

Videotapes are another informal assessment instrument that provide authentic information about how children perform individually, in social contexts, and in instructional settings with adults and other children.

Portfolio assessment. A portfolio is a purposeful collection of student work that exhibits to the student and others (such as families and other teachers) the student's efforts, progress, or achievement in given areas (Paulson, Paulson, & Meyer, 1991). Teachers can place test scores, checklists, rating scales, examples of systematic observations, a child's drawings, writing samples, tape recordings of the child reading or telling a story, or a videotape of a child playing in the block area in portfolios. Children can actively participate in the creation of the portfolio by meeting with the teacher to select work samples.

A portfolio can represent student accomplishments at selected time intervals and provide permanent or long-term records of children's progress (Puckett & Black, 1994). Work can be dated to allow teachers to follow the child's progress in different developmental areas. Once a portfolio is assembled, the teacher can write a summary of the work and observations for a specified time period. In preschool through third grade, development and learning are usually viewed as *evolving*, which means that using grades or comparing work and observation samples is not appropriate. Rather, portfolios at this level should focus on a child's developmental progress. Puckett and Black (1994) suggest that portfolios be evaluated on the basis of whether or not the content:

- Reflects different contexts in which learning occurs—cultural, home, school, large group, small group, and individual;
- Demonstrates progress toward specific behaviors or achievements or toward school or individual learning goals;
- Reflects individual capabilities and interests; and
- Informs decisions about instruction and curriculum.

There is no one, correct way to assemble, store, and retrieve portfolio contents. Teachers need to decide what type of container or containers can be used as well as how the containers can be used. For example, file folders, expandable folders, hanging files, pocket folders, oversized sheet of construction paper folded in half and stapled, stacking baskets, corrugated cubby-hole units, wall-filing units, and uniform-sized boxes are possibilities suggested by Puckett and Black (1994). The procedure for how students can gain access to their portfolios also need to be considered. If stationary units are used, students will need a way to transport their portfolio and its contents to the classroom or their home. Similarly, the ways that portfolios are organized can also vary. Portfolios can be organized by subject-matter area, developmental category, or by topics or themes if an integrated curriculum is used (Wortham, 1995). When portfolios are used mainly for assessment of children's academic progress, there should be a section for teacher assessment records and a section for child work. In some classrooms, portfolios may be used for a single purpose, such as a literacy portfolio or a mathematics portfolio. If that is the case, all of the work should focus on examples of children's work in a specific subject. If portfolios are organized using a developmental approach, there could be a section for motor or physical development, social and emotional development, language development, and cognitive development.

Once a teacher decides what to include in a portfolio and how to organize it, considerations of how the contents will be evaluated need to be made. Program goals and objectives and developmental checklists can serve as guides to children's developmental progress when assembling an evaluation profile (Wortham, 1995). The child's progress needs to be the focus of an evaluation of the portfolio. Information about the child's strengths, weaknesses, achievement, and instructional needs should be collected. By using all of the data collected in the portfolio, the teacher can then describe the child's developmental status and characteristics (Grace & Shores, 1991). The portfolio evaluation process needs to be appropriate for the children's level of development and should address how the information derived from the process can inform the teacher about the types of learning experiences that need to be provided.

CHAPTER SUMMARY

In this chapter, we discussed how critical assessment is to learning about and teaching young children. We have drawn from NAEYC's definitions and purposes of assessment, which focus on observing, recording, and documenting children's developmental progress in order to make decisions about curriculum and instruction in the early childhood classroom. In our discussion of assessment methods, we emphasized that standardized tests should be used mainly for determining eligibility for special education services. When assessing children's progress in the early childhood classroom, we recommended that informal methods of assessment that rely on observational techniques be used. In Activity 1, we ask you to think back to the philosophy you developed in Chapter 1 to see how the assessment techniques presented in this chapter match with how you think young children learn and develop. In the following chapters, we present ways to organize and manage an early childhood classroom and ways to develop and implement an integrated curriculum. As you begin to think about these aspects of teaching young children, keep in mind the relationship between assessing what children know and are able to do and the experiences you develop and implement for them.

ACTIVITIES

1. Using the philosophy that you developed in Chapter 1, describe in several sentences how you think children's development and learning should be assessed. What techniques from this chapter did you include? Discuss the assessment techniques that you chose with your classmates.
2. Interview a teacher about how standardized tests are used in his or her school or program. Are the tests used to determine placement for special education services or are they used to compare children's performance with others in their school, school district, or state? Using the information found on pp. 232–239 about the uses and misuses of standardized tests, write a brief summary of how this teacher uses standardized tests.

3. Observe a child for a period of 20 minutes. Before you begin your observation, decide what method you will use (such as anecdotal record, running record, event sampling, or time sampling). Summarize your observation by addressing the following questions: 1) What specific behaviors did you observe? 2) What information did you record? 3) What does the information tell you about this child? 4) What inferences can you make about the child's behaviors? 5) Did you have any difficulties with the method you used?

4. Interview a 5-year-old and an 8-year-old. Ask each child to tell you where rain comes from. What do the child's responses tell you about his or her understanding of ideas and concepts related to rain? How are the responses from the two children alike and different? You can also ask each child to draw a picture of where rain comes from and then compare the drawing to the child's verbal explanations.

5. Visit a classroom where portfolios are used. Identify the different contents of the portfolio that provide information about both what the child can do and what the child knows and understands.

chapter 10

Approaches to Early Childhood Curriculum

After reading this chapter you should be able to discuss the following questions:

❖ How is curriculum commonly defined in early childhood education?
❖ What are some of the typical attributes of curriculum models based on Montessori, behaviorism, constructivism, and developmentally appropriate practice?
❖ What are some of the differences between the four curricular approaches?

CHAPTER OVERVIEW

In this chapter, we provide a definition of early childhood curriculum, discuss the importance of thinking about families and the history of early childhood curriculum, and present four different approaches to curriculum in early childhood education. As we focus on specific approaches to early childhood curriculum, it is important to remember that the term *curriculum* can mean many different things to different people. To many educators, curriculum refers to the "what is taught" aspect of schooling. Currently, it is important to consider curriculum in terms of connections among educational programs, families, and communities.

DEFINING CURRICULUM

The term *curriculum*, as it applies to elementary, middle, and secondary schools, is open to many interpretations. Most educators acknowledge that there is no single definition of curriculum. The curriculum used in schools is usually outlined in a written document that suggests the educational content and other experiences to be pursued by students for whom the school accepts responsibility (Doll, 1992). Many educators consider the curriculum found in schools to be on a continuum (Doll, 1992). At one end of the continuum is a traditional approach with a well-defined and clearly specified plan for learning by means of goals, objectives, and lesson plans (Olivia, 1992). In this more traditional approach, curriculum: a) is planned in advance; b) is designed for student instruction under the direction of the school as a clearly delineated set of plans; and c) includes outcomes that can be described at the beginning of instruction and measured following instruction. At the other end of the continuum, curriculum is defined more broadly and is described as all of the experiences under the school's direction that lead to learning.

A more traditional curriculum predetermined by the school has been criticized for not taking into consideration a learner's previous experience, culture, and prior knowledge. In early childhood education, curriculum has been defined and approached differently from elementary, middle, and secondary schools. During the 20th century, theories of child development have greatly influenced early childhood curriculum development (Spodek, 1986).

The early childhood curriculum should consider content, or what will be taught, as well as the processes young children use or experience in acquiring new knowledge. In many early childhood programs, content refers to language, mathematics, social studies, and science concepts, as well as music, movement, creative arts, and dramatics. For young children, a curriculum that is focused only on specific skills in certain content areas such as language, mathematics, social studies, and science is often termed "academic curriculum." In contrast, a "developmental curriculum" is more concerned with the process of learning rather than specific content. A developmental curriculum is focused on: a) creating an environment that is responsive to children's individual needs and interests; b) preparing the environment so a teacher can then observe and guide children; and c) providing experiences that continually challenge and support the construction of new understandings (Spodek, 1991).

Many early childhood educators view a content-oriented curriculum focused on academic skills as "inappropriate" and a developmental curriculum as "appropriate." In this chapter, we examine four different approaches to early childhood curriculum. As we describe and discuss the different approaches, it is important to remember that a number of factors influence how teachers develop and implement activities and experiences in classrooms. When planning activities and experiences for young children, we define curriculum in a broad way because we believe it is important to consider a child's family, the community in which the child lives, and theories of child development. Our definition of curriculum is: *all of the experiences children encounter in educational settings that take into consideration the child's cultural background, previous experience and knowledge, family, and developmental level.*

As you read and learn more about different approaches to early childhood curriculum, it is essential to consider the similarities and differences in approaches. Deciding which approach is "best" is not a goal in our discussion. As Goffin (1994) suggests, we feel that it is important "to go beyond questions that ask 'what works best?' " (p. 27). Rather, we recognize the importance of examining how early childhood programs might be tailored to maximize the learning potential of children with differing characteristics (Goffin, 1994). We concur with current early childhood curriculum research that investigates the connections between the effects of different approaches and children's family environments (Goffin, 1994).

In Chapters 7 and 8 we discussed the importance of families and family involvement in early childhood programs. That is, we emphasized the need for schools and programs to adapt to different families and changes in family structures. Since we believe that the experiences that occur in a family context are critical when developing classroom experiences, we suggest that you think about the role that families play in each of the different approaches. At the end of this section, we have included questions about families for you to think about as you learn about each approach.

The history of curriculum approaches in early childhood education is also critical to consider when comparing different curricular approaches. At the end of the 20th century, early childhood programs are again viewed as being important in minimizing the impact of poverty and improving the chances of school success for all children. As educators, administrators, and policymakers continue to discuss the role of early education programs in social and educational arenas, we need to reflect on the social, political, and educational forces that have brought about the development and refinement of different curriculum approaches.

For example, the work of Hunt and Bloom in the early 1960s suggested that human intelligence could be modified and was influential in the emergence of Head Start and other early intervention programs. Developmental and educational psychologists then began to investigate whether early childhood was, in fact, a critical period for intellectual development and whether early childhood programs could compensate for disadvantaged environments (Goffin, 1994).

In Chapter 2, we discussed historical events that have had a lasting impact on the field of early childhood. As we compare and contrast four specific curriculum approaches in this chapter, we hope that you will think about how certain historical events continue to influence the implementation and refinement of these approaches. Figure 10.1 provides a summary of several historical influences on early childhood curriculum approaches.

Consider the following reflective questions as you read about each approach. The questions are provided to help you begin to understand the similarities and differences between and among the different approaches:

- Can you identify the type of curricular approach that was used in any of your early school experiences?
- Did the curricular approach that you experienced provide you with a positive experience?
- What roles are families expected to play in each approach?
- Are changes in family structure (i.e., single parents, children of divorced parents, nontraditional families) reflected in the expectations of the different approaches for family involvement?
- What family theoretical perspectives fit with the different approaches?

FIGURE 10.1   Summary of Historical Influences on Early Childhood Curriculum

Froebel

- Froebel conceptualized an established kindergarten in Germany.
- His beliefs about the importance of development and learning through self-activity and manipulation of objects influenced kindergarten programs in the late 19th century (Hewes, 1995).

Montessori

- Montessori developed curriculum designed to influence sensorimotor, intellectual, language, and moral development in the early 20th century (Weber, 1984).

Dewey

- Dewey's ideas on the social life of the community and democracy in the classroom caused early childhood educators to move away from a Froebelian approach.
- He believed that play was part of children's natural impulses and that children should have direct experiences with social and physical phenomena (Spodek, 1991).

The Child Development Movement

- This movement began to influence early childhood curriculum in the 1940s and 1950s. As a more scientific approach, the child development movement focused on stages of development and maturation as determinants of the types of experiences children should have in early education programs (Weber, 1984).

The 1960s and 1970s

- There was an increased interest in early childhood curriculum as research findings (Bloom, 1964; Hunt, 1961) suggested that intellectual development could be modified during the first 5 years of life. These findings, as well as the work of Piaget and Skinner, were used to support early intervention programs.
- A number of curriculum models for early childhood education were developed in university research centers or by private foundations as part of the planned variation curriculum models of Head Start and Follow Through. These models examined the effects of early intervention using different developmental orientations and beliefs about how and what to teach young children (Goffin, 1994).
- As different early education programs with different curricula were developed and disseminated to schools, teachers, and children, early childhood education was viewed as a way to help advance young children from low-income homes.

continues

FIGURE 10.1   *continued*

1980s and 1990s

- Early childhood programs with specific curricula experienced a period of limitation as federal and state funds declined (Goffin, 1994; Spodek, 1991).
- During the mid-1980s, many early childhood educators expressed concern about the academic focus, rigidity of curriculum, and standardization of programs in kindergarten and the primary grades. As public schools began to implement prekindergarten (4-year-olds) programs, early educators feared that the new programs would reflect existing public school programs designed for older children (Goffin, 1994).
- There was a major effort by NAEYC to promote DAP, which resulted in a successful attempt to reassert a developmental tradition into early childhood curriculum.
- In the early 1990s, early childhood programs expanded as early education was again viewed as a way to resolve social concerns such as the number of young children considered to be at risk of school failure, the increasing numbers of teenage mothers, and the number of employed mothers requiring child care for their children (Goffin, 1994).

THE MONTESSORI APPROACH

The Montessori approach is the oldest enduring approach that has withstood historical and societal changes as well as shifts in educational thought (Goffin, 1994). Montessori schools, both preschools and elementary schools, are now common in most American communities. Although many schools are private, the Montessori approach has increased tremendously in public school early childhood programs over the past decade (Morrison, 1997). Montessori schools vary widely, depending on the philosophy of the teachers and how closely a school tries to maintain the original philosophy.

As we discussed in Chapter 2, Montessori was a physician, anthropologist, and educator who believed that early education should be guided by a scientific approach. The Children's House in Italy was a very progressive approach for the early 20th century. In addition to such innovative methods as individual choice, mixed-aged grouping, and didactic materials, Montessori's original intent to serve the families and the community was a precursor to what we currently call a family resource center. Montessori's Children's House provided comprehensive childcare services that addressed children's nutritional and health-care needs. Montessori also advocated family involvement by opening the school to observation at any time, requiring parents to meet with their child's teacher at least once a week, and sending children home if they were unclean or unruly (Goffin, 1994).

Principles and Goals

One of the most important goals of Montessori education is recognizing the unique needs and capabilities of each individual child. Montessori believed that children should be given choices so that they can develop the skills and abilities necessary for effective learning, autonomy, and positive self-esteem (Morrison, 1997). Goffin (1994) summarized five recurring beliefs that dominate Montessori's writings:

> a) that her method represents a scientific approach to education; b) that the "secret of childhood" resides in the fact that through their spontaneous activity, children labor to "make themselves into men"; c) that mental development, similar to physical growth, is the result of a natural, internally regulated force; d) that liberty is the imperative ingredient that enables education to assist the "complete unfolding of (a child's) life"; and e) that order, most especially with the child, but also in the child's environment, is prerequisite to the child becoming an independent, autonomous, and rational individual (p. 49).

There has been a great deal written about the Montessori method, and Montessori herself wrote numerous works that have endured through time (e.g., Montessori, 1912/1964; 1949/1963; 1937/1966). In our description and explanation of the Montessori approach, we summarize the key concepts and ideas that are most commonly found in writings about the approach. We focus on the absorbent mind, sensitive periods, the prepared environment and auto-education.

The absorbent mind.   The concept of the *absorbent mind* pertains to the belief that mental growth, similar to physical growth, is the result of a natural, internally regulated force. Each child must educate herself rather than be educated by others. There are unconscious and conscious stages in the development of the absorbent mind (Lillard, 1972). From birth to 3 years of age, children are unconsciously absorbing all that is around them. Gradually, this process becomes conscious. The child's environment should be interesting and attractive since her personality is formed by absorbing what she finds in the world as a whole (Hainstock, 1986). According to Montessori, growth and development depend upon a continued narrowing of the relationships between a child and her environment. After taking in the world as a whole, the child then analyzes in the conscious stage. During the conscious stage, the child develops the ability to organize experiences and make generalizations such as distinguishing and matching colors (Morrison, 1997). The child constructs her mind in this way until, little by little, she has established memory, the power to understand, and the ability to reason. While the absorbent mind explains the quality and process by which the child acquires knowledge, the sensitive periods describe the pattern the child follows in gaining knowledge of her environment.

Sensitive periods.   The term *sensitive periods* refers to phases when children are more susceptible to certain behaviors and can learn specific skills more easily (Hainstock, 1986). Sensitive periods occur until a child is almost 5 years old during rapid physical, language, and cognitive growth (Morrison, 1997). During a sensitive period, the child: a) reacts in specific ways to certain stimuli; b) learns to adjust herself and make knowledge acquisitions; c) chooses what is suitable and necessary for growth from the complex environment; and d) absorbs one characteristic of her environment to the exclusion of all others (Hainstock, 1986; Lillard, 1972).

Montessori delineated sensitive periods in the child's life in areas such as the development of walking, the use of the hand and tongue (sensory and motor activity), and intense social interest. Sensory and motor activities were important to Montessori because of their contribution to the development of language. It is important to recognize sensitive periods in teaching because a child's desire to learn in the area of special sensitivity will be lost if she is prevented from following the interest that occurs in any given sensitive period (Lillard, 1972). Consequently, teachers must recognize sensitive periods when they occur and capitalize on them by providing the optimum learning setting to foster their development (Morrison, 1997).

The prepared environment and auto-education.   The purpose of the *prepared environment* is to enable children to be independent of adults. In the prepared environment, teachers arrange materials for instruction and demonstrate the procedures for using the materials. Children can then decide what materials they want to work with and how they want to work with them. This process leads children to organize their experiences and thinking through certain activities and consequently, educate themselves (Brewer, 1998; Morrison, 1997). Montessori referred to this process as *auto-education.* Since individual freedom is a key aspect of the Montessori philosophy, children will absorb the knowledge that they find in the environment when they are free to explore materials of their own choosing. According to Montessori, the prepared environment involves order, which is prerequisite to auto-education.

A prepared environment can be established in any setting such as a classroom or playground. In a prepared environment, the teacher is responsible for selecting and arranging the materials that encourage learning. Children can then ask questions and initiate activities. Montessori introduced child-sized furniture and lowered chalkboards, and created outside areas in which children could choose to participate in gardening and other outdoor activities (Goffin, 1994; Morrison, 1997). Montessori developed self-correcting materials so that the control of error guides the child in her use of the materials and permits her to recognize her own mistakes (Lillard, 1972). Specific characteristics of a prepared environment also include: a) everyday motor activities such as learning self-care skills; b) water activities in which children are taught to scrub tables and wash dishes to develop coordination; and c) practical life experiences such as polishing mirrors, dusting furniture, and peeling vegetables. As children become engaged in an activity, they gradually lengthen their span of concentration as they follow a regular sequence of actions and learn to pay attention to details (Morrison, 1997).

Criticisms of the Montessori approach.   As the Montessori method was embraced by more affluent families, many of the health, nutrition, and family

Montessori's prepared environment includes everyday activities such as scrubbing tables or washing dishes.

support components were omitted (Goffin, 1994). When the Montessori approach spread to other countries including the United States, the curriculum's focus tended to become more narrow. Montessori's followers focused primarily on her methods and materials rather than on a broader approach that included her beliefs about and understandings of young children. Many early childhood educators continue to express concern for the method's lack of interest in creative self-expression, the formality of the activities, the exact way in which children have to use the prepared materials, and the narrow scope of the curriculum (Feinburg & Mindess, 1994; Goffin, 1994; Weber, 1969).

Although Montessori has been recognized for her establishment of programs for "poor" families and a connection between the school and the community, Montessori programs in the United States do not commonly offer family and community involvement activities aimed at low-income children. Rather, Montessori programs typically address the needs of white, upper- and middle-income children. Currently, Montessori education continues to experience popularity in the United States although programs can vary widely and differences have surfaced among Montessori educators (Spodek, Saracho, & Davis, 1991). While the Montessori method has been an alternative to traditional early childhood programs for most of this century, there are few well-designed studies that have tested its effectiveness (Spodek, Saracho, & Davis, 1991). Typical experiences found during a day in a Montessori classroom are summarized in Box 10.1.

BOX 10.1 *A Typical Montessori Classroom for 3- to 6-Year-Olds*

A typical Montessori classroom for 3- to 6-year-olds incorporates language, mathematics, sensory-motor, and practical life centers as well as science, social studies, art, and computer areas. When students arrive (for example, between 8:15 and 8:30 A.M.), they participate in circle time to share stories and ideas. Since there is no set daily schedule, the remainder of the day is determined by student direction. Although each child has a voice in determining topics of study from day to day, writing, reading, mathematics, sensory exploration, and practical life skills are the primary areas of exploration and study.

A typical language activity consists of a set of geometric insets. Since writing is always done on a table, a child removes the geometric insets from a shelf to the table without waiting for teacher direction. The child, Marina, uses the frame and inset to create a geometric design of her choice. When the design is completed, she fills in the design with straight lines using colored pencils. Upon completion, Marina files her paper in her own file so that it can be made into a booklet or sent home at the end of the week.

Another language activity involves spelling and sentence construction. Marina takes a set of word pictures and a movable alphabet cabinet to the carpet. She then constructs a sentence using a picture card and portable letters. Her sentence is: "The man is fat." After Marina has constructed the sentence, she practices writing it and takes paper and pencil to the table, writes the sentence, and files it in her file.

At approximately 10:15 A.M., Marina chooses to take a break and have a snack. Marina is never forced to take a break and she can have her snack by herself or with other children. After the snack, Marina goes to the practical life area and polishes a table. Polishing the table incorporates gross motor development, as well as the setup of material in a specific order from left to right. Marina removes the materials herself, completes the task, and cleans up independently. This activity typically takes 15 minutes to complete.

Marina then goes to the math center and works for about 10 minutes with another student on an addition task. The two students set up an addition strip board and find as many ways as possible to construct "nine." Following the math activity, Marina joins a directed group lesson of six children and her "directress," or teacher. Each child is given a reading booklet. The children discuss the pictures and then read the story. The purpose of this activity is to encourage listening, sequencing, and comprehension skills. This activity typically takes 15 minutes to complete.

At approximately 11:00 A.M., the children play outside for 20 minutes. During the outside time, they have the opportunity to participate in free play and a directed movement experience that may include jumping rope or catching a ball. Children may also participate in nature walks or other types of field activities.

As Marina finishes playing outside, she joins her other classmates in a circle activity inside with her directress. The students typically sing songs, engage in finger plays and poetry readings, and play musical instruments. The circle time also encourages children to talk about topics of interest to the entire class. A child is not obligated to join the circle, and

continues

BOX 10.1	*A Typical Montessori Classroom for 3- to 6-Year-Olds continued*

may continue with a task while others are participating in circle time. However, most children want to join the circle since they have been working independently or at their own pace all morning long. Circle time typically takes 20 minutes to complete.

An hour-long lunch follows circle time. As part of the practical life aspect of the Montessori approach, Marina is responsible for setting the table, getting her own lunch, and cleaning up. Following lunch, Marina checks her work folder to determine whether or not she has any unfinished work. If there is no unfinished work, the directress suggests several things for her to do. On this particular day, Marina follows the directress's suggestion

to work with the geometry cabinet. This activity involves matching a set of cards to their corresponding geometric shapes.

While Marina is working with geometric designs, other children choose to nap. Each child is free to rest when he or she wants to since there is no attempt to force a rest period upon a child. Marina usually does not choose to rest. Upon completion of the geometric task, Marina chooses to paint at an easel. After painting, Marina participates in another directed activity that lasts about 30 minutes. The school day ends at 3:00 P.M. Because the class is a "community," each child is responsible for cleaning up at the end of each school day.

THE BEHAVIORIST APPROACH

Principles and Goals

The behaviorist approach to curriculum in early childhood education is rooted in the psychological theories of Pavlov, Watson, Thorndike, and Skinner. Behaviorism focuses on the influence of the environment in behavioral development. In a behaviorist approach, it is theorized that human behavior is learned as a result of the consequences of a specific behavior. Whenever a behavior is followed by positive consequences (reward), that behavior becomes stronger because it has been positively reinforced. If, on the other hand, a behavior is followed by no reinforcement (extinction) or by aversive events (punishment), that behavior is weakened (Todd, 1994; Weber, 1984).

Teachers often attempt to provide positive and negative consequences after a given child behavior. Consequently, behaviors can be changed rapidly when a teacher is systematic about providing consequences. The circumstances that exist when a behavior is reinforced become cues or signals for the behavior. These cues or signals are known as *stimulus control prompts.* Teachers can devise special signals to deliberately prompt specific behaviors. For example, teachers often use signals such as showing a picture of a green light, holding their hand in the air, or ringing a bell to "cue" children to pay attention, begin work, put away toys, and talk or not talk to one another.

Behavior analysis refers to the identification of the circumstances surrounding a behavior, such as the events before, during, and after the behavior (Todd, 1994). *Behavior modification* refers to the process of building and changing behavior (Weber, 1984). According to behaviorists, environmental circumstances play a pivotal role for behavioral development in early childhood education. Basic principles of behaviorism can be used to arrange environments to help children learn and grow intentionally (Weber, 1984). Teachers must think about providing a learning environment that offers predictable reinforcements of positive behavior and little or no support for negative behaviors (Morrison, 1997). In a behaviorist early childhood classroom, the teacher becomes a kind of engineer who manipulates environmental circumstances to measure, influence, or change behavior, and document the progress in changing child behavior (Weber, 1984).

The behaviorist curriculum approach in early childhood education emerged from B. F. Skinner's work on conceptualizing operant conditioning, or the idea of successive approximations (Goffin, 1994; Weber, 1984). In operant conditioning, emphasis is placed on environmental factors that increase, decrease, or maintain the rate of occurrence of specific behaviors (Alberto & Troutman, 1995). Operant conditioners are concerned primarily with the consequences of behavior and the establishment of relationships between behavior and consequences (Weber, 1984). If unwanted behavior is rewarded by unplanned reinforcement, then the unwanted behavior can be accidentally reinforced. In a behaviorist classroom, the environment is critical to modifying existing behavior through the use of positive and negative reinforcement (Goffin, 1994; Weber, 1984).

Behaviorism Applied to Early Childhood Education

As we discussed in Chapter 2, the notion that young children's intelligence could be modified by the environment emerged in the early 1960s when Hunt and Bloom published their work demonstrating the effects of environmental interventions. Behaviorism was applied to early childhood curriculum through the development of the *Direct Instruction* program model when models were developed for Head Start and Follow Through in the 1960s. Unlike most other program models, Direct Instruction was not built from child-development theories. The Direct Instruction model emerged from theories of instructional psychology, instructional design, and educational learning theory (Goffin, 1994). These theories explain behavioral changes and individual differences in terms of learning rather than development.

Direct instruction as a curriculum approach.   The Direct Instruction approach was originally established as a curriculum model in the mid-1960s by Bereiter and Engelmann (1966). This model was based on what is currently viewed as a "deficit model" for early education. Specifically, the model was established to address the needs of young children from economically disadvantaged homes who were believed to be "culturally deprived." This line of thinking reflected the premise that children from low-income families were deprived of adequate learning experiences and entered school with fewer intellectual skills and concepts than their advantaged peers (Goffin, 1994). This concept was a common explanation for the difference between performance levels of low-income and middle-class children in the 1960s. The approach is also based on the assumption that lower performing children could catch up with their more advantaged peers if their instructional programs were designed to teach more academic skills in less time.

Bereiter and Engelmann's curriculum aimed at stimulating children's cognitive development broadly and was designed to teach disadvantaged children 15 skills necessary for school success (White & Buka, 1987). The curriculum provided 18 "basic teaching strategies that have application in the preschool for culturally deprived children" (Bereiter & Engelmann, 1966, p. 120). The Direct Instruction approach is based on the belief that children can be taught competencies more rapidly if teachers are provided with well-planned educational procedures, such as pre-tested curriculum materials (Becker, Engelmann, Carnine, & Rhine, 1981). Teachers in the approach use small-group methods of instruction to present carefully sequenced daily lessons in reading, mathematics, and language. In a Direct Instruction kindergarten, these lessons are presented in a step-by-step manner to achieve the goal of student success in first grade.

According to Becker et al. (1981), the Direct Instruction model was derived from empirical behavior theory, logical analysis of concepts and tasks, and logical analysis of the use of resources in the classroom. The Direct Instruction model was published under the trade name *DISTAR* in the 1960s. DISTAR provided teaching procedures for eliciting and maintaining childrens' attention, securing their responses, and dispensing reinforcers (Goffin, 1994). It also offered guidance in classroom organization and management procedures for regulating the verbal behavior of teachers and children, and described ways to monitor children's academic progress and use reinforcers to encourage the acquisition of desirable behaviors.

Most early childhood educators associate scripted lessons and behavioral principles such as reinforcement, conditioned responses, stimulus control, prompting, and shaping with the Direct Instruction approach. Although the primary focus of the approach is on children's achievement, the original designers did acknowledge an interest in promoting children's affective and social development. However, the lack of attention to experiences that facilitate social and emotional growth has been a major criticism of the approach.

Many early childhood educators have long expressed a concern about a curriculum that was conceptualized by educational and behavioral psychologists rather than by developmental psychologists (Goffin, 1994). Some of the early applications of the behaviorist approach to preschool programs were char-

FIGURE 10.2 Description of Typical Experiences Found in Behaviorist Classrooms

A Direct Instruction classroom is organized to maximize drill and practice. Typically, rows of desks face a blackboard to facilitate large-group instruction. A specified amount of time is allotted for academic areas such as reading, English, spelling, mathematics, science, and social studies. Art and music may also be included. Lessons in each of the academic areas follow a teacher's guide or manual and can be characterized as structured. Students are expected to make appropriate or correct responses to teacher questions that have been planned before the lesson takes place. A Direct Instruction lesson consists of the following sequential steps:

1. *Review previously learned material.* In a lesson on plants, the teacher may review the parts of the plant discussed in a previous lesson before introducing the functions of different plant parts.

2. *State the objective of the lesson.* The teacher states the objective at the beginning of the lesson following the review. In the plant lesson, the teacher might say "Today we are going to identify the functions of leaves and roots."

3. *Present new material.* The new material is sequentially organized and presented in an engaging manner. During the presentation of new material, the teacher checks for student understanding. In the plant lesson, the teacher provides a clear and detailed description of the functions of leaves and roots. Frequent and varied examples are continually provided during the presentation.

4. *Conduct guided practice.* The teacher leads students through practice activities by providing feedback on correct and incorrect student responses. When conducting guided practice on the functions of plant parts, the teacher might say "Find the root of the plant, now show me where the root absorbs water that helps the plant grow."

5. *Provide independent practice.* The teacher allows the student to work independently, while checking for errors. Homework is provided if the teacher feels that the students can practice independently.

6. *Review periodically with corrective feedback to assure that knowledge is retained.* The teacher periodically administers different types of tests to see whether students remember the content knowledge that was originally taught.

acterized by teacher-directed, fast-paced, task-oriented lessons that emphasized drill and "repeated trial" sessions that were sometimes perceived to be similar to animal training (Goffin, 1994). It is important to remember that there are effective teaching methods and materials developed by behaviorists that can be used appropriately as well as inappropriately. Many teachers of young children use parts of the behaviorist approach when teaching specific concepts and skills or when devising techniques to manage inappropriate classroom behaviors. A description of typical experiences found in a behaviorist classroom are summarized in Figure 10.2.

Direct Instruction as an example of the behaviorist approach was originally devised for young children who were identified by educators as being at-risk for academic success. The approach was not designed to address the needs of families and assumes that all at-risk children enter early education programs with deficits. Currently, Direct Instruction is criticized for its lack of flexibility and adaptability to children from different cultural and family backgrounds. Direct Instruction provides no linkage to the family or community. The approach assumes that all academic learning takes place in school and does not provide for family input or participation in a child's educational program. Debates about the most appropriate curriculum for at-risk young children continue to focus on the question: Do all children thrive with similar learning experiences or do the needs of low-income children necessitate an academic curriculum that is structured and predetermined?

THE CONSTRUCTIVIST APPROACH

The constructivist approach to early childhood curriculum is based on Piaget's theory and contends that children actually construct their own knowledge of the world as well as their level of cognitive development. A constructivist teacher believes that children do this through active physical and mental activity. Processes that learners use to construct their own knowledge include active involvement with a variety of manipulative materials in problem-solving experiences and through interactions with others. The constructivist approach also incorporates Piaget's beliefs by encouraging the processes of assimilation, accommodation, and disequilibrium.

The constructivist approach can be linked to the translation of Piagetian theory into curriculum approaches by researchers and educators during the 1960s and 1970s. There are three influential preschool programs that connected Piagetian theory and practice: Lavatelli's (1970) *Early Childhood Curriculum: A Piaget Program;* the High/Scope *Cognitively Oriented Curriculum* (Weikart, Rogers, Adcock, & McClelland, 1971; Hohmann, Banet, & Weikart, 1979); and the Kamii-DeVries approach (Kamii & DeVries, 1976, 1977, 1978, 1980).

All of these programs incorporated ideas from Piaget's theory. Each program is based on the beliefs that children's thinking is different from that of adults and that cognitive development occurs in an invariant sequence of qualitatively different stages (DeVries & Kohlberg, 1987). DeVries & Kohlberg (1987) identify four points of agreement among the three programs:

- All contend that a basic objective to be drawn from Piaget's work is to foster structural change in children's reasoning in the direction of operational thought.
- All emphasize the fundamental importance of the child's action for learning and development.
- All borrow ideas from the child development tradition in early education for materials, equipment, and activities that permit children to be active (for example, painting and other art activities, block building, pretend play, singing, and sand and water play).

- None of the three Piagetian programs is just "Piagetian." Each recognizes certain limitations in using Piaget's theory alone as a basis for educational practice (DeVries and Kohlberg, 1987).

All of these approaches have been successful and can serve as specific examples of programs developed through the translation of Piagetian theory. For the purposes of this chapter, we focus on only one application—the Kamii-DeVries view of constructivism as an example of a constructivist approach.

Principles and Goals of the Kamii-DeVries Curriculum Approach

Because of the complexity of the Kamii-DeVries constructivist approach, we summarize only some of its key aspects in this section. The Kamii-DeVries approach is derived from Kamii's work in the 1960s and 1970s in which she used Piaget's theory as a framework for developing a cognitively oriented preschool curriculum. The Kamii-DeVries approach uses Piaget's theory for incorporating cognitive development into early education in a way that is compatible with early educators' beliefs that teaching and learning are interactive and developmental (Goffin, 1994).

The Kamii-DeVries approach is based on their belief that Piaget's theory has implications for children's moral, social, affective, and cognitive development (DeVries & Zan, 1995; Goffin, 1994). This constructivist orientation considers the development of social skills, personality, and self-esteem as critical to children's active involvement with their environment. The approach encourages cooperative activities for the purpose of respecting the feelings and rights of others and coordinating different points of view (decentering and cooperating) (DeVries & Kohlberg, 1987). Kamii and DeVries believe that a focus only on cognitive development is too narrow and neglects concern with motivation or personality (DeVries & Kohlberg, 1987; DeVries & Zan, 1995).

This constructivist perspective goes beyond early Piagetian programs that focused primarily on cognitively oriented tasks such as experiments with conservation of liquid (Lavatelli, 1970). The Kamii-DeVries approach believes that it is important to identify stages of cognitive development within daily classroom activities rather than focus solely on tasks that are unrelated to children's interests (DeVries & Zan, 1995; Goffin, 1994; Kamii & DeVries, 1976, 1977). In the Kamii-DeVries approach, children are encouraged to think for themselves, while teachers should be knowledgeable about their developmental theory. Teachers can then use the theory to understand how and if children are progressing as they learn in their own ways.

Two primary program components of the Kamii-DeVries approach are *physical knowledge activities* and *group games*. Physical knowledge activities "involve the child's action on and observation of the reactions of objects in the physical world" (DeVries & Kolberg, 1987, p. 91). Activities considered to be valuable to the construction of physical knowledge help children acquire knowledge of classification schemes and may involve the movement of objects and changes in objects. Physical knowledge activities that encourage actions on objects to make them move might include pulling, pushing, rolling, kicking, jumping, balancing, or dropping (DeVries & Zan, 1995). Activities involving changes include cooking, mixing paints, and freezing and thawing water. A third category of activities that share elements of action on objects and change in objects includes shadow play and sinking-and-floating objects. Many physical knowledge activities are often associated with typical science activities found in many preschool and primary classrooms. A description of a typical Kamii-DeVries physical knowledge activity involving moving objects is presented in Box 10.2.

A central purpose of group games is to promote children's adaptation to the social world. Group games are interactions during which children play together according to conventional rules that specify how players relate to each other and the preestablished result that is to be achieved (Goffin, 1994). Kamii and DeVries describe specific rules in which players assume roles that are interdependent, opposed, and collaborative (DeVries & Kohlberg, 1987; Kamii & DeVries, 1980). In the Kamii-DeVries approach, group games promote autonomy by giving children freedom to choose to follow or not follow rules, reflect on the consequences, and

Physical knowledge activities encourage actions on objects to make them move.

BOX 10.2	*Description of a Typical Kamii-DeVries Constructivist Activity*

A PHYSICAL-KNOWLEDGE ACTIVITY IN-VOLVING MOVING OBJECTS. In physical-knowledge activities, the purpose is for children to act on objects to see how they react or try to produce particular effects, and to structure observations of reactions. The following excerpt from a blowing activity illustrates the typical way in which opportunities occur to promote classificatory reasoning within the context of objectives pertaining to general cognitive development, and alongside other specific objectives.

In a blowing activity, for example, if the child tries to move a straw across the floor by blowing it with another straw, he finds out that he has to blow in the middle at a right angle to make it go straight. As a function of where one blows relative to the center of the straw, it turns more or less to the right or to the left, sometimes turning a complete 360 degrees. As the child sees how the straw reacts to different actions, he structures spatial and logical relationships. How this happens can be seen more clearly in the following description of a blowing activity. After giving each child a straw, Ms. Ellis showed them a box containing several of each of the following items: Kleenex, round Tinker Toys, popsicle sticks, straws, empty cans (frozen orange juice and one-pound coffee cans), marbles, and small blocks. She said, "Can you find something that you can blow across the floor?" This question prompted the children to look at objects with their "blowability" in mind and to think, at some vague, intuitive level, about considerations such as the following: Is the object's weight relevant? Is its shape important? Are both important? How can we find out?

These questions illustrate the logico-mathematical structuring that takes place during a physical-knowledge activity. The child constructs logico-mathematical structures in the course of structuring specific contents. In this blowing activity, the child has an opportunity to create at least three categories—"things that *never* move" (a block), "things that *always* move" (a Kleenex, marble, straw, and popsicle stick), and "things that *sometimes* move" (an orange juice can and tinker toy which move only when they are in a certain position). In addition, the child may observe that certain objects move by sliding, certain objects move by rolling, and still others (such as a straw) move in both ways. A classificatory scheme also becomes necessary to put into correspondence the result of blowing in the middle and the results of blowing on other parts of the straw. With this classificatory scheme the child can conclude that the only way to make the straw go straight is by blowing in the middle.

DeVries, R., & Kohlberg, L. (1987). *Programs of Early Education: A Constructivist View.* Longman, Inc: New York.

eventually grow to understand that the reasons for the rules are rooted in maintaining desired relations with others (DeVries & Zan, 1995; Goffin, 1994).

Games that are beneficial to children provide something interesting and challenging for them to figure out. Playing games allows children to determine their own success, and permits them to participate actively throughout the game. Teachers need to reduce their use of authority by encouraging children to regulate the games themselves (DeVries & Zan, 1995; Goffin, 1994). The Kamii-DeVries constructivist approach also addresses logico-mathematical knowledge by outlining specific techniques to teach children mathematical concepts such as numbers (Kamii & DeClark, 1985; Kamii & DeVries, 1976; Kamii & Joseph, 1989).

Children need to focus on "number" in routine situations in which number is a natural issue in order to construct logical-mathematical knowledge. For example, distributing materials, dividing objects, collecting things, keeping records, and cleaning up all provide opportunities to focus on number. In these situations, children should be asked to figure out the relationships involved. Some of the group games developed by Kamii and DeVries involve number by using boards, dice, and spinners.

The role of the teacher.

Teachers need to provide a supportive environment in which children are allowed to make decisions and rely on others to facilitate their thinking (DeVries & Zan, 1995). The teacher acts as a facilitator who creates equal relationships with children. It is critical that teachers be very knowledgeable about Piaget's theory so they can encourage children to progress to higher developmental levels of reasoning. Through a rich knowledge base of development, teachers can assess children's spontaneous activity, provide appropriate learning activities, and ask questions that will extend children's ideas and stimulate their reasoning (Goffin, 1994). In the Kamii-DeVries approach, the teacher respects what children know and allows them to construct personal interpretations and rules of behavior.

A constructivist approach to early childhood curriculum found in today's early childhood programs differs from the earlier Piagetian approaches established in the 1960s and 1970s. According to Kamii and DeVries, their approach represents a faithful implementation of Piaget's ideas (Goffin, 1994) because of its theoretical soundness. The Kamii-DeVries approach is also dependent upon the validity of Piaget's theory as an explanation for human development in general, and cognitive development in particular (Goffin, 1994).

In terms of diversity, the constructivist approach does provide for attention to individual needs in which both the child and the teacher respond to ideas, concepts, and themes developed by others. Since the approach is child-centered and focuses on the child's immediate environment, interests, and past experiences, the teacher has many opportunities to include relevant ethnic and cultural elements in the lesson (King, Chipman, & Cruz-Janzen, 1994). It is important to remember that

Piagetian theory was developed, normed, and tested on white, middle-class children. Consequently, the constructivist approach reflects the majority societal values, attitudes, and customs (King, Chipman, & Cruz-Janzen, 1994).

The constructivist approach allows for the involvement of families. As we have discussed previously, the approach encourages children to bring experiences from the home and community into the classroom. In most applications of the constructivist approach, families are encouraged to participate in classroom activities in traditional ways (i.e., parent volunteers, parent-teacher conferences).

Since the constructivist approach is so closely associated with Piaget and a traditional developmental approach, it is widely accepted by developmental psychologists and early childhood educators. As with all of the approaches we have presented, many teachers of young children use specific pieces or aspects of the approach in combination with other approaches. Developmentally appropriate practice, which will be discussed in the next section, is closely aligned to many of the key principles and ideas of the constructivist approach.

DEVELOPMENTALLY APPROPRIATE PRACTICE APPROACH

As we discussed in Chapter 3, developmentally appropriate practice (DAP) refers to the long-standing belief among early childhood educators that knowledge about child development, with the child as the primary source of the curriculum, should be the basis for making decisions about early childhood practices (Hart, Burts, & Charlesworth, 1997). In this section, we focus on the curriculum component of the position statement developed by the National Association for the Education of Young Children (NAEYC) in 1987 (Bredekamp, 1987) and NAEYC in 1997 (Bredekamp & Copple, 1997), as well as on two documents on appropriate curriculum and assessment developed by NAEYC (Bredekamp & Rosegrant, 1992, 1996).

Although the guidelines for developmentally appropriate practice are not considered to be the same type of curriculum approach as the Montessori, behaviorist, and constructivist approaches, we present the DAP guidelines because they are referred to or used in some fashion in many early childhood programs. The curriculum guidelines also continue to be discussed and debated among and between early childhood professionals (Lubeck, 1998). When the original DAP document was developed and published in 1987, many early childhood educators expressed concern about an overemphasis on formal instruction in public preschool and kindergarten programs (Bredekamp, 1987). The DAP document was an attempt to reassert the early childhood profession's developmental tradition into curriculum (Hart, Burts, & Charlesworth, 1997; Goffin, 1994). DAP curriculum guidelines assume a cognitive/interactive theory of intellectual development derived primarily from the work of Piaget (Kessler, 1991). We include developmentally appropriate curriculum guidelines in Tips for Teachers 10.1.

TIPS FOR TEACHERS 10.1

Constructing Appropriate Curriculum Following Developmentally Appropriate Practice Guidelines

- Provide for all areas of a child's development: physical, emotional, social, linguistic, aesthetic, and cognitive.
- Include a broad range of content across disciplines that is socially relevant, intellectually engaging, and personally meaningful to children.
- Build upon what children already know and are able to do (activate prior knowledge) to consolidate their learning and foster their acquisition of new concepts and skills.
- Frequently integrate curriculum plans across traditional subject-matter divisions to help children make meaningful connections and provide opportunities for rich conceptual development; focusing on one subject is also a valid strategy at times.
- Promote the development of knowledge and understanding, processes and skills, as well as the dispositions to use and apply skills and to go on learning.
- Provide curriculum content that has intellectual integrity, reflecting the key concepts and tools of inquiry of recognized disciplines in ways that are accessible and achievable for young

children, ages 3 through 8 (e.g., Bredekamp & Rosegrant 1992, 1996). Children should directly participate in study of the disciplines, for instance, by conducting scientific experiments, writing, performing, solving mathematical problems, collecting and analyzing data, collecting oral history, and performing other roles of experts in the disciplines.
- Provide opportunities to support children's home culture and language while also developing all children's abilities to participate in the shared culture of the program and community.
- Develop curriculum goals that are realistic and attainable for most children in the designated age range for which they are designed.
- Use technology that is physically and philosophically integrated in the classroom curriculum and teaching.

Bredekamp. S., & Copple, C. (Eds.). (1997). *Developmentally Appropriate Practice in Early Childhood Programs.* (Revised Edition). Washington, DC: National Association for the Education of Young Children.

Principles and Goals

The developmentally appropriate guidelines for curriculum are based on the belief that high-quality early childhood programs provide a safe and nurturing environment that promotes the physical, social, emotional, and cognitive development of young children while considering a child's gender, cultural background, ability, and family (Hart, Burts, & Charlesworth, 1997). According to DAP curriculum guidelines, program quality is determined by the extent to which knowledge about how children develop and learn is applied in program practices (Bredekamp & Copple, 1997). Developmental appropriateness results from the process of professionals making decisions about the well-being and education of children based on at least three types of information or knowledge:

- What is known about child development and learning;
- What is known about the strengths, interests, and needs of each individual child in the group; and
- What is known about the social and cultural contexts in which children live (Bredekamp & Copple, 1997).

Information about child development and learning is based on knowledge of human characteristics. Based on this information, general predictions within an age range are made about what activities, materials, interactions, or experiences will be interesting, healthy, safe, achievable, and challenging to children (Bredekamp & Copple, 1997). Consequently, in a program that employs DAP curriculum guidelines, teachers apply their knowledge of typical development to identify the range of appropriate behaviors, activities, and materials for a specific age group. When teachers are knowledgeable about the strengths, interests, and needs of each individual child in the group, they are able to adapt for and be responsive to individual variation. A DAP curriculum is responsive to individual differences and, at the same time, provides experiences that match the child's developing abilities. Knowledge of the social and cultural contexts in which children live ensures that learning experiences are meaningful, relevant and respectful for children and their families (Bredekamp & Copple, 1997; Charlesworth, 1998). According to DAP, teachers design the most appropriate learning environment based on their understanding of individual children's growth patterns, strengths, and interests while attending to each individual child's family, cultural, and community background (Bredekamp, 1991; Charlesworth, 1998).

The role of the teacher   A central role of the teacher in a DAP curriculum is to prepare the environment, and then observe, guide, and facilitate so that children are continually challenged and supported to construct new understandings for themselves (Charlesworth, 1998; Kessler, 1991). In a DAP curriculum, children's play is an essential means for mental growth. DAP guidelines stress that children develop intellectually, socially, physically, and emotionally through play. Therefore, child-initiated, child-directed, and teacher-supported play is a primary component of developmentally appropriate practice (Charlesworth, 1998). Box 10.3 describes a typical day in a developmentally appropriate classroom.

A curriculum framework for developmentally appropriate practice is outlined in the NAEYC document *Reaching potentials: Appropriate curriculum*

Family involvement is an important aspect of the Developmentally Appropriate Practice approach.

and assessment for young children, Vol. 1 (Bredekamp & Rosegrant, 1992). These more specific curriculum guidelines emphasize the themes of age-appropriateness and individual-appropriateness, and include providing play activities, choosing content based on children's interests, focusing on issues of diversity, and developing activities that build upon children's prior knowledge. The guidelines also highlight the fact that an integrated, thematic curriculum approach is essential to designing a developmentally appropriate curriculum. The NAEYC guidelines for appropriate curriculum content are provided in Figure 10.3.

Integrated curriculum.   The term *integrated curriculum* refers to activities and experiences that teach content from multiple disciplines such as mathematics, science, social studies, the arts, and language and literacy at the same time. According to the guidelines for appropriate curriculum, the concept of integration comes from the integrated nature of development (Bredekamp & Rosegrant, 1992). That is, what happens in one domain of development such as cognitive growth also influences the domains of physical and emotional development. Integrated curriculum includes a number of strategies that can be used

BOX 10.3 — *A Typical Day in a Developmentally Appropriate Prekindergarten Class*

A typical day begins by engaging children in interactions with peers and their environment. As children come into the classroom, they are allowed to choose an activity to work on until all of the class members have arrived. When all the children have arrived, the class participates in circle time activities. These activities include discussing the calendar, singing, and sharing time. For sharing time, children are encouraged to share personal news such as taking a family trip or experiencing the birth of a sibling. For example, one prekindergarten student, Leroy, shares the news about the birth of his new baby brother. After sharing, the teacher leads a discussion about the activities that have been organized for the day.

After circle time, Leroy moves to group time where children work with reading and writing activities and experiences related to the theme "All About Me," which the class is currently investigating. Leroy's teacher supports the whole language philosophy. As a teacher who follows developmentally appropriate curriculum guidelines, she believes that all areas of knowledge need to be integrated meaningfully and naturally. During group time, Leroy and his classmates will participate in integrated reading and writing activities such as shared reading, guided reading, partner reading, and process writing.

After approximately 50 minutes of group activities, Leroy and his classmates choose activities from a variety of learning centers. Learning center activities provide hands-on projects that vary from active to quiet and small group to large group, and employ small muscles to large muscles. Typical learning centers that are always available include a block area; manipulative games that focus on classifying, sorting, and number and letter identification; a housekeeping area; a reading and writing center; an easel for painting; and a sand-and-water table. Each child chooses the center he or she likes to go to and is encouraged to engage in meaningful play, interact with peers, solve problems, and pose questions about the materials in the centers.

Following center time, the teacher involves the children in music and movement activities for about 25 minutes. During these activities, children may listen to music, sing songs, play instruments, dance, or move freely. Children then walk to lunch in the cafeteria where they are encouraged to socialize for approximately 25 minutes. When the children finish eating, they are responsible for cleaning their eating area before using the bathroom and returning to their classroom.

When Leroy and his classmates return to the classroom, they work with mathematics materials for 30 minutes. They typically work with unifix cubes, pattern blocks, clay, buttons, and literature books to apply mathematical concepts such as sorting, classifying, counting, and comparing. Leroy then draws in his journal and writes about what his family did at home the night before. Since family involvement is important to Leroy's teacher, she attempts to facilitate family support and participation by asking Leroy to take his journal home each day and ask family members to help him record daily happenings in the home.

continues

BOX 10.3   *A Typical Day in a Developmentally Appropriate Prekindergarten Class* continued

After journal writing, Leroy and his class-mates participate in a quiet time for 30 minutes. During quiet time, children can silently read on a mat or lay quietly. Following quiet time, children have a snack and listen to a story and then play outside for 30 minutes. The last activity before going home is an-other circle time in which the teacher discusses activities that children participated in during the day. When children are dismissed to go home, Leroy's teacher attempts to say something encouraging and positive to each child as he or she walks out of the classroom.

to enhance meaningfulness and support conceptual development (Bredekamp & Rosegrant, 1992). We discuss specific strategies such as webbing across themes or content disciplines (Krogh, 1990) that can be used to develop an integrated curriculum in Chapter 13.

According to the appropriate curriculum guidelines, an integrated curriculum needs to address skill and concept development in different content disciplines such as mathematics. Additionally, an integrated curriculum needs to have "intellectual integrity" (Bredekamp & Rosegrant, 1992). Intellectual integrity means that activities and experiences are not trivial or meaningless; rather, they are relevant to knowledge found in content disciplines.

The document *Reaching potentials: Transforming early childhood curriculum and assessment, Vol. 2* (Bredekamp & Rosegrant, 1996) also addresses the need to teach skills and content in a meaningful context. Specific guidelines for content knowledge in mathematics, science, health, visual arts, music, social studies, physical education, and language and literacy are provided in this volume. The Volume 2 guidelines build on Volume 1, describing what content is of most worth, what content goals are accepted by educators in the disciplines (and have the greatest intellectual integrity), and what content goals are realistic and attainable for children of different ages (Bredekamp & Rosegrant, 1996). Separate disciplines establish a foundation for young children's knowledge acquisition by: 1) defining branches of knowledge; 2) providing systems for designing and organizing knowledge; 3) providing key concepts; and 4) providing perspectives on understanding the social, physical, and biological world. The Volume 2 guidelines also include the national standards that were developed in the early 1990s for all of the disciplines except language arts. The national standards delineate the knowledge that is considered to be essential for young children to learn in each of the disciplines.

FIGURE 10.3   NAEYC Guidelines for Curriculum Content

1. The curriculum has an articulated description of its theoretical base that is consistent with prevailing professional opinion and research on how children learn.

2. Curriculum content is designed to achieve long-range goals for children in all domains—social, emotional, cognitive, and physical—and to prepare children to function as fully contributing members of a democratic society.

3. Curriculum addresses the development of knowledge and understanding, processes and skills, dispositions and attitudes.

4. Curriculum addresses a broad range of content that is relevant, engaging, and meaningful to children.

5. Curriculum goals are realistic and attainable for most children in the designated age range for which they were designed.

6. Curriculum content reflects and is generated by the needs and interests of individual children within the group. Curriculum incorporates a wide variety of learning experiences, materials and equipment, and instructional strategies to accommodate a broad range of children's individual differences in prior experience, maturation rates, styles of learning, needs, and interests.

7. Curriculum respects and supports individual, cultural, and linguistic diversity. Curriculum supports and encourages positive relationships with children's families.

8. Curriculum builds upon what children already know and are able to do (activating prior knowledge) to consolidate their learning and to foster their acquisition of new concepts and skills.

9. Curriculum provides conceptual frameworks for children so that their mental constructions based on prior knowledge and experience become more complex over time.

10. Curriculum allows for focus on a particular topic or content while allowing for integration across traditional subject-matter divisions by planning around themes and/or learning experiences that provide opportunities for rich conceptual development.

11. Curriculum content has intellectual integrity; content meets the recognized standards of the relevant subject-matter disciplines.

12. Curriculum content is worth knowing; curriculum respects children's intelligence and does not waste their time.

13. Curriculum engages children actively, not passively, in the learning process. Children have opportunities to make meaningful choices.

14. Curriculum values children's constructive errors and does not prematurely limit exploration and experimentation for the sake of ensuring "right" answers.

15. Curriculum emphasizes the development of children's thinking, reasoning, decision making, and problem-solving abilities.

16. Curriculum emphasizes the value of social interaction to learning in all domains and provides opportunities to learn from peers.

continues

FIGURE 10.3 *continued*

17. Curriculum is supportive of children's physiological needs for activity, sensory stimulation, fresh air, rest, hygiene, and nourishment/elimination.

18. Curriculum protects children's psychological safety, that is, children feel happy, relaxed, and comfortable rather than disengaged, frightened, worried, or stressed.

19. Curriculum strengthens children's sense of competence and enjoyment of learning by providing experiences for children to succeed from their point of view.

20. Curriculum is flexible so that teachers can adapt to individual children or groups.

Bredekamp, S., & Rosegrant, T. (Eds.). (1996). *Reaching Potentials Through Appropriate Curriculum and Assessment.* (Vol. 2). Washington, DC: National Association for the Education of Young Children.

Since developmentally appropriate practice is so widely accepted as a framework for curriculum planning and implementation in early childhood programs, it is important for anyone who works with young children to become an "expert" on the approach. You can use Checklist 10.1 to help you determine whether or not a classroom is using a developmentally appropriate curriculum.

We use developmentally appropriate practice as a framework for curriculum planning and implementation in the remaining chapters of this text. However, it is important to note that there have been criticisms of the approach in the last 10 years. In some instances, teachers of young children have implemented an "integrated" curriculum that includes meaningless and trivial activities that lack a foundation in the content area disciplines (Bredekamp & Rosegrant, 1996). This lack of "intellectual integrity" has caused concern since children may leave early childhood programs lacking in foundational concept knowledge.

Since DAP provides a broader framework and philosophy than the other three approaches we have discussed, DAP addresses adult-child interactions, diversity issues, and inclusion of families in the day-to-day curriculum more explicitly. In Tips for Teachers 10.2, we provide suggestions for positive adult-child and child-child interactions that help develop the creation of a caring community of learners. As you read the next three chapters on specific components of early childhood curriculum, keep thinking about how DAP and the other approaches we discussed can be integrated into programs for young children.

CHECKLIST 10.1

Is This a Developmentally Appropriate Curriculum?

When observing an early childhood classroom, or preparing your own classroom, consider the following questions.

Does the Curriculum:

_____ Provide for all areas of a child's development—physical, emotional, social, and cognitive—through an integrated approach?

_____ Base decisions on teachers' observations and recordings of each child's special interests and developmental progress?

_____ Emphasize learning as an interactive process where teachers prepare the environment for children to learn through active exploration and interaction with adults, other children, and materials?

_____ Provide learning activities and materials that are concrete, real, and relevant to the lives of young children?

_____ Provide for a wider range of developmental interests and abilities than the chronological age range of the group would suggest, preparing to meet the needs of children who exhibit interests and skills outside the range of normal development?

_____ Provide opportunities for children to choose from among a variety of activities, materials, and equipment, and time to explore through active involvement?

_____ Provide multicultural and nonsexist experiences, materials, and equipment for children of all ages?

_____ Provide a balance of rest and active movement for children throughout the program day?

_____ Provide outdoor experiences for children of all ages?

Bredekamp, S. (Ed.). (1987). *Developmentally Appropriate Practice in Early Childhood Programs: Serving Children from Birth to Age 8.* Washington, DC: National Association for the Education of Young Children.

TIPS FOR TEACHERS **10.2**

Creating a Caring Community of Learners

- Provide a setting that functions as a community of learners in which all participants consider and contribute to each other's well-being and learning.
- Provide opportunities for children to play together, work on projects in small groups, and talk with other children and adults so that their own development and learning is enhanced.
- Provide a balance of rest and active movement for children throughout the program day. Children of all ages should have outdoor experiences.
- Protect children's psychological safety so that children feel secure, relaxed, and comfortable rather than disengaged, frightened, worried, or stressed.

- Provide an organized environment and an orderly routine (an environment that is dynamic and changing but predictable and comprehensible from a child's point of view).
- Provide a variety of materials and opportunities for children to have firsthand, meaningful experiences.

Bredekamp, S., & Copple, C. (Eds.). (1997). *Developmentally Appropriate Practice in Early Childhood Programs.* (Revised Edition). Washington, D.C.: National Association for the Education of Young Children.

CHAPTER SUMMARY

In this chapter, we discussed four different approaches to early childhood curriculum: the Montessori approach, the behaviorist approach, the constructivist approach, and developmentally appropriate practices. There are similarities and differences among the approaches in terms of how each approach considers how children learn and how teachers should develop curriculum. For example, the behaviorist approach is considered to be teacher-centered while developmentally appropriate practices are considered to be child-centered. In our discussion of curriculum approaches, we provided examples of typical experiences that can be found in classrooms that follow the different approaches. Activity 1 provides you with an opportunity to incorporate a particular approach or combination of approaches into your own philosophy of teaching. As you read the following chapters, think about how different techniques for guiding children's behavior, organizing classrooms, and integrating curriculum fit or do not fit with these particular curricular approaches.

ACTIVITIES

1. Reread your teaching philosophy and identify the curricular approach or combination of approaches that most closely matches your beliefs about the kinds of experiences that children should encounter in educational settings. Using information about the different approaches discussed in this chapter, write a brief rationale that explains why you believe children should encounter these types of experiences.

2. Arrange to observe in a Montessori classroom. How closely does the classroom reflect the characteristics described in the Montessori case discussed earlier in this chapter? How are the materials used in the classroom? Are there any children who have difficulty working independently? What are the strengths of the Montessori approach? What are the weaknesses?

3. Visit a preschool, kindergarten, or primary-grade classroom and consider the following questions: Can you identify any behavioristic techniques in use in the classroom? How are behavioristic techniques used? Does the teacher use behavior modification techniques such as rewards?

4. Talk with several preschool, kindergarten, or primary-grade teachers. Ask them to: 1) explain what the term "developmentally appropriate practice" means to them; 2) provide specific examples of activities from their classroom that are developmentally appropriate; and 3) describe how they involve their students' families.

5. Engage two to three young children in the physical knowledge activity found in Box 10.2. After considering the questions found in Box 10.2, were the children able to create three categories of things that move? How did the children respond to the questions you asked? Was the activity difficult or easy for the children?

chapter 11

Organizing Classroom and Outdoor Learning Environments

After reading this chapter you should be able to discuss the following questions:

❖ Why are the concepts of age-appropriateness and individual-appropriateness important in the organization of classrooms and playgrounds?
❖ Which principles of materials selection are most important to you?
❖ Which principles of classroom organization are most important to you?
❖ How might you incorporate outdoor learning centers into a playground?
❖ Why is the daily schedule an important component of classroom organization?

CHAPTER OVERVIEW

In this chapter we review principles for organizing developmentally appropriate early childhood learning environments. We begin with a review of general principles. Next, we review principles associated with the selection of materials and equipment, the organization of classroom learning centers, and the organization of outdoor learning centers. We end with a discussion of classroom schedules. At the end of the chapter, you will have an opportunity to write your own philosophy of quality learning environments (see Activity 1).

KEY ORGANIZATIONAL PRINCIPLES

The organization of a developmentally appropriate classroom and playground follow five key principles that reoccur throughout this chapter. Before reviewing these principles, we first must clarify a few terms:

• We define *materials* as disposable (e.g., construction paper, sand, crayons) and nondisposable items (e.g., blocks, balls, manipulatives) that children manipulate with their hands when engaged in educational activities. We define *equipment* as stationary (e.g., furniture, mats, sandbox) and moving items (e.g., globes, riding toys, swings) that children act upon when engaged in educational activities.
• We define *classroom learning centers* and *playground learning centers* as spaces that are designed to support and integrate learning activities across a range of content areas (e.g., science, math, art, music). Learning centers are clearly marked, and they are stocked with age-appropriate materials and equipment.

- We define *safety* as the physical, cognitive, and social-emotional well-being of children that results from a well-planned learning environment.
- We define *daily schedules* as the timetables by which children carry out their activities. In this chapter, you will discover how to design schedules that allow children to safely experience different learning activities throughout the day.

Principle 1: Developmentally Appropriate Learning Environments

Developmentally appropriate classrooms support developmentally appropriate practices (Bredekamp & Copple, 1997). This means that both age-appropriateness and individual-appropriateness are considered in selecting materials and arranging learning centers (Bredekamp & Copple, 1997; National Association of Elementary School Principals, 1993). *Age-appropriateness* refers to the general developmental skills and interests of a particular age group. *Individual-appropriateness* refers to the unique developmental skills and interests of individual children. Classroom and playground designs typically begin with a consideration of age-appropriate spaces, materials, and equipment. The design is then revised to reflect the needs and interests of individual children. One example of individual-appropriateness is the inclusion of children with diverse abilities.

Principle 2: Inclusion

Developmentally appropriate classrooms allow for the inclusion of all children who, as you recall from Chapters 1 and 4, display individual variations in their developmental skills and interests. Care is taken to select materials and create learning centers that are responsive to a range of abilities. Modeling clay, for example, is a material that allows for the inclusion of many abilities and interests. It can be used to pound away anger as well as to make objects (e.g., animals, self-portraits). It can also be used alone or combined with other materials to make abstract sculptures. Some suggestions for facilitating children's activities and use of materials that are respectful of diverse abilities include the following:

- Adapt activities, materials, and schedules so all children have equal opportunities for success.
- Consider the time that different children need to complete a task. Allow children who finish quickly to transition into another activity while the remaining children complete their work.
- Work with behavior specialists to help children with social-emotional or cognitive challenges to make smooth transitions between activities.
- Pair children together to work on projects so that they build upon each other's strengths.
- Modify doorways, equipment, and structures to allow children with physical handicaps access to all parts of the classroom and outdoors.

Developmentally appropriate classrooms allow for the inclusion of all children.

Gender is another important inclusion consideration. Boys and girls should be encouraged to pursue activities in all learning centers to maximize their learning experiences and social skills. For example, blocks may be included in the housekeeping center to encourage boys and girls to build a house for a family. Dolls can be included in the block center to encourage girls and boys to build an airport so that a group of children can fly to a holiday location.

Principle 3: Balance

A balance of materials, learning centers, and schedules provides children with a developmentally appropriate learning environment. For example, a balance between quiet and active periods helps children to regulate their energy. A balance between independent and group activities gives children opportunities to demonstrate their individuality and cooperation. A balance between private and public spaces provides children with storage space for their personal belongings and the public display of their work. A balance between safety and innovation encourages children to take "safe" risks in their exploration of new materials.

Principle 4: Continuity and Flexibility

The need for continuity and flexibility in the learning environment is one example of the principle of balance. Children become bored and restless with too much continuity and overwhelmed and confused with too much change. Achieving a balance between continuity and flexibility is best realized by continually monitoring children's reactions to the classroom environment. Introduce new materials when children begin to show signs of boredom. Alter or create new centers to maintain children's interests and encourage their experimentation. Other strategies for balancing continuity and flexibility include moving familiar materials from one learning center to another center and modifying daily schedules to allow children more time to pursue those projects in which they show an interest.

Principle 5: Safety

As noted earlier, safety is a holistic concept that reflects physical, cognitive, and social-emotional well-being. Damaged school equipment can result in physical harm, lead children to make inappropriate conclusions, and create barriers to children's sense of competence. We examine the theme of safety throughout this chapter. For now, we invite you to complete a reflective activity that we ask our students to conduct:

- Figure 11.1 illustrates an example of a safety and wellness scan. Use this scan to identify the potential physical, cognitive, and social-emotional safety risks within an early childhood learning environment. What steps might you take to improve upon the safety and wellness of the classroom environment that you scan?

SELECTION OF CLASSROOM MATERIALS AND EQUIPMENT

The materials that you select for your classroom may come from a number of sources. They may be purchased or homemade; they may be found at yard sales or donated by local businesses. A selective cross-listing of classroom materials and equipment by age group and learning center is provided in Table 11.1. In this section, we discuss principles to follow in your selection of materials and equipment (Bredekamp & Copple, 1997; National Association of Elementary School Principals, 1993).

Familiarity

Begin the year by observing children's play with materials and equipment. In some cases, children may use materials or equipment in an unsafe manner. Instruction in their safe handling will therefore be in order. In other cases, children may display an innovative use of materials. Your reinforcement of such innovative play will encourage children to engage in more elaborate play. As we noted in Chapter 8, it is also important to consider the materials found in children's homes. This knowledge will help you to achieve a better balance between familiar and novel classroom materials.

FIGURE 11.1 Safety and Wellness Scan of a Kindergarten Classroom

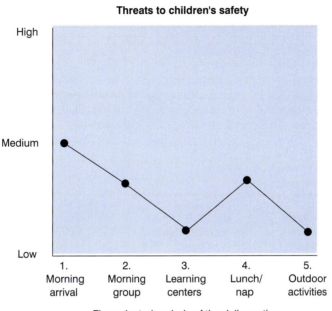

1. *Medium threat.* Ms. Garcia begins her kindergarten class by greeting children and families individually. Justin finds that not all learning center areas are open to the children. The centers that are open are well equipped. Ms. Garcia fails to help children transition into an activity, allowing Brianna and Malcolm to wander around the room.

2. *Low to medium threat.* The children understand the morning routine and readily take their places on a large carpet that was recently cleaned. The large-group area needs to be enlarged to reduce crowding. Michael, Katie, and Malea fidget and push each other due to overcrowding.

3. *Low threat.* Ms. Garcia helps each child to choose a learning center in which to work. Classroom materials are clean and safe. There are clear guides as to how many children can be in any one center. The teacher is actively involved with the children.

4. *Low to medium threat.* A nutritious lunch is served, and children are encouraged to engage in social conversation. The family-style seating arrangement invites cooperation. Transition into and out of lunch is still hectic. More student participation is needed in helping to facilitate lunch and nap time. More space is also needed for nap time, as children's mats are too close together.

5. *Low threat.* The transition from indoors to outdoors is smooth, and the playground environment is safe. Daily inspections are conducted to repair or remove damaged equipment. Malea and Katie lead the march to the sandboxes, which are inspected and cleaned daily. Children with disabilities, particularly Brianna, who walks with the aid of braces, have easy access to all playground areas.

TABLE 11.1   Classroom Learning Materials and Equipment

	Infant 6 weeks to 1 year	Toddler 1 year to 2 1/2 years	Preschool 2 1/2 years to 5 years	School Age 5 years to 8 years
Classroom Furnishings	Couch/futon Changing counter Adult rocker Cribs/cradles Infant bounce chair Cubbies/bins High chair/chair with tray Child access shelves Nest/wading pool	In addition: Book display Chairs/seating cubs Lunch tables Child rockers Block cart Small water table Cots/mats Pillows	In addition: Activity counters Small play tables Work bench Room dividers Small rugs Sand/water table	In addition: Easy chairs Bunk beds Tents Hammock
Dramatic Play	Baby dolls Stuffed animals Rubber animals Rubber people Puppets Hats Plexiglass mirrors	In addition: Large doll furniture Dress-up clothes and hats Child-size furniture Plastic cooking sets Blankets Tents Boxes Cars/trucks Pots/pans	In addition: Dollhouses Plastic food Clothespins Play money Cash register Kitchen utensils Prop boxes Purses/luggage Play telephone	In addition: Small dolls Castle sets Mobile Balance scale Microphone Stage Fabric Planks/boxes

Blocks/ Construction	Fiberboard blocks
	Foam blocks
	Bucket and blocks
		In addition:
		More blocks
		Large blocks
		Large train
		Snap blocks
		Waffle blocks
			In addition:
			Unit blocks
			Hollow blocks
			Planks
			Pulleys
			Wheelbarrow
			Woodworking tools/
			  hats/belts
			Dominoes/
			  lots of blocks
				In addition:
				More hollow
				  blocks
				More planks
				Plastic crates
				More tools
				Tri-wall
				  cardboard
				Traffic signs/train
				  set
				Plastic/wood
				  wheels, nuts,
				  bolts

Creative/Art	Finger paint
	Simple prints
	Wall hangings
	Sculpture
		In addition:
		Block crayons
		Large brushes
		Chalk/markers
			In addition:
			Easel
			Small brushes
			Watercolors
				In addition:
				Tri-wall
				  cardboard
				Styrofoam
				  pieces
				Clay

continues

TABLE 11.1 *continued*

	Infant 6 weeks to 1 year	Toddler 1 year to 2 1/2 years	Preschool 2 1/2 years to 5 years	School Age 5 years to 8 years
	Mobiles Messy mats	Chalkboard Ink stamps Paste	Modeling clay and wax Collage materials Glue Scissors	Sewing machine Badge maker Camera Camcorder

**Sensory/
Sand/
Water/
Science**
	Dish/garden tubs
	Tub toys
	Sponges
	Plants
	Aquariums/bird
	  feeders
	Animals
	Windchimes
		In addition:
		Buckets/jars
		Funnels/sifters
		Measuring cups/
		  pitchers
		Magnifiers
		Large magnets
		Flashlights
			In addition:
			Electric frying
			  pan (supervised)
			Incubator
			Ant farm
			Balance scales
			Thermometer
			Magnets/prisms
				In addition:
				Microscopes
				Rock tumblers
				Tape measures
				Oven
				Motors

**Books/
Language/
Music**
	Cloth books
	Hardboard books
	Posters
	Photos
	Records/tapes
	Music boxes
	Musical mobiles
		In addition:
		Picture books
		Play telephones
		Simple instruments
		Listening center
			In addition:
			More books
			Magnetic letters
			Typewriter
			Telephones
			Thick pencils
			Musical keyboard
			Instrument set
			Scarves/ribbons
				In addition:
				Computer and
				  software
				Easy-read books
				Chapter books
				Maps
				Dictionary/
				  encyclopedias
				Historical books
				Notebooks
				Reflective
				  journals
				Newspapers

Perceptual- Motor/ Games/ Manip- ulatives/ Math	Mobiles Cradle gyms Busy boxes Rattles Prisms	In addition: Pop beads Stack/nesting toys Large pegboards Lock boards Pounding bench Poker chips Sorting boxes	In addition: Small pegboards Puzzles Thread boards Table blocks/ parquet blocks Lego/Lazy blocks Abacus Lacing boards Nuts and bolts	In addition: Board games Skill games Cards/checkers Dominoes Looms Cuisenaire rods Calculators Models

Adapted from Childcraft's Guide to Equipping the Developmentally Appropriate Center, by J. Greenman (1990). From *Child Care Information Exchange, 76* 31–34. Reprinted with permission from Child Care Information Exchange, P. O. Box 3249, Redmond, WA 98073 — 1–800–221–2864.

Durability

Materials and equipment should be able to withstand the active and sometimes rough play of children. Make note of the warranty that accompanies any toy or piece of equipment. When possible, play with a toy before making a purchase. Reflect upon children's developmental skills and behavior when purchasing materials and equipment.

Consider the selection of reading materials. Cloth and plastic books, which are easily cleaned, are usually chosen for infants and toddlers. Preschool and kindergarten children tend to be less responsible than school-age children in their care of materials. This explains why most of their books have hard covers. Although magazines and books with soft covers are also included in preschool and kindergarten classrooms, it is with the understanding that they are likely to be torn. Teachers also purchase a number of oversized or "big" books that allow preschool and kindergarten children to turn pages easily and carry books to and from storage areas. Finally, reading materials for school-age children usually include more expensive magazines as well as paperback books. These choices reflect school-age children's more responsible behavior and desire for more detailed information about their world.

Safety

Avoid mistaking durable materials as safe materials. A dart made of wood and steel may be durable but it is certainly not safe. A ball made of socks is relatively safe, but it may not be very durable. Some safety issues to consider when selecting materials for your classroom include the following:

- **Corners.** Some common classroom materials with sharp corners include scissors, rulers, pencils, blocks, puzzles, and hardback books. Materials with sharp corners should be avoided or kept to a minimum for infants and toddlers. More of these materials are needed in preschool classrooms, but their use should be carefully monitored. In some cases substitutions can be made (e.g., rounded, plastic scissors). Even primary-grade children should be warned of the risks associated with the misuse of materials with sharp corners.
- **Surfaces.** Select smooth surfaces whenever possible, keeping in mind that some textured surfaces are necessary to stimulate children's sense of touch and to provide variety in the classroom.
- **Paint.** Toys and materials made of toxic paint should be avoided. Read all labels carefully before making a purchase. Children's use of painted items that are donated should be carefully monitored. Children should never be allowed to place these objects in their mouths.
- **Size.** Choking is of special concern in the early childhood classroom. Special devices can be purchased to determine if the size of an object might cause a breathing obstruction. We advise teachers to use these devices as one means of determining which toys and materials to include in a classroom. Although some small toys and materials (e.g., crayons) are necessary, others (e.g., toys with detachable parts) are not.

- **Parts.** As a general rule, the fewer parts associated with a toy the better. The durability and safety of toys and equipment are reduced when one or more parts are broken or missing. For example, broken items can become safety hazards when swallowed or thrown. We advise teachers to immediately remove any item with a missing or broken part until it can be repaired or replaced.

Scale

Materials and equipment should reflect the height, weight, and manipulative abilities of the children for whom they are selected. For example, furniture should be "child-sized" so that it fits children's physical dimensions. Blocks and movable equipment (e.g., cots, mats) should be made of light materials so that children can manipulate them easily.

Manipulatives should also be "child-sized" and responsive to children's abilities and interests. Crayons and books should be of varied sizes to exercise children's small-motor skills. As a general rule, preschool children need larger crayons and books than do older children. Likewise, a few small-, medium-, and large-sized soft balls suffice for preschool children. School-age children require a greater variety of ball sizes, shapes, and weights. Simple musical instruments (e.g., recorder, bongos, noise cans) meet the interests and skills of preschool children, but school-age children make better use of more sophisticated musical instruments (e.g., trumpet, drums, keyboard).

Two other scale considerations include the storage of materials and the display of children's work. Storing classroom materials at children's eye level allows for easier access and reinforces their sense of self-sufficiency. Displaying children's work (e.g., art, dictation, writing samples, models) at their eye level encourages them to share their work with others.

Finally, make sure that children have a clear view of the outside. Avoid the use of heavy window treatments, as they collect dust and obstruct children's view. Also consider the placement of video monitors, computers, lights, and other visual stimuli. Bringing such visual objects down to children's eye level is necessary to fully engage their attention and avoid eye strain.

Variety and Supply

A variety of classroom materials supports the diverse interests of children represented within a classroom. It also challenges children to make independent choices, encourages them to think about activities in novel ways, encourages their experimentation, and cuts down on disagreements over sharing. It is especially important to maintain a variety of disposable materials like construction paper, paints, crayons, glue, and glitter. Preschool children use large amounts of such materials to experiment. School-age children also use large amounts of disposable materials in their pursuit of elaborate projects.

Open-ended materials can be used for many different purposes.

Open-Ended Materials

Open-ended materials include items that can be used for a variety of different purposes in different locations. Many disposable materials (e.g., construction paper, sand, scrap cloth, weaving materials, and crayons) are open-ended. For example, children can use construction paper to make collages in the art center or maps in the science center. Sand can be used to develop math concepts (e.g., children measure sand into different-sized beakers) or to explore environmental principles (e.g., water filters through sand faster than through clay).

Nondisposable materials and equipment (e.g., Legos, blocks, balls, mats, musical tapes) also have open-ended qualities. For example, Legos can be used to construct buildings in the block center or design patterns in the manipulative center. Musical tapes can be used for dance or as a basis for introducing children to song writing. Mats can be used to take naps or to practice tumbling activities. Colored blocks can be used for constructing buildings, counting, and sorting.

Teachers as Educational Material

As a teacher, you will act as an extension of the materials found in your classroom. For example, failure to prepare children for their involvement with new materials will result in these materials being ignored or used in inappropriate ways. Some of the ways in which you can support children's creative use of classroom materials follow.

Facilitation. Plan your lessons around classroom materials. As we noted earlier, most teachers begin by observing children's involvement with materials and equipment. They then plan ways to incorporate familiar and new materials into their lesson plans to accomplish specific learning objectives. Finally, teachers facilitate children's involvement with materials and equipment by providing directions or labels, asking questions, pointing out opportunities for new discoveries, noting possible play options, and guiding children's observations.

Expansion. Expand children's learning by providing them with choices. New materials can be added to support new activities. It is also important to introduce new ideas for using familiar materials and to help children identify ways to use new materials to expand their understanding of familiar ideas. For example, you might demonstrate the use of an abacus for counting after children have become familiar with counting chips. Or, you might move colorful, small blocks from the manipulative center to the block center to expand children's building activities.

Guidance. It is also important to consider your behavior management plan when selecting materials. As noted earlier, interesting and developmentally appropriate materials help children to focus their attention so that they do not become bored. Children's knowledge of materials also allows them to engage in activities with less direct supervision.

Demonstrations. We advise teachers to demonstrate new materials and equipment to ensure that children follow safety guidelines. Demonstrations also help to ensure the maintenance of new materials and equipment.

Collaboration. Actively joining with children in their learning activities helps them to see the value of sharing and cooperation. As a result, they begin to offer suggestions to one another, observe each other's use of materials, and ask one another questions about their use of materials.

Even the best materials will be of little use if the classroom is organized in a haphazard manner. It is for this reason that we now turn to principles for organizing classroom learning centers.

ORGANIZING CLASSROOM LEARNING CENTERS

Any number of criteria can be used to select and organize classroom learning centers. Not all teachers use all learning centers, and some teachers may phase in and out different centers throughout the year. Box 11.1 summarizes the characteristics of a variety of learning centers that you may choose to include in your classroom.

BOX 11.1 — *Classroom Learning Centers*

Some of the types of learning centers that teachers consider when organizing their classrooms are summarized here. To remain open to the numerous educational opportunities associated with all learning centers, we suggest that you discuss with your peers ways in which the learning experiences associated with one center can also be facilitated in other centers.

Block Center

Blocks are open-ended materials, as they support the educational needs of the whole child. For example, blocks exercise children's small- and large-motor skills, as well as their eye-hand perceptual skills. Children's construction activities also promote social cooperation and creativity. Basic educational concepts associated with math (counting, comparisons) and science (gravity, predictions) are likewise easily introduced into the block center.

The block center should include a large, open space in which children can conduct their construction activities easily. A full complement of unit blocks should be placed on low, open shelves for easy access. *Unit blocks* consist of wooden blocks that come in different shapes and sizes. They are used by children to represent various construction projects like buildings, bridges, towers, highways, landing pads, and ramps. Hollow blocks are also present in the block center, along with block accessories like small dolls, toy farm animals and equipment, toy cars, trucks, and vehicles, levers and pulleys, toy helicopters and airplanes, and toy people.

Reading and Listening Center

Children's enjoyment of reading is encouraged within a quiet, comfortable environment that is located away from noisy centers. Although not necessary, some teachers construct reading lofts to help ensure quietness and privacy. Whatever your design, the reading center should be well-supplied with a variety of books (e.g., pictorial, historical, art, rhythms, informational, resource) and magazines. You may also want to include simple writing materials (paper, pencils, markers, crayons) for children who wish to write about their reading experiences. Headphones, tapes, and tape recorders are also included in reading centers so that children can listen to music or "talking books," as well as record and interpret sounds.

Writing and Computer Center

Children of all ages benefit from their learning experiences in the writing center. Some of the materials that support children's writing interests and skills include paper of different sizes, lined and unlined paper, notecards, glue and tape, pencils and markers, crayons, books, business cards, labels, stickers and stamps, envelopes of various sizes, rulers, newspapers and magazines, ink blots, stencils, typewriters, computers and software, and posters. Both individual and small-group activities can take place in this center. For example, children may work on individual letters or join with others to dictate a story to their teacher. They may trace business logos or design their own logos for use in the dramatic play center.

The writing center is typically located next to the reading center and computer station, as all these centers involve relatively quiet activities. This placement also makes it easier to integrate activities across the three centers. For example, children may look at or

continues

| BOX 11.1 | *Classroom Learning Centers continued* |

read a story book and then move to the writing center to write about or dictate their reading experiences. They may also choose to write or dictate their own story using a computer or typewriter. It is important to post these and other writing products around the classroom to acknowledge and reinforce children's interest in writing.

Art Center

The art center is one of the busiest centers in an early childhood classroom. Some of the materials present in the art center include paper of different sizes and for different uses (watercolor, drawing, construction, painting), pastels and crayons, colored chalk, paints of different kinds (watercolor, fingerpaint, tempera paint, oil paint), brushes of different sizes, pencils and markers, easels, smocks, glue and tape, glitter and confetti, scissors, magazines and newspapers, sand of different colors, and modeling clay.

The open-ended nature of art materials encourages children to express their thoughts and feelings. Children also show great pride in the products that result from their art activities. As with their other products, children's artwork should be proudly displayed throughout the room.

We have observed art centers located near both quiet and noisy areas. One compromise is to use the art center as a barrier station between a noisy area (e.g., woodworking center) and a quiet area (e.g., writing center). Note also that activities from both of these centers can be incorporated easily into the art center. Children's woodworking products might be brought to the art center for painting. Children's writing products can also be brought to the art center for coloring or stenciling.

Dramatic Play Center

The dramatic play center allows children to try out new roles and express their feelings about their own life experiences. This center can also be used to introduce children to specific life situations. For example, one of the most common dramatic center themes involves home life, allowing children to practice social roles that they will one day assume as adults. A sampling of other possible themes includes the following:

- A cardboard box can be used to create a post office mail drop.
- A toy doctor's kit and small table or chair can be used to create a doctor's office.
- A bench with a few potted plants can be used to create a gardening center.
- A collection of children's artwork can be arranged to create an art gallery.
- A cardboard box and a few hand or finger puppets can be used to create a puppet show.

Science and Math Center

Children's curiosity about their physical world is supported in the science and math center. Basic science and math concepts like classification, counting, observation, and prediction are reinforced when children are surrounded by items like the following: insect collections, magnets, prisms, dried leaves, bark, plants, living insects, paper and scissors, soils and rocks, cubes, gears and gadgets, filters, vegetable dyes, colored chips, pegboards, calculators, strings of different strength and length, pulleys, terrariums, magnifying glasses, measuring equipment, petri dishes, and scales. These are just some of the items that can be

continues

BOX 11.1 *Classroom Learning Centers* continued

stored on open shelves. Likewise, science magazines and books can add to children's understanding of these materials.

Placing the science center next to a window allows children to experiment with light. The science center can also be placed next to the block, manipulative, sand/water, or art centers to encourage children to expand and integrate their activities. For example, pulleys might be used to construct a block building. Sand might be used with rocks, water, and plants to construct a container garden. Children can also use pens and crayons from the art center to draw a map of their home or neighborhood. Small balls and sticks from the manipulative table might be used with clay to make insect models.

Social Sciences Center

The purpose of a social science center is to advance children's understanding and appreciation of human behavior and its relationship to civilization. Any number of themes can be introduced into a social science center throughout the year, including the customs and languages of other countries, agricultural products from around the world, the influence of geography on clothing and housing, historical depictions of family and community life, simple polls and surveys regarding social issues of interest to young children (e.g., favorite flavors of ice cream, television programs, favorite times of school day), and musical instruments, songs, and dances from around the world. Some of the permanent materials and equipment associated with the social sciences center include maps, globes, travel catalogs, science magazines that address human life, simple bar graphs showing

results from polls, computers with software related to different cultures and geography, children's books dealing with family lives and ethnic groups, models of different climates and terrains, and displays of agricultural and cultural products.

Woodworking Center

The woodworking center reinforces and combines activities found in the block, dramatic, science, and manipulative centers. For example, children use small- and large-motor skills as they saw, cut, clamp, and hammer. They may also choose to turn the woodworking center into a hardware store or lumber yard. They may test the softness of different types of wood, or experiment with the best way to attach small decorations to different types of wood. When children are angry, the woodworking center becomes a perfect location for them to let out their feelings.

The woodworking center is usually noisy and should therefore be placed away from quiet centers. As noted in Table 11.1, more realistic woodworking tools can be added to the center as children mature. However, children should demonstrate an ability to follow safety rules and have a knowledge of tool safety before pursuing activities in this center. Their activities should also be closely monitored by adults.

Manipulative and Math Center

The manipulative center includes Legos, small colored blocks, nested beakers, pipe cleaners, colored beads, puzzles, board games, table looms, pegs and pegboards, lacing boards, unifix cubes, geoblocks, sequencing cards, and other small materials that encourage small-motor skills, eye-hand coordination, ex-

continues

BOX 11.1 *Classroom Learning Centers* continued

perimentation, cooperation, math skills, and creativity. For example, small-motor skills are exercised by lacing boards, constructing puzzles, and playing with nuts and bolts. Experimentation with math concepts and geometric patterns is encouraged through stacking and sorting beakers, adding and subtracting colored chips, manipulating an abacus or calculator, making designs with unifix cubes or colored pegs, and sorting and sequencing beads. Cooperation and creativity are encouraged as children work together to build a structure out of Legos or use a small table loom to weave a piece of fabric.

Manipulatives are usually stored in open containers on low shelves that are located next to work tables. This allows children to quickly identify and gain access to the materials that interest them. We consider the manipulative center to be somewhat like the art center in that it can be quiet or noisy. We therefore view it as another center that might mediate between a quiet and noisy center. For example, we have already noted the benefits of locating the manipulative center next to the science center. It might also be placed next to the art center, thereby allowing children to incorporate three-dimensional objects (e.g., pipe cleaners, pegs, pop beads) into their art designs.

Sand and Water Center

Sand and water play provides children with sensory experiences and creative expression. It also reinforces science and math concepts. For example, young children's play in this center can introduce them to the textures of different sands and the sounds that water makes when flowing over gravel. They can create sand castles and waterfalls, and they can observe the effects of falling water on dry and wet sand. Children also learn that not all solid items sink, and that some hollow items can sink when filled with water. They learn that gravity pulls water downward, but a water pump makes water go upstream. They learn about evaporation and the importance of keeping sand and water areas clean. Children learn to measure and divide sand and water into fractions as they pour and build. They count the number of cans needed to fill a small bucket with water, and they learn that many small sandpiles can be further reduced to individual grains of sand. Children can also duplicate in sand the geometric patterns that they make in the manipulative center. They can also expand their understanding of geometric figures by designing miniature sand or rock gardens.

Like the art center, it is important that sand and water tables be located near a water source. Most teachers also prefer that the tables be located near an exit to the outside so that children can carry sand and water materials easily between the classroom and playground. Vinyl or tile floors are helpful in cleanup, and the sand and water tables should be cleaned routinely to maintain a sanitary and safe work environment.

Pets

A pet center may include insects, as well as small mammals, birds, and reptiles. A pet center can prove very useful in a number of ways. It can help children learn firsthand about concepts introduced in the science center (e.g., metamorphosis of insects, favored living conditions of different animals). Pets can also reinforce math and science concepts. For example, children might be asked to predict how

continues

BOX 11.1	*Classroom Learning Centers* continued

far two frogs of different species or sizes can jump. Children might then measure the length of jumps made by each frog and compare the results with their predictions.

Pet centers allow children to respect and assume responsibility for other living things. In addition, pets can help create a soothing classroom environment. For example, one of the authors found that a young child with emotional problems was able to control his emotional outbursts when holding the classroom rabbit.

Of course, pet centers also require special attention. Cages must be cleaned, appropriate food and living conditions must be provided, children must be taught how to play with classroom pets appropriately, some children's fear of animals must be considered, and the potential for a pet's death must be considered. All of these issues should be thought through prior to deciding upon the introduction of a pet center and the selection of an appropriate pet. We advise teachers to seek the advice of experts prior to purchasing any classroom pet to make this center a positive experience.

Music Center

The music center allows children to create and experiment with sounds. Instruments typically found in music centers include cymbals, rhythm sticks, recorders, bells, miniature versions of musical instruments (e.g., horns, pianos, drums), compact discs or musical tapes, blank music sheets for writing songs, song books, and streamers and balls for creative movements.

A variety of activities can occur in the music center. Some children may choose to experiment with different musical instruments. Other children may choose to listen to music or write their own music. And still other children may choose to create dance movements. Typically, the music center is located near an open space so that children can dance and march to music. This means that children who want to engage in quiet activities should be allowed to take their listening and writing materials to the reading center. In some cases, it may be possible to move shelves to create a temporary quiet area for these activities.

Cubbies and Lockers

Classroom cubbies or lockers allow children a private space in which to store their jackets, extra clothing, and work products that they are to take home. Children's names should be clearly printed on each cubby to avoid confusion. It is best to place cubbies next to the door in which children enter the classroom in the morning and depart in the afternoon. Parent bulletin boards and an information center can also be located close by for easy access to center newsletters, educational flyers, and other important information.

Equally important as the selection of learning centers is their organization and relationship to each other. In this section, we use a scheme suggested by Lowman and Ruhmann (1998) to review principles of classroom organization. Although originally presented in a discussion of toddler environments, we have adapted the model for use in all early childhood learning environments from birth through age 8. The model is based on a "multi-s" approach to room organization that includes simplicity, softness, senses, stimulation, stability, safety, and sanitation. All of these principles are supported by early childhood professionals (Bredekamp & Copple, 1997; Koralek, Newman, & Colker, 1995; National Association of Elementary School Principals, 1993).

Simplicity

Avoid overcrowding children by keeping the classroom design simple. Although children need an enriching environment, it is best not to go too far. We have visited cluttered classrooms in which teachers attempted to include too many learning centers in a small space. The resulting classrooms were characterized by confusion, disagreements, and a general sense of tension. This should not be surprising. Most children (as well as adults) become overwhelmed and frustrated when presented with crowded situations. For this reason, we suggest you take a reflective approach in designing your learning centers. It is also beneficial to work with a colleague who can provide you with feedback on your organizational plans.

Identify an age group with which you would like to work. Arrange a classroom learning environment for these children from the selection of learning centers in Box 11.1. Keep the principle of simplicity in mind as you organize your classroom. Do not worry about making your classroom perfect, as you will be modifying your original design throughout this section.

Softness

An increasing number of children are spending large amounts of time away from home before, during, and after school. It is therefore important to bring a homelike softness to the classroom. This principle challenges teachers to focus on more than the educational qualities of learning centers. Consideration must also be given to the creation of "soft spots." For example, wall hangings might be included in the science center. Upholstered furniture and stuffed toys might be selected for a housekeeping center. Carpet might be placed in the reading center. Children's cubbies might be decorated with family pictures.

The inclusion of classroom soft spots does more than provide a homelike environment. Some soft spots help to absorb noise; others provide comfort. And still other soft spots have a sensory appeal that helps to focus children's attention.

Return again to your classroom design. How might you introduce two or more soft spots into your classroom? Share your examples with your peers.

Senses

Because children, like adults, are attracted to sensory experiences, it is important to consider the sensory qualities of learning centers. Learning centers should have a variety of materials for children to look at, feel, smell, listen to, or taste. Consider how the five senses might be incorporated into a construction center as you ask children to:

* Look at the color of wood, leaves, and bark.
* Feel the texture of bark.
* Smell different varieties of wood (e.g., birch, cedar, pine).
* Distinguish between the sounds of different construction techniques (e.g., nailing, sawing).
* Taste edible products from trees (e.g., nuts, syrup).

Not all senses need to be so pronounced in every learning center, but it is best to think through as many sensory experiences as possible to maximize children's learning opportunities. With this in mind, you are now ready to further modify your classroom design.

How might you introduce the five senses into one of your learning centers? Share your ideas with your peers.

Stimulation

A number of factors define the degree to which early childhood classrooms are interesting and stimulating. For example, the principles of simplicity, softness, and sensory experiences all help to influence the type and degree of stimulation present within a classroom. Other factors include the following.

Accessibility.   Children are stimulated to become involved in activities when materials are readily accessible on open shelves that are placed at their eye level. Open containers likewise provide easier access than closed containers.

Color.   The color of classroom walls and ceilings also helps to create different classroom moods. For example, reds create a mood of excitement, deep purples and greens are soothing, and yellows are restful (Caples, 1996). Caples (1996), an architect specializing in school facilities, also recommends the use of "ethnic" color palettes to create pride of and connection to children's communities.

Self-selection.   Children are stimulated to engage in learning activities when they are given choices. For example, rather than assigning children to learning centers, allow them to self-select. As centers fill, you can help children make other selections with the assurance that they too will have a turn in those centers that are currently filled.

Keeping track of the number of children in a learning center is necessary in maintaining safety, cooperation, and a quality learning experience. Different techniques can be used to alert children and adults as to the availability of space in a learning center. One common technique is for children to hang a laminated name tag outside each center. When all the hooks at a center are filled, children know that they must make another selection. Children move their tags as they move between

Children are stimulated to become involved in classroom activities when materials are readily available.

learning centers. This technique is effective in stimulating children to assume self-responsibility for their choices and to cooperate with others in maintaining an orderly classroom environment.

> *Incorporate an ethnic or cultural design into one of your learning centers. Consider the following groups: African American, Cuban American, Appalachian, Native American, and Vietnamese. To accomplish this task, you will need to learn about the ethnic and cultural backgrounds of your group. Visit museums and local ethnic or cultural neighborhoods, read books, or view videotapes. Consult with sociologists or anthropologists at your college or university. Do not depend upon popular culture (e.g., television and magazines), as it sometimes presents stereotyped images of ethnic and cultural groups.*

Stability

One of the most important elements in classroom organization is the creation of a stable, consistent environment in which children with diverse abilities are afforded equal access to all activities. Balance is one element that helps to create a stable environment. Other factors that contribute to a stable learning environment include the following.

Center arrangements.   Certain types of activities are especially important to consider when arranging a stable classroom space that provides children with a sense of security and consistency. These include messy and clean activities, individual and group activities, independent and cooperative activities, and quiet and loud activities. Begin with a consideration of the types of activities that occur in these centers. For example, quiet and noisy centers should be separated. Placing the block center (noisy) next to a reading center (quiet) is not wise. Placing the reading center next to a writing center (two quiet centers) is a better combination. Note the arrangement of learning centers in Figure 11.2. Can you identify an organizational pattern that reflects mutually supportive activities? Remember that no one design is perfect. What changes might you make in Figure 11.2?

Another consideration is specific to messy centers like the art, cooking, and sand/water centers. All of these centers should be placed close to a water source to more easily facilitate learning activities that involve the use of water. Cleanup is also easier if these centers are located next to water. Likewise, tile or vinyl floors can facilitate cleanup in these centers.

Finally, teachers often note that their classrooms never have enough windows or that the windows are located in the wrong locations. In fact, a justification can be made for placing windows within any learning center. Windows in the science and art centers allow for experimentation with natural light (e.g., heat value of sun, effect of light on prisms or transparent art materials). Windows also provide natural lighting for reading, music, and writing centers. As a teacher, you must decide how windows best fit the interests of the children in your classroom.

Group meetings.   Large-group meetings are an important component of the day. Children and teachers often meet as a group in the morning to review the daily schedule, make announcements, share experiences, and make plans for transitions into learning centers. Group meetings likewise are conducted throughout the day to dictate or read stories, sing songs, and review group projects.

Many teachers use a large, colorful rug or carpet for group meetings. Children may arrange themselves on the carpet or they may be assigned a special place to sit in order to ease their transition into and out of group. Teachers with limited classroom space often incorporate group meetings next to learning centers. In these cases, it is best to place the group meeting space next to centers that can be quickly cleared. For example, the block or reading center might double as a group meeting space.

Displays.   The amount and type of children's work displayed in a classroom is a good indicator of a developmentally appropriate classroom. Consider Figure 11.2. How many different places might you exhibit children's work in this classroom? The ceiling is one place to display mobiles (wind chimes), artwork (e.g., drawings), and models (e.g., planets). However, the ceiling is most suitable for adult viewing. In what other parts of the classroom might you display children's work so that is at their eye level?

FIGURE 11.2 A Classroom Design *(Adapted and reprinted by permission of Rebecca Olson, University of Georgia.)*

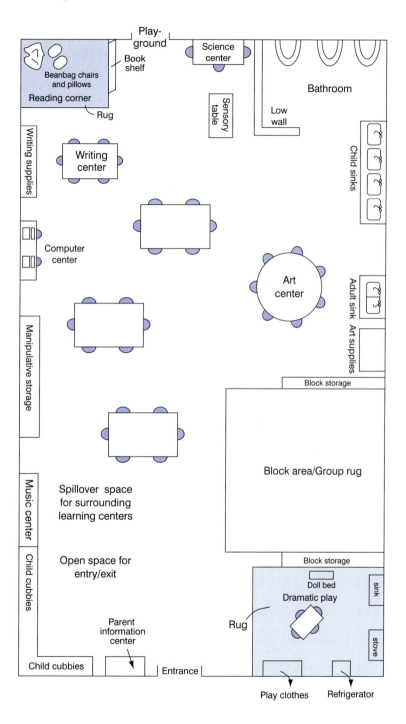

Inclusion.   Stable environments are also characterized by the inclusion of children with diverse abilities. As we noted in Chapter 3, this need not be difficult. Simply reducing the number of children allowed in a learning center at one time may safely accommodate a child in a wheelchair. Another example involves inclusion of the same child in the block center. Since the child sits higher up than her peers, she has an advantage that will contribute to her success and that of her peers. She can serve as a construction manager (since she has a better view of the construction work taking place on the floor), and she is also better placed to add higher blocks. So, as the building rises, she figures ever more prominently in the more difficult aspects of construction. Note that in Checklist 11.1 and Figure 11.3 we have modified our earlier classroom design to address the needs of a child in a wheelchair. Can you identify other organizational modifications that might be made to better accommodate this child?

Of course, not all handicaps are physical in nature. For example, children who are excessively shy must also be afforded equal access to classroom activities. Simply arranging a space for such a child to observe and quietly discuss his activity options with a teacher may make it easier for him to eventually join an activity. Also, teachers are often successful in identifying an adult or peer who can gently approach and join a shy child, thus allowing the child to structure his own learning environment. How might you further modify Figure 11.3 to accommodate the potential needs of a child who is socially withdrawn?

How might you further modify your classroom to accommodate a child who is hearing impaired?

Safety

Just as safety is important in the selection of materials and equipment, it is also an essential component of classroom organization. The following principles are routinely considered when assessing classroom safety.

Traffic flow.   Traffic should flow smoothly between learning centers so that classroom noise and the potential for accidents are reduced. Consider Figures 11.2 and 11.3, both of which reflect some essential elements of good traffic flow. Note first that learning centers tend to be located next to walls with open spaces in the middle of the floor. This allows children and adults to more easily navigate between centers. Second, the dividers between learning centers are low (at or below children's eye level) to allow children and adults to see one another's movements. Third, each area contains its own storage area. This helps children to restrict their movements to the areas in which they are conducting their activities. Finally, entrances into the room are clear of obstructions, visible, and separated from learning centers. It is also important that sufficient space be provided around doorways to accommodate the entry and departure of children and parents.

CHECKLIST 11.1

Is This Classroom Wheelchair Accessible?

When observing an early childhood classroom, or preparing your own, check for the following. What other modifications might you make?

Inclusion and Classroom Organization

_____ Adjustable table legs to raise table height

_____ Table size and shape modified for easier wheelchair access

_____ Wide paths created to accommodate wheelchair movement

_____ Adjustable storage shelves for easier wheelchair access

_____ Rearrangement of toilets for easier wheelchair access

_____ Handrails added to facilitate child's transfer from wheelchair to the toilet

_____ Toilets raised to facilitate child's transfer from wheelchair to the toilet

_____ Wheelchair-accessible sinks

Spacing between centers. We have already noted the importance of restricting the number of children in a learning center to avoid overcrowding and confusion. It is also important to provide adequate space between learning centers so that the activities of one group do not impinge on those of another group.

Toileting. Bathroom facilities may be located within or outside early childhood classrooms. When located within the classroom, it is a general rule that the toileting area for kindergarten and younger children be as open as possible to allow teachers to help children with their toileting needs. However, it is also important to follow state regulations and school policies in this matter, especially in regard to children's privacy rights.

When toilets are located outside the classroom, guidelines are needed for helping children gain easy access to them. Keep in mind both the age-appropriateness and individual-appropriateness of this situation. Some children, regardless of their age, may need more help than others.

Daily inspections. It is a good habit to inspect the classroom every morning for potential safety hazards. Conduct the inspection before children arrive, as hazards may be easily overlooked once the daily routine begins. Look for objects that

FIGURE 11.3   Inclusion and Classroom Organization (*Adapted and reprinted by permission of Rebecca Olson, University of Georgia.*)

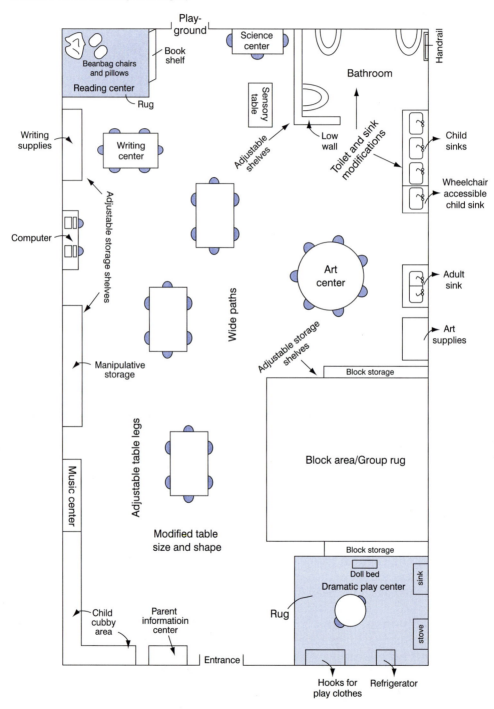

may have been dropped on the floor, cleaning solutions that may have been left out on counters, and broken materials and equipment that may need to be replaced or repaired.

Revise your room organization to take into account safety precautions, especially traffic flow. Share your revision with your peers.

Sanitation

One special aspect of safety is sanitation. Daily use of the classroom by children and adults results in soiled floors, materials, and equipment. Key sanitation principles to keep in mind follow.

Cleaning routines. Some materials require more frequent cleaning than others. Cloth books and toys, for example, often find their way into the mouths of infants and toddlers. These materials require daily washing. Materials and equipment for older children require less frequent cleaning, but they too must be routinely cleaned to avoid the spread of illnesses.

Washable equipment and materials can be cleaned with detergent and water, then sprayed with a solution of 1 tablespoon of bleach to 1 quart of water (Kendrick, Kaufmann, & Messenger, 1991). Surfaces likewise should be wiped down with soapy water and sprayed with a bleach/water solution.

Windows, walls, floors, and curtains also require routine cleaning to keep dust and other potential pollutants at a manageable level. Officials from your local health department can make suggestions about cleaning schedules, solutions, and procedures for the specific materials and equipment found in your classroom.

Washing hands. Nothing succeeds better in keeping a classroom clean than effective hand washing. Frequent hand washing also helps to control the spread of infectious diseases. We suggest that you invite a health professional to your classroom to instruct you on hand washing techniques and the advantages and disadvantages of liquid and bar soap.

Cooking. As we noted in Chapter 4, cooking activities provide children with valuable lessons involving math (measuring), art (food presentation), socialization (cooperation), and reading (recipes). However, care must be taken to ensure that food is properly washed and handled to avoid the spread of illnesses. We suggest that you speak to a food scientist or school nutritionist prior to each cooking experience to identify the particular sanitation steps to take to keep children healthy.

Sand and water tables. It is a standard rule that water tables and sandboxes remain covered when not in use. Otherwise, they can easily become contaminated. In addition, sharp items may become hidden, resulting in cut or bruised hands. Covering water tables and sandboxes also prevents cats and dogs from using them as litter boxes. Finally, it is important to drain and clean water tables and toys after each use. This will cut down on the growth of germs.

Identify two potential sanitation challenges associated with your learning centers and explain how you might address them. Share your ideas with your peers.

Now that you have had practice in designing a classroom learning environment, we next address principles for organizing an outdoor learning environment.

ORGANIZING OUTDOOR LEARNING CENTERS

The education of young children does not end in the classroom. Playgrounds also provide opportunities to support and expand children's understanding of their world. Many of the principles that govern classroom design are also applicable to playgrounds, including balance, safety, and inclusion (Bredekamp & Copple, 1997; National Association of Elementary School Principals, 1993). In this section, we review a number of playground design principles recommended by experts in the field (Frost, 1992; Koralek et al., 1995; Kutska & Hoffman, 1992; Marotz, Cross, & Rush, 1993; Payne & Rink, 1997).

Principles of Playground Design

We have provided an example of a playground design in Figure 11.4. You will have an opportunity to design your own playground while reading this section. Do not be surprised if you need to reconsider various components of your design. Playgrounds, like classrooms, are works in progress.

Design for the whole child.   Traditionally, playgrounds were associated primarily with children's physical development. Today, playgrounds are designed to support children's physical, cognitive, and social-emotional development. Playground learning centers include opportunities for art activities, nature studies, quiet activities, dramatic play, construction, gardening, and science activities. It is therefore possible for teachers to link classroom and outdoor learning experiences.

How might you link a classroom learning experience with one on the playground?

Consider access points.   Access to the playground is both a logistical and safety issue. Consider, for example, children's behavior. Children can transition more easily between indoor and outdoor activities when classrooms open directly onto playgrounds. In contrast, asking children to walk down halls or to use stairs to access playgrounds involves a complicated set of transitions that can result in behavior management problems.

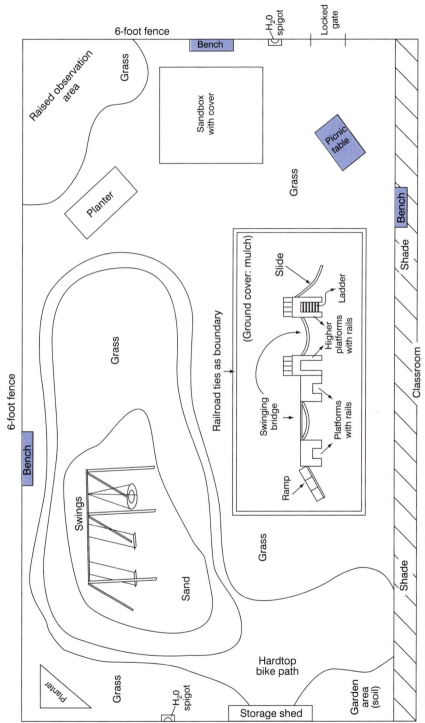

FIGURE 11.4 A Playground Design *(Adapted and reprinted by permission of Rebecca Olson, University of Georgia.)*

313

Consideration must also be given to the relationship between the playground environment and street traffic. Construction workers and landscapers need periodic access to playgrounds to install or remove heavy equipment and to work on the grounds. Yet, children's activities must be protected from street noise and interference from visitors. It is generally recommended that service access be limited to one gate. This reduces the number of opportunities for children to leave the playground or for strangers to enter the playground.

Other access considerations include the placement of bathroom facilities, water spigots, and storage sheds. The ease of access to these areas must be balanced with safety considerations. For example, how will children be supervised while using bathroom facilities located on the playground or while returning to the classroom? Might children trip over water spigots if they are placed in the middle of the playground?

> *Use the classroom design that you developed earlier and decide how children will gain access to and from the playground. What type of access will be permitted from the street? What type of perimeter barrier will you use to maintain children's privacy (e.g., fencing, shrubs, walls)? Finally, decide how children will gain access to bathrooms and playground storage facilities.*

Consider the arrangement of outdoor learning centers.   The arrangement of outdoor learning centers begins with a consideration of overall space needs. One recommendation is that playgrounds should provide a range of 75 to 100 square feet per child (Marotz et al., 1993). Next, consider the space needed for individual centers. The active play that takes place on large-motor equipment (e.g., swings) requires more space that a quiet resting or reading area. It is likewise important to keep in mind that some learning centers may actually be located outside the playground. For example, a small hill or platform on the playground can be used as an observation point from which to record wildlife activities in an adjacent wooded area.

The grouping of outdoor learning centers is also important. As in the classroom, playground learning centers that support active play (e.g., climbing, swinging, running, riding) should be grouped together and separated from less active play areas (e.g., gardening, sandbox, reading, nature study). Other factors to consider when grouping centers include the following:

- **Water activities.**   Outdoor learning centers that make use of water include gardens, sandboxes, nature studies, and art. Each of these centers requires a water source.
- **Movement activities.**   Certain activities require large, open spaces in which children can move freely. Grassy areas with small hills can accommodate children's need to run, tumble, crawl, dance, and hop. Paved areas are needed on which to ride wagons and tricycles. Grassy and paved areas should be separated or have a sizable buffer zone so that one set of activities does not interfere with the other. Likewise, riding paths should be located away from

Like classrooms, playgrounds can be divided into separate learning centers.

water and sandy areas so that children are not tempted to ride their wagons or tricycles into them.

- **Supervision.** Activities that involve large-motor equipment, water, and sand often require more adult supervision than those in which children read quietly or make nature observations. Teachers must consider how best to group these different centers so that they can most effectively supervise children's activities.
- **Transitions.** Some activities require a longer transition period than others, especially in regard to the storage of materials and equipment. Outdoor materials and equipment that require storage are most often used during sand, riding, art, nature, water, and gardening activities. It is thus important that these centers are located next to storage facilities. In contrast, few if any special materials are needed to accompany children's play on swings, slides, and climbing platforms. Subsequently, these large pieces of equipment can be located farther away from storage facilities.

Another consideration involves the placement of boundaries to separate and indicate entry into different outdoor learning centers. Landscape timbers, low vine-covered fences, bridges, low shrubs and small trees, tires, open sandy and green spaces, graveled or other textured pathways, tunnels, low mounds, a small stream, and benches are just some of the boundaries that may be used to define and separate learning centers while allowing for a flow of traffic between centers.

Boundaries can also be used to prevent entry into certain areas by younger children. This is especially important when playgrounds are used by multiple age groups. For example, you may choose to widen the intervals between steps leading up to platforms. Small intervals can first be used to allow younger children access to a lower platform. The intervals between steps can then gradually increase to allow only older children access to a higher platform.

Whatever the exact use of boundaries, the result should allow children and adults to move easily between learning centers. One recommendation is to space pieces of playground equipment no less than 8 feet apart (Marotz et al., 1993).

Design and organize a playground to accompany your classroom. First, keep in mind the access and perimeter barriers that you have already established. These may need to be altered as you work through this exercise. Now consider the total amount of space that you will need for your playground. What are the ages of the children who will use the playground? How many children will be on the playground at any given time? Identify the interest centers that you will include in your playground, again remembering not to overcrowd the available space. Decide where your learning centers will be placed. Finally, describe the types of boundaries that will be used to define the learning centers.

Choose quality outdoor equipment and material.   Developmentally appropriate playgrounds provide children with a variety of natural and mass-produced landscape elements. Large rocks can be used for climbing. Grassy areas invite children to conduct group games. Paved paths can be used for riding or chalk drawings. Wading pools or fountains can be used for their calming effects.

The selection of large pieces of equipment is also important. The more variety associated with a piece of equipment, the more children will be challenged to think creatively. Today, complex structures are available that encourage multiple play activities like climbing, swinging, hanging, jumping, and balancing. Such complex structures are preferable to separate pieces of equipment (e.g., a slide, a swing), which tend to be used in isolation.

Complex structures can also be used in dramatic play. Consider, for example, the symbolic representation of animal habitats. Interconnected pieces of large-motor equipment (e.g., slides, swings, balance beams) can be used to represent different parts of a habitat. The slide might be used as a waterfall, the swing as vines, the climbing platform as the tops of trees, and the balance beam as a log that crosses a stream.

Finally, consider the selection of outdoor play equipment like shovels, balls, ropes, and riding toys. A few examples of outdoor equipment to support large-motor skills are presented in Table 11.2. What small-motor materials and equipment might you add to this list?

TABLE 11.2	**Outdoor Equipment***			
	Infant 6 weeks to 1 year	Toddler 1 year to 2 1/2 years	Preschool 2 1/2 years to 5 years	School Age 5 years to 8 years
Large motor Equipment	Mats/pillows Beach balls Push/pull toys Small wagon Foam rolls Tunnel 4- to 6-passenger carts Strollers Sling/backpack	In addition: Stairs/slide Rocking boat Barrel Wheelbarrows Variety of balls Simple climber	In addition: Balance beam Pedal wheel toys Larger wagons Shovels/rakes Hula hoops Planks/triangles	In addition: Sports balls Roller/ice skates Basketball hoop Jump ropes Scooters

*Adult supervision is important to ensure children's safety when playing with large-motor equipment.

Adapted from Childcraft's Guide to Equipping the Developmentally Appropriate Center, by J. Greenman (1990). From *Child Care Information Exchange, 76* 31–34. Reprinted with permission from Child Care Information Exchange, P. O. Box 3249, Redmond, WA 98073 — 1–800–221–2864.

Make a list of playground materials and equipment that you will place in each of your learning centers. Use Tables 11.1 and 11.2 as beginning points. Supplement these lists using catalogs that are available, often for free, from early childhood supply companies. Keep in mind the principles that we have reviewed so far in this chapter.

Include transitional spaces.

Classroom and outdoor spaces need not be separated. A classroom with large doors that open onto the playground, a porch, overhang, or even a covered sidewalk provide transitional spaces that can support learning activities. Perhaps the most obvious advantage of a transitional space is that it allows some outdoor activities to continue during inclement weather (e.g., riding, games). Examples of more unique activities that can be pursued in transitional spaces include the following:

- An art activity that begins in the classroom (e.g., watercolors) can be moved outdoors to observe the changes that result from exposure to sun, wind, and rain.
- Observation of changes in animal behavior across seasons is more easily accomplished in a transitional space.
- Transitional spaces provide a good venue for hanging large and messy artwork, as well as for building large structures out of cardboard.
- Transitional spaces can serve as a retreat from the harsh sun, wind, and snow.
- A shade garden can be established to compliment a sunny flower garden.
- In some environments, pets may be more easily cared for in transitional spaces.

You are now ready to consider the addition of a transitional space to link your classroom and playground.

Design your transitional space, justifying its placement and potential use. Give one example of an activity that you might plan for this space during each of the four seasons.

Consider children with diverse abilities.   Playgrounds, like classrooms, should accommodate children with diverse skills and needs. Wide door and gate openings, ramps, and oversized paths can be installed to accommodate wheelchairs. Pruned branches prevent children with limited vision from hurting themselves. Level bridges are useful for children who have difficulty climbing. Shallow-water pools allow children in wheelchairs easy access to water activities. Swing straps securely hold children who need support. Pull tunnels made of light materials can be used by children who can't use their legs. Raised sandboxes and garden boxes of different heights can be used by children who have difficulty bending or standing. Note that in Figures 11.5 and 11.6 we have used some of these options to address the inclusion of a child in a wheelchair. What other changes might you make?

Decide how two children with different types of disabilities (e.g., attention deficit, limited vision, hearing impairment, or use of one arm) will be accommodated in your playground design.

Outdoor safety is especially important.   We now briefly review some of the common factors involved in playground safety that reflect the Consumer Products Safety Commission Playground Safety guidelines (CPSC) (Consumer Products Safety Commission, 1991). We limit our discussion to only a few of the key CPSC guidelines (Kutska & Hoffman, 1992), as specialists should be consulted to address the specific safety issues associated with any particular playground space.

FIGURE 11.5   Inclusion Within a Playground

The modifications made to accommodate a child in a wheelchair are listed below. What other modifications might you make?

- Raised planters to accommodate a wheelchair
- Ramps and transfer points on playground structures and at observation area
- Surfaces throughout playground that a wheelchair can be pushed over, including the gate area
- Picnic table with space for a wheelchair
- Raised sandbox to accommodate a wheelchair

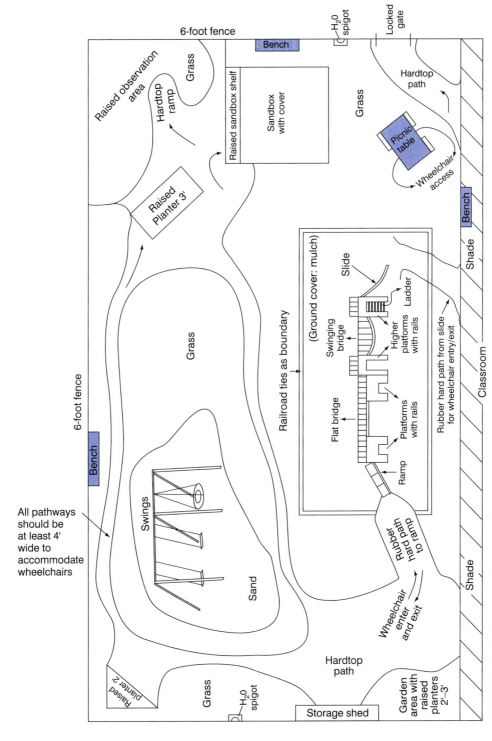

FIGURE 11.6 Inclusion Within a Playground *(Adapted and reprinted by permission of Rebecca Olson, University of Georgia.)*

319

- **Review existing equipment.**   Establish a schedule for taking inventory of all playground equipment to identify maintenance needs. Steps should be taken immediately to replace those pieces of equipment that cannot be repaired.
- **Remove inappropriate equipment.**   Some items are not recommended for use by the CPSC and should therefore be removed. These include animal figure swings, multiple occupancy swings, and rope swings. In addition, concrete footings should be covered or replaced. Cement landing pads should also be removed.
- **Use ground cover.**   It is estimated that about 70 percent of all playground injuries can be minimized by providing soft landing materials underneath playground equipment. Jumps and falls from equipment can be cushioned by using ground covers like wood mulch, wood chips, and small and coarse sand. There are advantages and disadvantages associated with each of these materials, including durability, resistance to wind, cost, ease of maintenance, and the depth of materials required to adequately cushion falls.
- **Schedule inspections and maintenance.**   A routine schedule of playground inspection is needed to ensure the safety of all playground areas. Failure to carry out such inspections can result in legal action should an accident occur.
- **Plan for upgrades.**   The school budget should include sufficient funds to repair and replace playground equipment.
- **Develop activity guidelines.**   It is also important that teachers, school administrators, parents, and children work together to develop a list of basic safety guidelines to address children's use of playground materials and equipment. One set of safety guidelines includes the following (Frost, 1992; Marotz et al., 1993):

Children should sit on climbing equipment, not hang by their knees. Children should keep their hands to themselves when playing on tall pieces of equipment. They should avoid pulling on the legs or arms of children who are playing on climbing equipment and platforms.
Children should not throw objects from playground equipment and platforms.
Children should climb only on those pieces of equipment that have been approved by teachers and school officials.
Children should face forward when swinging and swing in a straight line. There should be only one child on a swing at a time.
Children should wait until the swing comes to a stop before getting on or off.
Children should hold onto swings with both hands.
Children should only climb up the slide ladder. Only one child should be on the slide ladder and slide at one time. Children should face forward when sliding. No objects should be placed on slides or slide ladders.

As with other guidelines, these safety precautions must be adapted to each group of children. Some children will need to be introduced to the guidelines one at a time. Other children may need demonstrations to help them understand the need for safety guidelines.

List three safety guidelines that, as a teacher, you would suggest to parents and children. Swap your list with others. On what points do you agree? Give an example of how you might introduce a guideline to a particular age group.

Up to this point, we have primarily discussed the structural components of classroom and playground designs. In the following section, we discuss daily schedules.

DAILY SCHEDULES

Daily schedules provide many organizational benefits. They:

- Define the order of activities and determine how long each activity is to last.
- Ensure a balance between active and quiet activities.
- Define which areas of the classroom are to be used at different times of the day.
- Help teachers to identify the types of assistance they need to carry out activities.
- Inform teachers of the types of materials and equipment that are needed at different times of the day.
- Alert teachers to potential behavior management issues that may arise while transitioning between activities.
- Help teachers to ensure that their assessment of children encompasses different types of activities throughout the day.

Some examples of daily schedules are presented in Figure 11.7. The following principles support developmentally appropriate schedules (Bredekamp & Copple, 1997; Koralek et al., 1995; National Association of Elementary School Principals, 1993).

A Balanced Schedule

The learning materials and centers that you organized earlier in this chapter have the potential to influence your daily schedule. If you designed a large and well-supplied art center, chances are you will want to make the most of this center. Subsequently, other centers may be ignored. Likewise, if you took great pride in your playground design, it is likely that you will plan for extended periods of outdoor activities. Such influences should be recognized and steps taken to present children with a balanced schedule of activities. Remember that

FIGURE 11.7 Daily Classroom Schedules

All of the following time periods include time for cleanup and transitions.

Primary Grades (First, Second, Third)

7:30–8:00	*Arrival:* All interest centers open for self-selection
8:00–8:30	*Group Meeting:* Sharing, discussions, review of daily plans
8:30–9:30	*Reading & Writing:* Spelling group, reading group, writing center group
9:30–10:30	*Planned Outdoor Activity/Free Play*
10:30–11:30	*Arts:* Art center, dramatic center, writing center, music center
11:30–12:30	*Lunch (family style)/Rest Period/Outdoor Play*
12:30–1:30	*Math & Science:* Math group, computer center, science center, block center, social sciences center, woodworking center
1:30–2:30	*Library/Music/Children's Center Choice (alternates throughout the week)*
2:30–3:00	*Group Meeting:* Sharing, discussion, planning
3:00–3:30	*Departure:* Collect belongings, transition into after-school program, transportation home

Prekindergarten and Kindergarten

7:30–8:00	*Arrival:* All interest centers open for self-selection
8:00–8:30	*Small Groups:* Planned interest center activities to reflect weekly theme (e.g., community life, the weather, the seasons)
8:30–9:00	*Morning Snack/Bathroom*
9:00–10:15	*Planned Outdoor Activities/Free Play*
10:15–11:30	*Interest Centers:* Self-selection
11:30–12:00	*Lunch/Bathroom*
12:00–12:30	*Large-Group Time (Storybooks, songs, finger plays)*
12:30–1:30	*Rest or Nap Time/Bathroom*
1:30–2:00	*Small Groups:* Planned interest center activities to reflect weekly theme
2:00–2:30	*Group Meeting:* Sharing, discussion, planning
2:30–3:00	*Departure:* Collect belongings, transition into after-school program, transportation home

continues

FIGURE 11.7   *continued*

After-School Program

3:00–3:30	*Arrival/Snack*
3:30–4:30	*Planned Outdoor Activities/Free Play*
4:30–5:30	*Small-Group Activities:* Group projects (e.g., plays, murals, gardening)
5:30–6:30	*Self-Selected Interest Centers/Homework/Departures*

Classrooms for 2- and 3-Year-Olds

7:30–8:00	*Arrival/Free Play:* All interest centers open for self-selection
8:00–8:30	*Large Group:* Stories, finger plays, games
8:30–9:00	*Morning Snack/Bathroom*
9:00–9:30	*Small Group:* Planned interest center activities
9:30–10:30	*Planned Outdoor Activity/Free Play*
10:30–11:00	*Storytime/Bathroom*
11:00–11:30	*Lunch*
11:30–12:45	*Rest or Nap Time/Bathroom*
12:45–1:30	*Outdoor Free Play*
1:30–2:00	*Afternoon Snack/Bathroom*
2:00–2:30	*Interest Centers:* All centers open for self-selection
2:30–3:00	*Departure:* Collect belongings, transportation home

Infants and Toddlers (Half-Day Program)

7:30–8:15	*Arrival/Transition Into Classroom Environment*
8:15–9:00	*Teacher-Facilitated Play*
9:00–9:45	*Snack/Toileting*
9:45–10:00	*Circle Time:* Music, finger plays, songs, sensory experiences
10:00–10:30	*Teacher-Facilitated Outdoor Play*
10:30–11:15	*Snack/Toileting*
11:15–12:15	*Quiet Activities/Departure*

children's involvement with a range of materials and centers helps them to link their learning experiences and to look at educational concepts from different perspectives.

Other balance considerations include the scheduling of quiet and active periods, snacks and lunch, indoor and outdoor activities, and individual and group activities. Although it is usually not included on the daily schedule, time must also be allotted for cleanup. Finally, special events and field trips should follow a relaxed schedule.

Developmental Needs of Children

As is true of other aspects of classroom organization, classroom schedules should reflect the developmental needs and interests of children. For example, preschool and kindergarten children require shorter story times than do primary-grade children. Also remember that there will be differences even within the same age groups. You may find that your 6-year-olds need a slightly longer morning circle time in order to smoothly transition into the school day than do children in other first-grade classrooms. Or, as a kindergarten teacher, you may want to lengthen the snack times of your daily schedule to incorporate special learning activities. Other kindergarten teachers may find that their children become distracted when such activities are introduced into snack time.

Flexibility

Although children need continuity in their daily activities, some flexibility is needed to account for certain realities. In particular, classroom schedules must fit around school routines like recess, lunch, trips to the library, and visits by educational specialists. Classroom schedules should also accommodate children's need to pursue activities that are interesting to them. Forcing young children to adhere to a strict schedule can interfere with their developing sense of initiative and industry. It is better to allow children the extra time they need when they are heavily engaged in an activity and skip or shorten other activities.

Transitions

One of the most challenging aspects of the daily schedule is the transition between activities. Helping children to switch their focus between activities can be made easier if, as we mentioned earlier, the schedule is treated with some degree of flexibility and enough time is allotted to help children bring closure to one activity and begin another. Teachers who actively involve children in transitions also find that these periods go more smoothly. Some of the transition techniques that are commonly used by teachers include the following:

- Give children advanced warning as to when an activity is to end. Engage their senses. Familiar music or a simple clapping sound can become a routine signal that children are to begin wrapping up their activities.

- Involve children in cleanup activities. Children can help to wipe down tables, clear surfaces, and pick up the remains of their art activity. Preschool and older children can even brainstorm creative ways to move themselves from large group to learning centers.
- Facilitate cleanup by verbally reinforcing children's efforts, pointing out overlooked objects left on a table, introducing a cleanup song, and helping out yourself. Teachers' active involvement in cleanup is effective for at least three reasons. First, it allows teachers to be more empathic with the challenges that children encounter in carrying out cleanup tasks. Second, it provides an opportunity to assess children's ability to follow directions and cooperate. Finally, children are more likely to cooperate with cleanup if they see it as a fun task that involves everyone.
- Asking children younger than age 5 to maintain a line when walking down a hall is usually not very effective. Rather, teachers can best gain children's cooperation when moving outdoors or to another part of the building through "follow me" songs, finger plays, or simple games. Preschool children can also be moved in small groups according to the color of their clothing or their demonstrated ability to sit quietly. As children reach kindergarten, they can be introduced gradually to lines when they are out of their classroom. However, it is important that they understand the necessity of such lines (e.g., safety, crowding, respect for quiet zones). Transitions within the classroom should remain informal and respectful of children's abilities to display responsible group behavior.

Time Periods

The following time periods are used by teachers to organize the daily schedule. However, it is important to remember that not all teachers treat the time periods in exactly the same way.

Arrival/free choice.   Morning arrival sets the tone for the day and is critical to helping children transition into the daily schedule. It is therefore important that you plan each learning center for morning arrival just as you would during other parts of the day. Place materials on tables and arrange equipment so that children can begin their work easily while you continue to greet arriving children. Infants and toddlers will, of course, require more individual attention than will preschool and primary-grade children.

Reflect back on your earlier classroom design. Use this design to plan for morning arrival. What materials will you place in different learning centers to help children make a smooth transition into the classroom upon their morning arrival?

Group activity.   Keep group activities for infants and toddlers simple and short. They are not as interested in group activities as are older children. Likewise, they lack the social skills to truly cooperate as a cohesive group.

Group activities become more important for older children. For example, morning group for preschool and kindergarten children often involves reviewing the calendar (e.g., day of the week, month) and the weather, singing a group song, conducting a finger play, and reviewing the daily schedule. Group activities can also be used with primary-grade children to plan and review class projects, discuss an upcoming field trip or review a completed field trip, prepare holiday cards for parents or residents of a neighborhood nursing home, plan and produce plays, conduct show-and-tell, conduct reflective writing exercises, listen to community speakers, view educational videos, conduct group reading exercises, hold discussions of behavior guidelines, and hold discussions of current events (e.g., television shows, holidays, fundraisers).

Planning and transition.   Planning also represents an important part of the school day for preschool and primary-grade children. Children in younger-age classrooms (e.g., preschool and kindergarten) often plan in large or small groups, identifying the learning center in which they will begin their day. Teachers facilitate this process by providing each child a turn in identifying a center and a plan of action. The plan need not be elaborate. A child may simply state, "I want to draw a picture of my cat."

Flexibility is again key to making the plans of young children work. The main objective associated with planning is that children have some idea of where they are going and what they plan to do. Allowing children to change their plans is part of the learning process, especially as children discuss the reasons for their change of mind.

Planning for children in the first, second, and third grades is usually more informal than that for younger children. Primary-grade children are more accustomed to classroom expectations regarding the pursuit of constructive activities and behavior management guidelines. They are also able to act more independently. Simply reviewing the options available for morning activities is often sufficient to allow primary-grade children to make informed and independent choices.

Learning center activities.   Note in Figure 11.7 that a considerable amount of time is devoted to learning center activities. These are important periods of the day for preschool and primary-grade children, allowing them the freedom to explore and take full advantage of your organizational work. As a teacher, you will perform a number of support tasks during these periods:

• Observe and assess children's understanding of the materials and equipment located in different centers, making adjustments as needed to ensure that children's activities are developmentally appropriate. For example, you may find that your second-grade class needs more or less sophisticated materials and equipment in the science center to support their learning activities.

- Introduce new educational concepts through planned activities and by helping children recognize the significance of their own self-discoveries.
- Respond to questions and requests for assistance.
- Provide information and resources to help children accomplish their tasks.
- Encourage children's industriousness.
- Assist children in working through disagreements.
- Point out ways in which children can cooperate.
- Suggest new activities that can result from combining activities taking place in two or more learning centers.

Snacks and lunch. Snacks and lunch are perfect times for helping children develop good nutritional habits, safety and hygiene practices, and social skills. Likewise, involving children in various aspects of food preparation and cleanup helps them to appreciate the value of caring for others.

Academic concepts can also be incorporated into snack and lunchtimes. Preschool and kindergarten children may help pour each child "a-half" a glass of milk, or they might be asked to lay out "two napkins for each child." They can also help prepare snacks by following simple recipes that combine familiar words with pictures. Primary-grade children can work with teachers to plan budgets for different types of snacks. They can also read and discuss information about the nutritional value of different snacks.

Rest and nap time. This is a period of the day that is sometimes given cursory thought. Yet, a period of rest is essential to the well-being of children. A quality rest period depends upon attention to lighting, noise levels, and the spacing of mats. Some teachers assist children as they transition into rest time by singing a soft song with them. Other teachers play soothing music. It is not necessary that all children sleep during rest time, but it is important that they quietly read or color so as not to disturb other children. The actual length of the rest period varies depending upon school or state policies.

Outdoor play. Outdoor play, like the rest period, is also sometimes overlooked. Our earlier discussion of the importance of organizing outdoor learning centers attests to the developmental and educational significance of this period of the day. This is a period in which children not only exercise their large-motor skills, but also have opportunities to develop new insights into their world. As a teacher, you will want to monitor and facilitate children's outdoor play, just as you do within the classroom.

CHAPTER SUMMARY

Key organizational principles to address when designing classroom and playground spaces include developmentally appropriate practices, balance, inclusion, and safety. The selection of classroom materials involves consideration of children's familiarity with materials, the durability and safety of materials, variety, and the educational benefits of open-ended materials. Teachers must also consider how they will introduce and facilitate children's involvement with materials. Finally, organizational principles associated with classroom learning centers can be summarized using a "multi-s" model that includes simplicity, softness, senses, stimulation, stability, safety, and sanitation.

Outdoor playgrounds and daily schedules are also important components of quality learning environments. Many of the principles associated with organizing outdoor learning centers are similar to those for organizing classroom learning centers. Two unique playground considerations include access points and transitional spaces. Daily schedules help to define the structure and flow of activities throughout the day.

ACTIVITIES

1. Classroom organization is one of the most visible aspects of a teacher's educational philosophy. Reflect back on your educational philosophy from Chapter 1, as well as your design of learning environments from this chapter. Then write your philosophy of a quality learning environment for young children. The following questions may help guide you in this activity:
   - What was the most difficult part of organizing your classroom and playground? What was the easiest part?
   - Which organizational principles are most important to you?
   - How might you use your philosophy of education from Chapter 1 to support your organization of an early learning environment?
2. Observe the organization of two classrooms within the same grade level. Interview the teachers about the factors they considered when organizing their respective classrooms. What similarities and differences do you find?
3. Compare a kindergarten and a third-grade classroom. What differences do you see in classroom organization, materials, and schedules?
4. Is there a playground company in your community? If so, interview a representative about playground basic design and safety considerations that teachers should be aware of.
5. Ask a group of children to design their ideal classroom or playground. Is there a pattern of likes and dislikes?
6. Identify an unused outdoor community space to make into a "dream playground." Assume that money is no object. Divide into small groups and make a model or draw a diagram of your "dream playground." Playground professionals, teachers, or children might serve as judges

to award a series of "best of" awards. You can also repeat this activity by designing a "dream classroom" in an unused community indoor space.

7. Now think realistically. As a class, agree upon a realistic budget for equipping a new classroom or playground. Identify the age group that will occupy these spaces. Collect early childhood supply catalogs. Divide into small groups and use the catalogs to design learning centers and supply them with materials. Compare your results. Which group made the most creative use of the class budget?

chapter 12

Guiding and Managing the Behavior of Young Children

After reading this chapter you should be able to discuss the following questions:

❖ What is the goal of behavior management?
❖ What is the difference between child guidance and child obedience?
❖ What is the difference between behavior management models based on low, medium, and high teacher-control practices?
❖ What is your personal philosophy of behavior management?

CHAPTER OVERVIEW

The management of an early childhood classroom is one of the most challenging aspects of teaching. When attending professional conferences, we often find that the demand for workshops on behavior management far exceeds conference offerings. We also find that teachers who attend such workshops sometimes have unrealistic expectations. They may request solutions to "problem" behaviors, instead of first seeking an understanding of those behaviors. They may expect behavior management practices to generalize to all children, instead of remembering that each child is unique. And, they may fail to reflect upon how the advice of "experts" relates to their own "expert" understanding of the children in their classrooms.

Our goal in this chapter is to examine issues and concepts that will allow you to develop an informed philosophy of behavior management. We begin with an examination of your personal experiences and thoughts. Next, we review the goal of behavior management. We then compare the differences between behavior management practices that are based upon principles of child guidance versus child obedience. Four behavior management models are also reviewed. A series of guides is provided in Activity 1 at the end of the chapter to assist you in writing your own philosophy of behavior management.

PERSONAL EXPERIENCES

Teachers and parents alike often justify their use of behavior management practices based upon their own experiences. Some follow the same practices used by their teachers and parents. Others use completely different practices as a reaction against those used by their teachers and parents. It is therefore appropriate to begin our discussion of behavior management with a reflective task:

• Think back to your own childhood. Describe the behavior management practices used by your parents, caregivers, and teachers. In what ways were these practices similar and different? How did you respond to the different practices? In what ways have your childhood experiences shaped your own thoughts about behavior management? You may find it interesting to compare your experiences and thoughts with those of your peers. Do not be surprised to find differences within your peer group.

Defining Behavior Management

We define *behavior management* as a socialization process whereby teachers help children to have their needs met in socially responsible ways. In practical terms, behavior management may be approached as a science, an art form, and as a game. Think back once again to your own childhood as you read the following sections. In what ways did your parents and teachers approach behavior management as a science, an art form, and a game?

Behavior management as a science.   The "science" of behavior management is reflected in the different models that we review later in this chapter. Bookstores are filled with child-guidance books that reflect these "scientific" approaches to behavior management. Each model represents a different interpretation of the types of teacher-child interactions that are needed to support children's early development and education. As a teacher, you must decide how each model fits your own philosophy of behavior management.

Behavior management as an art.   It is unrealistic to believe that all children will respond to all behavior management practices in the same way. It is likewise unrealistic to expect teachers to be equally successful when implementing each and every behavior management practice. Teachers must decide how their personal strengths and personality fit with different practices. This is the "art" of behavior management. "Creative" teachers are reflective, adapting their personal style of social interaction and teaching to meet the needs of individual children and the classroom as a whole.

Behavior management as a game.   It is a fact that throughout the year, children change, teachers change, and the classroom environment changes. It is for these reasons that experienced teachers know that behavior management must also be seen as a "game." Even behavior management practices that worked perfectly well in the morning may no longer be effective in the afternoon. They may need to be modified to fit a new situation, adapted to children's changing physical or social-emotional states, or combined with other practices. Your success as a teacher will, in part, depend upon your ability to remain flexible and open to using a range of developmentally appropriate behavior management practices. The development of this skill begins with your understanding of the goal of behavior management.

THE GOAL OF BEHAVIOR MANAGEMENT

Although a number of goals can be associated with behavior management, one goal in particular is important. Teachers, parents, and youth leaders all assume responsibility for socializing children for life in a democratic society. It is therefore important that teachers use behavior management practices that guide children's social learning so that they are able to make a healthy adult adjustment to American democracy. This idea is not new, as reflected in the following 1974 quote:

> (Behavior management) is the fulcrum of education. Without (behavior management) both teacher and pupil become unbalanced and very little learning takes place. . . . The successful formula for guiding children in the classroom is based on the belief that democracy is not just a political ideal, but a way of life. This freedom is not license. It is a shared responsibility which must be taught.*

We have identified three socialization objectives that reflect life in a democratic society in general and a democratic classroom in particular (see Tips for Teachers 12.1). These three objectives are determination, dependability, and diligence.

Determination

Children, as well as adults, encounter all types of challenges in their personal lives. Healthy individuals develop a sense of determination to overcome challenges, discover truths, seek justice, and defend those who are unable to defend themselves. Such determination may at times even go against popular opinion. Nevertheless, a democratic society depends upon individuals who assert their right to be heard and respected.

A sense of determination is developed when teachers respect children's feelings and ideas, help children to identify their personal strengths, serve as experienced guides to help children think through their actions, and expose children to role models who themselves display determination.

Dependability

A democratic society depends upon family systems, employment environments, and communities in which individuals are dependable and trustworthy. Children who live in a democratic society must therefore learn to demonstrate that they can be trusted by their families, teachers, and peers to "do the right thing."

Young children are often unable to see how their words and actions impact those around them. Teachers help children develop a sense of dependability when they encourage children to reflect upon the consequences of their behavior and to assume responsibility for their behavior. Children also learn dependability when they

*From *Discipline without Tears* by Rudolf Dreikurs and Pearl Cassel. Copyright © 1972 by Pearl G. Cassel. Used by permission of Dutton, a division of Penguin Putnam, Inc.

TIPS FOR TEACHERS 12.1

Nurturing Determination, Dependability, and Diligence

Determination

- Encourage children to persist at tasks that they find frustrating.
- Help children to reflect upon their abilities and strengths.
- Help children to think through their alternatives before acting.
- Expose children to role models who display determination.
- Read stories or conduct plays that include themes of determination.

Dependability

- Allow children to help establish classroom rules.
- Encourage children to assume responsibility for their behavior.
- Help children to reflect upon the consequences of their behavior.

- Make games inclusive of all abilities.
- Provide time in class to discuss the importance of cooperation and dependability.

Diligence

- Encourage children's sense of initiative and industry.
- Help children to think of ways to consistently complete their assigned responsibilities.
- Provide sufficient time, material, and support for children to complete their activities.
- Encourage effort and success equally.
- Include themes of diligence in classroom lesson plans.

---

are able to understand and function within appropriate limits. Finally, children develop a sense of dependability by learning to work cooperatively with their peers.

Diligence

A democratic society depends upon individuals who are diligent in carrying out their family, career, and civic roles. They pay attention to their own needs as well as to the needs of others. Diligent individuals also have a sense of achievement. They seek to accomplish the tasks they undertake rather than to simply "get by."

Teachers help children develop a sense of diligence by allowing them to persist at a task rather than interrupting or forcing them to prematurely end their activity. Children's efforts and accomplishments are equally encouraged. Children are also given developmentally appropriate responsibilities. When necessary, teachers help children to think through ways in which to carry out their responsibilities in a timely and responsible manner.

One challenge to helping children develop a sense of determination, dependability, and diligence is to decide upon the degree to which teachers should guide or control children's behavior. We next examine the difference between child guidance and child obedience as agents of behavior management.

CHILD GUIDANCE VERSUS CHILD OBEDIENCE

You may have already observed that behavior management is a broad term. This can sometimes lead to confusion. For example, some people consider *child guidance* and *child discipline* to be synonymous. Others do not. In general, professionals take two approaches to dealing with this dilemma. Some scholars attempt to reconcile what they see as simple semantic differences between the two phrases by equating "child guidance" with "positive discipline" practices (Marion, 1995). This is a valid approach in that the concept of discipline has its origin in Latin and is roughly defined as meaning "guidance" or "instruction." The problem with this approach is that it is rarely followed in practice. Instead, a "semantic slide" takes place in which teachers confuse discipline with punishment (Gartrell, 1997):

> . . . teachers have a hard time telling where discipline ends and punishment begins. . . . when most teachers use discipline, they tend to include acts of punishment; they mix up discipline and punishment out of anger or because they feel the child "deserves it." The very idea of "disciplining" a child suggests punishment, illustrating the easy semantic slide of the one into the other.*

A second approach makes a clearer distinction between positive child "guidance" practices and negative child "obedience" practices. In this approach, references to "discipline" are dropped. Our experience leads us to agree with Gartrell's (1997) analysis of guidance and discipline. It is for this reason that we distinguish between child "guidance" and "obedience."

We see *child guidance* as being synonymous with democratic behavior management in that teachers and children discuss their feelings and thoughts as a means of resolving disputes, clarifying misunderstandings, and meeting individual needs. The behavior management models of Ginott and Dreikurs, which we review later in this chapter, represent examples of child guidance. We define *child obedience* as a unilateral process in which teachers make demands of children and administer some type of punishment when those demands are not met. The behavior management model of Canter, which we review later in this chapter contains elements of child obedience. A summary of the distinguishing characteristics of child-guidance and child-obedience practices follows.

Punishment versus Understanding

Obedience practices often involve punishment as a means of control. *Punishment* is characterized by a loss of rights or a taking away of something that is valued. Missing recess and spending time alone in a corner of the room are two popular types of punishment. In the first instance (missing recess), children are denied their right to physical exercise. In the second instance (time out), children are held up for public ridicule.

---

*Adapted from "Beyond Discipline to Guidance," by D. Gartrell from *Young Children* (Sept. 1997). Copyright © 1997 by Daniel J. Gartrell. Reprinted by permission.

Corporal punishment.   This is a more extreme version of punishment that can involve physical force (e.g., slapping, spanking), emotional ridicule (e.g., name calling), isolation, and denial of basic needs (e.g., food, rest, clothing). Although still sanctioned by some states, corporal punishment is considered developmentally inappropriate (Bredekamp & Copple, 1997) in that it does not teach self-control or build self-esteem (Gartrell, 1994; Marion, 1995). It thus runs counter to the goals of a democratic society. There are also practical reasons why teachers should never use or endorse any type of punishment:

- Children may internalize the force and intimidation that accompanies punishment and subsequently use them against their peers.
- Parents may view punishment as their exclusive right and responsibility.
- Although parents may endorse the use of punishment, they may not agree with your decision to use it in a given situation and/or your delivery of punishment.
- Parents may define punishment quite differently than do you or your school. For example, your endorsement of punishment may lead some parents to believe that you support the use of physical and/or emotional abuse.
- Parents who believe that a teacher has employed "excessive" punishment can take legal action, even in states that allow for corporal punishment.

     In contrast to the punishment that accompanies obedience practices, guidance practices focus on understanding the motivations behind children's behavior so that appropriate steps can be taken to help children learn socially appropriate behaviors:

> The teacher believes in the positive potential of each child. He recognizes that mistaken behaviors are caused by inexperience in social situations, the influence of others on the child, or by deep, unmet physical or emotional needs. Understanding why children show mistaken behavior permits the teacher to teach social skills with a minimum of moral judgement about the child. He takes the attitudes that "we all make mistakes; we just need to learn from them."*

Short-Term External Control versus Long-Term Internal Control

Obedience practices have a short-term focus on maintaining classroom control through external pressure from the teacher. Although classroom control is also an objective of child-guidance practices, it is not the major objective. It is instead viewed as a secondary effect of teachers helping children to achieve internal control through learning communication and problem-solving skills. In short, teachers use child-guidance practices to help children develop responsible behavior patterns that will endure over the long term and will be self-initiated.

*Adapted from "Beyond Discipline to Guidance," by D. Gartrell from *Young Children* (Sept. 1997). Copyright © 1997 by Daniel J. Gartrell. Reprinted by permission.

Focus on Conformity Versus Self-Expression

Obedience practices focus only on whether or not behaviors conform to rules established by teachers. Children's angry outbursts are seen as confrontational and disrespectful. Punishment usually follows. Guidance practices help children to express their thoughts and feelings in appropriate ways. Children's angry outbursts are seen as opportunities for teaching children how to express themselves using appropriate communication skills.

Teacher-Centered Versus Team-Centered

We already have implied that obedience practices are teacher-centered—the teacher sets and enforces classroom rules. As a result, numerous classroom rules may accrue throughout the year, making it difficult for young children to keep them all in mind.

Guidance practices rely upon a team-centered approach that acknowledges the expectations of teachers, parents, and children themselves (Gartrell, 1997) (see Figure 12.1). Because of the different expectations that often exist among these groups, it is usually best to begin the year with only a few simple rules of conduct upon which everyone can agree (Gartrell, 1997). For example, many of the most important rules established by children and teachers throughout the year revolve around issues of safety. Consider the following safety rules:

- I will take care of myself.
- I will take care of others.
- I will take care of the classroom.

Note that these rules are short and vague. This is intentional. Such simple rules provide children and teachers an opportunity to discuss situations and engage in problem solving. In contrast, specific rules may not apply to every situation. What types of classroom situations might arise in which teachers and children would need to discuss these rules?

Group Focus Versus Individual Focus

Obedience practices that rely upon teacher-centered rules and the short-term consequences of misbehavior lend themselves to a focus on the group. Few considerations are given to the circumstances surrounding broken rules, and few exceptions are made for children who are unfortunate enough to have overlooked a classroom rule.

Teachers who employ guidance practices take into account both the context of the behavior and the individual personalities of children. These considerations are used to form an alliance with children to discuss why classroom rules were ignored and to explore potential behavioral alternatives that children might choose in the future. In addition, teachers attempt to avoid embarrassing children by discussing behaviors, not personalities. You will learn how to develop this skill later in this chapter.

FIGURE 12.1   A Team Approach to Child Guidance

Parents, teachers, and children often have different perspectives of early childhood classrooms. What other thoughts might you add to these three lists?

Teacher's Perspective

• Others judge my teaching skills by the behavior of the children in my classroom.

• I am responsible for the safety of all the children in my classroom.

• I must maintain classroom order if I am to successfully carry out my lesson plans.

• Classroom projects require children to listen, follow directions, and cooperate.

Parent's Perspective

• I expect to be consulted about classroom behavior management practices.

• I can help my child's teacher to avoid conflict by providing her with information about my child's life experiences, interpersonal skills, interests, and fears.

• Teachers should respect the values and life goals that I hold for my child.

• Teachers should be prepared to answer my questions about behavior management issues.

Children's Perspective

• We want to have fun.

• We like having options and choices.

• We respond best to those rules that we help to develop.

• We need time to learn about new environments and rules.

• We are eager to please those who treat us with respect.

• We have bad days when we just want to be left alone.

• We don't always get along with all of our peers.

Reactive Versus Proactive

Teachers who use obedience practices take a reactive approach to behavior management. They wait for a misbehavior and then respond with some type of punishment. In contrast, teachers who use guidance practices are proactive in their attempts to understand the children in their classroom, the motivations behind their behavior, and ways in which classroom situations may create opportunities for misbehavior (e.g., overcrowding, a rushed schedule, a lack of materials).

In closing this section, we should note that teachers who use guidance practices are sometimes accused of being too "soft," allowing children to "rule," or of having "no discipline standards." These allegations are not true. It is true that the teacher-child interactions associated with child-guidance practices take time, energy, and patience. In contrast, child-obedience practices are much easier to administer since they focus only upon the needs of the teacher and the short-term objective of classroom control. In the long term, however, helping children to internalize socially appropriate behavior standards that support the values of a democratic society is time, energy, and patience well spent.

The characteristics that distinguish child guidance and child discipline form the foundation for understanding the "science" of implementing behavior management models. We now turn to an examination of behavior management models found in classrooms.

BEHAVIOR MANAGEMENT MODELS

Behavior management models provide teachers with a structure for their interactions with children. In particular, behavior management models promote three reflective functions that are critical to developing and applying an informed philosophy of behavior management:

- **Behavioral motives** provide teachers with a reference point from which to consider the motives behind children's behavior.
- **Personal experiences and beliefs** challenge teachers to systematically think through their personal experiences and thoughts regarding children in general and teacher-child interactions in particular.
- **Applications** allow teachers to consider how different behavior management practices might be applied within a classroom.

Many more behavior management models exist than we can cover in this chapter. We therefore limit our discussion to three models that reflect low, medium, and high degrees of teacher involvement in maintaining classroom control and order (Burden, 1995). Put another way, the models that follow move from a pure child-centered classroom (low control) to a reciprocal child-teacher classroom (medium control), to a pure teacher-centered classroom (high control).

Haim Ginott: A Low-Control Perspective of Behavior Management

You will recall from Chapter 1 that a nature perspective of child development and education emphasizes innate forces. The behavior of children naturally unfolds as children mature. This perspective is typically associated with a low degree of teacher involvement in classroom behavior management (Burden, 1995). Child-guidance practices are based on the belief that an accepting environment enables children to realize their innate ability to control their behavior and make decisions that will promote their personal development. Teachers thus accept children as they present themselves, looking for the good in every child. They encourage children to explore and express their thoughts and natural abilities.

Respect for children's emerging self-esteem is a hallmark of a low control approach to behavior management.

Haim Ginott's (1969; 1993) humanistic model of behavior management represents a low-control perspective of behavior management in which teachers respect, protect, and promote young children's emerging self-concept. Rather than taking the lead, teachers follow the lead of children. Teachers who follow this perspective serve as reflective mirrors of children's feelings and behaviors, listening to children's concerns, inquiring as to their interests, and reflecting back the feelings that children express. In this sense, Ginott's behavior management practices represent the most pure form of a child-centered classroom. The importance of supportive teacher-child interactions is reflected in Ginott's "cardinal principle":

> At their best, teachers address themselves to the child's situation. At their
> worst, they judge his character and personality. This, in essence, is the differ-
> ence between effective and ineffective communication.*

In this statement, Ginott is advising teachers to address themselves to children's behavior while protecting children's self-worth. Ginott's focus on communication is of particular importance in that it reflects his belief in the need to guide children's exploration and expression of self through dialogue:

*Adapted from *Teacher and Child: A Book for Parents and Teachers* by H. G. Ginott. Copyright © (1993) by Alice Ginott. Reprinted by permission.

Emotions are part of our genetic heritage. . . . While we are not free to choose the emotions that arise in us, we are free to choose how and when to express them, provided we know what they are. That is the crux of the problem. Many people have been educated out of knowing what their feelings are. . . . Emotional education can help children to know what they feel. It is more important for a child to know what he feels than why he feels it. . . . How can we help a child to know his feelings? We can do so by serving as a mirror to his emotions. . . . The function of an emotional mirror is to reflect feelings as they are, without distortion.*

"Emotional education" is thus achieved when teachers communicate their unwavering support and acceptance of children while at the same time helping children to understand their own feelings. The following communication and support practices affirm children's "emotional education" (Burden, 1995; Gartrell, 1994; Ginott, 1969; 1993).

Encourage children's efforts and successes.
Encouragement involves recognizing not only children's successes, but also their efforts. Encouraging remarks are tied to specific behaviors and events, not just outcomes. Encouragement of children's efforts and socially appropriate behaviors also reinforces their understanding of democratic values like determination, dependability, and diligence.

In contrast, praise for being a "good boy" or a "perfect student" sounds nice, but it is not linked to specific behaviors or events that children can point to as concrete indicators of their self-worth. Praise also focuses only upon children's accomplishments or character. Consider the following exchange involving Miesha's first-place award for her art project. Which exchange is more encouraging?

Mr. Simon: "Miesha, I am so proud of you. You're the best."

(versus)

Ms. Goldman: "Miesha, you made a very interesting sculpture that was recognized by the judges as the best in our school. That shows a real talent. You must feel very proud right now."

Mr. Simon's praise was void of facts regarding Miesha's efforts. Ms. Goldman was much better at helping Miesha to connect her efforts and feelings. Her encouragement focused on facts regarding specific behaviors and their consequences. We will have more to say about encouragement versus praise later in this chapter when we discuss Dreikurs's behavior management model.

Identify and accept children's feelings.
Children's statements sometimes have less to do with their words than the feelings behind those words. Consider the following examples. Which teacher is better at focusing on the heart of Beth's communication?

*Adapted from *Between Parent and Child: New Solutions to Old Problems* by H. G. Ginott. Copyright © (1969) by Alice Ginott. Reprinted by permission.

| Beth: | "You never choose me to go first. I hate you." |
| Mr. Simon: | "Oh, I know you don't really hate me. Come sit by me." |

(versus)

| Ms. Goldman: | "I can hear that you are really angry with me." |

Mr. Simon denied Beth the right to feel angry. As an adult, think about how you feel when someone dismisses your feelings. It can be very frustrating. Ms. Goldman recognized that children too want to be heard and began by first acknowledging that she had heard and accepted Beth's feelings. Now they can move on to discuss those feelings.

Focus on relationships first, then on the situation.   Effective teachers allow "statements of understanding (to) precede statements of advice or instruction" (Ginott, 1969, p. 20). Consider the following exchange. Which response follows this communication practice?

| Randy: | "You never choose me to go first." |
| Mr. Simon: | "Randy, it sounds like you feel that I don't treat you fairly." |

(versus)

| Ms. Goldman: | "I'll choose you first tomorrow." |

Mr. Simon provided a relationship frame of reference. He recognized that Randy's statement involves more than just the event Randy described; it also involves a relationship issue. In contrast, Ms. Goldman ignored Randy's relationship message and instead focused only on the situation. Even if Randy does go first tomorrow, his feelings about his relationship with Ms. Goldman will not have been addressed.

Empathize without protest.   When children express negative images of themselves, our first response is often to deny or protest. A better response is to indicate that we understand the feelings expressed. Again, consider the following exchange. Which teacher is responding appropriately?

| Ti: | "I'm such a loser." |
| Mr. Simon: | "You don't really like yourself right now." |

(versus)

| Ms. Goldman: | "You are not a loser. We are all winners." |

Mr. Simon began by acknowledging Ti's feelings. This may not make Ti feel any better, but it did let her know that she was heard. Mr. Simon may now choose to follow up by helping Ti to identify what she likes about herself. On the other hand, Ms. Goldman protested Ti's statement by offering faint praise. Not only did she deny Ti her feelings, but her general statement that "we are all winners" may have confirmed Ti's feelings that she is a loser among a group of winners.

Invite cooperation.   Cooperation in the classroom is achieved by giving children choices and allowing children to make their own decisions. These practices help children to gain a sense of self-reliance by discovering that they can make responsible decisions independent of adults. The following example demonstrates one way to invite cooperation:

Mr. Simon:	"We need to begin cleaning up. Decide who at your table will put away materials and who will wipe down the table. I'll walk by each table to answer any questions."

Mr. Simon clearly demonstrated his trust in children by inviting their cooperation in the cleanup activity. He left the decision-making process up to the children while letting them know that he was available to answer their questions. Mr. Simon realized that young children can live up to our expectations when we send simple and clear messages that we trust their ability to cooperate with us.

Attack the behavior, not the child.   Although it is sometimes difficult to do, teachers should keep in mind that it is children's behavior that angers them, not children themselves.

> The realities of teaching . . . make anger inevitable. Teachers need not apologize for their angry feelings. . . . An enlightened teacher is not afraid of his anger, because he has learned to express it without doing damage. He describes what he sees, what he feels, and what he expects. He attacks the problem, not the person. . . .*

When we fail to make this distinction between behavior and child, we run the risk of attacking children with statements like "You are so clumsy" or "This would never have happened if you would learn to follow directions." Both of these statements attack children's character while ignoring the actual behavior that led to our anger. One common strategy for attacking the behavior and not the child is the use of "I" or "me" messages. Two examples follow:

Mr. Simon:	"Jessie, I am angry that my instructions were ignored."
Ms. Goldman:	"Danielle, it makes me angry when others jump ahead."

Note that both teachers communicated their feelings about a behavior while avoiding attacks on the children's characters.

State your expectations.   Stating your expectations of children following the use of "I" or "me" messages is especially important for young children who may not fully understand the consequences of their behavior or who may not know how to correct their behavior. Consider how Mr. Simon and Ms. Goldman follow up their initial "I" and "me" messages with statements regarding their expectations.

*Adapted from *Teacher and Child: A Book for Parents and Teachers* by H. G. Ginott. Copyright © (1993) by Alice Ginott. Reprinted by permission.

Mr. Simon: "Jessie, I am angry that my instructions were ignored. It is important that we work together on this. I need for you to repeat my instructions so that I know you understand me."

Ms. Goldman: "Danielle, it makes me angry when others jump ahead. I need for you to raise your hand before getting out of line."

Provide behavioral alternatives to direct children's behavior. Simply criticizing children's behavior provides no educational instruction as to appropriate behavior. "Emotional education" is provided when children are given appropriate behavioral alternatives. Consider how Mr. Simon and Ms. Goldman respond when they observe Julio jumping on his cot:

Mr. Simon: "Julio, you know better than that. Stop it."

(versus)

Ms. Goldman: "Julio, remember that we do not jump on our cots. You may sit or lay on your cot. You can jump when we go outside."

Mr. Simon criticized without providing direction other than a stern "Stop it." In contrast, Ms. Goldman took the time to remind Julio of a classroom rule, to provide two appropriate behavioral alternatives, and to remind Julio that jumping was allowed outside. Who provided the better "emotional education" in this situation?

Accept children's comments. Children sometimes make statements that have nothing to do with the activity under way. Teachers should nevertheless acknowledge these statements as they might have some unknown importance. For example, some aspect of an activity might remind children of recent home experiences. Or, the activity might lead to feelings that children themselves can't explain. In either case, it is important that young children be allowed to share their feelings. Both of the following examples demonstrate the practice of accepting students' comments:

Mr. Simon: "I appreciate you telling me about your baby brother. Maybe you could draw me a picture of him later. What do you think of our story so far?

Ms. Goldman: "I also think that blue is a pretty color. What do you think about the green frog that we are looking at?"

Note that in both examples, the teachers first acknowledged the children's statements and then gently brought them back to the activity at hand. In both cases, the teachers recognized that some underlying motivation lay behind the children's statements. In the first example, it may be that something in the story led the child to think about her baby brother. In the second example, the green frog may have frightened the child who managed his fear by attempting to mentally create his favorite color of blue.

It is equally important to note what the teachers did not do. They did not attempt to second-guess the children or to question them at length about their comments. They also avoided criticizing the children for not paying attention.

Help children to solve their own problems.

As we noted earlier, children learn to be self-reliant when teachers help them to solve their own problems. Teachers may provide suggestions, offer options, point out possible consequences, clarify the situation, or simply listen. Consider the following comments made by Mr. Simon and Ms. Goldman when observing two students arguing over the use of a computer:

Mr. Simon: "John and Will, remember our discussion about sharing. Please think of some ways that you can share the computer."

(versus)

Ms. Goldman: "John and Will, you need to share. Take turns. John, you go first; then it will be Will's turn."

Mr. Simon clarified a classroom rule and then made the children jointly responsible for thinking of ways to share the computer. Ms. Goldman likewise stated her expectations, but she took sole responsibility for their application. John and Will had no say in the matter. How do you think John and Will may have felt in these two situations?

Keep your comments and directions brief.

Children, like adults, do not need or want long lectures about their behavior. Neither do they need or want long directives. They do need brief, clear statements that are oriented to solving a problem or resolving a dispute. Consider the following two examples:

Mr. Simon: "Tedra, I am happy that you are working so hard on this project. I know that you only want to use the really small pieces of paper to make your collage, but we only have about 10 minutes left before we go to lunch. That means that in 5 minutes we will need to put away our materials and wash our hands. Otherwise, we will be late for lunch. I know that you like to finish your work on time, and I don't want you to feel rushed. You may find it easier to use some bigger pieces of paper, or you may want to make your collage smaller. Don't worry, though, if you don't have time to finish just now. You will have more time later today."

(versus)

Ms. Goldman: "I am happy to see that you are working so hard on this project. We have about 5 minutes before we stop to prepare for lunch. If you don't have time to finish just now, you will have more time this afternoon."

Ms. Goldman communicated basically the same message as did Mr. Simon, but in fewer words. Both teachers recognized that Tedra likes to deal with detail and she often runs into time barriers. Unfortunately, there is nothing that can be done about the school lunch schedule. How do you think Tedra might have felt about these two different messages? How might she have responded to the two messages?

We think it important to end our discussion of Ginott by returning to two issues raised earlier in this chapter. First, the communication practices just summarized represent a "science," an "art," and a "game." Although Ginott provided a systematic approach to behavior management based upon communication practices ("science"), Mr. Simon and Ms. Goldman had varying degrees of success in adapting the different practices ("art"). Each teacher also had to decide when and how to use each behavior management practice ("game").

Second, you may have already noted that many of these communication practices do not come easily. They take time and practice to perfect. In fact, teachers sometimes admit to feeling uncomfortable when attempting to use Ginott's communication practices. Others feel that they lack the time and energy to become skilled in their use. It may help you to know that, as students, we too felt uncomfortable at first when implementing Ginott's practices. However, we can also assure you that with a little practice, these communication techniques will quickly become a valued part of your behavior management plan. Just remember that "practice makes perfect" and that the long-term goal of preparing children for life in a democratic society is not an easy task. It requires time and energy.

Rudolf Dreikurs: A Medium-Control Perspective of Behavior Management

You will recall from Chapter 1 that an interactionist perspective emphasizes the combined forces of nature and the environment in children's development and education. Teachers who adopt this perspective take into account children's natural abilities as well as their social environments. They use a medium level of classroom control that is characterized by reflection and flexibility (Burden, 1995). For example, teachers are accepting of children's internal feelings while also recognizing that learning best takes place within an orderly classroom. Behavior management is thus viewed as a joint teacher-child responsibility, and children and teachers work together to develop classroom rules. Although teachers take the feelings, interests, and needs of individual children into account, the ultimate goal is to help all children appreciate the need for and adaptation to group guidelines.

Rudolf Dreikurs based his behavior management model on a "democratic" style of teacher-child interaction. Can you identify elements of determination, dependability, and diligence in the following passage?

> Cooperation in the democratic classroom is based on consideration for the other's rights and interests while standing up for one's own rights. . . . Respect implies the recognition that the other person has something to offer, as well as the right to offer it. . . . Respect for oneself implies not letting oneself be put into another person's services forcibly, standing up for

A democratic classroom represents a medium-control approach to behavior management.

one's beliefs without getting into a fight, not abusing those who are weaker or younger, or punishing others for not accepting one's ideas. . . . In a democratic classroom the pupils and the teacher are united in planning, organizing, implementing, and participating in their common activities. . . . Essential to a democratic classroom is a combination of firmness and kindness expressed in the teacher's attitude toward her class. *Firmness* implies self-respect; *kindness* implies respect for others. Neither one alone achieves a harmonious relationship of equals. We can resolve our conflicts without either fighting or yielding, by both respecting others and respecting ourselves. This is the foundation upon which satisfactory classroom relationships are built (Dreikurs, Grunwald, & Pepper, 1982, pp. 68–69).

As reflected in this quote, Dreikurs's model of democratic behavior management is characterized by both specific guidance practices and a dialogue model. In this chapter, we focus primarily on his guidance practices.

Encouragement. Similar to Ginott, Dreikurs endorsed the use of encouragement. Some examples of encouraging practices noted by Dreikurs follow (Dreikurs & Cassel, 1972; Dreikurs, Grunwald, & Pepper, 1982). You will note that many of the practices support or extend Ginott's views.

- Teachers focus on improvement, not perfection.
- Teachers commend effort, not just results.

- Teachers separate the deed from the doer. They reject a child's behavior without rejecting the child.
- Teachers build on children's strengths, not their weaknesses. Success is seen as a result of encouragement, and is not its primary goal.
- Teachers show faith in all children.
- Mistakes are viewed as learning opportunities, not mistakes. Teachers use children's mistakes to modify or plan new learning experiences.
- Teachers reinforce and stimulate children, but they do not push. Children are allowed to move at their own pace.
- Teachers allow children to take care of themselves. They encourage age-appropriate self-sufficiency.
- Teachers use nonverbal and verbal encouragement. For example, different messages can be delivered in the grading of a 10-item exam (Dreikurs, Grunwald, & Pepper, 1982). The teacher may write "+6" or "−4" on a paper to indicate the same grade. Which grade is an example of nonverbal encouragement?

Can you think of how each of these examples might translate into specific classroom practices? A few examples follow (Dreikurs, Grunwald, & Pepper, 1982):

- Allow children turns at instructing the class on something they know how to do well, no matter how insignificant the activity.
- Assign special jobs to children that match their unique talents.
- Display children's work for which they express pride.
- Let children who show a disinterest in writing help you write down daily assignments.

Encouragement also involves verbal communication. Some examples of verbal encouragement include the following.* Can you think of others?

- "You have improved in . . ."
- "Let's try it together."
- "We now know that you made a mistake. What can you do differently?"
- "You would like me to think you can't do this, but I think you can."
- "What did you learn from this activity?"
- "What do you like about your story?"
- "How did you figure this out?"

Children who receive such verbal encouragement are prompted to reflect upon both their efforts and their accomplishments. As a result, they learn to think beyond their self-perceived inadequacies to identify their strengths (Dreikurs & Cassel, 1972). In contrast, children who are discouraged dwell upon how others see them, often downplaying their true abilities.

Praise versus encouragement.   One practice that can lead to discouragement is praise. The difference between encouragement and praise can be

*From *Discipline without Tears* by Rudolf Dreikurs and Pearl Cassel. Copyright © 1972 by Pearl G. Cassel. Used by permission of Dutton, a division of Penguin Putnam, Inc.

seen in the following comparison statements. Note how encouragement focuses on children's efforts and/or feelings, while praise focuses only on children's accomplishments and/or teacher judgements (Dreikurs, Grunwald, & Pepper, 1982):

Praise	*Encouragement*
• "Im so proud of you."	• "You must feel proud of your work."
• "You are always so good."	• "I really appreciate your help."
• "Congratulations! You're the best in math."	• "Your hard work in math really shows."
• "You're the best."	• "You take your work seriously."

These differences, while subtle, send very different messages and result in different behaviors. Some of the behaviors that can result from encouragement and praise follow (Dreikurs, Grunwald, & Pepper, 1982):

Praise	*Encouragement*
• Reinforces competition	• Reinforces cooperation
• Focuses on the quality of performance	• Focuses on effort and enjoyment
• Causes students to feel judged	• Causes students to feel accepted
• Fosters fear of failure	• Fosters acceptance of personal strengths and challenges
• Fosters dependence	• Fosters independence

Logical consequences.   The distinguishing characteristic of this practice is that children are allowed to experience the consequences of their behavior. Also, both teachers and children are empowered through the use of logical consequences. A few examples of logical consequences are shown in Box 12.1. How are both teachers and children empowered in these examples?

Natural consequences.   Whereas logical consequences are arranged by teachers, natural consequences are arranged by nature (Dreikurs, Grunwald, & Pepper, 1982). A child who fails to follow a teacher's request to walk, not run, on an icy sidewalk experiences the natural consequence of falling. The "teacher" in this situation is the natural event that results from running on an icy sidewalk. Two other examples of natural consequences follow. Can you think of others?

- **Case 1:** Jacqui ignores the teacher's directions to "not touch the hot plate" and burns her hand.
- **Case 2:** Chi fails to pay attention while instructions are being given on building kites. Later in the day, her kite breaks apart on its first launching.

Natural consequences should be used with extreme caution. In particular, teachers should avoid using natural consequences as a form of punishment. For example, allowing a child to experience the natural consequence of going outside in freezing weather because she does not want to wear a jacket is inappropriate.

BOX 12.1 | *Logical Consequences*

Logical Consequences in Ms. Fraser's Kindergarten

Five-year-old Lea makes colorful designs on the wall near the art center. Ms. Fraser reminds Lea of the rule that we write "only on paper" unless otherwise instructed by a teacher. She gives Lea the choice of helping to wash or paint the wall.

Six-year-old Rosa runs into the street during a field trip to a local park. Ms. Fraser reminds Rosa of field trip rules. She offers Rosa the choice of holding hands with an adult for the rest of the trip or sitting with the secretary in the park office.

Logical Consequences in Mr. Herrera's First-Grade Classroom

Seven-year-old Steven quickly says, "I'm sorry" after throwing a toy across the room and hitting the teacher assistant. Mr. Herrera responds, "Thank you for saying you are sorry. Now what are you going to do to fix this situation?"

Eight-year-old Rob pushes another child off a swing during recess. Mr. Herrera reminds himself to address the deed and not the child and asks Rob what he thinks should be done to make amends.

* * *

It is important to note that although logical consequences seem simple, they require planning. The following characteristics define the effective use of logical consequences (Dreikurs & Cassel, 1974; Dreikurs, Grunwald, & Pepper, 1982):

- **They should be logically related to the inappropriate behavior.** Requiring Lea to skip recess will not result in a clean wall. It is not a logical consequence of Lea's behavior. Helping to clean or paint the wall does correct the situation. Both activities represent logical consequences of Lea's behavior.
- **They should be discussed with and understood by children.** Logical consequences are effective only when children understand the link between their behavior and the resulting consequences. Seven-year-old Steve and 8-year-old Rob are old enough to help identify the logical consequences of their behavior. In contrast, the teacher provided the two younger children with choices to help them understand the logical consequences of their behavior.
- **They are effective only when a good teacher-child relationship exists.** A trusting and respectful teacher-child relationship forms the foundation for discussion and implementation of logical consequences. Otherwise, a power struggle can result.
- **They should be applied consistently.** Teachers are consistent when applying logical consequences. Otherwise, children will not take them seriously.

Allowing children to experience an electrical shock because they fail to follow instructions about playing with electrical sockets is inappropriate. And, allowing children to be ridiculed by their peers for failing to follow directions is inappropriate. In all of these situations, teachers must intervene to protect children's social-emotional and physical safety.

TIPS FOR TEACHERS 12.2

Facilitating Classroom Group Discussions

- Begin the classroom discussion by writing agenda items on the blackboard.
  1. Good things of the past week
  2. Ways in which we can improve next week
  3. Personal problems
  4. Responsibilities
  5. Future plans
- Let students take the lead in addressing each item.
- Keep the discussion solution-focused and constructive.
- Keep the discussion behavior-focused, not personality-focused.

- Focus the discussion on group behavior, not individual behavior.
- Follow communication guidelines like turn-taking.
- Remember, solutions should come from the group, not from the teacher.
- Concentrate on the benefits of group discussions to children: belonging, communication, cohesion, expression of feelings, respect, and reflection.

From *Discipline Without Tears* by Rudolf Dreikurs and Pearl Cassel. Copyright © 1972 by Pearl G. Cassel. Used by permission of Dutton, a division of Penguin Putnam Inc.

Group discussions.   Group discussions are an important component of democratic education, promoting problem-solving and communication skills (Dreikurs, Grunwald, & Pepper, 1982). It is recommended that they be conducted on a weekly basis (Dreikurs & Cassel, 1972). As is true of other child-guidance practices, group discussions must be planned and facilitated. We summarize the agenda and facilitation guidelines associated with group discussions in Tips for Teachers 12.2.

Lee Canter: A High-Control Perspective of Behavior Management

You will recall from Chapter 1 that a nurture perspective of development emphasizes social forces in children's development and education. Teachers who adopt a nurture perspective therefore take personal responsibility for shaping children's behavior. They likewise assert a high degree of control within their classrooms, giving little attention to children's thoughts, feelings, or preferences (Burden, 1995). Canter's "assertive discipline" model reflects a teacher-centered classroom.

Assertive discipline follows a three-step process, with each step representing a higher level of teacher control over children's behavior. Some children may respond to the first step, while others may respond only to step two or step three. Take time to compare the practices of this model to those of Ginott and Dreikurs. The comparison will help you to develop your own philosophy of behavior management in Activity 1 at the end of this chapter.

A teacher-centered classroom represents a high-control approach to behavior management.

Step 1: Communicate assertively.

Teachers begin by making short, direct statements regarding their needs or expectations (Canter & Canter, 1985). Firm statements like the following send a clear message that teacher requests are to be taken seriously:

- "Put away your books now."
- "Turn in your assignments immediately."
- "You will not talk to each other during this lesson."

Nonverbal assertive communication accompanies and strengthens the seriousness of teachers' verbal statements. In particular, three nonverbal practices are recommended. First, teachers remain calm to demonstrate their control over the situation. Second, teachers look children in the eye when speaking. Third, teachers use slight gestures of the body to emphasize the statement. For example, a slight touch on the arm or shoulder reinforces the sincerity and forcefulness of the teacher's statement.

Two other practices associated with assertive communication include the "broken record" and "praise." Teachers use the "broken record" to avoid arguments with children by repeating their requests over and over:

Mr. Simon:	"Boys and girls, it is time to go to lunch. Go wash your hands."
El:	"But I'm not finished."
Teacher:	"I understand, El, but it is time to go to lunch. Wash your hands."
El:	"Ok, in a couple of minutes."
Teacher:	"No, now. Wash your hands now."
El:	"I'm almost finished."
Teacher:	"El, go wash your hands now."

Note that the "broken record" is used to reassert the teacher's expectations. There is no attempt to negotiate or discuss the situation with the child.

Also contrary to the Ginott and Dreikurs models, praise is used as an assertive communication practice. Three types of praise are recognized (Canter & Canter, 1985):

• **Simple praise** involves simple statements like, "I'm proud of your grade" or "You did a great job." Three rules are followed when delivering praise. First, teachers are specific. A statement like, "I like the way you pay attention" is more specific than "I like your behavior." Second, teachers look children in the eye and/or gently touch them when delivering praise. Finally, teachers avoid the use of qualifiers that can turn their praise into sarcasm. Can you identify the qualifier in the following statement?

> "Kyle, I like the way you pay attention. Now if you would just follow directions."

• **Super praise** involves praising children in multiple settings. For example, the teacher who first witnesses a behavior delivers praise. Next, the teacher praises the child in front of another significant adult, like a parent. Finally, the other adult praises the child.
• **Nonverbal praise** involves winks, smiles, nods, and gentle touches that immediately follow positive behavior. These are used to reinforce the verbal praise delivered by teachers.

Step 2: Action. We have noted previously that children do not always respond to spoken words. Followers of assertive discipline therefore use "disciplinary consequences" to back up their assertive communication. Some of these consequences are summarized in Figure 12.2.

FIGURE 12.2 Disciplinary Consequences Associated with Assertive Discipline

The following "disciplinary consequences" are recommended by followers of the assertive discipline model when children fail to follow teacher requests (Canter & Canter, 1985; 1993).

Time out. Separate children from their peers and place them in a "nonstimulating" situation (e.g., children sit alone at an isolated desk). A timer may be used to let children know how long they are to remain in time out. Children may also be sent to another well-disciplined classroom. It is important to note that Canter does not address what type of interaction should take place between the teacher and child prior to, during, or following the separation period. Rather, he recommends that children who are separated from the group should listen to the lesson and continue with their work.

Physical action. Younger children can be held and physically made to follow teachers' directions. Schools often teach appropriate positions for holding children who need restraining. It is important that teachers understand and follow school policies when using any physical action with children.

"Do what I want first." Children comply with the teacher's expectations before they engage in their preferred activity.

Take away privileges. Privileges are taken away for failing to follow teacher expectations. Some of the privileges mentioned by Canter include TV, outside play, use of telephone, and snacks.

Logical consequences. Consequences are provided to children in the form of choices that are logically tied to the behavior in question.

> I can't let you tear up these magazines. You have a choice. You can sit quietly and read or you can go to another center.

Logical consequences should be delivered as soon as possible after the disruptive situation, they should be used consistently, and they should be delivered in a calm manner. Consequences that do not work should be changed until they do work.

Place students next to you. Stand by or sit next to students who fail to pay attention or who are disruptive.

Call students by their names. Include the names of students in your lesson when you observe that they are being inattentive or disruptive.

> I want everyone, including Winston, to spend the next few minutes looking at our map.

Give reminders. Some students benefit from reminders of their tasks and responsibilities.

> "Lynn, remember to ask Ms. Johnson for the atlas before taking it from the library. Be sure to tell her we will bring it back tomorrow morning. Come straight back to the classroom."

Think sheet. This reflective exercise involves students listing their misbehavior, the reasons why they chose to misbehave, the impact of their behavior on others, and alternative behaviors that they might choose from in the future. The think sheet provides a beginning point for child-teacher conferences.

Have students contact their parents. Teachers sometimes choose to have students contact their parents to explain their misbehavior. This can be done by phone or in a letter. This is not recommended in situations in which parents may respond with hostility toward the child.

Adapted from *Assertive Discipline for Parents* (revised edition) by L. Canter, and M. Canter. Copyright © 1988 by Canter & Associates, Inc. Reprinted by permission.
Adapted from *Succeeding with Difficult Students* by L. Canter, and M. Canter. Copyright © 1988 by Canter & Associates, Inc. Reprinted by permission.

The importance of reinforcing children's behavior is also recognized. In addition to praise, special privileges and special rewards are used to reinforce children's behavior (Canter & Canter, 1985, 1993).

- **Special privileges**   allow children access to something they value.

  Teacher: "Monty, you and Jamie have been very cooperative this morning. You can have the first choice during free time today."

- **Special rewards**   are tangible reinforcers. They may include a star, pencil, token, decal, art supplies, or food. Teachers, not children, decide which rewards to use, although children's interests must obviously be taken into consideration. The selected reward immediately follows observation of children's positive behavior.

Step 3: Establish a plan.

Children who do not respond to steps 1 and 2 may require a formal plan of assertive discipline. Such a plan is viewed as a "confidence builder" because it allows teachers to feel more confident in their ability to control children's behavior (Canter & Canter, 1985). The assertive discipline plan involves three components (Canter & Canter, 1993). First, the behavior expected of children is specified. Second, the reward that will result when children display the expected behavior is specified. Children's interests are kept in mind when developing a list of potential rewards. Finally, the consequences that will result when children fail to follow the expected behavior are specified. Two examples of assertive discipline plans are given in Figure 12.3, one for an individual and one for a classroom.

We should note that there is considerable debate over the interpretation and application of assertive discipline. This model has been criticized in at least four ways (Gartrell, 1994). How might the following criticisms apply to the assertive discipline practices listed in Figures 12.2 and 12.3?

- The model overemphasizes obedience at the expense of negotiation and cooperation.
- The model does not take into account individual differences.
- The model's focus on rewards and privileges reinforces a competitive environment.
- The model reinforces an authoritarian style of behavior management.

You may find yourself agreeing with some of Canter's recommendations and disagreeing with others. Chances are you had the same response to Ginott and Dreikurs. In reality, teachers often find that their behavior management philosophies reflect a combination of behavior management models. In Activity 1, we provide you with guidelines for developing your own personal philosophy of behavior management.

FIGURE 12.3   Assertive Discipline Plans

Ty's Individual Discipline Plan (Age 7)

Expected Behavior	Resulting Reward	Discipline Consequences
Following directions	Verbal praise	Complete class assignment during recess
Listening to teacher	Notebook sticker	Write an apology to teacher
Cooperating with students	Lunch with friend	Time out in "opportunity room"

Grade Two Classroom Discipline Plan

Classroom Rules
- Pay attention
- Follow directions
- Keep your hands and feet to yourself
- Do not speak out of turn
- Remain quiet while in the classroom
- Cooperate with others

Daily and Weekly Rewards
- Teacher praise (daily)
- 10 extra minutes of computer time (daily)
- Points toward a weekly class reward (this week, pizza)

Discipline Consequences
- First warning: Students review classroom rules.
- Second warning: Students complete a "Think Sheet" (see Figure 12.2).
- Third warning: Students lose extra computer time and 10 minutes of recess.
- Fifth warning: Students lose weekly points.

CHAPTER SUMMARY

Behavior management can be viewed as a science, an art form, and a game. The goal of behavior management is to help children make a successful adjustment to life in a democratic society. The socialization objectives associated with this goal include determination, dependability, and diligence.

Child guidance is defined as a reciprocal form of behavior management in which children internalize long-term behavior patterns by working with teachers to solve problems and negotiate solutions. Child obedience is defined as a unilateral form of behavior management in which teachers control children through short-term, often punishing, means.

Behavior management models are useful in helping teachers to identify and justify their behavior management practices. Low teacher-control models emphasize the role of teacher as a communicator and supporter of children's natural strengths. Medium teacher-child control models emphasize the role of teacher as a facilitator of children's adjustment to group expectations. High teacher-control models emphasize the role of teacher as a controlling agent who defines and enforces classroom behaviors based primarily upon personal expectations.

ACTIVITIES

1. Jot down your immediate response to at least five of the following behaviors that children sometimes exhibit:
   - Crying
   - Whining
   - Tattling
   - Arguing
   - Fighting
   - Name calling
   - Becoming easily distracted
   - Displaying rigid gender roles
   - Shyness
   - Refusing to comply with requests
   - Acting before thinking; impulsive
   - Seeking immediate gratification of needs
   - Saying inappropriate things to classroom guests
   - Failing to share or cooperate with others
   - Comparing self with others constantly
   - Being slow to begin a task
   - Failing to pay attention
   - Asking questions constantly
   - Comparing teachers
   - Cursing
   - Bullying other children
   - Displaying mood swings
   - Displaying silly behavior
   - Being easily influenced by others

   Use the following reflective questions to write your philosophy of behavior management. We suggest that you keep your philosophy statement short (i.e., no more than a couple of paragraphs). A succinct philosophy is easier to explain than one that is long.

   - Which of the behaviors in the list do you find most disturbing? Why?
   - To what degree should individual differences be taken into account when developing a behavior management plan?
   - To what extent should families be consulted when developing a behavior management plan?
   - To what extent should children be consulted when developing a behavior management plan?
   - Which practices listed in this chapter might you use to deal with these behaviors?

2. Observe teachers' behavior management practices. To what degree do their practices reflect behavior management as a "science," an "art," and a "game"?

3. Keep a week-long log of your observations of teachers interacting with children. Identify examples of encouragement and praise, and logical and natural consequences.

4. As a class, collect the behavior management philosophies of teachers or schools. Divide into small groups to compare the different philosophies. To what degree are different behavior models reflected in the philosophies?

5. Interview children of different ages about the types of behavior management practices they like and dislike. Why do they like and dislike particular practices?

TIPS FOR TEACHERS 13.1

Planning an Integrated Curriculum

- Take into account the needs and interests of each child when constructing a learning environment.
- Plan learning environments that reflect the diversity of children's life experiences.
- Create educational activities for young children that reflect children's home and school learning environments.

- Take into account the social context of children's lives and its possible influence on their development and classroom performance rather than holding all children accountable to one standard.
- Integrate reading, writing, music, science, and other subject-matter areas into all activities throughout the day rather than dividing them into different time slots.

families, assessment, developmentally appropriate curricular approaches, and an integrated early childhood curriculum.

When beginning teachers think about planning activities, they are often only concerned about developing and implementing activities that will keep children occupied. In our discussion of curriculum in Chapter 10, we focused on the idea that early childhood curriculum should consider the content, or what will be taught, as well as the processes young children use or experience in acquiring new knowledge. We hope that you will keep in mind both the content that you are teaching and the processes young children use in learning, since an effective curriculum includes experiences that continually challenge and support the construction of new understandings.

Integrated Curriculum

In Chapter 10 we also introduced the term *integrated curriculum.* As you may recall, integrated curriculum refers to activities and experiences that teach content from different subject-matter disciplines such as mathematics, science, social studies, the arts, and language and literacy. It is also important to remember that the concept of integration comes from the integrated nature of development—what happens in one domain of development, such as cognitive growth, influences other domains of development, such as the physical and emotional. Consequently, a developmentally appropriate curriculum provides for all areas of a child's development: physical, cognitive, social, and emotional (Bredekamp & Copple, 1997). An integrated curriculum also addresses content from various subject-matter disciplines so that children develop an understanding of concepts and make connections across disciplines (Bredekamp & Copple, 1997).

According to DAP, teachers facilitate the development of children's knowledge and skills in all content areas when they use a curriculum that is organized and integrated so that children acquire deeper understanding of key concepts, skills, and tools of inquiry in each subject area. When teachers integrate across traditional subject-matter disciplines, children participate in the study of the disciplines directly by conducting scientific experiments, writing, performing, solving mathematical problems, or collecting and analyzing data (Bredekamp & Copple, 1997). An integrated curriculum can also provide opportunities to bring children's home language and culture into the school. Similarly, many teachers find that an integrated curriculum can help them meet the identified special needs of individual children, including children with disabilities and those who exhibit unusual interests and skills.

Thematic Units

A *thematic unit* is a collection of materials, activities, and techniques organized around a concept or theme. A thematic unit can be used as an organizational tool to link different subject-matter content and, consequently, assist the learner in making connections between the different content areas. As a beginning teacher, we suggest that you first develop a theme and then integrate activities around that theme. According to Seefeldt (1997), units organized around a theme can:

- Relate the activities to the daily lives of children;
- Accomplish the teaching and learning that follow children's interests;
- Provide activities that build on children's previous experiences;
- Meet individual needs through a variety of experiences and opportunities; and
- Provide opportunities for children to build a sense of community by working together.

Historical perspectives.   Thematic units and an integrated approach to curriculum are not new or unique to early childhood education. The belief that new ideas and concepts can be taught by connecting real life to school activities can be traced to Carolyn Pratt and John Dewey in the 1920s and 1930s. For example, Pratt (1924) advocated the use of real-life experiences, such as a trip to the New York City waterfront, as a way to facilitate map making and boat building. You may recall from our discussion of Dewey in Chapter 2 that he advocated the use of project activities, field trips, and group work.

One aspect of Dewey's philosophy that contributed to the conceptualization and use of themes in curricular planning is his belief about the importance of children's interest in formulating curriculum. Dewey believed that through children's interests, activities would emerge spontaneously and differentiate into separate areas of study (White, Fein, Manning, & Daniels, manuscript submitted for publication). Dewey's ideas about the classroom being a community of learners in which curriculum was discovered in the social life of the class, also support the use of thematic units and integrated curriculum. By participating in active learning classroom experiences, such as creating a city with different services, children are engaged in activities that promote understanding of different community roles and responsibilities. Similarly, Kilpatrick (1918) urged teachers to build units on the study of real institutions such as the post office. According to Kilpatrick, concrete experiences, such as a visit to the post office, encourage the classroom to reach out to the community, and the community to come into the classroom.

The *project approach,* which was developed by Katz and Chard (1989), involves an in-depth study of a particular topic that one or more children undertake for an extended period of time. Investigation is emphasized in the project approach, and children are encouraged to act as data collectors. A wide variety of concepts and skills in different subject-matter areas can be found in a project such as writing, reading, building, calculating, problem solving, analyzing, and observing (Katz & Chard, 1989). In the project approach, children choose the focus, activities, and amount of time the topic is studied. Projects that have been proposed by Katz and Chard include baskets, shadows and light, shoes, homes, chairs, water, and school buses. In a project on the school bus, for example, children go outside of the classroom to study specific aspects of school buses, such as the types of wheels and tires. They may also engage in activities inside the classroom such as constructing a school bus out of clay or cardboard. Consequently, children link what they have learned outside of the classroom to the tasks and activities in which they are engaged inside the classroom.

Another recent approach that uses children's interest as the primary focus for planning curriculum is the one used by the municipal schools in Reggio Emilia, Italy. In the Reggio Emilia approach, projects emerge from simple, concrete experiences such as a visit to a poppy field. Activities that result from such an experience include examining flowers, drawing them, sculpting them, discussing them, and creating murals over an extended period of time (Brewer, 1998; Staley, 1998). A theme is used in the Reggio Emilia approach as the main cognitive support for learning, but then the direction of the activities depends on the children, the unfolding of events, and the teachers (Staley, 1998). Teachers act as facilitators by asking questions, providing different materials, and guiding children to improve and revise their work (Staley, 1998). Both the project approach and the Reggio Emilia curriculum provide us with concrete applications of how children's interest can lead to a study of a topic or theme that integrates subject-matter content.

Theories of cognitive development.   In our discussion of cognitive development in Chapter 5, we discussed the works of Piaget, Vygotsky, and information-processing theorists. These theories about the role of cognitive development in learning and teaching provide a foundation for the use of a thematic unit approach that emphasizes an integrated curriculum. Piaget's theory tells us that it is necessary to begin with meaningful real-life experiences, questions rather than answers, and an accepting attitude toward errors. According to Piaget, children construct knowledge through active involvement in their own learning. His theory of knowledge construction provides a foundation for the design of early childhood activities that provide opportunities to integrate new information and knowledge into a learner's existing knowledge structure. Thematic units often can facilitate this construction of knowledge by providing a variety of materials and activities that are conceptually linked and address children's developmental level.

From a Vygotskian perspective, adults and more experienced members of society mediate the acquisition of knowledge and skills needed to live in a particular culture. Through scaffolding, children advance in consciousness and control as a result of the aid provided by adults and more competent peers. When children work together on a common theme, they have the opportunity to scaffold learning tasks for each other. They can share information and prior knowledge, and offer feedback to one another. Consequently, children internalize new knowledge through engaging in social activity with others.

Information-processing theory also supports thematic units as a vehicle for organizing an integrated curriculum. When topics for potential lessons are related to a common theme or context, children's ability to learn is much better than when lessons are presented in an isolated and unconnected format. A child is more likely to remember new concepts when the concepts are connected to prior knowledge and previous experience:

> Conceptual organizers such as themes, units, or projects give children something meaningful and substantive to engage their minds. It is difficult for children to make sense of abstract concepts such as colors, mathematical symbols, or letter sounds when they are presented at random or devoid of any meaningful context (NAEYC, 1991, p. 30).

When teachers use themes to develop integrated approaches to curriculum, they can contribute to knowledge construction by framing activities in ways that help children see the relationships between concepts. This relationship, according to information-processing researchers, is the basis for conceptual understanding. In our discussion of planning, we present different ways that teachers can use thematic units to link different concepts and the relationships between those concepts. We begin our discussion of planning for an integrated curriculum by discussing how to develop individual lesson plans.

PLANNING INDIVIDUAL LESSONS

In planning individual lessons, we remind you that teachers need to consider a) the experiences that children bring with them to school; b) the activities that children are interested in; c) the differences in physical, cognitive, and social/emotional developmental levels; d) children's families and cultural background; and e) knowledge of the children's community. Planning individual lessons is complex and also involves a teacher's personal philosophy. Think back to the philosophy you have developed and refined while reading this text—what

Beginning teachers often write out detailed plans to help guide their thinking about what they will teach.

implications does your philosophy have for planning? When you begin the planning process, ask yourself two essential questions: What do I want the children to learn? and How will I know if a child has learned something?

In our explanation of planning individual lessons and thematic units, we provide a framework for you to use as you begin learning how to plan. Beginning teachers find that writing out their lesson plans helps to guide their thinking. Consequently, we suggest that you start by writing out all of the different components of a lesson plan. As planning becomes more automatic, you may not include as much detail, however, you will always need to write lesson plans. Experienced teachers continue to write lesson plans and use them to help inform parents, administrators, and other teachers about what they are teaching (Seefeldt & Barbour, 1994). The framework we suggest includes goals and objectives, developmental activities, and evaluation. We also provide other examples of planning that address families and individual needs.

Goals and Objectives

Goals.   Goals are broad statements that describe the general purposes of the experiences and activities you plan to teach. Objectives are related to general goals; however, objectives are specific statements that identify the behaviors you want children to demonstrate after they have participated in your lesson. Both goals and objectives are important because administrators, fellow teachers, and families will want to know the objective of the lesson and what you expect the children to learn during a lesson. The goals should consider the nature of the children you teach, the values of the community in which the children live, and your own educational philosophy.

In many situations, teachers are given goals and objectives that have been developed by the state, local school district, or child-care center. Teachers may also be given curriculum guides; preselected reading; mathematics, social studies, and science textbooks; or published curriculum kits (Seefeldt, 1997). Although it can be difficult to address the developmental characteristics and needs of young children while addressing mandated goals and objectives, teachers who understand the underlying concepts that need to be taught are successful.

Throughout this discussion of planning an individual lesson, we use an example of a mathematics lesson that was developed by Mrs. Sweeney, an early childhood education student. We chose this lesson example because it is an integrated lesson on specific mathematics and social studies concepts that was taught during a thematic unit on ancient Egypt. Mrs. Sweeney's example also incorporates mandated curriculum goals and objectives that were developed outside her classroom by the state and local school district. We refer to Mrs. Sweeney's lesson plan as we explain each of the different parts of a lesson plan. The complete lesson plan can be found in Figure 13.1. An example of a goal statement from this lesson on ancient Egypt is "To know about the culture and contributions of ancient Egypt."

FIGURE 13.1   Individual Lesson Plan on Counting Like an Egyptian

Lesson Topic/Subject

This lesson is part of a month-long thematic unit on ancient Egypt. The Egyptian number system will be investigated in the unit. This lesson corresponds to several goals of the school district's curriculum for third grade in both mathematics and social studies.

Goals

Goal 1 (Mathematics).   To investigate different ways of grouping and writing numbers.

Goal 2 (Mathematics).   To understand how to read and write numbers through the hundred thousands.

Goal 3 (Social Studies).   To know about the culture and contributions of the ancient Egyptians.

Goal 4 (Social Studies).   To understand the influences of ancient Egyptian geography, its economic system, and its government.

Concepts

1. The ancient Egyptians developed a number system using symbols that are different from the Indo-Arabic numerals we use today.

2. There are similarities between the two systems. For example, both systems are based on groups of 10.

3. There are differences between the two systems. For example, there is no place value and no symbol for zero in the ancient Egyptian system.

Objectives

1. Students will convert ancient Egyptian numerals to Indo-Arabic numerals and Indo-Arabic numerals to ancient Egyptian numerals.

2. Students will compare and contrast the ancient Egyptian number system with the Indo-Arabic system that we use today.

Procedures

Introductory activities.   The class will meet as a group on the rug to begin the lesson. The teacher will read excerpts from pages 24 to 34 of *Science in Ancient Egypt* by Geraldine Woods. The teacher will then lead a discussion about how numbers can be written in different ways (Roman numerals, tally marks). She will ask the students if they have ever tried to solve a secret code or write messages in a code; she will explain that figuring out numbers from ancient Egypt is a lot like trying to decipher a secret code.

Developmental activities.   The students will return to their table groups. Each student will be given half of one file folder, a paper fastener, and a "Make Your Own Number Decoder" sheet. Students will be instructed to cut out the circles, color the top circle of their number decoder, and then glue both circles to their file folder. They will then cut out the mounted circles, cut out the two "windows" on the circles, and push the fastener through the middle of both circles.

continues

FIGURE 13.1   *continued*

Once their decoders are complete, students will work in pairs to play the "Egyptian Number Game." One partner will call out a number from his decoder (130, 15, 72, etc.) and the other partner will spin his decoder to find the right Egyptian numeral and then will write it down on a piece of paper. After a few turns, one partner will then write a number on the paper Egyptian style, and the other partner will have to find the correct Indo-Arabic number. Students will play this game for 15 minutes.

Students will return to their desks. The teacher will show an overhead transparency of the Egyptian numerals, and will model a few examples of how to convert the symbols into numbers the students can understand, and how to change our numbers into Egyptian numerals. Students will then complete a sheet to practice these concepts.

Summary activities.   As a class, with the teacher as scribe, the students will complete a Venn diagram on the board to compare Egyptian and American mathematics. They will discuss what they learned while trying to use the Egyptian numerals, and will brainstorm similarities and differences between the ancient Egyptian system and the system we use today. To conclude, students will brainstorm new facts learned through the lesson that can be added to our class "Learning Pyramid" bulletin board.

Evaluation

1. The teacher will take anecdotal notes during the "Egyptian Number Game" to determine whether students can convert ancient Egyptian numerals to Indo-Arabic numerals and Indo-Arabic numerals to ancient Egyptian numerals.

2. The teacher will collect completed sheets at the end of the lesson to determine whether students converted ancient Egyptian numerals to Indo-Arabic numerals and Indo-Arabic numerals to ancient Egyptian numerals.

3. The teacher will observe and note student comments and participation in discussion during the creation of the Venn diagram to determine where students can compare and contrast the ancient Egyptian number system and the Indo-Arabic system that we use today.

Relevant Children's Literature

Cushman, D. (1996). *The mystery of King Karfu.* USA: Guild Books.

Lattimore, D. N. (1992). *The winged cat.* New York: Harper Collins.

Walsh, J. P. (1994). *Pepi and the secret names.* New York: Lothrop, Lee & Shepard Books.

Objectives.   Instructional or behavioral objectives are different from the goals of the lesson because they specifically state what the children will be able to do after the learning activity. The goals that you select should serve as a framework for the specific objectives. Consequently, there needs to be a connection between the goals and objectives—objectives are more specific statements of the goals. A behavioral objective, unlike a lesson goal, is an explicit statement of behavior that will be accepted as evidence of the child's having achieved what was set out to be accomplished (Seefeldt, 1997). By writing behavioral objectives, teachers can identify what they will teach and how they will know if the children have learned what has been taught. When writing objectives, it is important to use specific language. Mager (1962) suggests using words that clearly communicate what will be taught and learned. Examples of specific words that convey a definitive reference to what has been learned include *identify, classify, construct, compare, name, describe,* and *define.* An example objective that uses specific terminology to communicate a definitive reference to what has been learned is "Students will identify the shapes—circle, square, and rectangle—while playing a shape game." Similarly, Mrs. Sweeney used specific terminology when she wrote the objective: "Students will convert ancient Egyptian numerals to Indo-Arabic numerals and Indo-Arabic numerals to ancient Egyptian numerals."

It is important for you to know about and be comfortable using objectives, as they help teachers to plan precisely and many schools and child-care centers require that teachers use them. Behavioral objectives have been used for many years and are often criticized for being too narrow and constraining for teachers. Some educators believe that objectives can limit children's learning by influencing teachers to ignore children's behaviors or outcomes not prespecified by an objective (Seefeldt, 1997). Similarly, when behavioral objectives are too specific, they may cause teachers to focus on the specific procedures of an activity or lesson rather than considering the broader experience of an entire lesson.

Concepts

If you think back to our discussion of cognitive development in Chapter 5, we discussed how concepts help us organize, reorganize, and categorize the information and experiences that our brain processes. "Concepts are fundamental ideas that children form about objects and events in their world" (Kostelnik et al., 1991, p. 2). They are the cognitive categories that allow people to group together perceptually distinct information, events, or items (Wellman, 1988). Concepts serve as the building blocks of knowing, thinking, and reasoning. Categorizing and classifying information based on similarities and differences helps children develop conceptual knowledge. By identifying the most important concepts in a lesson, the teacher can facilitate children's understanding of those concepts by providing experiences that help them compare and categorize the information.

In planning lessons, concepts refer to the important ideas; that is, the significant content in different subjects. Since teachers need to be knowledgeable about the content they are teaching, the identification of the concepts in a particular subject-matter area can help them sequence and structure a lesson. As we have mentioned previously, teachers may be given curriculum guides that include concepts that need to be taught in conjunction with specific objectives. When teachers create their own lessons (without support from commercial materials or a mandated curriculum), they must use their knowledge of subject-matter content as well as their knowledge of the children, their families, and their community to determine the concepts that will be included in a specific lesson. In Mrs. Sweeney's lesson on "counting in ancient Egypt," there are three important concepts: 1) the ancient Egyptians developed a number system using symbols that are different from the Indo-Arabic numerals that we use today; 2) there are similarities between the two systems; and 3) there are differences between the two systems. In our discussion of lesson procedures, we will discuss how concepts can be introduced and how different experiences such as participating in a teacher-led discussion and playing a game are planned to help children understand the concepts.

Procedures

The procedures of a lesson include the activities that you and the children are engaged in to achieve the goals and objectives and teach the concepts. Before you begin teaching the activities that are described in the procedures, you need to: 1) prepare all of the materials that you will need, and 2) review the subject-matter content that you will be teaching (i.e., the content knowledge that is relevant to the concepts you are teaching). In Mrs. Sweeney's lesson on ancient Egypt, she prepared the following materials list and then checked to see that she had everything ready before she began the lesson.

Student Materials:

- 20 copies of the "Make Your Own Decoder" sheet
- 20 copies of the "Numbers in Ancient Egypt" sheet
- 10 manilla file folders
- 20 paper fasteners
- Glue, scissors, and crayons for 20 students

Teacher Materials:

- *Science in Ancient Egypt* by Geraldine Woods (with page 24 marked)
- Transparency of the "How the Egyptians Worked with Numbers" sheet
- Chart paper with blank Venn diagram labeled "Egyptian Math" and "American Math"
- Markers
- Index cards on a ring for anecdotal note taking

Learning Activities

Introductory activities.   Teachers need to recognize children's previous experiences and knowledge when introducing new ideas and concepts. By connecting new and unfamiliar information to what is familiar and known, teachers can be more confident that young children will understand the new ideas and concepts. Consequently, the introductory part of a lesson needs to include activities that help the teacher find out what the children already know about the concepts she plans to teach. The introduction also needs to create interest in the lesson ideas and concepts. Mrs. Sweeney chose to read from a book about science in ancient Egypt, lead a discussion about how numbers can be written in different ways (which focuses the children on the concepts of the lesson), ask questions, and explain one of the concepts of the lesson.

Developmental activities.   The developmental activities are the "meat" of the lesson. These activities should connect to children's previous experiences that relate to the concepts of the lesson, be interesting to the children, and provide different opportunities and experiences that will facilitate the children's understanding and ability to apply the concepts. In Mrs. Sweeney's lesson, the children made a number decoder sheet, played a game using the decoder sheet, listened and watched as Mrs. Sweeney modeled how to convert symbols into understandable numbers and how to change familiar numbers into Egyptian numbers, and then completed a practice sheet independently. You can see that Mrs. Sweeney varied the activities by including teacher explanation, teacher modeling, group work, and independent work.

Summary activities.   The purpose of the summary activities is to assure that students achieve some type of closure to the lesson and are not left "hanging." In this part of the lesson, the concepts can be reviewed while the teacher thinks about whether or not the students have achieved the lesson objectives. There are different ways to summarize the lesson. Mrs. Sweeney chose to have her students complete a Venn diagram on the board to compare Egyptian and American mathematics. During this activity, the children discuss similarities and differences between the two number systems, which were the concepts she was teaching in this lesson. In the last activity, the children add facts to a unit bulletin board that will help connect this particular lesson to previous lessons on ancient Egypt.

Evaluation

The final component of a lesson plan focuses on whether or not the goals and objectives of the lesson have been accomplished. If behavioral objectives have been stated specifically, then the teacher can simply check the children's behavior in relation to the objective statements and evaluate the lesson. We discussed a number of assessment techniques in Chapter 10 that can be used in conjunction with objectives. For example, a checklist can be used to determine whether or not a child is able to sort attribute blocks by size, color, and shape. Children can also be interviewed to determine whether or not they can explain how to solve two-digit addition problems. In Mrs. Sweeney's lesson, she used a combination of assessment techniques to determine whether or not she met her objectives. For the objective "Students will convert ancient Egyptian numerals to Indo-Arabic numerals and Indo-Arabic numerals to Egyptian numerals," Mrs. Sweeney decided to take anecdotal notes during the "Egyptian Number Game" and collect completed worksheets at the end of the lesson to determine whether students could convert ancient Egyptian numerals to Indo-Arabic numerals and Indo-Arabic numerals to Egyptian numerals. She planned to observe and note student comments and participation in discussion during the creation of the Venn diagram to determine whether or not she met the second objective, "Students will compare and contrast the ancient Egyptian number system and the Indo-Arabic system that we use today."

PLANNING INTEGRATED UNITS USING THEMES

The burning question for most beginning teachers is "What will I teach?" Many teachers (especially beginning teachers) find that organizing curriculum by themes instead of by subject-matter content areas such as mathematics and science can be difficult and frustrating. Consequently, in this section we provide you with a structure that is parallel to the format we discussed in planning individual lessons. Most beginning teachers express a need for the support of specific guidelines as they try to decide what they will teach. This support may be provided via specific curriculum guidelines from school systems and state departments of education. However, we believe that teachers must plan their own curriculum by relying on their personal philosophy, their knowledge of child development, the children themselves, the children's families, and the children's lives in the community.

Throughout our discussion on thematic units, we use examples from a thematic unit developed by a student teacher. This unit is organized around a theme that facilitated an integrated curriculum; however, the theme and corresponding activities were developed to follow guidelines from the school system and state department of education. We chose this unit because it provides examples of how thematic units can address many of the principles we have presented in this text and still address school district and state guidelines.

When you begin to plan curriculum using thematic units, it is important to remain focused on the needs and interests of the children you are teaching. In addition to the content (i.e., the concepts and ideas you plan for the children to learn) of the activities, you also need to consider the types of experiences you want the children to become involved in. As we begin our discussion about planning what to teach, think about the following questions: What centers can be used as part of the theme? How will I use large-group, small-group, and individual activities when teaching concepts related to the theme? How can I incorporate the children's life experiences? How will I provide for choices that facilitate student interest, motivation, and involvement? How can I encourage the children to work together? How can I promote children's self-management? All of these questions are critical parts of planning an integrated curriculum that exemplifies developmentally appropriate practice. As we discuss different ways to answer the question "What will I teach?" we encourage you to remember that child choice, active learning experiences, decision-making and problem-solving skills, and opportunities for children to work together are all aspects of developmentally appropriate curriculum.

Teachers can encourage children's involvement in the learning process by seeking their input.

One of the most significant aspects of a thematic unit is the subject-matter content and associated concepts that will be taught. Thematic units often allow children to study subject-matter content in-depth. That is, children have opportunities to pursue their interests and questions about different aspects of the theme in comprehensive ways over a period of time. As you may recall in Chapter 10, we introduced the idea of intellectual integrity. When a thematic unit has intellectual integrity, the activities and experiences are not trivial or meaningless; rather, they are relevant to knowledge found in the content disciplines. You may want to refer back to Chapter 10 and review the developmentally appropriate curriculum guidelines, the guidelines for curriculum content, or the document, *Reaching potentials: Transforming early childhood curriculum and assessment, Vol. 2* (Bredekamp & Rosegrant, 1992), to review what content goals are accepted by educators in the disciplines as having the greatest intellectual integrity.

Teachers may draw from different sources when selecting a theme for an integrated unit. In addition to school district and state guidelines, many teachers consider the interest of their children in different topics. Children's involvement in the planning of a thematic unit can occur in different ways. Many teachers brainstorm areas of interest in a particular theme to determine subtopics and specific unit activities. By offering input, the children are more involved in the learning process, more enthusiastic about what they experience in school, and more able to exert a sense of ownership of their own learning experiences (Krough, 1990). When children are involved in brainstorming, the teacher can also think about how children might learn from different experiences such as going on field trips and interviewing resource people. The teacher can determine what children already know and what they would like to learn about the theme.

When teachers consider children's interest in and previous knowledge about a particular theme, they also think about practical considerations such as the availability of resources, materials, and the amount of time that can be allocated to different types of experiences. Once the theme is determined, we suggest that you use the same framework for planning the unit as we suggested for planning an individual lesson. Think about goals, objectives, and the specific concepts (from subject-matter content) that can be included in the unit. At the same time, determine the activities and experiences you will use to teach these goals and concepts. Other components of the unit include evaluation, family involvement, and plans for individual children with special needs. A strategy that many beginning teachers find useful as they begin to organize a thematic unit is planning with a web.

Webbing

Webbing is an approach to organizing themes that helps teachers incorporate most, or even all, of the required or desired curriculum (Krough, 1990). Planning with a web can provide an overview of the entire unit, representing different subject-matter areas, activities, or concepts. Or it can help organize children's interest in a particular theme. Before writing out detailed lesson plans, many teachers use

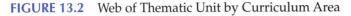

FIGURE 13.2   Web of Thematic Unit by Curriculum Area

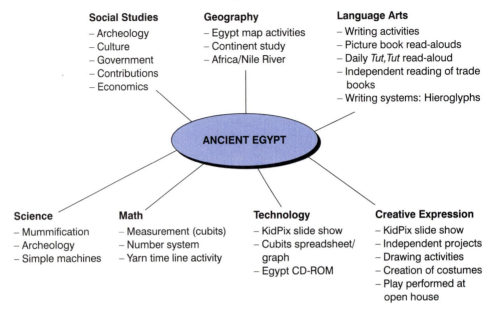

webbing because it is less structured and more tentative than an outline (Krough, 1990). For example, when Mrs. Sweeney began planning her thematic unit on ancient Egypt, she used a web to help her organize the unit by subject-matter area. In Figure 13.2, you can see that Mrs. Sweeney began listing potential topics and activities to include in each subject-matter area.

Teachers often use webs to see that each subject area in the curriculum is adequately represented. Planning with a web helped Mrs. Sweeney develop an overview of the entire third-grade curriculum. After Mrs. Sweeney finished planning the activities for her unit on ancient Egypt, her cooperating teacher asked her to develop a web that showed how the activities addressed the school district and state curriculum guidelines. The web is depicted in Figure 13.3.

Mrs. Sweeney's webs were more structured because of the district and state requirements and expectations for learning at the third-grade level. In preschool and kindergarten, webs may be built on a more loosely structured theme. Some teachers in preschool, kindergarten, and the primary grades use webs to involve children either in the planning process or during the unit itself. By beginning the web with a set of basic concepts, children can be encouraged to see connections among the concepts and can begin to think in terms of the relationships between the concepts.

Another student teacher, Mr. Meyer, developed a thematic unit for kindergarten on foods and nutrition and used webs as part of his planning process. He developed a concept web on fruits and vegetables that is depicted in Figure 13.4.

FIGURE 13.3   Web of Overall Unit by School District and State Curriculum Guidelines

Geography and Archeology
Week One

– Literature: *Croco'Nile, I Can Be an Archeologist, Magic School Bus Shows and Tells*
– Map activities
– Archeological dig activity and writing activity
– Personal artifact exchange and writing activity

Government
Weeks Two & Three

– Make the red & white crowns of upper & lower Egypt
– Color-code the Power Pyramid with writing activity
– Pharaoh read-alouds: *Temple Cat, The Egyptian Cinderella,* and *The Golden Flower*; Venn diagram of the two legends

ANCIENT EGYPT

Culture
Weeks Two & Three

– November 4th: Anniversary of the discovery of King Tut's tomb—read the *Curse of the Mummy* legend and debate if it is true or not true (T-charts)
– Read-alouds: *Egyptian Pyramids, Mummies Made in Egypt, King Karfu, Pepi and the Secret Names*
– Reading Rainbow video of *Mummies Made in Egypt*
– *Ancient Egypt* laser disc—building of the pyramids and training of the scribes
– Afterlife activities
– Hieroglyphics activities
– Gods and goddesses

Economics & Contributions
Week Four

– Continue with the Power Pyramid—apply to our school
– Bartering activity with M & Ms
– Read-aloud: *Zekmet the Stone Carver*
– Travel brochures activity
– Make and play Senet
– Venn diagram: Ancient Egypt vs. modern day
– Writing activity: postcards home

After he studied several curriculum guides and talked with his cooperating teacher, he decided to divide the topic of fruits and vegetables into types, sources, seed, health and nutrition, and preparation and taste. He then listed the concepts that he wanted the children to learn. Mr. Meyer connected the concepts he wanted to teach in each topic. For example, in Figure 13.5, he developed a web to help him organize what he was going to teach about seeds. He organized his lessons on seeds by focusing on size and color, color, growth, associated seeds, and location and number on or in the fruit. By using webs to organize the concepts, Mr. Meyer was able to see the connections between the concepts. This helped him to explain these connections to the children.

During his unit, Mr. Meyer presented the web to his class. After they had studied types of fruits and vegetables and different seeds, he used the web to show the connections between different types of fruits and vegetables and different types of seeds. Mr. Meyer also observed his cooperating teacher as she presented a web to the children and asked them to help her create connections between the concepts.

Webbing can be used in different ways to facilitate the process of planning and graphically represent the connections within the unit. Mr. Meyer created

FIGURE 13.4 Conceptual Web with Accompanying Concepts to be Learned

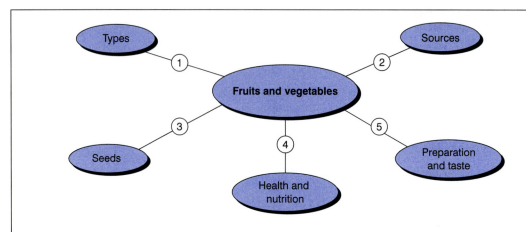

Numbers indicate order of presentation.

- There are many kinds of fruits and vegetables. (1)
- Fruits and vegetables have different names. (1)
- Fruits and vegetables come in many shapes, sizes, and colors. (1)
- Fruits and vegetables can be bought fresh, frozen, or canned. (2)
- Some people grow fruits and vegetables in gardens. (2)
- Fruits and vegetables need sunlight and water to grow. (3)
- Some fruits have seeds. (3)
- People need certain amounts of fruits and vegetables to stay healthy. (4)
- Most fruits and vegetables can be eaten raw or cooked. (5)
- Some fruits and vegetables need to be peeled before they are eaten. (5)

Note: Numbers in parentheses refer to Conceptual Outline Web.

another web for an assignment in a class on applying theories of development and learning to curriculum. In his class, Mr. Meyer was asked to think about how he could apply Gardner's theory of multiple intelligences to his thematic unit. As you can see in Figure 13.6, he organized the activities according to Gardner's different intelligences after he developed a number of activities for the unit.

In Mr. Meyer's class on "Children and Their Families," he was assigned to a small group with several of his classmates and asked to develop family involvement activities that could be used in kindergarten and the primary grades. Since

FIGURE 13.5   Foods and Nutrition Activity Web

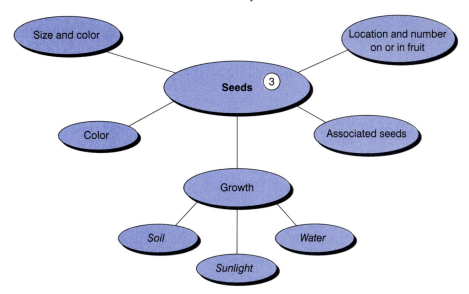

the students in Mr. Meyer's group were developing different thematic units, his group decided to start with a web of family involvement activities that could be used in different units at different times of the year. The web that Mr. Meyer's group developed is shown in Figure 13.7. Mr. Meyer and his fellow group members were then able to use the family web as an organizing tool for constructing family involvement activities in their thematic units.

Many beginning and experienced teachers find that webs can be used in a variety of ways to facilitate the planning process. Webs can also be used to introduce the content and corresponding concepts of a thematic unit. The introduction of a thematic unit is critical to eliciting interest and excitement in the children and connecting that interest to children's prior knowledge. In the next section, we discuss the introduction to a thematic unit as well as the other unit components. We discuss the same components and format that were introduced in the previous section on planning individual lessons: 1) goals and objectives; 2) concepts; 3) learning activities; and 4) evaluation. Throughout our discussion we provide examples from Mr. Meyer's kindergarten unit on "Foods and Nutrition."

Components of a Thematic Unit

Goals and objectives.   After using the webbing strategy to develop an overview of the entire unit, the next step is the development of unit goals. As we discussed in the section on planning individual lessons, goals are broad statements

FIGURE 13.6   Food and Nutrition Unit Webbed According to the Multiple Intelligences

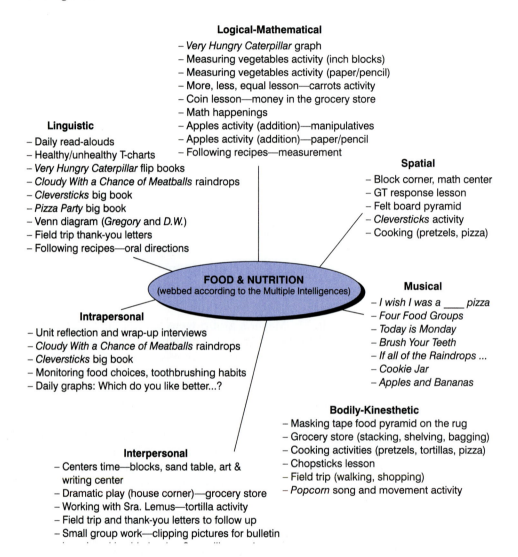

Logical-Mathematical
– *Very Hungry Caterpillar* graph
– Measuring vegetables activity (inch blocks)
– Measuring vegetables activity (paper/pencil)
– More, less, equal lesson—carrots activity
– Coin lesson—money in the grocery store
– Math happenings
– Apples activity (addition)—manipulatives
– Apples activity (addition)—paper/pencil
– Following recipes—measurement

Linguistic
– Daily read-alouds
– Healthy/unhealthy T-charts
– *Very Hungry Caterpillar* flip books
– *Cloudy With a Chance of Meatballs* raindrops
– *Cleversticks* big book
– *Pizza Party* big book
– Venn diagram (*Gregory* and *D.W.*)
– Field trip thank-you letters
– Following recipes—oral directions

Spatial
– Block corner, math center
– GT response lesson
– Felt board pyramid
– *Cleversticks* activity
– Cooking (pretzels, pizza)

FOOD & NUTRITION
(webbed according to the Multiple Intelligences)

Musical
– *I wish I was a ____ pizza*
– *Four Food Groups*
– *Today is Monday*
– *Brush Your Teeth*
– *If all of the Raindrops ...*
– *Cookie Jar*
– *Apples and Bananas*

Intrapersonal
– Unit reflection and wrap-up interviews
– *Cloudy With a Chance of Meatballs* raindrops
– *Cleversticks* big book
– Monitoring food choices, toothbrushing habits
– Daily graphs: Which do you like better...?

Bodily-Kinesthetic
– Masking tape food pyramid on the rug
– Grocery store (stacking, shelving, bagging)
– Cooking activities (pretzels, tortillas, pizza)
– Chopsticks lesson
– Field trip (walking, shopping)
– *Popcorn* song and movement activity

Interpersonal
– Centers time—blocks, sand table, art & writing center
– Dramatic play (house corner)—grocery store
– Working with Sra. Lemus—tortilla activity
– Field trip and thank-you letters to follow up
– Small group work—clipping pictures for bulletin

that describe the general purposes of the activities and experiences you plan to teach. The goals tell what the unit is to accomplish and describe how the children will change following the unit experience (Seefeldt, 1997). They should also be reflected in the objectives and activities of individual lessons across the entire unit. The goals should be flexible and allow for the incorporation of children's interest into specific activities as the unit evolves. After Mr. Meyer developed his webs to help him organize the theme of foods and nutrition, he developed a list of goals, which are presented in Figure 13.8.

FIGURE 13.7 Web on Different Ways to Involve Families

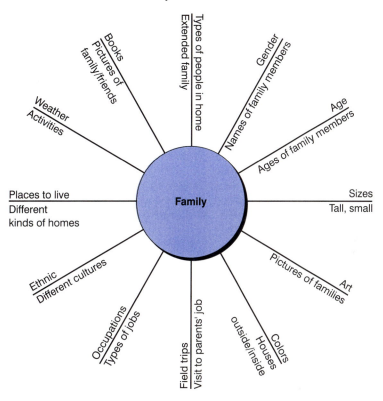

Some teachers develop a separate list of objectives, while others focus on the objectives for the individual plans that they develop for each day. Mr. Meyer began constructing a list of objectives to guide his individual plans. However, he found it difficult to list every objective for every lesson before he started developing his activities and daily plans. His tentative list included:

- Students will identify fruits and vegetables by color, shape, and size.
- Students will describe how fruits and vegetables keep our bodies healthy.
- Students will investigate how recipes are written.
- Students will represent their favorite food pictorially and will explain it orally.
- Students will observe and predict how brushing teeth influences dental health.
- Students will investigate how food and drink choices affect dental health.
- Students will prepare different foods such as fruits before eating.
- Students will classify different foods into groups of healthy and nonhealthy foods.
- Students will describe different foods that their families eat at home.
- Students will describe where foods such as fruits and vegetables come from.

FIGURE 13.8 Subject-Matter Discipline Goals for Foods and Nutrition Unit

---

Social Studies
- Children will explore places where fruits and vegetables come from—the grocery store, farms, and gardens—through field trips.
- Children will be exposed to food preparations from a variety of countries and cultures through our annual "Fruits and Vegetables Feast."
- Children will learn to appreciate differences through exposure to the customs of a variety of cultures, both through the feast, and through carefully selected children's literature.

Language Arts
- Children will have rich language experiences about fruits and vegetables built around our trip to a community garden and a grocery store and follow-up language experience activities. Emphasis will be placed on vocabulary related to different types of fruits and vegetables, food preparation techniques, and nutrition.
- Children will have fun with language by making up a group story about our trip to a community garden.
- Children will have the opportunity to match word and print by listening to appropriately selected book-and-tape sets, including *Blueberries for Sal*.

Math and Science
- Children will make observations about fruits regarding shape, number of parts, color, and similarities of structures.
- Children will be exposed to science vocabulary about fruits and plants.
- Children will learn how plants grow by planting seeds and vegetative cuttings and watching them develop.
- Children will learn how scientists make observations by recording their plants' growth.
- Children will learn about sorting and matching with fruits and vegetables.

Movement/Physical Development
- Children will learn creative expression in movement through activities such as *Grow Like a Seed* and *Peanut Butter and Jelly*.
- Children will learn to feel and express beat through numerous finger plays and songs, such as *My Garden Finger Play*.

Concepts

In our discussion of concepts in the section on planning individual lessons, we discussed how concepts refer to the important ideas and significant content in different subjects. As you may recall, Mr. Meyer used webbing to determine concepts that he planned to teach. As seen in Figure 13.4, he delineated 10 different concepts that were specific to fruits and vegetables. As he began planning specific activities that involved cooking and the children's families, he added the following concepts:

- Cooking involves following directions.
- Directions for cooking are listed in the form of a recipe.
- Recipes are printed in newspapers and magazines and are bound together in books called cookbooks.
- The food and drink choices we make can affect our health.
- Scientists make predictions and observations.
- People from different cultures have different ways and styles of eating.

Although Mr. Meyer did not determine all of the concepts he would be teaching before he developed his individual plans, he checked to make sure that he was including the concepts required by school district and state guidelines.

Procedures

Introductory activities.   An introduction to a unit should motivate and stimulate children's interest in the theme you have chosen. In addition, teachers need to assess what children already know about the concepts they plan to teach. The following experiences are examples of ways to introduce a thematic unit:

- Initiate a discussion that includes questions designed to stimulate children's interest and thinking (Seefeldt, 1997). Mr. Meyer could ask the following questions to begin his unit: "What foods do you like to eat at home?" "Where do you get these foods?" "Are there any foods that come from plants?"
- Create an experience such as putting eggs in several jars containing different liquids like milk, Coca-Cola, and vinegar. Tell the children that you would like them to observe what happens to the eggs after they have been in the jars for a period of time. Mr. Meyer used this activity as an introduction to concepts on dental health that evolved from his foods and nutrition thematic unit.
- Use an audiovisual resource such as a videotape, CD-ROM, slides, or a record.
- Create an arranged environment (Seefeldt, 1997). Mr. Meyer talked with his cooperating teacher about displaying pictures of different foods or an open book that was related to the topic to introduce his unit. His cooperating teacher also suggested that he prepare a bulletin board on the foods and nutrition theme.
- Discuss a web to elicit children's interest. Mr. Meyer also considered using his web on different types of fruits and vegetables. Since he is teaching kindergarten, he planned to also use pictures of different fruits and vegetables as he introduced the web.
- Read a story that is related to the theme. Mr. Meyer found a number of books from the school's library that he could use to begin a discussion about foods and nutrition.

Developmental activities.   The developmental activities are the core of a thematic unit. Beginning teachers often find it confusing and frustrating to develop activities that address all of the principles of a developmentally appropriate curriculum. It can be tricky to move from webbing an overview of a unit to actually generating a sequence of individual plans that address all developmental areas—family involvement, child-child interactions, opportunities for individual choice, active learning experiences, and opportunities to develop decision-making and problem-solving skills. In addition, remember that the developmental activities need to include experiences that facilitate the understanding of the concepts and relationships between the concepts.

In our explanation of developmental activities, we continue to use examples from Mr. Meyer's foods and nutrition theme. As Mr. Meyer thought about how he could connect the different subject-matter content areas and provide developmentally appropriate experiences, he used his webs, his list of goals and objectives, and his list of concepts. He also relied on advice from his cooperating teacher and fellow students. Consequently, Mr. Meyer generated a list of major learning experiences that he divided by subject-matter area:

- **Social studies.**   Social studies activities included field trips to a grocery store and a community garden to connect the concepts the children were learning to their community. At the grocery store, Mr. Meyer planned for the children to

A field trip in the children's community can provide connections to real-life experiences.

see how different foods are displayed and the variety of foods that are available for purchase. He also planned for each child to purchase an ingredient for a cooking project. At the community garden, he anticipated that the children would see how people grow their own food and what types of food are grown. He also planned to invite two resource people from the community, a master gardener and the produce manager from the local grocery store, to talk to the children about growing, harvesting, and marketing different foods.

- **Science.** Science activities included using tools such as a magnifying glass and microscope to examine different foods. Mr. Meyer also planned for the children to grow plants and to follow recipes to make different foods. For example, he found recipes for fruit kabobs, fruit salad, and salsa. These activities would lead to the children eating different foods and discussing their food preferences. Mr. Meyer also wanted to discuss and compare foods that are healthy and unhealthy.

- **Language and literacy.** For language and literacy, Mr. Meyer compiled a list of children's books that he could read on a regular basis throughout the unit, which is displayed in Figure 13.9. In addition to reading books, Mr. Meyer planned activities in which the children would participate in oral discussions that incorporated asking open-ended questions, listening to tapes and records, recording ideas in writing, dictating and writing letters, and dictating to an adult or tape recorder. He planned to generate a list of favorite foods during one of the initial activities and then use the words the children contributed during subsequent lessons.

- **Mathematics.** Mr. Meyer planned to have the children use mathematics in their daily classroom life. For example, he planned to provide opportunities for the children to sort foods by color, sort and count seeds from various foods, identify shapes found in foods, compare foods by weight, discuss the sequence of different food-preparation processes, predict how many seeds are in an apple or orange, and measure different foods.

- **Art.** Mr. Meyer found a number of ideas that would incorporate art into his unit. He planned experiences such as painting with pudding, printing with apples, creating collages from seeds and magazine pictures, creating a favorite food booklet, creating prints with vegetables, and using carrots and celery as paint brushes.

- **Movement and music.** For movement and music, Mr. Meyer compiled a list of songs and finger plays that he could use throughout the unit. Figure 13.10 includes the songs and finger plays Mr. Meyer collected. For movement, Mr. Meyer planned to ask the children to imitate how certain plants grow and to move in different ways while singing the songs, "My Garden" and "Peanut Butter, Jelly."

- **Technology/multimedia.** Mr. Meyer wanted to incorporate technology and multimedia resources into his unit. With the help of the technology specialist in his school, he listed different computer activities that he found to be

FIGURE 13.9   Unit-Related Children's Literature Books*

A Spike of Green, Barbara Baker

A Very Young Gardener, Jill Krementz

Apples and Pumpkins, Anne Rockwell

Bert's Little Garden, Tom Cooke

Billy the Bean, Maria Buria

Blueberries for Sal, Robert McCloskey

Bread and Jam for Frances, Russell Hoban

Carrot Seed, Ruth Krauss

Cheese, Peas, and Chocolate Pudding, Betty Van Wittsen

Cherries and Cherry Pits, Vera Williams

Chicken Sunday, Patricia Polacco

Cloudy With a Chance of Meatballs, Judith Barrett

Cranberry Thanksgiving, Wendi Devlin

Curious George Goes to a Restaurant, Margaret and H. A. Rey

Follow the Drinking Gourd, Jeanette Winter

Grandma's Soup, Nancy Karkowsky

Green Eggs and Ham, Dr. Seuss

Gregory, The Terrible Eater, Mitchell Sharmat

Growing Vegetable Soup, Lois Ehlert

How a Seed Grows, Helene Jordan

I Will Tell You Peach Stone, Nathan Zimelman

Little Pear, The Story of a Little Chinese Boy, C. Lattimore

Little Seeds, Else Holmelund Minarek

Maytime Magic, Mabel Watts

Mousekin's Golden House, Edna Miller

My Kitchen, Harlow Rockwell

Pumpkin, Pumpkin, Jeanne Titherington

Ruby Mae Has Something To Say, David Small

Soup for Supper, Phyllis Root

Stone Soup, Marcia Brown, Heather Forest, Ann McGovern, and Tony Ross

The Biggest Pumpkin Ever, Steven Kroll

The Buried Treasure, Djemma Bider

The Emperor's Plum Tree, Michelle Nikly

The Great Big Enormous Turnip, Alexsei Tolstoy

The Pea Patch Jig, Thatcher Hurd

The Very Hungry Caterpillar, Eric Carle

This Years Garden, Cynthia Rylant

Three Apples Fell From Heaven, Virginia A. Tashjian

Three Stalks of Corn, Leo Politi

Under the Blackberries, Rachel Pank

Note: Multicultural books are in **bold** print

developmentally appropriate along with possible videotapes that he could use. His list of technology resources is shown in Figure 13.11.

In addition to these large- and small-group activities, Mr. Meyer also made a list of possible learning centers that incorporate his foods and nutrition theme:

- **Block center**   with plastic foods, farm trucks, and tractor trailer trucks.
- **Home living and dramatic play center**   with a grocery store cash register, play money, play food, grocery bags, grocer's apron, and shopping cart; and a fruit stand with plastic fruits, baskets, bags, scales, and play money.
- **Farm center**   with rake, hoe, shovel, hay bale, seeds, wagon, plastic foods, boxes/crates, and overalls.
- **Sand table**   with potting soil and seeds, Jell-O, or cornmeal.

FIGURE 13.10 Unit-Related Music and Finger Plays

The Vegetable Garden

(Sing to the tune of *Mulberry Bush*)

Here we go 'round the vegetable garden,
The vegetable garden, the vegetable garden,
Here we go 'round the vegetable garden,
So early in the morning.

Other verses:
This is the way we pull the weeds. . .
This is the way we water the plants. . .
This is the way we eat the vegetables. . .

My Garden

This is my garden
  (extend one hand forward, palm up)
I'll rake it with care
  (make raking motion on palm with three
  fingers of other hand)
And then some seeds
  (planting motion)
I'll plant in there.
The sun will shine
  (make circle with arms)
And the rain will fall
  (let fingers flutter down to lap)
and my garden will blossom
  (cup hand together, extend upward slowly)
And grow straight and tall.

Little Apples

(Sing to the tune of *Ten Little Indians*)

One little, two little, three little apples,
Four little, five little, six little apples,

Seven little, eight little, nine little apples
All fell to the ground.

Bananas

Bananas are my favorite fruit.
  (make fists as if holding a banana)
I eat one every day.
  (hold up one finger)
I always take one with me
  (act as if putting one in pocket)
When I go out to play.
  (wave good-bye)
It gives me lots of energy
  (make a muscle)
To jump around and run.
  (move arms as if running)
Bananas are my favorite fruit.
  (rub tummy)
To me they're so much fun!
  (point to self and smile)

Two Little Apples

Two little apples hanging on a tree
  (arms out with hand turned down)
Two little apples smiling at me
  (turn hands up)
I shook that tree as hard as I could
  (shaking motion)
Down came the apples. Mmmmmmmm
Were they good!
  (falling motion: rub tummy)

---

continues

In Mr. Meyer's class on "Children and Their Families," he developed a web and then planned a number of activities to encourage family involvement. He suggested home activities that would facilitate a connection between the concepts learned in his class and the children's homes. Figure 13.12 shows the different family involvement activities that Mr. Meyer planned.

FIGURE 13.10 Unit-Related Music and Finger Plays *continued*

Peanut Butter, Jelly

The words are a variation of popular play rhyme about making a peanut butter and jelly sandwich, from kneading the bread dough, to mashing the peanuts, to finally eating the whole thing. In between each of the verses (which include suggested hand and body actions), the rhythmic refrain—with motions—is repeated.

Peanut	butter,	peanut	butter,	jelly	jelly.
(clap,	*slap knees,*	*clap,*	*slap knees,*	*clap, slap knees,*	*clap, slap knees)*

First you take the dough and knead it, knead it.
  (push with heels of hands)   [Refrain]

Pop it in the oven and bake it, bake it.
  (extend arm toward "oven")   [Refrain]

Then you take a knife and slice it, slice it.
  ("saw" back and forth with side of hand)   [Refrain]

Then you take the peanuts and crack them, crack them.
  (pound fists together)   [Refrain]

Put them on the floor and mash them, mash them.
  (push fists into palm of other hand)   [Refrain]

Then you take a knife and spread it, spread it.
  (move hand back and forth as if spreading)   [Refrain]

Next you take some grapes and squash them, squash them.
  (stamp feet)   [Refrain]

Glop it on the bread and smear it, smear it.
  (spreading motion again)   [Refrain]

Then you take the sandwich and eat it, eat it.
  (open and close mouth as if biting)   [Refrain]

Mr. Meyer's cooperating teacher also asked him to think about how he could adapt the different activities to meet any special needs of his students. For the five students who are non-native English or English-as-a-Second-Language (ESL) learners, Mr. Meyer talked with an ESL specialist in his school building and generated a list of techniques that he could use with some of his major learning activities. Mr. Meyer's list included:

- **Reading.** After reading a story to the class, read it again, encouraging the children to repeat passages of the book together. During reading, translate the names of some of the different foods in the languages represented in the class; ask ESL students to translate for the class as well.

FIGURE 13.11   Unit-Related Media and Technology Resources

Computer Activities

Mickey's 123's: The Big Surprise Party, Disney Software

Reader Rabbit 1, The Learning Company

The Tree House, Leslie Grimm

ABC's, Fisher Price

Sammy's Science House, Edmark

Baby ROM, American Baby

Videos

Barney Rhymes with Mother Goose, 1993, The Lyons Group. Includes "Peas, Porridge, Hot," and "Mary, Mary, Quite Contrary."

Barney Songs, 1995, The Lyons Group. Includes "Alphabet Soup," "Make the Bread," and "Have a Snack."

Counted Higher: Great Music Videos from Sesame Street, 1988, CTW/Random House. Includes "The Ten Commandments of Health."

Jack and the Bean Stalk, 1995, HBO/Random House. Narrated by Robert Guillaume.

Madeline at Cooking School, 1993, DIC Video, Golden Book Video and Design, Western Publishing Company, Inc.

The Very Hungary Caterpillar and Other Stories by Erik Carle, 1995, The Illuminated Film Company, Ltd./Scholastic.

FIGURE 13.12   Foods and Nutrition Family Involvement Activities

1. Families will be invited to visit the classroom to share or prepare a favorite food.
2. Families will be asked to provide empty boxes or cans to be used in the home living/dramatic play center. Families will also be asked to provide old props related to food preparation such as hats, aprons, plastic baking tools, etc.
3. Families may contribute recipes that will be distributed as a class cookbook to the children and their families.
4. A letter explaining the Foods and Nutrition unit will be sent home to inform families of planned projects.
5. Families will be asked to involve their children in home cooking projects.
6. Families will be invited to join the field trips to the grocery store and community garden. In addition, families will be welcomed to visit the classroom throughout the unit.
7. Students' work will be collected and sent home to share with their families.
8. A list of children's books about fruits and vegetables will be sent home.

- **Art.**   After the ESL students have finished painting different foods, ask them to say the name of the foods they painted in their native language and in English. Label the pictures in the native language and in English.
- **Mathematics.**   Ask the ESL students to say the names of the foods in the sorting, grouping, and patterning activities. Ask for the food names in their native language and in English.
- **Language.**   When playing "Simon Says" with plastic fruit props, say the name of the fruits in the ESL students' native languages and encourage other children to repeat the names. Say the names of the fruits in English and ask all children to repeat the names.

As Mr. Meyer continued to develop his unit, he worked with his cooperating teacher to assure that the activities would be connected. That is, he ensured that each activity built on another so the children would see how the concepts in one activity were related to the next activity. He then worked on the sequence of his activities and began to think about how he would summarize or conclude the unit so that he could encourage the children to reflect on what they had experienced.

Summary activities.   Summary activities help children to organize, present, or summarize the ideas and concepts they have learned (Seefeldt & Barbour, 1994). The summary activity can also provide an opportunity for the teacher to assess what concepts and ideas the children have learned during the unit. Examples of summary activities include asking children to create products or displays of their work that present particular concepts, dictating stories or thank-you letters, or compiling a book of dictated stories and pictures. In the primary grades, children can create graphs or diagrams that depict the relationship between different concepts (Seefeldt, 1997).

Mr. Meyer decided to make a class book that he could laminate and keep in the classroom as his summary activity. He planned to include the children's recipes of their favorite foods, pictures the students drew, and dictated stories about activities they participated in. As the unit evolved, Mr. Meyer saved pictures and stories about activities such as the field trip to the grocery store and the visit by the grocery store produce manager. By keeping the book in the classroom, Mr. Meyer referred to the concepts the students learned when he discussed related ideas in future thematic units.

Evaluation

Evaluation of the children's learning is another critical component of a thematic unit. Evaluation should include a variety of assessment techniques that are used throughout the unit. Many of the different assessment techniques that we discussed in Chapter 10 can be used to determine whether or not the children understand the concepts you are teaching in your unit. Teachers typically use observation, portfolios, informal interviews, videotapes, anecdotal records, and checklists throughout the unit. In keeping with our focus on developmentally appropriate practice, we remind you that informal methods of assessment used throughout the unit will provide the most relevant and meaningful evaluation of children's learning.

Mr. Meyer planned to use a combination of assessment techniques throughout his thematic unit. He planned to take anecdotal records during discussions and while students participated in certain activities such as sorting and classifying different foods, weighing different objects, and during dictation activities. He also planned to collect pictures and accompanying dictations during the unit. His cooperating teacher also suggested that he take anecdotal records as students dictated stories for their recipes to ensure that they could orally explain what they had dictated. Mr. Meyer also thought about periodically asking the children what their favorite activities were to ensure that he was aware of their interest in the different unit experiences.

CHAPTER SUMMARY

It can be challenging, and at times frustrating, to successfully plan an integrated early childhood curriculum. Planning is more than developing activities that are interesting, appealing, and satisfying to young children. In this and other chapters, we discussed a number of principles that influence and are influenced by careful and thoughtful planning. For example: 1) an integrated curriculum provides for all areas of a child's development as well as content from various subject-matter disciplines; 2) teachers facilitate the development of children's knowledge and skills in all content areas when they use an integrated curriculum; 3) teachers need to consider the experiences children bring with them to school, activities children are interested in, differences in developmental levels, children's families and cultural background, and knowledge of the children's community; and 4) a thematic unit has intellectual integrity and can be used as an organizational tool to link different subject-matter content. Now that you have finished reading this text, we would like you to revisit the philosophy of teaching that you developed in Chapter 1.

 ### Revisiting Your Teaching Philosophy

Work in small groups with your classmates. Before you begin the group work, reflect on all of the philosophies and related activities that you have worked on while reading this text. Highlight or rewrite issues you feel strongly about.

To guide your reflections in small groups, address the following questions and activities:

- How do your philosophies address children, their families, and their communities?
- Identify two theorists who have been discussed in previous chapters and explain why their theories match with your beliefs about how young children learn and develop.
- Share your classroom designs (from Chapter 12) with others in your class in small groups. The small groups should consist of class members who chose the same age level for their classroom design. Now:

    1. Identify design elements that might need to be addressed regarding classroom management issues (for example, an area of the room that might become too crowded during center time)
    2. Provide an example of types of behaviors that might occur as a result of the classroom design
    3. Use one of the three behavior management models from Chapter 12 to address how you would respond to these behaviors
    4. Identify the most important aspect of organizing learning environments according to your philosophy.

- If you and your peers were teachers in the same school, would it be possible to combine your individual philosophies into one philosophy? Give it a try! As you begin your discussion, remember the four teaching philosophies discussed in Chapter 1: humanistic, ecological, developmental, and instructional.

ACTIVITIES

1. Assume that you have been assigned to develop a plan for teaching a lesson on "Our Community" to first graders. One of the concepts in the curriculum guidelines is: "There are many types of cars, trucks, and buses." Write a general goal, a specific objective, and a learning activity to use with these first-grade children.
2. Obtain school district or state curriculum guidelines for prekindergarten, kindergarten, and the primary grades. Compare the guidelines to unit plans from a teacher at any of these levels. Answer the following questions:
   - Can you identify the concepts that should be taught?
   - How are the activities organized?

- If the teacher uses thematic units, can you determine lessons that integrate different subject-matter areas?
- Can you identify specific lessons that you could easily teach?
- Are there any family involvement activities?
- Are the needs of special learners addressed?

3. Interview a teacher who uses thematic units. Consider asking some of the following questions:
   - How does she plan?
   - Does she ever use webbing as a strategy to organize her planning?
   - How does she determine the concepts and objectives she plans to teach in her units?

- How does she address children's interest in her thematic units?
- Does she plan family involvement activities as part of her thematic units?
- What does she do if she cannot incorporate every subject-matter area in her thematic units?
- Does she include activities that promote children working together to solve problems?
- What types of assessment techniques does she use during and at the end of her thematic units?

4. Observe in a classroom that uses an integrated curriculum approach in preschool or the primary grades.

- What types of learning activities are the children engaged in?
- Do the children have the opportunity to make decisions about the activities they participate in?
- How is the classroom organized?
- What are the assessment techniques that are used?
- Are different developmental areas addressed in the activities you observed?

5. Assume that you have been assigned the topic, "The Rainforest" to teach in second grade. After looking over school district or state curriculum guidelines, create a conceptual web of possible concepts you would teach in this unit.

References

Adams, W. C. (1991). *Foundations of physical education, exercise, and sport sciences.* Philadelphia: Lea & Febiger.

Ainsworth, M. D. S., Blehar, M. C., Waters, E., & Wall, S. (1978). *Patterns of attachment: A psychological study of the strange situation.* Hillsdale, NJ: Erlbaum.

Alberto, P. A., & Troutman, A. C. (1995). *Applied behavior analysis for teachers* (4th ed.). Englewood Cliffs, NJ: Prentice-Hall.

Allen, K. E., & Marotz, L. (1994). *Developmental profiles: Birth to six* (2d ed.). Albany, NY: Delmar.

Allred, K. W., Briem, R., & Black, S. J. (1998). Collaboratively addressing needs of young children with disabilities. *Young Children, 53,* 32–35.

Amado, A. (1993). Steps for supporting community connections. In A. Amado (Ed.), *Friendships and community connections between people with and without disabilities* (pp. 299–326). Baltimore, MD: Paul Brookes.

Ames, L. B. (1989). *Arnold Gesell: Themes of his work.* New York: Human Sciences Press.

Anderson, J. D. (1988). *The education of Blacks in the South, 1860–1935.* Chapel Hill: University of North Carolina Press.

Anglin, J. M. (1993). Vocabulary development: A morphological analysis. *Monographs of the Society for Research in Child Development, 58* (10, Serial No. 238).

Auxter, D., & Pyfer, J. (1989). *Principles and methods of adapted physical education and recreation.* St. Louis: Times College Publishing.

Azmitia, M. (1988). Peer interaction and problem solving: When are two heads better than one? *Child Development, 59,* 87–96.

Baldwin, E. A., & Markman, E. M. (1989). Establishing word object relations: a first step. *Child Development, 60,* 1291–1306.

Barber, B. K. (1992). Family, personality, and adolescent behavior problems. *Journal of Marriage and the Family, 54,* 69–79.

Barnes, G. M., & Farrell, M. P. (1992). Parental support and control as predictors of adolescent drinking, delinquency, and related problem behaviors. *Journal of Marriage and the Family, 54,* 763–776.

Barton, M. L., & Zeanah, C. H. (1990). Stress in the preschool years. In L. E. Arnold (Ed.), *Childhood stress.* New York: John Wiley & Sons.

Bates, E., Camaioni, L., & Volterra, V. (1975). The acquisition of performatives prior to speech. *Merrill-Palmer Quarterly, 21,* 205–226.

Bates, J. E. (1989). Application of temperament concepts. In G. A. Kohnstamm, J. E. Bates, & M. K. Rothbart (Eds.), *Temperament in childhood* (pp. 321–356). New York: Wiley.

Baumrind, D. (1967). Child care practices anteceding three patterns of preschool behavior. *Genetic Psychology Monographs, 75,* 43–88.

Baumrind, D. (1971). Current patterns of parental authority. *Developmental Psychology Monographs, 4* (1, Part 2).

Baumrind, D. (1991a). Parenting styles and adolescent development. In R. M. Lerner, A. C. Petersen, & J. Brooks-Gunn (Eds.), *Encyclopedia of adolescence* (pp. 746–758). New York: Garland.

Baumrind, D. (1991b). The influence of parenting style on adolescent competence and substance use. *Journal of Early Adolescence, 11,* 56–95.

Beal, C. R. (1994). *Boys and girls: The development of gender roles.* New York: McGraw-Hill.

Becker, W. C., Engelmann, S., Carnine, D. W., & Rhine, W. R. (1981). Direct instruction model. In W. R. Rhine (Ed.), *Making schools more effective: New directions from Follow Through* (pp. 95–154). New York: Academic Press.

Beckman, P. J., Barnwell, D., Horn, E., Hanson, M. J., Gutierrez, S., & Lieber, J. (1998). Communities, families, and inclusion. *Early Childhood Research Quarterly, 13,* 125–150.

Bee, H. (1997). *The developing child* (8th ed). New York: Longman.

Bell, R. Q. (1968). A reinterpretation of the direction of effects in studies of socialization. *Psychological Review, 75,* 81–95.

Bell, R. Q. (1971). Stimulus control of parent or caretaker behavior by offspring. *Developmental Psychology, 4,* 63–72.

Bellah, R. N., Sullivan, W. M., Swidler, A., & Tipton, S. M. (1985). *Habits of the heart: Individualism and commitment in American life.* New York: Harper & Row.

Bereiter, C., & Engelmann, S. (1966). *Teaching disadvantaged children in the preschool.* Englewood Cliffs, NJ: Prentice-Hall.

Berger, E. H. (1991). Parent involvement: Yesterday and today. *The Elementary School Journal, 91,* 209–220.

Berk, L. E. (1992). Children's private speech: An overview of theory and the status of research. In R. M. Diaz & L. E. Berk (Eds.), *Private speech: From social interaction to self-regulation* (pp. 17–53). Hillsdale, NJ: Erlbaum.

Berk, L. E. (1996). *Infants, children and adolescents* (2d ed.). Needham Heights, MA: Allyn & Bacon.

Berk, L. E., & Landau, S. (1993). Private speech of learning disabled and normally achieving children in classroom academic and laboratory contexts. *Child Development, 64,* 556–571.

Berk, L. E., & Spuhl, S. T. (1995). Maternal interaction, private speech, and task performance in preschool children. *Early Childhood Research Quarterly, 10,* 357–377.

Berk, L. E., & Winsler, A. (1995). *Scaffolding children's learning: Vygotsky and early childhood education.* Washington, DC: National Association for the Education of Young Children.

Berndt, T. J. (1997). *Child development.* Madison, WI: Brown & Benchmark Publishers.

Billman, J., & Sherman, J. A. (1996). *Observation and participation in early childhood settings.* Boston: Allyn & Bacon.

Birch, L. L., Johnson, S. L., Andresen, G., Peters, J. C., & Schulte, M. C. (1991). The variability of young children's energy intake. *New England Journal of Medicine, 324,* 232–235.

Bivens, J. A., & Berk, L. E. (1990). A longitudinal study of the development of elementary school children's private speech. *Merrill-Palmer Quarterly, 36,* 443–463.

Black, J., Puckett, M., & Michael, J. (1992). *The young child: Development from birth through age eight.* New York: Merrill.

Block, J. H., & Everson, S. T., & Guskey, T. R. (1995). *School improvement programs.* New York: Scholastic.

Blom, G. E., Cheney, B. D., & Snoddy, J. E. (1986). *Stress in childhood: An intervention model for teachers and other professionals.* New York: Teachers College Press.

Bloom, B. S. (1964). *Stability and change in human characteristics.* New York: John Wiley & Sons.

Bloom, L., Beckwith, R., & Capatides, J. B. (1988). Developments in expression of affect. *Infant Behavior and Development, 11,* 169–186.

Bohannon, J. N., III, & Stanowicz, L. (1988). The issue of negative evidence: Adult responses to children's language errors. *Developmental Psychology, 24,* 684–689.

Bowen, J. (1981). *A history of western education.* London: Methuen.

Bowman, B., & Brady, E. H. (1982). Today's issues: Tomorrow's possibilities. In S. Hill & B. J. Barnes (Eds.), *Young children and their families: Needs of the nineties.* Lexington, MA: Lexington Books.

Boyd, W. (1914). *From Locke to Montessori.* London: Harrap & Company.

Boyd, W. (1965). *The history of western education* (7th ed.). New York: Barnes & Noble.

Boyer, E. L. (1992). *Ready to learn: A mandate for the nation.* Princeton, NJ: The Carnegie Foundation for the Advancement of Teaching.

Bredekamp, S. (Ed.). (1987). *Developmentally appropriate practice in early childhood programs serving children from birth through age 8.* Washington, DC: National Association for the Education of Young Children.

Bredekamp, S. (1991). Redeveloping early childhood education: A response to Kessler. *Early Childhood Research Quarterly 6*, 199–209.

Bredekamp, S., & Copple, C. (1997). *Developmentally appropriate practice in early childhood programs serving children from birth through age 8: Revised edition.* Washington, DC: National Association for the Education of Young Children.

Bredekamp, S., & Rosegrant, T. (Eds.). (1992). *Reaching potentials: Appropriate curriculum and assessment for young children* (Vol. 1). Washington, DC: National Association for the Education of Young Children.

Bredekamp, S., & Rosegrant, T. (Eds.). (1996). *Reaching potentials: Transforming early childhood curriculum and assessment* (Vol. 2). Washington, DC: National Association for the Education of Young Children.

Bredekamp, S., & Shepard, L. (1989). How best to protect children from inappropriate expectations, practices, and policies. *Young Children, 44*(3), 14–24.

Brewer, J. A. (1998). *Introduction to early childhood education* (3d ed.). Boston: Allyn & Bacon.

Bronfenbrenner, U. (1979). *The ecology of human development.* Cambridge, MA: Harvard University Press.

Brown, A. L., Bransford, J. D., Ferrara, R. A., & Campione, J. C. (1983). Learning, remembering, and understanding. In J. H. Flavell & E. M. Markman (Eds.), *Handbook of child psychology: Vol. 3. Cognitive development* (pp. 77–166). New York: Wiley.

Brown, J. S., Collins, A., & Duguid, P. (1989). Situated cognition and the culture of learning. *Educational Researcher, 18*(4), 32–42.

Bryant, D. M., Clifford, R. M., & Peisner, E. S. (1991). Best practices for beginners: Developmental appropriateness in kindergarten. *American Educational Research Journal, 28*, 783–803.

Bryant, D. M., Peisner-Feinberg, E. S., & Clifford, R. M. (1993). *Evaluation of public preschool programs in North Carolina: Final report.* Chapel Hill, NC: Frank Porter Graham Child Development Center.

Burchfield, D. W. (1996). Teaching all children: Four developmentally appropriate curricular and instructional strategies in primary-grade classrooms. *Young Children, 52*, 4–10.

Burden, P. R. (1995). *Classroom management and discipline.* White Plains, NY: Longman.

Butts, R. F. (1973). *The education of the west: A formative chapter in the history of civilization.* New York: McGraw-Hill.

Buysse, V., Wesley, P. W., & Keyes, L. (1998). Implementing early childhood inclusion: Barrier and support factors. *Early Childhood Research Quarterly, 13*, 169–184.

Calhoun, A. W. (1945). *A social history of the American family: From colonial times to the present.* New York: Barnes & Noble.

Campbell, F. A., & Taylor, K. (1996). Early childhood programs that work for children from economically disadvantaged families. *Young Children, 51*, 74–80.

Canter, L., & Canter, M. (1985). *Assertive discipline for parents (revised ed.).* New York: Harper & Row.

Canter, L., & Canter, M. (1993). *Succeeding with difficult students.* Santa Monica, CA: Lee Canter & Associates.

Caples, S. E. (1996). Some guidelines for preschool design. *Young Children, 51*, 14–21.

Caspi, A., Henry, B., McGee, R. O., Moffitt, T. E., & Silva, P. A. (1995). Temperamental origins of child and adolescent behavior problems. *Child Development, 66*, 55–68.

Caspi, A., & Silva, P. A. (1995). Temperamental qualities at age three predict personality traits in young adulthood: Longitudinal evidence from a birth cohort. *Child Development, 66*, 486–498.

Charlesworth, R. (1998). Developmentally appropriate practice is for everyone. *Childhood Education, 74*, 274–282.

Charlesworth, R., & Lind, K. L. (1995). *Math and science for young children* (2d ed.). Albany, NY: Delmar.

Chavkin, N. (1994). *Families and schools in a pluralistic society.* New York: SUNY Press.

Cherlin, A. J. (1996). *Public and private families: An introduction.* New York: McGraw-Hill.

Cherlin, A. J. (1997). A reply to Glenn: What's most important in a family textbook? *Family Relations, 46*, 209–211.

Chomsky, C. (1969). *The acquisition of syntax in children from five to ten.* Cambridge, MA: MIT Press.

Cizak, G. J. (1997). Learning, achievement, and assessment: Constructs at a crossroads. In G. D. Phye (Ed.), *Handbook of classroom assessment* (pp. 1–32). San Diego, CA: Academic Press.

Clark, E. (1983). Meanings and concepts. In J. Flavell and E. Markman (Eds.), *Handbook of child psychology: Vol. III. Cognitive Development* (pp. 789–837). New York: Wiley.

Clark, E. V., & Hecht, B. F. (1982). Learning to coin agent and instrument nouns. *Cognition, 12,* 1–24.

Cleverly, J., & Phillips, D. (1986). *Visions of childhood.* New York: Teachers College Press.

Cochran, M., & Dean, C. (1991). Home-school relations and the empowerment process. *The Elementary School Journal, 91,* 261–270.

Colby, A., & Kohlberg, L. (1987). *The measurement of moral judgement* (Vol. 1). Cambridge, England: Cambridge University Press.

Colby, A., Kohlberg, L., Gibbs, J., & Lieberman, M. (1983). A longitudinal study of moral development. *Monographs of the Society for Research in Child Development* (Serial no. 200, Vol. 48, Nos. 1–2).

Coleman, J. S. (1988). Social capital in the creation of human capital. *American Journal of Sociology, 94,* (Supplement 95), S95–S120.

Coleman, M. (1991). Planning for the changing nature of family life in schools for young children. *Young Children, 46,* 15–20.

Coleman, M. (1997). Families and schools: In search of a common ground. *Young Children, 52,* 14–21.

Coleman, M., & Churchill, S. (1997). Challenges to family involvement in early childhood education: Opportunities for involving family professionals. *Childhood Education, 73,* 144–148.

Coleman, M., & Wallinga, C. (in press). Teacher training in family involvement: An interpersonal approach. *Childhood Education.*

Coleman, M., Wallinga, C., & Toledo, C. (1998). *Life skills training within school-age child care programs: Patterns of delivery.* Manuscript submitted for publication.

Columbia University College of Physicians and Surgeons (1990). *Columbia University College of Physicians and Surgeons Complete Guide to Early Child Care.* New York: Crown Publishers.

Comenius, J. A. (1623/1956). *The school of infancy.* Chapel Hill, NC: University of North Carolina Press.

Comer, J. P., & Haynes, N. M. (1991). Parent involvement in schools: An ecological approach. *The Elementary School Journal, 91,* 271–278.

Congressional Quarterly Service. (1985). *Congress and the Nation* (Vol. 6). Washington, DC: Author.

Consortium of Family Organizations. (1990, March). What criteria should be used to implement a family perspective? *The COFO Family Policy Report, 1,* 3.

Consumer Products Safety Commission (1991). *1991 handbook for public playground safety.* Washington, DC: Author.

Coontz, S. (1988). *The social origins of private life.* New York: Verso.

Coontz, S. (1992). *The way we never were: American families and the nostalgia trap.* New York: Basic Books.

Cowan, P. A. (1993). The sky is falling, but Popenoe's analysis won't help us do anything about it. *Journal of Marriage and the Family, 55,* 548–553.

Crabtree, C., Nash, G. B., Gagnon, P., & Waugh, S. (Eds.). (1992). *Lessons from history: Essential understandings and historical perspectives students should acquire.* Los Angeles: National Center for History in the Schools, The University of California.

Crain, W. (1992). *Theories of development: Concepts and applications* (3d ed.). Englewood Cliffs, NJ: Prentice-Hall.

Cremin, L. A. (1964). *The transformation of the school.* New York: Vintage Books.

Cremin, L. A. (1988). *American education: The metropolitan experience.* New York: Harper & Row.

Cryer, D., & Phillipsen, L. (1997). Quality details: A close-up look at child care program strengths and weaknesses. *Young Children, 52,* 51–61.

Cuffaro, H. K. (1995). *Experimenting with the world.* New York: Teacher's College Press.

Curriculum changes stir debate on numerous issues. (1994, October 16). *The Atlanta Journal and Constitution,* p. D10.

Datta, L. (1976). Watchman, how is it with the child? In E. H. Grotberg (Ed.), *200 years of children* (pp. 221–279). Washington, DC: U.S. Government Printing Office.

Davies, D. (1991). Schools reaching out: Family, school, and community partnerships for student success. *Phi Delta Kappan, 72,* 376–382.

Dawson, G., Hessl, D., & Fry, K. (1994). Social influences on early developing biological and behavioral systems related to risk for affective disorder. In *Development and Psychopathology* (pp. 759–779). Cambridge, England: Cambridge University Press.

Demo, D. H. (1992). Parent-child relations: Assessing recent changes. *Journal of Marriage and the Family, 54,* 104–117.

de Villiers, J. G., & de Villiers, P. A. (1973). A cross-sectional study of the acquisition of grammatical morphemes in child speech. *Journal of Psycholinguistic Research, 2,* 267–278.

DeVries, R., & Kohlberg, L. (1987). *Programs of early education.* New York: Longman.

DeVries, R., & Zan, B. (1995). Creating a constructivist classroom atmosphere. *Young Children, 51,* 4–13.

Dewey, J. (1938). *Experience and education.* New York: Macmillan.

Dill, B. T. (1988). Our mothers' grief: Racial ethnic women and the maintenance of families. *Journal of Family History, 13*(4), 415–431.

Doll, R. C. (1992). *Curriculum improvement: Decision making and process* (8th ed.). Boston: Allyn & Bacon.

Dreikurs, R., & Cassel, P. (1972). *Discipline without tears.* New York: Dutton.

Dreikurs, R., Grunwald, B. B., & Pepper, F. C. (1982). *Maintain sanity in the classroom: Classroom management techniques* (2d ed.). New York: Harper & Row.

Dunn, L., & Kontos, S. (1997). What have we learned about developmentally appropriate practice? *Young Children, 52,* 4–13.

Dryfoos, J. G. (1994). *Full-service schools: A revolution in health and social services for children, youth, and families.* San Francisco: Jossey-Bass.

Dyson, A. H., & Genishi, C. (1993). Visions of children as language users: Language and language education in early childhood. In B. Spodek (Ed.), *Handbook of research on the education of young children* (pp. 122–136). New York: Macmillan.

Eby, F. (1952). *The development of modern education.* New York: Prentice-Hall.

Eckenrode, J., Laird, M., & Doris, J. (1993). School performance and disciplinary problems among abused and neglected children. *Developmental Psychology, 29,* 53–62.

Eisenberg, E., & Rafanello, D. (1998). Accreditation facilitation: A study of one project's success. *Young Children, 53,* 44–48.

Elkind, D. (1981). *The hurried child: Growing up too fast too soon.* Reading, MA: Addison-Wesley.

Elkind, D. (1987). The child yesterday, today, and tomorrow. *Young Children, 42,* 6–11.

Ellis, A. K., & Fouts, J. T. (1994). *Research on school restructuring.* Princeton Junction, NJ: Eye on Education.

Enns, J. T. (Ed.). (1990). *The development of attention: Research and theory.* Amsterdam: North-Holland.

Epstein, J. L. (1987a). What principals should know about parent involvement. *Principal, 66,* 6–9.

Epstein, J. L. (1987b). Parent involvement: What research says to administrators. *Education and Urban Society, 19,* 119–136.

Epstein, J. L. (1991). Paths to partnership: What we can learn from federal, state, district, and school initiatives. *Phi Delta Kappan, 72,* 344–349.

Epstein, J. L. (1995). School/family/community partnerships: Caring for the children we share. *Phi Delta Kappan, 76,* 701–712.

Epstein, J. L., & Dauber, S. L. (1991). School programs and teacher practices of parent involvement in inner-city elementary and middle schools. *The Elementary School Journal, 91,* 289–306.

Erikson, E. H. (1963). *Childhood and society* (2d ed.). New York: W. W. Norton.

Erikson, E. H. (1964). *Insight and Responsibility.* New York: W. W. Norton.

Erikson, E. H. (1980). *Identity and the life cycle.* New York: W. W. Norton.

Erikson, E. H. (1994). *Identity: Youth and crisis.* New York: W. W. Norton.

Feinburg, S. G., & Mindess, M. (1994). *Eliciting children's full potential.* Pacific Grove, CA: Brooks/Cole.

Feldman, D. H. (1991). *Nature's gambit.* New York: Teacher's College Press.

Fennimore, B. S. (1989). *Child advocacy for early childhood education.* New York: Teachers College Press.

Ferber, M. A., & O'Farrell, B. (1991). *Work and family: Policies for a changing work force.* Washington, DC: National Academy Press.

Fernald, A., & Mazzie, C. (1991). Prosody and focus in speech to infants and adults. *Developmental Psychology, 27,* 209–221.

Flavell, J. H. (1985). *Cognitive development* (2d ed.). Englewood Cliffs, NJ: Prentice-Hall.

Flavell, J. H. (1988). The development of children's knowledge about the mind: From cognitive connections to mental representations. In J. W. Astington, P. L. Harris, & D. R. Olson (Eds.), *Developing theories of mind* (pp. 244–267). New York: Cambridge University Press.

Footlick, J. K. (1990, Winter/Spring). What happened to the family? *Newsweek* (special edition), pp. 15–20.

Frauenglas, M. H., & Diaz, R. M. (1985). Self-regulatory functions of children's private speech: A critical analysis of recent challenges to Vygotsky's theory. *Developmental Psychology, 21,* 357–364.

Froebel, F. (1887). *The education of man.* (W. N. Hailmann, Trans.) New York: D. Appleton and Company.

Frost, J. L. (1992). *Play and playscapes.* Albany, NY: Delmar.

Fuhr, J. E., & Barclay, K. H. (1998). The importance of appropriate nutrition and nutrition education. *Young Children, 53,* 74–80.

Furstenberg, F. F., & Hughes, M. E. (1995). Social capital and successful development among at-risk youth. *Journal of Marriage and the Family, 57,* 580–592.

Galinsky, E., Howes, C., Kontos, S., & Shinn, M. (1994). *The study of family child care and relative care: Highlights of findings.* New York: Families and Work Institute.

Ganong, L. H., Coleman, M., & Mapes, D. (1990). A meta-analytic review of family structure stereotypes. *Journal of Marriage and the Family, 52,* 2887–2897.

Garbarino, J., & Abramowitz, R. H. (1992). The ecology of human development. In J. Garbarino (Ed.), *Children and families in the social environment* (2d ed.). Hawthorne, NY: Aldine De Gruyter.

Garcia, E. E. (1997). The education of Hispanics in early childhood: Of roots and wings. *Young Children, 52,* 5–14.

Gardner, H. (1983). *Frames of mind: The theory of multiple intelligence.* New York: Basic Books.

Garmezy, N. (1991). Resilience and vulnerability to adverse developmental outcomes associated with poverty. *American Behavioral Scientist, 34,* 416–430.

Garmezy, N. (1993). Children in poverty: Resilience despite risk. *Psychiatry, 56,* 127–136.

Garmezy, N., Masten, A. S., & Tellegen, A. (1984). The study of stress and competence in children: A building block of developmental psychopathology. *Child Development, 55,* 97–111.

Garrison, W., & Earls, F. (1987). *Temperament and child psychopathology.* Newbury Park, CA: Sage.

Gartrell, D. (1994). *A guidance approach to discipline.* Albany, NY: Delmar.

Gartrell, D. (1997). Beyond discipline to guidance. *Young Children, 52* (6), 34–42.

Garvey, C. (1975). Requests and responses in children's speech. *Journal of Child Language, 2,* 41–63.

Gelberg, D. (1997). *The business of reforming American schools.* Albany, NY: State University of New York Press.

Genovese, E. D. (1981). Husbands and fathers, wives and mothers, during slavery. In M. Albin & D. Cavallo (Eds.), *Family life in America: 1620–2000.* St. James, NY: Revisionary Press.

Gesell, A. (1924). *Infancy and human growth.* New York: Macmillan.

Gesell, A. (1946). The ontogenesis of infant behavior. In L. Carmichael (Ed.), *Manual of child psychology,* New York: John Wiley & Sons.

Ginott, H. G. (1969). *Between parent and child: New solutions to old problems.* London: Staples.

Ginott, H. G. (1993). *Teacher and child.* New York: Collier.

Glenn, N. D. (1997). A critique of twenty family and marriage and family textbooks. *Family Relations, 46,* 197–208.

Goelman, H., & Pence, H. R. (1987). Effects of child care, family, and individual characteristics on children's language development. In D. A. Phillips (Ed.), *Quality in child care: What does research tell us?* Washington, DC: National Association for the Education of Young Children.

Goffin, S. G. (1994). *Curriculum models and early childhood education: Appraising the relationship.* New York: Maxwell Macmillan International.

Goodwin, W. L., & Goodwin, L. D. (1993). Young children and measurement: Standardized and nonstandardized instruments in early childhood education. In B. Spodek (Ed.), *Handbook of research on the education of young children* (pp. 441–463). New York: Macmillan.

Goodwin, W. L., & Goodwin, L. D. (1997). Using standardized measures for evaluating young children's learning. In B. Spodek & O. N. Saracho (Eds.), *Issues in early childhood evaluation and assessment. Yearbook in Early Childhood Education* (Vol. 7) (pp. 92–107). New York: Teachers College Press.

Gordon, I. J. (1977). Parent education and parent involvement: Retrospect and prospect. *Childhood Education, 54,* 71–77.

Grace, C., & Shores, E. F. (1991). *The portfolio and its use.* Little Rock, AR: Southern Association on Children Under Six.

Greenawalt, C. E. (Ed.), (1994). *Educational innovation: An agenda to frame the future.* Lanham, MD: University Press of America.

Greenberg, P. (1989). Parents as partners in young children's development and education: A new American fad? Why does it matter? *Young Children, 44,* 61–75.

Greenwood, G. E., & Hickman, C. W. (1991). Research and practice in parent involvement: Implications for teacher education. *The Elementary School Journal, 91,* 279–288.

Grotberg, E. H. (1976). Child development. In E. H. Grotberg (Ed.), *200 years of children* (pp. 391–420). Washington, DC: U.S. Government Printing Office.

Gullo, D. F. (1997). Assessing student learning through the analysis of pupil products. In B. Spodek & O. N. Saracho (Eds.), *Issues in early childhood evaluation and assessment. Yearbook in Early Childhood Education* (Vol. 7) (pp. 129–148). New York: Teachers College Press.

Gutek, G. L. (1968). *Pestalozzi and education.* New York: Random House.

Gutman, H. G. (1976). *The black family in slavery and freedom: 1750–1925.* New York: Pantheon.

Gutman, H. G. (1983). Persistent myths about the Afro-American family. In M. Gordon (Ed.), *The American family in social-historical perspective* (3rd ed.). New York: St. Martin's Press.

Hadley, P. A., Wilcox, K. A., & Rice, M. L. (1994). Talking at school: Teacher expectations in preschool and kindergarten. *Early Childhood Research Quarterly, 9,* 111–129.

Hagen, J. W. (1967). The effect of distraction on selective attention. *Child Development, 38,* 685–694.

Hainstock, E. G. (1986). *The essential Montessori.* New York: Plume.

Hanson, J. B. (1998). How far should I go in advocating for one of my first-graders? *Young Children, 53,* 57.

Hanson, M. J., Wolfberg, P., Zercher, C., Morgan, M., Gutierrez, S., Barnwell, D., & Beckman, P. (1998). The culture of inclusion: Recognizing diversity at multiple levels. *Early Childhood Research Quarterly, 13,* 185–209.

Hareven, T. K. (1984). Themes in the historical development of the family. In P. B. Baltes & O. G. Brim (Eds.), *Life-span development and behavior* (Vol. 6). New York: Academic Press.

Harry, B. (1992). *Cultural diversity, families, and the special education system.* New York: Teachers College Press.

Hart, C. H., Burts, D. C., & Charlesworth, R. (1997). Integrated developmentally appropriate curriculum. In C. H. Hart, D. C. Burts, & R. Charlesworth (Eds.), *Integrated curriculum and developmentally appropriate practice.* Albany, NY: State University of New York Press.

Haseloff, W. (1990). The efficacy of the parent-teacher partnership of the 1990s. *Early Child Development and Care, 58,* 51–55.

Hasson, J. B. (1998). How far should I go in advocating for one of my first-graders? *Young Children, 53,* 57.

Hayes, C. D., Palmer, J. L., & Zaslow, M. J. (Eds.). (1990). *Who cares for America's children: Child care policy for the 1990s.* Washington, DC: National Academy Press.

Helburn, S. W. (Ed.). (1995). *Cost, quality, and child outcomes in child care center. Technical report.* Denver, CO: Department of Economics, Center for Research in Economics and Social Policy, University of Colorado at Denver.

Hewes, D. W. (1995). *Early childhood education: It's historic past and promising future.* Speech presented at the Annual Graduation Celebration: Early Childhood Education, Long Beach, CA. (ERIC DOCUMENT # PS 023 394).

Hing, B. O. (1993). *Making and remaking Asian America through immigration policy 1850–1990.* Stanford, CA: Stanford University Press.

Hogan, D. (1997). ADHD: A travel guide to success. *Childhood Education, 73,* 158–160.

Hohmann, M., Banet, B., & Weikart, D. (1979). *Young children in action: A manual for preschool educators.* Ypsilanti, MI: The High/Scope Press.

Holloway, S. D., & Fuller, B. (1992). The great child-care experiment: What are the lessons for school improvement? *Educational Researcher, 21,* 12–19.

Holt, K. S. (1991). *Child development: Diagnosis and assessment.* London: Butterworth-Heinemann.

Horgan, D. (1978). The development of the full passive. *Journal of Child Language, 5,* 65–80.

Howes, C., & Matheson, C. C. (1992). Sequences in the development of competent play with peers: Social and social pretend play. *Developmental Psychology, 28,* 961–974.

Hunt, J. M. (1961). *Intelligence and experience.* New York: Ronald Press.

Hymes, J. L. (1991). *Early childhood education: Twenty years in review.* Washington, DC: National Association for the Education of Young Children.

Illingworth, R. S. (1987). *The development of the infant and young child: Normal and abnormal* (9th ed.). Edinburgh, England: Churchill Livingstone.

Ishwaran, K. (1989). *Family and marriage: Cross-cultural perspectives.* Toronto, Ontario: Wall & Thompson.

Jacklin, C. N., & Maccoby, E. E. (1983). Issues of gender differentiation in normal development. In M. D. Levine, W. B. Carey, A. C. Crocker, & R. T. Gross (Eds.), *Developmental-behavioral pediatrics* (pp. 175–184). Philadelphia: Saunders.

Jennings, J. F. (1995). *National issues in education: Goals 2000 and school-to-work.* Washington, DC: Phi Delta Kappa International and The Institute for Educational Leadership.

Jewsuwan, R., Luster, T., & Kostelnik, M. (1993). The relation between parents' perceptions of temperament and children's adjustment to preschool. *Early Childhood Research Quarterly, 8,* 33–51.

Johnson, J. H. (1990). *The new American family and the school.* Columbus, OH: The National Middle School Association.

Johnston, B. J. (1993). The transformation of work and educational reform policy. *American Educational Research Journal, 30,* 39–65.

Johnston, L., & Mermin, J. (1994). Easing children's entry to school: Home visits help. *Young Children, 49,* 62–68.

Kail, R. V., Jr. (1984). *The development of memory in children* (2d ed.). San Francisco: Freeman.

Kamii, C. K., & DeClark, G. (1985). *Young children reinvent arithmetic: Implications of Piaget's theory.* New York: Teachers College Press.

Kamii, C., & DeVries, R. (1976). *Piaget, children, and number.* Washington, DC: National Association for the Education of Young Children.

Kamii, C., & DeVries, R. (1977). Piaget for early education. In M. C. Day & R. K. Parker (Eds.), *The preschool in action: Exploring early childhood programs* (2d ed., pp. 365–420). Boston: Allyn & Bacon.

Kamii, C., & DeVries, R. (1978). *Physical knowledge in preschool education: Implications of Piaget's theory.* Englewood Cliffs, NJ: Prentice-Hall.

Kamii, C., & DeVries, R. (1980). *Group games in early education: Implications of Piaget's theory.* Washington, DC: National Association for the Education of Young Children.

Kamii, C., & Joseph, L. (1989). *Young children continue to reinvent arithmetic, 2nd grade.* New York: Teachers College Press.

Kamii, C., & Kamii, M. (1990). Why achievement testing should stop. In C. Kamii (Ed.), *Achievement testing in the early grades: The games grown-ups play* (pp. 15–38). Washington, DC: National Association for the Education of Young Children.

Katz, L. G., & Chard, S. C. (1989). *Engaging children's minds: The project approach.* Norwood, NJ: Ablex.

Kelley-Laine, K. (1998). Parents as partners in schooling: The current state of affairs. *Childhood Education, 74,* 342–345.

Kendrick, A. S., Kaufmann, R., & Messenger, K. P. (1991). *Healthy young children: A manual for programs.* Washington, DC: National Association for the Education of Young Children.

Kessler, S. A. (1991). Alternative perspectives on early childhood education. *Early Childhood Research Quarterly, 6,* 183–197.

Kilpatrick, W. (1918). The project method. *Teachers College Record, 19,* 319–335.

King, E. W., Chipman, M., & Cruz-Janzen, M. (1994). *Educating young children in a diverse society.* Boston: Allyn & Bacon.

Kitano, H. H. L., & Daniels, R. (1988). *Asian Americans: Emerging minorities.* Englewood Cliffs, NJ: Prentice-Hall.

Klahr, D. (1992). Information-processing approaches in cognitive development. In M. H. Bornstein & M. E. Lamb (Eds.), *Developmental psychology: An advanced textbook* (3d ed., pp. 273–335). Hillsdale, NJ: Erlbaum.

Knapp, M. S. (1995). How shall we study comprehensive, collaborative services for children and families? *Educational Researcher, 24,* 5–16.

Kohlberg, L. (1969). Stage and sequence: The cognitive developmental approach to socialization. In D. A. Goslin (Ed.), *Handbook of socialization theory and research.* Chicago: Rand McNally.

Kohlberg, L., & Kramer, R. (1969). Continuities and discontinuities in childhood and adult moral development. *Human Development, 12,* 93–120.

Koralek, D. G., Newman, R. L., & Colker, L. J. (1995). *Caring for children in school-age programs (Vol. 1).* Washington, DC: Teaching Strategies.

Kraemer, G. W. (1992). A psychobiological theory of attachment. *Behavioral and Brain Sciences, 15*(3), 493–511.

Kreutzer, M. A., Leonard, C., & Flavell, J. H. (1975). An interview study of children's knowledge about memory. *Monographs of the Society for Research in Child Development, 40* (Serial No. 159).

Krough, S. (1990). *The integrated early childhood curriculum.* New York: McGraw-Hill.

Kutska, K. S., & Hoffman, K. J. (1992). *Playground safety is no accident: Development of a public playground safety and maintenance program.* Alexandria, VA: National Recreation and Park Association.

Lamb, M. E. (1981). *The role of the father in child development.* New York: Wiley.

Lamb, M. E., & Oppenheim, D. (1989). Fatherhood and father-child relations. Five years of research. In S. H. Cath, A. Gurwitt, & L. Gunsberg (Eds.), *Fathers and their families.* Hillsdale, NJ: Erlbaum.

Lamborn, S. D., Mounts, N. S., Steinberg, L., & Dornbusch, S. M. (1991). Patterns of competence and adjustment among adolescents from authoritative, authoritarian, indulgent, and neglectful families. *Child Development, 62,* 1049–1065.

Lavatelli, C. (1970). *Piaget's theory applied to an early childhood curriculum.* Boston: American Science and Engineering.

Lave, J., & Wenger, E. (1991). *Situated learning: Legitimate peripheral participation.* New York: Cambridge University Press.

Leiter, J., & Johnsen, M. C. (1994). Child maltreatment and school performance. *American Journal of Education, 102,* 154–189.

LeMasters, E. E., & DeFrain, J. (1989). *Parents in contemporary America: A sympathetic view.* New York: Wadsworth.

Lempert, H. (1989). Animacy constraints on preschoolers' acquisition of syntax. *Child Development, 60,* 237–245.

Lerner, J. V., & Lerner, R. M. (1983). Temperament and adaptation across life: Theoretical and empirical issues. In P. B. Bates & O. G. Brim, Jr. (Eds.), *Life span development and behavior* (Vol. V, pp. 197–231). New York: Academic Press.

Levin, I. (1993, November). *The model monopoly of the nuclear family.* Paper presented at the

National Conference on Family Relations, Baltimore, MD.

Lewit, E. M., & Baker, L. S. (1995). Child indicators: School readiness. In R. E. Behrman (Ed.), *Critical issues for children and youth.* Los Altos, CA: The Center for the Future of Children.

Lifshitz, F., Finch, N. M., & Lifshitz, J. Z. (1991). *Children's nutrition.* Boston: Jones and Bartlett Publishers.

Lightburn, A., & Kemp, S. P. (1994). Family-support programs: Opportunities for community-based practice. *Families in Society, 75,* 16–26.

Lillard, P. P. (1972). *Montessori.* New York: Schocken.

Litowitz, B. (1977). Learning to make definitions. *Journal of Child Language, 8,* 165–175.

Locke, J. (1964). *John Locke on education.* New York: Teachers College Press.

Logan, T. (1998). Creating a kindergarten community. *Young Children, 53,* 22–35.

Lonman, L. H., & Ruhmann, L. H. (1998). Simply sensational spaces. A multi-"s" approach to toddler environments. *Young Children, 53,* 11–17.

Lowman, L. H., & Ruhmann, L. H. (1998). Simply sensational spaces: A multi-"S" approach to toddler environments. *Young Children, 53,* 11–17.

Lubeck, S. (1998). Is developmentally appropriate practice for everyone? *Childhood Education, 74,* 283–292.

Maccoby, E., & Hagen, J. W. (1965). Effects of distraction upon central versus incidental recall: Developmental trends. *Journal of Experimental Child Psychology, 2,* 280–289.

Maccoby, E. E., & Martin, J. A. (1983). Socialization in the context of the family: Parent-child interaction. In P. H. Mussen (Ed.), *Handbook of child psychology, Vol. 4: Socialization, personality, and social development.* New York: Wiley.

Mager, R. (1962). *Preparing instructional objectives.* Palo Alto, CA: Freeman.

Main, M., & Hesse, E. (1990). Parents' unresolved traumatic experiences are related to infant disorganized attachment status: Is frightened and/or frightening parental behavior the linking mechanism? In M. T. Greenberg, D. Cicchetti, & E. M. Cummings (Eds.), *Attachment in the preschool years.* Chicago: University of Chicago Press.

Main, M., & Solomon, J. (1990). Procedure for identifying infant as disorganized/disoriented during the Ainsworth Strange Situation. In M. Breenberg, D. Cicchetti, E. M. Cummings (Eds.), *Attachment during the preschool years: Theory, research, and intervention* (pp. 121–160). Chicago: University of Chicago Press.

Mallory, B. L. (1994). Inclusive policy, practice, and theory for young children with developmental differences. In B. L. Mallory & R. S. New (Eds.), *Diversity and developmentally appropriate practices* (pp. 44–61). New York: Teachers College Press.

Marion, M. (1995). *Guidance of young children* (4th ed.). Englewood Cliffs, NJ: Merrill.

Markman, E., & Gorin, L. (1981). Children's ability to adjust their standards for evaluation comprehension. *Journal of Educational Psychology, 73,* 320–325.

Marotz, L. R., Cross, M. Z., & Rush, J. M. (1993). *Health, safety, & nutrition for the young child* (3d ed.). Albany, NY: Delmar.

Martin, C. L. (1993). New directions for investigating children's gender knowledge. *Developmental Review, 13,* 184–204.

Martin, C. L., & Halverson, C. F. (1983). The effects of sex-typing schemas on young children's memory. *Child Development, 54,* 563–574.

McCall, A. L., & Ford, M. P. (1998). Why not do something? Literature as a catalyst for social action. *Childhood Education, 74,* 130–135.

McCarthy, M. A., & Houston, J. P. (1980). *Fundamentals of early childhood education.* Cambridge, MA: Winthrop.

McClurg, L. G. (1998). Building an ethical community in the classroom: Community meeting. *Young Children, 53,* 30–35.

Mejia, D. (1983). The development of Mexican American children. In G. J. Powell, J. Yammomoto, A. Romero, & A. Moreles (Eds.), *The psychological development of minority group children* (pp. 77–114). New York: Brunner/Mazel.

Melaville, A. I., & Blank, M. J. (1991). *What it takes: Structuring interagency partnerships to connect children and families with comprehensive services.* Washington, DC: Education and Human Services Consortium.

Melaville, A. I., & Blank, M. J. (1993). *Together we can: A guide for crafting a profamily system of education and human services.* Washington, DC: Office of Educational Research and Improvement, U.S. Department of Education.

Menig-Peterson, C. L. (1975). The modification of communicative behavior in preschool-aged children as a function of the listener's perspective. *Child Development, 46,* 1015–1018.

Menyuk, P. (1977). *Language and maturation.* Cambridge, MA: MIT Press.

Meriwether, L. (1997). Math as the snack table. *Young Children, 52,* 69–73.

Miller, G. A. (1991). *The science of words.* New York: Scientific American Library.

Mintz, S., & Kellogg, S. (1988). *Domestic revolution: A social history of American family life.* New York: Free Press.

Mizio, E. (1983). The impact of macrosystems on Puerto Rican females. In G. J. Powell, J. Yammomoto, A. Romero, & A. Moreles (Eds.), *The psychological development of minority group children* (pp. 77–114). New York: Brunner/Mazel.

Montessori, M. (1912/1964). *The Montessori Method* (A. E. George, Trans.). New York: Schocken.

Montessori M. (1937/1966). *The secret of childhood* (M. Joseph Costelloe, Trans.). Notre Dame, IN: Fides.

Montessori, M. (1949). *The absorbent mind.* Adyar, Madras, India: Vasanta Press.

Montessori, M. (1949/1963). *The absorbent mind* (C. A. Claremont, Trans.). Adyar, Madras, India: The Theosophical Publishing House.

Morrison, G. S. (1997). *Fundamentals of early childhood education.* Upper Saddle River, NJ: Prentice-Hall.

Morrison, J. W., & Rodgers, L. S. (1996). Being responsive to the needs of children from dual heritage backgrounds. *Young Children, 52,* 29–33.

National Association for the Education of Young Children. (1988). NAEYC position statement on standardized testing of young children 3 through 8 years of age. *Young Children, 43,* 42–47.

National Association for the Education of Young Children. (1995). Position statement on quality, compensation, and affordability. *Young Children 51* (1), 39–41.

National Association for the Education of Young Children. (1996). Be a children's champion. *Young Children, 51,* 58–60.

National Association for the Education of Young Children. (1998). NAEYC position statement on licensing and public regulation of early childhood programs. *Young Children, 53,* 43–50.

National Association of Elementary School Principals (1993). *Standards for quality school-age child care.* Alexandria, VA: Author.

National Commission on Children. (1991). *Beyond rhetoric: A new American agenda for children and families.* Washington, DC: Author.

Nelson, K. (1973). Structure and strategy in learning to talk. *Monographs of the Society for Research in Child Development, 38* (1–2, Serial No. 149).

Nelson, K. (1981). Individual differences in language development: Implications for development and language. *Developmental Psychology, 17,* 170–187.

Neuman, S. B., Hagedorn, T., Celano, D., & Daly, P. (1995). Toward a collaborative approach to parents' involvement in early education: A study of teenage mothers in an African-American Community. *American Educational Research Journal, 32,* 801–827.

New, R. S., & Mallory, B. S. (Eds.). (1994). *Diversity and developmentally appropriate practices.* New York: Teachers College Press.

Newman, C. (1993). *School health practices.* St. Louis, MO: Mosby.

Newport, E. (1990). Maturational constraints on language learning. *Cognitive Science, 14,* 11–28.

Newport, E. L., Gleitman, H., & Gleitman, L. R. (1977). Mother, I'd rather do it myself: Some effects and non-effects of maternal speech style. In C. A. Ferguson & C. E. Snow (Eds.), *Talking to children* (pp. 109–149). New York: Cambridge University Press.

Nichols, B. (1990). *Moving and learning: The elementary school physical education experience.* St. Louis, MO: Times Mirror/Mosby College Publishing.

Nolen-Hocksema, S., Girgus, J. S., & Seligman, M. E. P. (1992). Predictors and consequences of childhood depressive symptoms: A 5-year longitudinal study. *Journal of Abnormal Psychology, 101,* 405–422.

Nolen-Hocksema, S., Wolfson, A., Mumme, D., & Guskin, K. (1995). Helplessness in children of depressed and nondepressed mothers. *Developmental Psychology, 31,* 377–387.

Noyes, D. (1987, September). Indoor pollutants: Environmental hazards to young children. *Young Children, 42,* 57–65.

O'Connor, S. M. (1995). Mothering in public: The division of organized child care in the kindergarten and day nursery, St. Louis, 1886–1920. *Early Childhood Research Quarterly, 10,* 63–80.

Ogbu, J. G. (1992). Understanding cultural diversity and learning. *Educational Leadership, 21,* 5–14.

Olivia, P. F. (1992). *Developing the curriculum* (3d ed.). New York: HarperCollins.

Olmstead, P. P. (1991). Parent involvement in elementary education: Findings and suggestions from the Follow Through project. *The Elementary School Journal, 91,* 221–232.

Olson, D. H., & DeFrain, J. (1994). *Marriage and the family: Diversity and strengths.* Mountain View, CA: Mayfield.

Ornstein, P. A., Baker-Ward, L., & Naus, M. J. (1975). The development of mnemonic skill. In F. Weinert & M. Perlmutter (Eds.), *Memory development: Universal changes and individual differences* (pp. 31–50). Hillsdale, NJ: Erlbaum.

Osborn, D. K. (1991). *Early childhood education in historical perspective.* Athens, GA: Daye Press.

Padilla, A. M., & DeSnyder, N. S. (1985). Counseling Hispanics: Strategies for effective intervention. In P. B. Deduson (Ed.), *Handbook of cross-cultural counseling and therapy.* Westport, CT: Greenwood Press.

Pallas, A. M. (1993). Schooling in the course of human lives: The social context of education and the transition to adulthood in industrial society. *Review of Educational Research, 63,* 409–447.

Palmer, R. R., & Colton, J. (1992). *A history of the modern world.* New York: McGraw-Hill.

Paris, S. G., & Myers, M. (1981). Comprehension monitoring, memory, and study strategies of good and poor readers. *Journal of Reading Behavior, 13,* 5–22.

Paris, S. G., & Winograd, P. (1990). How metacognition can promote children's academic learning. In B. Jones & L. Idol (Eds.), *Dimensions of thinking* (pp. 15–51). Hillsdale, NJ: Erlbaum.

Parten, M. B. (1932). Social participation among preschool children. *Journal of Abnormal and Social Psychology, 27,* 243–269.

Patterson, C. J. (1992). Children of lesbian and gay parents. *Child Development, 63,* 1025–1042.

Paulson, E. F., Paulson, P. R., & Meyer, C. A. (1991). What makes a portfolio a portfolio? *Educational Leadership, 48*(5), 60–63.

Payne, V. G., & Rink, J. E. (1997). Physical education in the developmentally appropriate integrated curriculum. In C. H. Hart, D. C. Burts, & R. Charlesworth (Eds.). *Integrated curriculum and developmentally appropriate practice: Birth to age eight.* Albany, NY: State University of New York Press.

Peters, D. L., & Klinzing, D. G. (1990). The content of early childhood teacher education programs. In B. Spodek & O. N. Saracho (Eds.), *Yearbook in early childhood education: Early childhood teacher preparation.* New York: Teachers College Press.

Petitto, L., & Marentette, P. (1991). Babbling in the manual mode. *Science, 251,* 1493–1494.

Piaget, J. (1950). *The psychology of intelligence.* London: Routledge & Kegan Paul.

Piaget, J. (1963). *The origins of intelligence in children* (2d ed.). (M. Cook, Trans.) New York: Norton.

Piaget, J. (1973). *The child and reality.* New York: Viking Press.

Piaget, J., & Inhelder, B. (1969). *The psychology of the child.* New York: Basic Books.

Pillow, B. H. (1989). The development of beliefs about selective attention. *Merrill-Palmer Quarterly, 35,* 421–443.

Plank, D. N., & Boyd, W. L. (1994). Antipolitics, education, and institutional choice: The flight from democracy. *American Educational Research Journal, 31,* 263–282.

Podrouzek, W., & Furrow, D. (1988). Preschoolers' use of eye contact while speaking: The influence of sex, age, and conversational partner. *Journal of Psycholinguistic Research, 17,* 89–93.

Pollock, M. B. (1994). *School health instruction: The elementary and middle school years* (3d ed.). St. Louis, MO: Mosby.

Popenoe, D. (1993). American family decline, 1960–1990: A review and appraisal. *Journal of Marriage and the Family, 55*, 527–555.

Powell, D. R. (1991). How schools support families: Critical policy tensions. *The Elementary School Journal, 91*, 307–319.

Pratt, C. (1924). *Experimental practice in the city and country school.* New York: E. P. Dutton.

Prior, M. (1992). Childhood temperament. *Journal of Child Psychology and Psychiatry, 33*, 249–279.

Procidano, M. E., & Fisher, C. B. (1992). *Contemporary families: A handbook for school professionals.* New York: Teachers College Press.

Puckett, M. B., & Black, J. K. (1994). *Authentic assessment of the young child.* New York: Macmillan.

Radziszewska, B., & Rogoff, B. (1988). Influence of adult and peer collaboration on the development of children's planning skills. *Developmental Psychology, 24*, 840–848.

Ratner, N., & Bruner, J. S. (1978). Social exchange and the acquisition of language. *Journal of Child Language, 5*, 391–402.

Reznick, J. S., & Goldfield, B. A. (1992). Rapid change in lexical development in comprehension and production. *Developmental Psychology, 28*, 406–413.

Rohacek, M. H., & Russell, S. D. (1998). Child care subsidy yield returns. *Young Children, 53*, 68–71.

Rosenblith, J. F. (1992). *In the beginning: Development from conception to age two* (2d ed.). Newbury Park, CA: Sage.

Rosenthal, D. M., & Sawyers, J. Y. (1996). Building successful home/school partnerships: Strategies for parent support and involvement. *Childhood Education, 72*, 194–200.

Rutter, M., Maughan, N., Mortimore, P., & Ouston, J. (1979). *Fifteen thousand hours: Secondary schools and their effects on children.* Cambridge, MA: Harvard University Press.

Ryan, B. A., & Adams, G. R. (1995). The family-school relationships model. In B. A. Ryan, G. R. Adams, T. P. Bullotta, R. P. Weissberg, & R. L. Hampton (Eds.), *The family-school connection: Theory, research, and practice.* Thousand Oaks, CA: Sage.

Sameroff, A. J. (1987). The social context of development. In N. Eisenberg (Ed.), *Contemporary topics in developmental psychology,* New York: Wiley.

Sanders, M. G., & Epstein, J. L. (1998). International perspectives on school-family-community partnerships. *Childhood Education, 74*, 340–341.

Sanson, A., Oberklaid, F., Pedlow, R., & Prior, M. (1991). Risk indicators: Assessment of infancy predictors of pre-school behavioral maladjustment. *Journal of Child Psychology and Psychiatry, 32*, 609–626.

Santrock, J. W. (1997). *Children.* Madison, WI: Brown & Benchmark Publishers.

Scanzoni, J. (1987). Families in the 1980s: Time to refocus our thinking. *Journal of Family Issues, 8*, 394–421.

Scanzoni, J. (1997). A reply to Glenn: Fashioning families and policies for the future—not the past. *Family Relations, 46*, 213–217.

Scarr, S., & McCartney, K. (1983). How people make their own environments: A theory of genotype-environment effects. *Child Development, 54*, 253–259.

Schaefer, E. S. (1991). Goals for parent and future parent education: Research on parental beliefs and behavior. *The Elementary School Journal, 91*, 239–248.

Schaffer, H. R., & Emerson, P. E. (1964). The development of social attachments in infancy. *Monographs of the Society for Research in Child Development, 29* (3, Serial No. 94, 1–77).

Schmidt, C. R., & Paris, S. G. (1984). The development of verbal communicative skills in children. In H. W. Reese (Ed.), *Advances in child development and behavior* (Vol. 18, pp. 1–47). New York: Academic Press.

Schwartz, M. A., & Scott, B. M. (1994). *Marriages and families: Diversity and change.* Englewood Cliffs, NJ: Prentice-Hall.

Scott-Jones, D. (1995). Parent-child interactions and school achievement. In B. A. Ryan, G. R. Adams, T. P. Bullotta, R. P. Weissberg, & R. L. Hampton (Eds.), *The family-school connection: Theory, research, and practice.* Thousand Oaks, CA: Sage.

Sears, S. J., & Milburn, J. (1990). School-age stress. In L. E. Arnold (Ed.), *Childhood stress.* New York: John Wiley & Sons.

Seefeldt, C. (1997). *Social studies for the preschool-primary classroom* (5th ed.). Columbus, OH: Prentice-Hall.

Seefeldt, C., & Barbour, N. (1990). *Early childhood education: An introduction* (2d ed.). Columbus, OH: Merrill.

Seefeldt, C., & Barbour, N. (1994). *Early childhood education* (3d ed.). New York: Merrill.

Selman, R. L. (1980). *The growth of interpersonal understanding.* New York: Academic Press.

Selman, R. L. (1981). The child as friendship philosopher. In S. R. Asher & J. M. Gottman (Eds.), *The development of children's friendships.* New York: Cambridge University Press.

Selye, H. (1974). *The stress of life* (2d ed.). New York: McGraw-Hill.

Serbin, L. A., Powlishta, K. K., & Gulko, J. (1993). The development of sex typing in middle childhood. *Monographs of the Society for Research in Child Development, 58* (2, Serial No. 232, 1–99).

Shatz, M., & Gelman, R. (1973). The development of communication skills: Modifications in the speech of young children as a function of listener. *Monographs of the Society for Research in Child Development, 38* (2, Serial No. 152).

Shepard, L. A., & Smith, M. C. (1986). Synthesis of research on school readiness and kindergarten retention. *Educational Leadership, 48,* 78–86.

Shepard, L. A., & Smith, M. L. (1988). Escalating academic demand in kindergarten: Counterproductive policies. *The Elementary School Journal, 89,* 135–145.

Sherrill, C. (1993). *Adapted physical activity, recreation, and sport: Crossdisciplinary and lifespan* (4th ed.). Madison, WI: Wm C. Brown.

Shonkoff, J. P. (1995). Child care for low-income families. *Young Children 50,* 63–65.

Shore, R. (1997). *Rethinking the brain.* New York: Families and Work Institute.

Silvern, S. B. (1988). Continuity/discontinuity between home and early childhood education environments. *The Elementary School Journal, 89,* 147–159.

Skolnick, A. (1997). A response to Glenn: The battle of the textbooks: Bringing in the culture war. *Family Relations, 46,* 219–222.

Slonim, M. B. (1991). *Children, culture and ethnicity: Evaluating and understanding the impact.* New York: Garland.

Smith, H. (1995). *Rethinking America: A new game plan from the American innovators: Schools, business, people, work.* New York: Random House.

Snow, C. E. (1977). The development of conversation between mothers and babies. *Journal of Child Language, 4,* 1–22.

Snow, C. W., Teleki, J. K., & Reguero-de-Atiles, J. T. (1996). Child care center licensing standards in the United States: 1981 to 1995. *Young Children, 51,* 36–41.

Solomon, Z. P. (1991). California's policy on parent involvement: State leadership for local initiatives. *Phi Delta Kappan, 72,* 359–362.

Soriano-Nagurski, L. (1998). And the wall came tumbling down: Including children who are differently abled in typical early childhood educational settings. *Young Children, 53,* 40.

Spillane, J. P. (1998). State policy and the non-monolithic nature of the local school district: Organizational and professional considerations. *American Educational Research Journal, 35,* 33–64.

Spodek, B. (1986). Development, values, and knowledge in the kindergarten curriculum. In B. Spodek (Ed.), *Today's kindergarten: Exploring the knowledge base, Expanding the curriculum* (pp. 32–47). New York: Teachers College Press.

Spodek, B. (1991). Early childhood curriculum and cultural definitions of knowledge. In B. Spodek & O. N. Saracho (Eds.), *Issues in early childhood curriculum* (pp. 1–20). New York: Teachers College Press.

Spodek, B., Saracho, O. N., & Davis, M. D. (1991). *Foundations of early childhood education* (2d ed.). Boston: Allyn & Bacon.

Stacey, J. (1993). Good riddance to "the family": A response to David Popenoe. *Journal of Marriage and the Family, 55,* 545–547.

Staley, L. (1998). Beginning to implement the Reggio philosophy. *Young Children 53,* 20–25.

Stallings, J. A. (1995). Ensuring teaching and learning in the 21st century. *Educational Researcher, 24,* 4–8.

Stamp, L. N., & Groves, M. M. (1994). Strengthening the ethic of care: Planning and supporting family involvement. *Dimensions, 22,* 5–9.

Staples, R. (1981). *The world of black singles.* Westport, CT: Greenwood.

Steinberg, L., & Meyer, R. (1995). *Childhood.* New York: McGraw-Hill.

Steinberg, L., Lamborn, S. D., Darling, N., Mounts, N. S., & Dornbusch, S. M. (1994). Over-time changes in adjustment and competence among adolescents from authoritative, authoritarian, indulgent, and neglectful families. *Child Development, 65,* 754–770.

Steinberg, L., Lamborn, S. D., Dornbusch, S. M., & Darling, N. (1992). Impact of parenting practices on adolescent achievement: Authoritative parenting, school involvement, and encouragement to succeed. *Child Development, 63,* 1266–1281.

Steinberg, L., Mounts, N. S., Lamborn, S. D., & Dornbusch, S. M. (1991). Authoritative parenting and adolescent adjustment across various ecological niches. *Journal of Research on Adolescence, 1,* 19–36.

Sternberg, R. J. (1996). *Intelligence applied.* New York: Harcourt Brace Jovanovich.

Sternberg, R. J. (1996). Myths, countermyths, and truths about intelligence. *Educational Researcher, 25* (2), pp. 11–15.

Sternberg, R. J., & Davidson, J. E. (1986). Cognitive development in the gifted and talented. In F. D. Horowitz & M. O'Brien (Eds.), *The gifted and talented: Developmental perspectives* (pp. 37–74). Washington, DC: American Psychological Association.

Sternberg, R. J., & Wagner, R. K. (1993). The geocentric view of intelligence and job performance is wrong. *Current Directions in Psychological Science, 2,* 1–5.

Strong, B., DeVault, C., & Sayad, B. W. (1998). *The marriage and family experience: Intimate relationships in a changing society.* Belmont, CA: Wadsworth.

Sue, D. (1981). *Counseling the culturally different.* New York: John Wiley.

Sutherland, P. (1992). *Cognitive development today.* London: Paul Chapman Publishing.

Swick, K. (1984). Family involvement: An empowerment perspective. *Dimensions, 22,* 10–13.

Swick, K. J., & Graves, S. B. (1993). *Empowering at-risk families during the early childhood years.* Washington, DC: National Education Association.

Talley, K. (1997). National accreditation: Why do some programs stall in self-study? *Young Children, 52,* 31–37.

Tanner, J. M. (1990). *Fetus into man: Physical growth from conception to maturity.* Cambridge, MA: Harvard University Press.

Teti, D. M., Messinger, D. S., Gelfand, D. M., & Issabella, R. (1995). Maternal depression and the quality of early attachment: An examination of infants, preschoolers, and their mothers. *Developmental Psychology, 31,* 364–376.

Thomas, A., & Chess, S. (1977). *Temperament and development.* New York: Brunner/Mazel.

Thomas, A., & Chess, S. (1981). The role of temperament in the contributions of individuals to their development. In R. M. Lerner & N. A. Busch-Rossnagel (Eds.), *Individuals as producers of their development: A life-span perspective.* New York: Academic Press.

Thomas, R. M. (1985). *Comparing theories of child development* (2d ed.). Belmont, CA: Wadsworth.

Thomas, R. M. (1996). *Comparing theories of child development* (4th ed.). Pacific Grove, CA: Brooks/Cole.

Thompson, S. H. (1998). Working with children of substance-abusing parents. *Young Children, 53,* 34–37.

Thorndike, E. L. (1910). *Educational psychology.* New York: Teachers College Press.

Thornton, A. (1989). Changing attitudes toward family issues in the United States. *Journal of Marriage and the Family, 51,* 873–893.

Todd, J. T. (1994). What psychology has to say about John B. Watson: Classical behaviorism in psychology textbooks, 1920–1989. In J. T. Todd & E. K. Morris (Eds.), *Modern perspectives on John B. Watson and classical behaviorism* (pp. 75–107). Westport, CT: Greenwood Press.

Trawick-Smith, J. (1997). *Early childhood development.* Upper Saddle River, NJ: Prentice-Hall.

Tronick, E. (1989). Emotions and emotional communication in infants. *American Psychologist, 44,* 112–119.

Tschann, J. M., Kaiser, P., Chesney, M. A., Alkon, A., & Boyce, W. T. (1996). Resilience and vulnerability among preschool children: Family functioning, temperament, and behavior problems. *Journal of the American Academy of Child and Adolescent Psychiatry, 35,* 184–192.

U. S. Bureau of the Census. (1996). *Statistical abstract of the United States* (116th ed.). Washington, DC: U. S. Government Printing Office.

U. S. Department of Agriculture. (1998). *Unlocking the barriers: Keys to communicating with underserved customers.* Washington, DC: Office of Communication.

Van der Veer, R., & Valsiner, J. (1991). *Understanding Vygotsky: A quest for synthesis.* Cambridge, MA: Blackwell.

Vaughan, V. C., & Litt, I. F. (1990). *Child and adolescent development: Clinical implications.* Philadelphia: W. B. Saunders.

Vurpillot, E. (1968). The development of scanning strategies and their relation to visual differentiation. *Journal of Experimental Child Psychology, 6,* 632–650.

Vygotsky, L. S. (1930, 1933, 1935/1978). *Mind in society: The development of higher psychological processes.* Cambridge, MA: Harvard University Press.

Vygotsky, L. S. (1934/1986). *Thought and language* (A. Kozulin, Trans.). Cambridge, MA: MIT Press.

Waddington, C. H. (1957). *The strategy of the genes.* London: Allen & Unwin.

Walker, A. J., Martin, S. S. K., & Thompson, L. (1988). Feminist programs for families. *Family Relations, 37,* 17–22.

Wang, M. C., Haertel, G. D., & Walberg, H. J. (1993). Toward a knowledge base for school learning. *Review of Educational Research, 63,* 249–294.

Warman, B. (1998). Trends in state accreditation policies. *Young Children, 53,* 52–55.

Warren-Leubecker, A., & Bohannon, J. N., III. (1989). Pragmatics: Language in social contexts. In J. Berko Gleason (Ed.), *The development of language* (pp. 327–368). Columbus, OH: Merrill.

Wasley, P. (1993). A response. *Educators College Record, 94,* 720–729.

Weber, E. (1969). *The kindergarten: Its encounter with educational thought in America.* New York: Teachers College Press.

Weber, E. (1984). *Ideas influencing early childhood education.* New York: Teachers College Press.

Wehren, A., DeLisi, R., & Arnold, M. (1981). The development of noun definition. *Journal of Child Language, 8,* 165–175.

Weikart, D. P., Rogers, L., Adcock, C., & McClelland, D. (1971). *The cognitively oriented classroom—A framework for preschool teachers.* Urbana, IL: University of Illinois Press.

Wellman, H. M. (1988). First steps in the child's theorizing about the mind. In J. Astington, P. L. Harris, & D. R. Olson, (Eds.), *Developing theories of mind.* New York: Cambridge University Press.

Werner, E. E. (1993). Risk, resilience, and recovery: Perspectives from the Kauai Longitudinal Study. *Development and Psychopathology, 5,* 503–515.

Werner, E. E., & Smith, R. S. (1977). *Kauai's children come of age.* Honolulu, HI: University of Hawaii Press.

Werner, E. E., & Smith, R. S. (1989). *Vulnerable but invincible: A longitudinal study of resilient children and youth.* New York: Adams-Bannister-Cox.

Werner, E. E., & Smith, R. S. (1992). *Overcoming the odds: High risk children from birth to adulthood.* Ithaca, NY: Cornell University Press.

Wertsch, J. V. (1985). *Vygotsky and the social formation of mind.* Cambridge, MA: Harvard University Press.

Wertsch, J. V., & Tulviste, P. (1992). L. S. Vygotsky and contemporary developmental psychology. *Developmental Psychology, 28,* 548–557.

White, C. S., Fein, G. G., Manning, B. H., & Daniels, A. (manuscript submitted for publication). The thematic unit: Old hat or new shoes? *Advances in early education and day care.*

White, K. R., Taylor, M. J., & Moss, V. D. (1992). Does research support claims about the benefits of involving parents in early intervention programs? *Review of Educational Research, 62,* 91–125.

White, S. H., & Buka, S. L. (1987). Early education: Programs, traditions, and policies. In E. Z. Rothkopf (Ed.), *Review of Research in Education* (Vol. 14, pp. 43–91). Washington, DC: American Educational Research Association.

Whitebrook, M., Phillips, D., & Howes, C. (1989). *Who cares? Child care teachers and the quality of care in America: Final report of the national child care staffing study.* Oakland, CA: Child Care Employee Project.

Whitson, A. (1998). Are local school boards obsolete? *Childhood Education, 74,* 172–173.

Wilds, E. H., & Lottich, K. V. (1961). *The foundations of modern education.* New York: Holt, Rinehart and Winston.

Wiley, A. R., Rose, A. J., Burger, L. K., & Miller, P. J. (1998). Constructing autonomous selves through narrative practices: A comparative study of working-class and middle-class families. *Child Development, 69,* 833–847.

Willer, B., Hofferth, S. L., Kisker, E., Divine-Hawkins, P., Farquhar, E., & Glantz, F. (1991). *The demand and supply of child care in 1990.* Washington, DC: National Association for the Education of Young Children.

Williams, E. R., & Caliendo, M. A. (1984). *Nutrition: Principles, issues, and applications.* New York: McGraw-Hill.

Williams, K. R. (1992). Social sources of marital violence and deterrence: Testing an integrated theory of assaults between partners. *Journal of Marriage and the Family, 54,* 620–629.

Wilson, R. (1980). *Criterion-referenced testing.* Test Service Notebook 37. New York: Psychological Corporation.

Wortham, S. C. (1992). *Childhood 1892–1992.* Wheaton, MD: Association for Childhood Education International.

Wortham, S. C. (1995). *Measurement and evaluation in early childhood education.* Englewood Cliffs, NJ: Prentice-Hall.

Zaller, R. (1984). *Europe in transition.* New York: Harper & Row.

Zigler, E. F., & Stevenson, M. F. (1993). *Children in a changing world: Development and social issues* (2d ed.). Pacific Grove, CA: Brooks/Cole.

Zimmerman, M. A., & Arunkumar, R. (1994). Resiliency research: Implications for schools and policy. *Social Policy Report: Society for Research in Child Development, 8,* 1–19.

Zimmerman, S. L. (1992). Family trends: What implications for family policy? *Family Relations, 41,* 423–429.

Zimmerman, S. L. (1995). *Understanding family policy: Theories and applications* (2d ed.). Thousand Oaks, CA: Sage.

Zinn, M. B., & Eitzen, D. S. (1990). *Diversity in families* (2d ed.). New York: Harper & Row.

Index